THE
STORY
OF THE
ARMORY
SHOW

THE
STORY OF THE

ARMORY SHOW

MILTON W.
BROWN

ABBEVILLE PRESS · PUBLISHERS · NEW YORK
THE JOSEPH H. HIRSHHORN FOUNDATION

Editor: Nancy Grubb
Designers: Julie Rauer, with Susanne Geppert
Production manager: Dana Cole

Front cover: Marcel Duchamp. *Nude Descending a Staircase, No. 2*, 1912.
See plate 9.
Back cover: Henri Matisse. *Blue Nude (Souvenir de Biskra)*, 1907.
See plate 6.
The pine tree, used on flags during the American Revolution, was the
official emblem of the Armory Show.

Second edition

LIBRARY OF CONGRESS
Library of Congress Cataloging-in-Publication Data

Brown, Milton Wolf, 1911-
The story of the Armory show/Milton W. Brown.
p. cm.
"The Joseph H. Hirshhorn Foundation."
Bibliography: p.
Includes index.
ISBN 0-89659-795-4: $29.95
1. Armory Show (1913: New York, N.Y.)—History. 2. Art,
Modern—19th century—Exhibitions. 3. Art, Modern—20th century—
Exhibitions. I. Title.
N6448.A74B7 1988
709'.041'0740147—dc 19   87-33441
CIP

To the members of the
Association of American Painters and Sculptors,
in memory

CONTENTS

Preface

My interest in the Armory Show of 1913 goes back more than fifty years. In 1963, the fiftieth-anniversary restaging of that exhibition, known more formally as the International Exhibition of Modern Art, figuratively dragged me out of the more or less cloistered atmosphere of teaching and scholarship into public view as an expert. *Time* magazine then characterized me as "Armory Show expert, Milton Brown." However, after it was all over, there did not seem much future in being "Armory Show expert, Milton Brown," and I retired back to academic anonymity, with the hope that if I lived until the seventy-fifth anniversary, they might dust me off again and I would have another opportunity to bask in the light of public recognition. I am very happy to be making it to the seventy-fifth anniversary and to see published a new edition of *The Story of the Armory Show*. The book was originally issued in connection with the fiftieth-anniversary celebration, which was held at the Munson-Williams-Proctor Institute, in Utica, New York, and, under the sponsorship of the Henry Street Settlement, at the 69th Regiment Armory in New York City, the site of the original exhibition. This revised publication has been made possible by the cooperation of Abbeville Press and the Joseph H. Hirshhorn Foundation, sponsor of the first edition.

To a certain extent, the book initially took shape because of the fortuitous emergence in 1962 of documentary material that had been thought nonexistent: the papers of Elmer MacRae, treasurer, and Walt Kuhn, secretary, of the Association of American Painters and Sculptors, which organized the 1913 exhibition. These documents are now preserved, respectively, in the Collection Archive of the Hirshhorn Museum and Sculpture Garden, and the Archives of American Art, both part of the Smithsonian Institution, Washington, D.C. A full account of the discovery of these papers and a description of their contents appear in the introduction. These documents, including almost complete records as well as diverse memorabilia of the Association and the Exhibition, made it possible to reconstruct the historic events from the birth of the Association, through the Show itself, to the demise of the Association, as well as all the repercussions caused in cultural and popular circles. The facts and the attendant relationships have been fairly accurately established, although many of the works and some of the participating artists have still not been identified.

The importance of the Armory Show can hardly be questioned, although the Fiftieth Anniversary Exhibition did spark some revisionist criticism, most of it directed at deflating the Show's central role in introducing modern art to the United States or its influence in changing the course of American art. These remain questions of interpretation, evaluation, and judgment. It is rather pointless to insist that American art would have evolved as it did without the Armory Show. The fact is that the Armory Show did occur, and there is plenty of evidence that it had a profound effect on the art world—artists, collectors, dealers, museums, and the public. Probably the most important art exhibition in our history, it was certainly the most exciting one.

Shortly after the publication of *The Story of the Armory Show* in

9

1963, Brenda Kuhn gave the Archives a batch of letters from her father to her mother covering the period from late 1911 to 1914, when he was traveling in connection with the Association and the Show. Dealing exclusively with those activities, the letters are nonetheless very private, though they deal with a public event; they are also psychologically revealing in unsuspected ways. However, they add very little to our previous knowledge of the events. These letters as well as the more formal documents of the Association were in Kuhn's possession when he wrote his own account entitled *The Story of the Armory Show,* and the letters reveal some aspects of his relationships that he preferred to suppress (for more information about these letters, see my article in the *Archives of American Art Journal,* Winter 1987–88). Any data pertinent to the Armory Show has been added to the text of this second edition.

Except for such minor emendations, this text is substantially the same as the first. Every effort has been made to bring the bibliography and the catalogue raisonné up to date. There are, of course, elements in the latter that are subject to constant change and very difficult to document, especially since many private collectors prefer anonymity. The revision was done under severe time limitations, and I owe a great debt of gratitude to all the registrars and curators of museums who answered our call for help. I am beholden as well to John Rewald, whose knowledge of Impressionism and Post-Impressionism is legendary, for his help in identifying the present location of several works in question. I am also grateful to Nancy Grubb, senior editor, and the staff of Abbeville Press for undertaking the new edition of this book and for producing it in such a timely manner. I have leaned heavily on the research talents of Dominic Madormo, who has done much of the updating of the catalogue and bibliography. Last, my special thanks go to Olga Hirshhorn, whose gracious intercession made the project possible.

10

Preface
to the First
Edition

This book, written fifty years after the Armory Show, is intended to commemorate that event and to document it in the light of the most recently discovered information, as described in the introduction. It includes a narrative account of the Association of American Painters and Sculptors (AAPS) and of the International Exhibition of Modern Art, which it organized. Added is a catalogue raisonné, whose intention is to supplement the original enigmatic catalogue with all the pertinent information now available; and appendixes containing important documents which could find no place in either the text or the catalogue.

Considering the limited time in which the book had to be prepared in order to synchronize with the Fiftieth Anniversary Exhibition held at the Munson-Williams-Proctor Institute in Utica and at the original Armory in New York, under the joint auspices of the Institute and the Henry Street Settlement, I owe a more than normal debt of gratitude to all those who helped.

I would like first of all to acknowledge the support of Joseph H. Hirshhorn and the Joseph H. Hirshhorn Foundation, which is publishing this book, and especially to thank my dear friend Abram Lerner, curator of the collection and vice-president of the Foundation, whose dogged insistence and unremitting faith persuaded both Mr. Hirshhorn and myself that it was possible; we all felt it was desirable. I am also indebted to the Foundation for the exclusive use of the MacRae Papers in its possession.

One aspect of the catalogue, the present location of works in the Armory Show, would not have been possible without the co-operation of the Munson-Williams-Proctor Institute and the Henry Street Settlement. The monumental work of rediscovery and reassembly undertaken by Joseph S. Trovato, assistant to the director, and by his staff revealed a wealth of new information. Special credit must go to two researchers, Samuel Sachs II and Martin Lerner, in discovering many previously unknown works. All of this information was generously made available before the publication date of the exhibition catalogue. For this courtesy, I thank Edward H. Dwight, director of the Institute, and Mrs. Winslow Carlton and Mrs. Jacob M. Kaplan, co-chairwomen of the Armory Show Committee of the Henry Street Settlement. My appreciation is also extended to Margaret Cogswell, who permitted us to use the proofs of the catalogue amid the turmoil of going to press.

I owe a great debt, as do all who are interested in the history of American art, to Brenda Kuhn, daughter of Walt Kuhn, first for conserving and then making public the Armory Show records that were in her father's possession during his lifetime; second, and very personally, for permitting me to use the title of her father's pamphlet, *The Story of the Armory Show*, for this book; and last, for her cooperation in discussing her memories of her father. I am indebted also to Virginia Myers Downes, daughter of Jerome Myers, for her kindness in permitting me access to her father's papers; to Ronnie Owen, daughter of Arthur B. Davies, for the candid revelation of one little-known aspect of his life, which she has given me permission to use; and to Nikifora L. Pach for her gracious help in all matters relating to her late husband, Walter Pach, and for permission to study his papers.

Mary Lescaze, Lydia Powel, and Frederic Lake were very helpful in identifying for me the many members of New York society who were connected in one way or another with the Armory Show; and Mrs. Lescaze turned up innumerable leads which, unfortunately, I could not always follow.

The professional assistance and courtesy one gets in art collections and libraries is an important part of scholarship, and William E. Woolfenden, assistant director of the Archives of American Art; James Humphry III, chief librarian of the Metropolitan Museum of Art; and Bernard Karpel, librarian of the Museum of Modern Art Library; as well as the staffs of these institutions, all extended a helping hand.

Two young art historians, formerly my students, Martin Lerner and Jerome Viola, acted as alter egos in searching for and checking on those minute bits of information without which the larger work is impossible. I would like also to thank my typists, Sandra Hogan, Martica Sawin, and Doris Palca, not for their skill, for which I paid them, but for their interest and intelligence in translating a mass of accumulated material and almost illegible copy into a manuscript. My wife, who is my greatest admirer and severest critic, managed, in spite of her own deadline, to read portions of the manuscript and offer astringent though sage advice.

Eugene Santomasso has been of enormous help in checking proof, as have Margot and Peter Jefferys.

Special acknowledgment is made to all those museums, collections, and private owners who have supplied information, given me permission to quote from documents, or allowed me to reproduce works of art in their possession.

For Burton Cumming, director of publications for the New York Graphic Society, and myself, this book has been more than a labor of love; it has been an exercise in nostalgia. We were fellow students in Paul J. Sachs' Museum Class at Harvard twenty-five years ago, when Mr. Cumming suggested that we reconstruct the Armory Show as our project. The idea was rejected then but, through one of those curious caprices of chance, we have joined forces to realize it now.

13

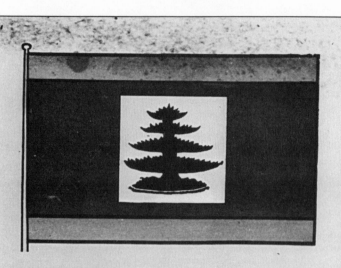

NEW YORK

1913

International Exhibition
of Modern Art

Association of American Painters
and Sculptors, Inc.

February Seventeenth to March Fifteenth

Catalogue 25 Cents

Catalogue of the Armory Show.

Introduction:
The
Documents

Until recently all accounts of the Armory Show have been based largely on the twenty-five-page pamphlet written by Walt Kuhn, the secretary of the Association of American Painters and Sculptors, which organized the Show. Twenty-five years after it happened, Kuhn reconstructed, in *The Story of the Armory Show*, the outlines of that enterprise in all its color and excitement. Other versions of the event were recorded by various participants: Jerome Myers in *Artist in Manhattan*, Guy Pène du Bois in *Artists Say the Silliest Things*, and Walter Pach in *Queer Thing, Painting*. These sources plus the great body of contemporary comment in newspapers and magazines have served as the basis for all subsequent reconstructions and evaluations of the Exhibition, but it was always the Kuhn pamphlet which remained the core of our knowledge of the event.

Some twenty years ago, when I first began to work on my book *American Painting from the Armory Show to the Depression*, I visited Kuhn to talk to him about his art and the role he played in the organization of the Armory Show. At that time he told me there were no extant records of the Association or the Exhibition. Similarly, Elmer MacRae, the treasurer, in a letter of November 29, 1951, to Bernard Karpel, librarian of the Museum of Modern Art, denied having anything in his possession that would be new to the Museum. However, the very material which was supposed not to exist, the records of the Association and the Armory Show, has recently come to light.

In 1958, the Greenwich Historical Society, in the course of restoring the Bush-Holley House at Cos Cob, Connecticut, discovered the records belonging to Elmer MacRae. The Holley Inn, originally a colonial homestead, was a favorite summering place for many artists at the turn of the century, and Elmer Mac-Rae, one of the frequent visitors, married Constant, the only daughter of Mr. and Mrs. Edward P. Holley. MacRae lived there from the time of his marriage in 1900 until his death in 1955, and it was to and from Cos Cob that he commuted during the days of the Armory Show, as the entries in his diary attest— "commutation book, $10.30." All the treasurer's records, along with a variety of other material, seem to have been packed into an old orange crate, stored in the barn behind the house, and then completely forgotten.

Walt Kuhn was aware that he had all the secretary's records, since he must have used them to write his story of the event. He denied them to me, perhaps because he did not know me and because there were things among the papers that might reopen the wounds of the old unpleasantness surrounding the dissolution of the Association. Kuhn made no mention of the falling-out in his account, and Myers closed his chapter on the Armory Show, "As always, time has smoothed out whatever differences there may have been, and the Armory Show remains a great tradition in our art history." All of them seem to have recognized the fact that the Exhibition had an importance far beyond their personal disagreements, and perhaps Kuhn did not want to rake the embers of an old dispute while some of the members were still alive. It is only in the past year that Brenda Kuhn has bequeathed these papers to the Archives of American Art and thus made them available to the public.

The MacRae Papers were exhibited at the Milch Gallery in 1959 along with a retrospective exhibition of his paintings and pastels. In order to raise money to carry on the restoration of the Holley House, the Greenwich Historical Society decided to sell the material pertaining to the Armory Show to the Joseph H. Hirshhorn Collection. Early in 1962, I was commissioned to publish these papers as a memorial volume on the fiftieth anniversary of the Armory Show. It seemed at that time a limited project that could be completed and published by February 17, 1963, fifty years after the date of the Armory Show opening. I began work in June and almost immediately learned from the June *Bulletin of the Archives of American Art* that the Kuhn Papers had come to light. A hurried trip to Detroit and an examination of the papers indicated that the original plan to publish the MacRae Papers as a separate entity no longer made sense. Both sources together now could supply the documentary information for an almost complete archaeological reconstruction of the Association and the Armory Show. This was an exciting possibility, but time had become a major consideration.

To add to both the pressures and the possibilities, we learned that the Munson-Williams-Proctor Institute was planning a Fiftieth Anniversary Exhibition and was anxious to find as many of the original works as they could for their show, and the information in the documents now made the identification of a great many more items possible. My decision was not to compete with the Institute in locating works but to write a narrative account of the Armory Show and a catalogue raisonné to include the great wealth of data which could find no place in the story itself. As the undertaking grew in magnitude, it became apparent that my January 1, 1963, deadline could not be met and the Foundation agreed to extend the date to February 15. Although something in timeliness was thereby lost, the book as it now stands, greatly increased in scope, will, I hope, have more permanent value.

The Kuhn Papers are the secretary's records and thus include most of the official transactions and correspondence of the society, whereas the MacRae Papers comprise the financial records and correspondence. Among the former are the original constitution and articles of incorporation of the Association; the minutes of many of the meetings, including a notebook which

17

The President and Members of the
Association of American Painters and Sculptors
invite you to be present
at the formal opening of the
International Exhibition of Modern Art
Monday afternoon February seventeenth, 1913
from three to seven o'clock
at the Armory
69th Regiment of Infantry, N.G.N.Y.
Lexington Avenue, 25th and 26th Streets

Invitation to the Armory Show.

contains the official report of the first two meetings; the note-book of the Domestic Committee, which records all of the works submitted and the action of the Committee on them; the entry blanks accompanying all the foreign works; manuscripts of Paul Gauguin's *Noa-Noa* translated by Kuhn, selected letters of Vincent van Gogh translated by Kuhn, and the record of a conversation with Odilon Redon by Pach; the brief submitted by John Quinn in the fight for duty-free art; and correspondence with artists, lenders, buyers, shippers, insurers, merchants, etc., including the transactions with the Armory authorities, the Art Institute of Chicago, and the Copley Society. Some items are missing, such as the domestic entry cards, but it is virtually a complete record of the secretary's activities. Pach's correspondence as an agent of the Association is also included, since he seems to have considered it the proper affair of the Association and to have given the material to Kuhn for the files.

There is also in the Kuhn Papers a collection of printed material: all the invitations, statements, blank forms, and form letters; the catalogues of all the exhibitions, including one of the New York Exhibition with prices noted; the various publications of the Association, pamphlets, and post cards; two scrapbooks of

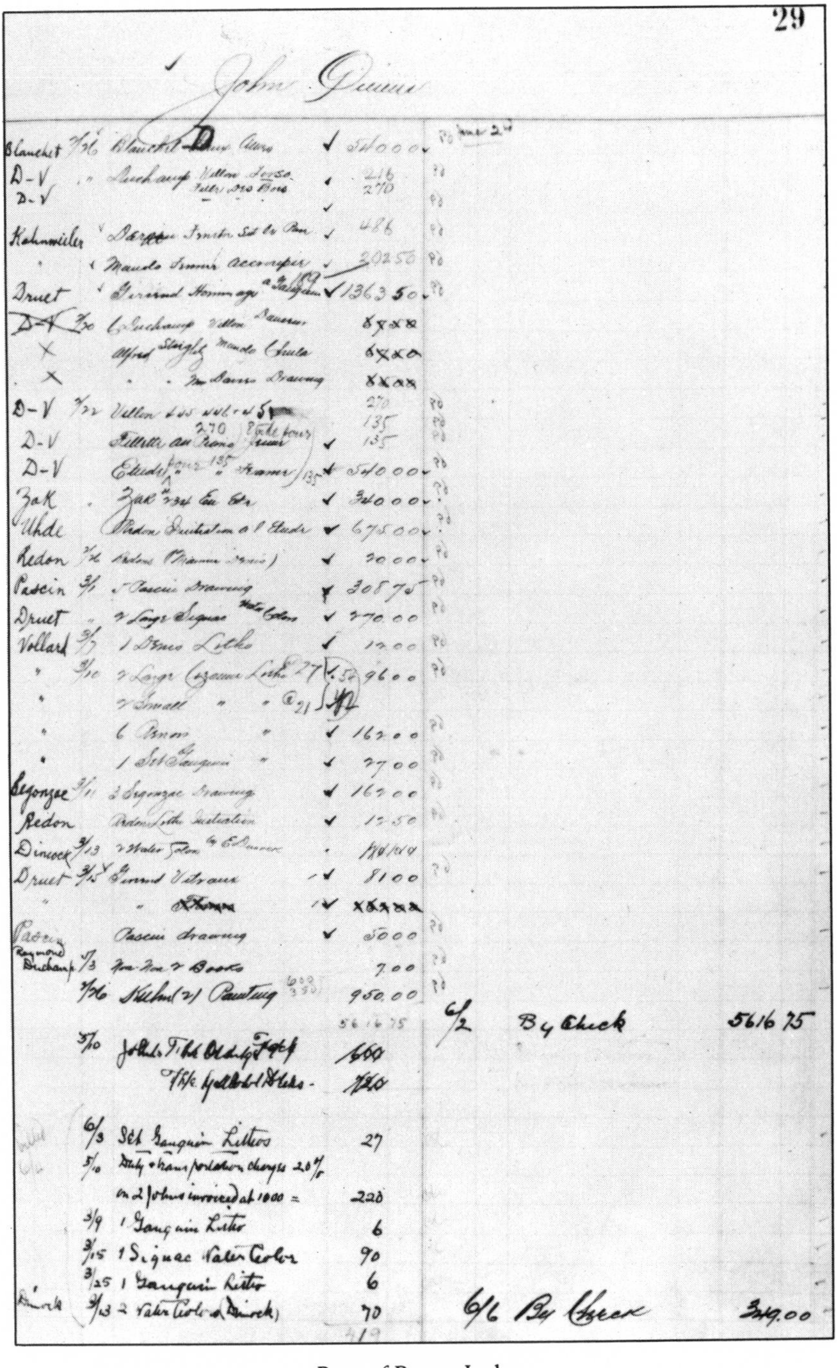
29

John Quinn

6/2 By Check 5616 75

6/6 By Check 319.00

Page of Buyers Ledger.

press clippings, including those from the Henry Romeike press service to which the Association subscribed, the most complete extant collection of critical comment on the Armory Show; and a scrapbook containing photographs for sale and distribution to the press. It should be noted here that these photographs are not exclusively of works in the Armory Show, although they are of works by the artists represented. Among the photographs are also several views of the interior of the Armory during the Exhibition and one of the exterior.

The MacRae Papers are those of the treasurer and are therefore more limited. They consist of all the financial documents, a set of personal diaries, some personal letters relating to the Armory Show, and a collection of press clippings. Among these items are three financial ledgers, which include all the financial transactions of the Association, ranging from an entry of twenty cents for thumbtacks to a payment of $5,616.75 for art purchased by John Quinn. One of these, the cashbook, records all the credit and debit payments made during the life of the Association. Another ledger covers foreign lenders to the Exhibition, including the artists, and lists the works lent, the prices asked, and payments made for works sold. The third ledger contains a list of donors and their contributions to the Association and one of buyers, the works they purchased, and the prices paid. There is also a fourth and smaller ledger, which covers MacRae's petty-cash expenses. Other financial documents include two checkbooks of the Greenwich Trust Company, a receipt book, four small notebooks recording admission receipts at the entry booths of the Armory Show, and a series of receipts covering foreign payments through the Astor Trust Company. Of special interest are two diaries—one for 1911 with entries covering the first week of January, 1912; one for 1913 detailing MacRae's activities down to the opening of the Show—and a small memo book with the minutes of the Executive Committee.

There are also among the MacRae Papers all the bills covering the financial transactions of the Association, from a bill for a party given for the press to the final Customs settlement; a variety of tally sheets covering wages and office expenses, sales of catalogues, pamphlets, and post cards, and admission fees; financial settlements with Chicago and Boston; insurance records;

REDON, ODILON (Continued)

273 Fleurs (fond rouge) *1350*
274 Pegase sur un roe *2700*
275 Fecondite (etude) *2700*
    Lent by M. Marcel Kapferer
276 Vase de fleurs avec geranium, No. 115 *1680*
277 Papillons, No. 121 *405*
278 Roses sur fond vert, No. 116 *810*
279 Papillon, No. 38 *1350-*
280 Profil noir sur fond or No. 111 *1350*
281 Fleurs, No. 75 *2700*
282 Phaeton, No. 114 *2160*
    Lent by M. Jos. Hessel
283 Deux têtes dans les fleurs
    Lent by M. Marcel Kapferer

284 Veillard *1350*
285 Muse sur Pegase No. 110 *2160*
286 Bargue *2700*
287 Le char d'Apollon *4050*
288 Fleurs dans un jut de gres *2160*
    Lent by M. Jos. Hessel
289 Initiation à l'Etude *675*
290 Fleurs (Pastel) *205*
    Lent by M. Wilhelm Uhde

291 Profil mystique (Pastel) *780*
292 Songe d'Orient (Pastel) *650*
293 Corbeille de Fleurs *195*
294 Coquelicots *Sold* *520*
295 Barque *890*
296 Vase de fleurs. bleu *Sold* *570*
297 Vase de fleurs. gris *Sold* *570*
298 Prometheus *390*
299 Tête en fleurs *300*
300 Le Silence. *Sold* *340*
301 Monstre et Angelique *455*
302 Deux êtres sublunaires ailes dans l'espace *585*
303 Ohannès *570*
    Lent by M. Artz & de Bois

304 Tête de femme (Pastel) *N. F. S.*
    Lent by Mme. Chadbourne

31

21

Page of MacRae's priced catalogue of the Armory Show.

lists of works in transit from abroad and in this country; and a variety of miscellaneous items covering every aspect of the venture. There are also items of a less financial nature, such as thanks from artists who had been paid for works sold, receipts for works delivered, and letters which are more personal although still related to the Show. Finally, the collection includes examples of the publications and post cards, a limited number of press clippings, a box of pine-tree buttons, the cuts for the post cards and the poster, the blueprint of the Armory Show layout, and a dusty and tattered fragment of the bunting which decorated the Armory.

These two collections in themselves, since they constitute in essence a complete record of the Armory Show, are enough to make a reconstruction possible. However, in the course of my research as well as that of the people working on the Fiftieth Anniversary Exhibition, a variety of new material was unearthed which either corroborated, clarified, or extended our knowledge. The Myers Papers, although not extensive, supplied some interesting sidelights. In the course of working with these papers, I learned from Mrs. Downes that Mary Mowbray-Clarke, wife of the vice-president of the Association, was still living. After some correspondence we finally arranged a meeting, but when I arrived she was already sinking into the coma from which she never recovered. Whatever she might have remembered was not communicated, and among the mass of mementos in a disordered attic no documents of any value could be found, although fragments of several of John Mowbray-Clarke's sculptures were discovered. Perhaps in that accumulation of the discarded remnants of more than a half-century of life, someone will someday turn up the things we were looking for. Not all our efforts were as fruitless. A notation in the cashbook that Kuhn had paid $18.50 to have the Chicago installation photographed led to the discovery of twelve photographs in the Art Institute which made possible the identification of many works previously unknown. The two small memo books in which Pach kept a daily account of sales helped clear up many of the obscurities in the MacRae Papers. Unfortunately, the Quinn Papers at the New York Public Library include only a few and not very important references to the Armory Show. Aside from these items, the Museum of Modern

Art has a collection of some memorabilia and a scrapbook of press clippings. No doubt the Fiftieth Anniversary Exhibition and a renewed interest in the Armory Show will eventually bring forth other material of importance. Among the items known to have existed that are still undiscovered, the most important are the entry blanks of the American section and the photographic record of works that once belonged to Hagelstein Brothers, official photographers to the Exhibition.

All this new information does not materially alter Kuhn's story of how the Armory Show happened or the generally accepted evaluation of its importance for American art. It has, however, supplied the detail to transform what had become a myth into a documented historical event. It is now possible to give an almost day-by-day account of the affair and to recapture something of that electric moment which stirred the American art world to unprecedented excitement.

I regret that time did not permit interviewing the many people who might have memories or knowledge of the Armory Show or following the many leads which were uncovered and could not be pursued. Most deeply I regret that time did not permit a study of the archives of the Chicago Art Institute or the Copley Society. There are, therefore, still a few footnotes to be written.

Which brings me to an explanation of why this book has no footnotes. This was a decision made after careful deliberation. Every fact in the book is documented, but the exact source is not given for two reasons. First, any such precise scholarly documentation would make the text unreadable, and most of all, as a memorial to the men who arranged it, I would like this book to awaken again some of the interest which the Show itself generated. This is a book directed to the general public and not to the scholar, though I hope it will be illuminating to both. Second, since most of the documentation is based on the unpublished material described above and all of it is uncatalogued, a precise identification of sources would have been extremely cumbersome and not very valuable. It could have been done, but I chose not to for these reasons, and I accept any censure which my more pedantic brethren may feel is my due. I would like to remind the reader again that this is not an unscholarly book; it is only an unfootnoted one. Now, on with the Show!

23

COLOR PLATES

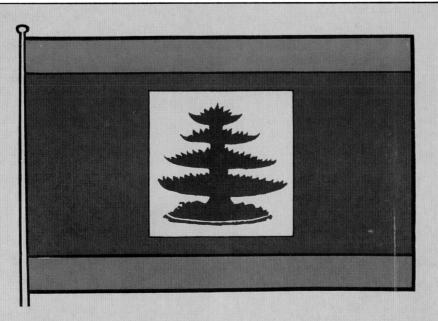

1. Armory Show poster.
Hirshhorn Museum and Sculpture Garden, Smithsonian Institution, Washington, D.C.

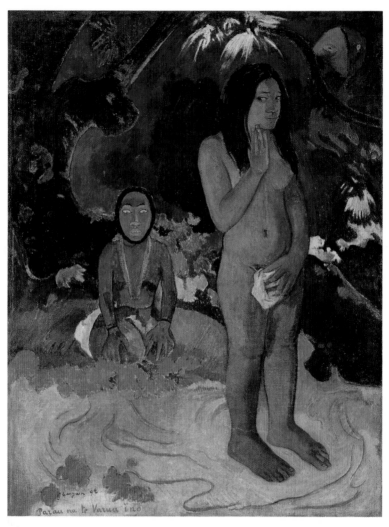

2. Paul Gauguin (1848–1903). *Words of the Devil*, 1892.
Oil on canvas, 36⅛ × 27 in. National Gallery of Art, Washington, D.C.;
Gift of Averell Harriman Foundation in memory of Marie N. Harriman.

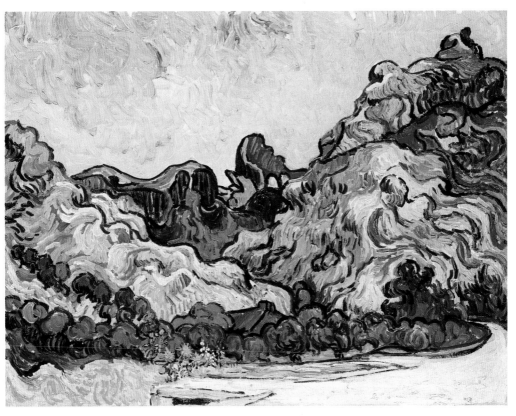

3. Vincent van Gogh (1853–1890). *Mountains at Saint-Rémy*, 1889.
Oil on canvas, 28¼ × 35¾ in. Solomon R. Guggenheim Museum, New York;
The Justin K. Thannhauser Collection.

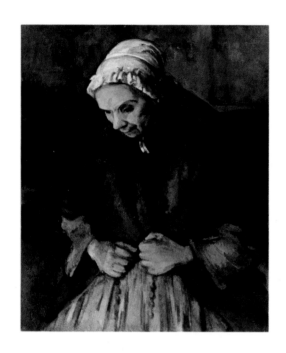

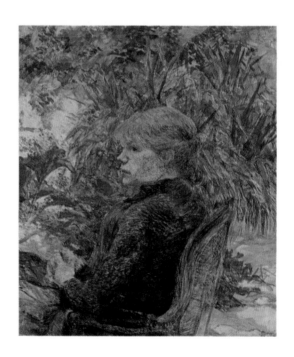

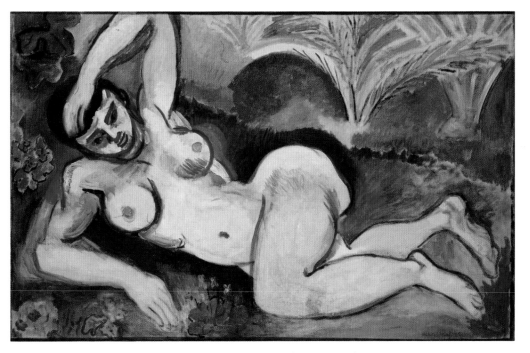

6. Henri Matisse (1869–1954). *Blue Nude* (*Souvenir de Biskra*), 1907.
Oil on canvas, 36¼ × 55¼ in. The Baltimore Museum of Art;
The Cone Collection formed by Dr. Claribel Cone
and Miss Etta Cone of Baltimore, Maryland.

Opposite, top:
4. Paul Cézanne (1839–1906). *An Old Woman with a Rosary*, c. 1896.
Oil on canvas, 31¾ × 25¾ in. The National Gallery, London.

Opposite, bottom:
5. Henri de Toulouse-Lautrec (1864–1901).
Red-Haired Woman Sitting in Conservatory, 1889.
Oil on canvas, 25½ × 20⅛ in. Private collection, U.S.A.

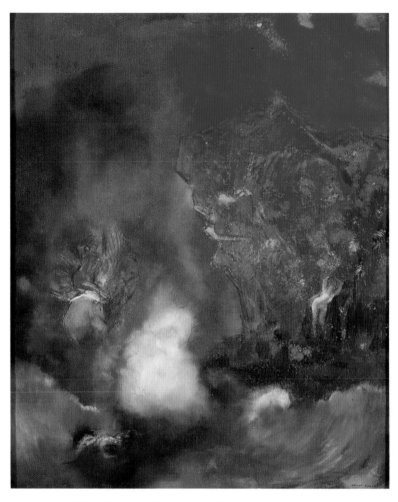

7. Odilon Redon (1840–1916). *Roger and Angelica*, c. 1910.
Pastel, 36½ × 28¾ in. Collection, The Museum of Modern Art, New York;
Lillie P. Bliss Collection.

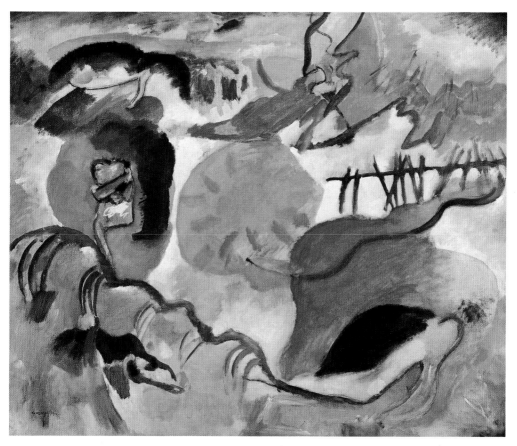

8. Wassily Kandinsky (1866–1944). *Garden of Love (Improvisation #27)*, 1912.
Oil on canvas, 47⅜ × 55¼ in. The Metropolitan Museum of Art, New York;
The Alfred Stieglitz Collection, 1949.

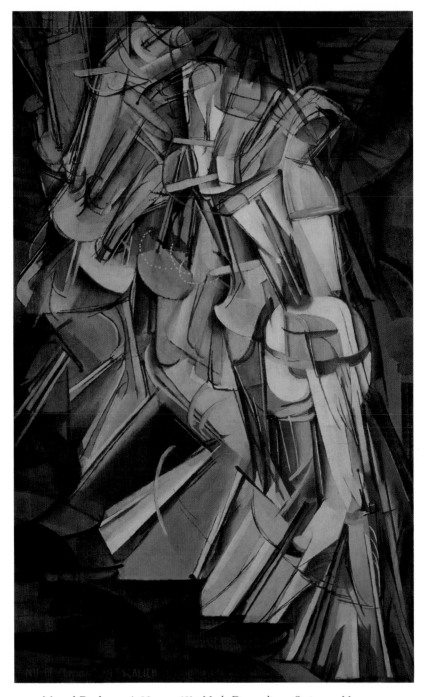

9. Marcel Duchamp (1887–1968). *Nude Descending a Staircase, No. 2,* 1912.
Oil on canvas, 58 × 35 in. Philadelphia Museum of Art;
Louise and Walter Arensberg Collection.

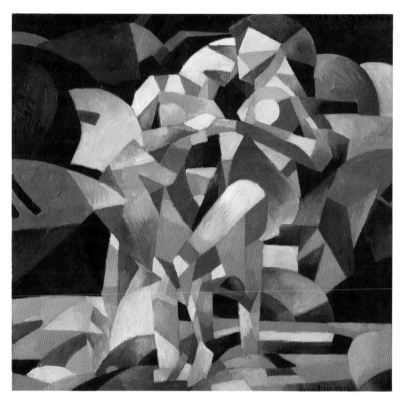

10. Francis Picabia (1879–1953). *Dances at the Spring,* 1912. Oil on canvas, 47½ × 47½ in. Philadelphia Museum of Art; Louise and Walter Arensberg Collection.

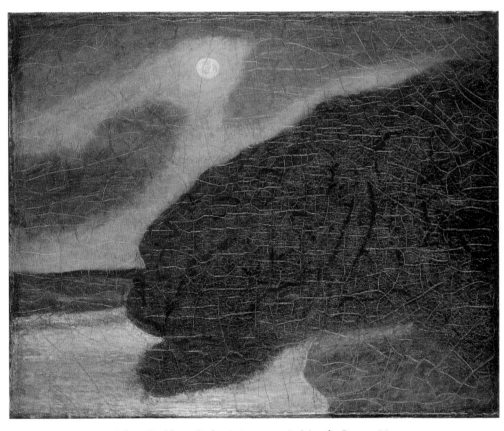

11. Albert Pinkham Ryder (1847–1917). *Moonlit Cove*, 1880–90.
Oil on canvas, 14⅛ × 17⅛ in. The Phillips Collection, Washington, D.C.

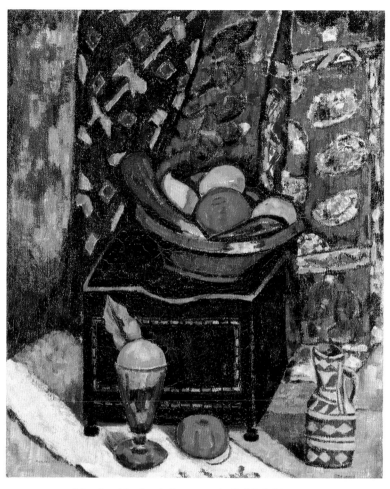

12. Marsden Hartley (1877–1943). *Still Life No. 1*, 1912.
Oil on canvas, 31 ½ × 25 ⅝ in. Columbus Museum of Art, Columbus, Ohio;
Gift of Ferdinand Howald.

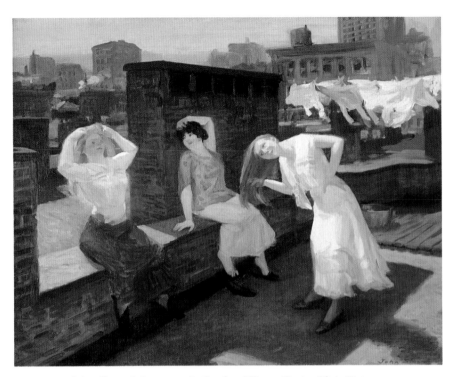

13. John Sloan (1871–1951). *Sunday, Women Drying Their Hair,* 1912.
Oil on canvas, 25½ × 31½ in. Addison Gallery of American Art,
Phillips Academy, Andover, Massachusetts.

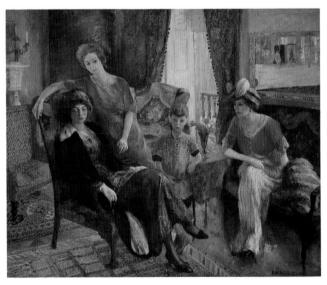

14. William Glackens (1870–1938). *Family Group,* 1910–11.
Oil on canvas, 72 × 84 in. National Gallery of Art, Washington, D.C.;
Gift of Mr. and Mrs. Ira Glackens.

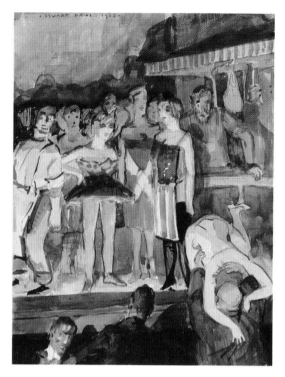

15. Stuart Davis (1892–1964). *Babe La Tour*, 1912.
Watercolor and pencil on paper, 15 × 11 in. National Museum of American Art,
Smithsonian Institution, Washington, D.C.; Gift of Henry M. Ploch.

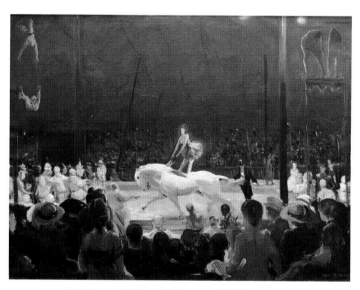

16. George Bellows (1882–1925). *Circus*, 1912.
Oil on canvas, 33⅞ × 43⅞ in. Addison Gallery of American Art,
Phillips Academy, Andover, Massachusetts.

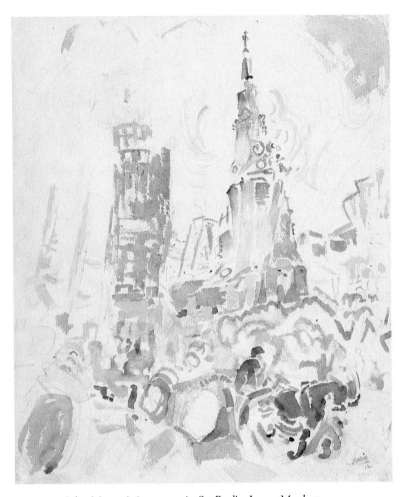

17. John Marin (1870–1953). *St. Paul's, Lower Manhattan*, 1912.
Watercolor on paper, 18⅛ × 14¾ in.
Delaware Art Museum, Wilmington, Delaware.

Opposite, top:
18. Charles Sheeler (1883–1965). *Landscape*, 1913.
Oil on panel, 10½ × 13⅞ in. Private collection, Boston.

Opposite, bottom:
19. Maurice Prendergast (1858–1924). *Landscape with Figures*, 1912.
Oil on canvas, 19¾ × 42⅞ in.
Munson-Williams-Proctor Institute, Utica, New York.

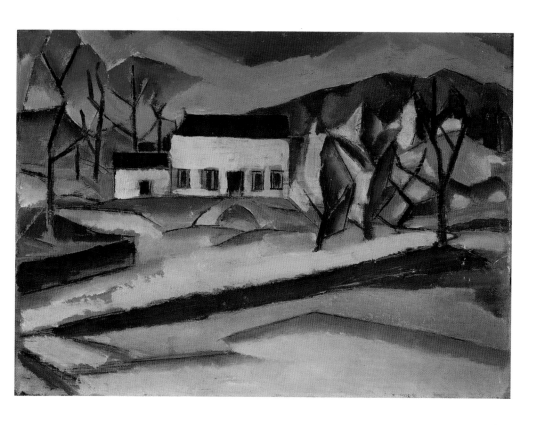
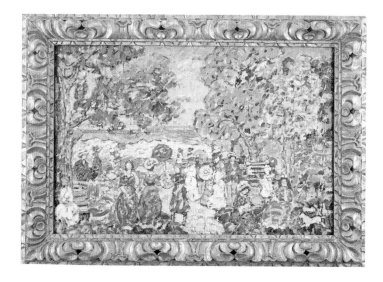

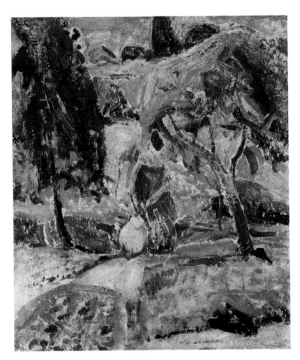

20. Alfred Maurer (1868–1932). *Autumn,* c. 1911.
Oil on board, 18 × 15 in. Nancy and Ira Glackens.

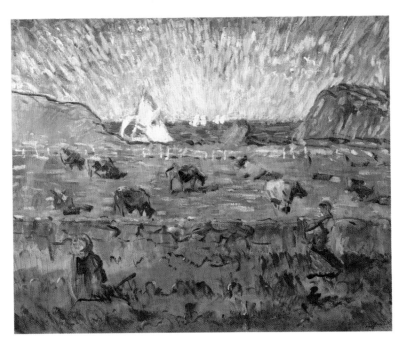

21. Walt Kuhn (1880–1949). *Morning,* 1912.
Oil on canvas, 33 × 40 in.
Norton Gallery and School of Art, West Palm Beach, Florida.

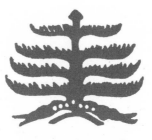

1

Success
to the Young
Society

On the evening of February 17, 1913, with four thousand guests milling around in the eighteen improvised rooms within the shell of the 69th Regiment Armory, the International Exhibition of Modern Art, more familiarly known as the Armory Show, was formally opened to the public. This sensational exhibition, which included examples of the most advanced movements in European art, was the first of its kind held in the United States and was the result of more than a year's planning and organization by a small group of artists, the Association of American Painters and Sculptors (AAPS). It was the culmination of a dream that had gotten out of hand.

Few of those who crowded the octagonal-shaped rooms formed

by a network of burlap-covered panels could have had any inkling of the impact that this event would have upon the future of American art. But everyone who wandered about in the din compounded of excited talk, laughter, and the strains of Bayne's 69th Regiment Band ensconced in the balcony and who looked at the pictures on the walls and the sculptures spotted around the floor must have felt the electric excitement of that moment. The partitions festooned with greenery, the pine trees, the flags and bunting, the yellow-hued streamers that formed a tentlike cap to the exhibition space, the richly dressed and gay crowd, the bright floodlights, and the brassy blare of the band, all helped create a festive air. Congratulations were in order. The AAPS had done the impossible. They had, all on their own, collected and exhibited more than twelve hundred American and foreign works of art for the edification and education of the American

Exterior of the 69th Regiment Armory, New York.

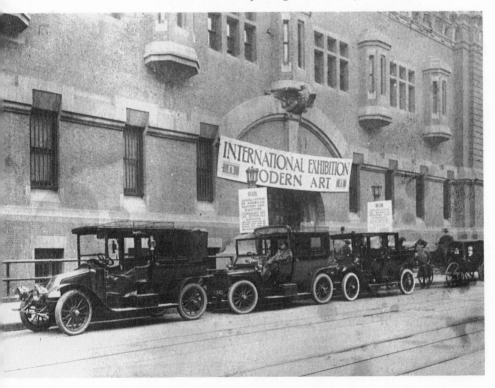

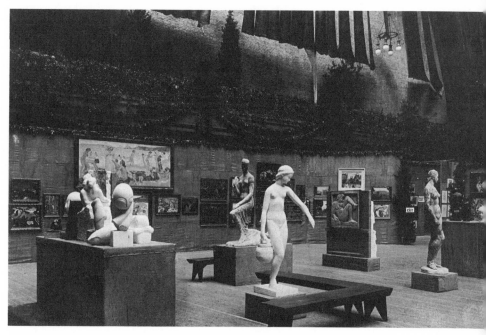

Gallery H, French painting and sculpture, New York.

art world and public. The Exhibition had been calculated from the beginning as a mental jolt to stir America out of its long esthetic complacency. So it was with an air of exultation that, after a fanfare of trumpets and a few modest words of introduction by Arthur B. Davies, the Association's president and the Exhibition's guiding genius, John Quinn formally opened the Show:

The members of this association have shown you that American artists—young American artists, that is—do not dread, and have no need to dread, the ideas or the culture of Europe. They believe that in the domain of art only the best should rule. This exhibition will be epoch making in the history of American art. Tonight will be the red-letter night in the history not only of American but of all modern art.

The members of the Association felt that it was time the American people had an opportunity to see and judge for themselves concerning the work of the Europeans who are creating a new art. Now that the exhibition is a fact, we can say with pride that it is the most complete art exhibition that has been held in the world during the last quarter century. We do not except any country or any capital.

This association has had no official, municipal, academic or other public backing. Thousands of dollars have been collected and expended by the members and its friends, who thus far have been too modest to permit the disclosure of their names. The members have had no axes to grind, no revenges to take. They have been guided by one standard— merit—and they have had the courage of their convictions.

It is difficult to be certain whether the Armory Show was the largest exhibition of art held in the last quarter-century here or in any other country, and one can pardon Quinn's sweeping assertion, but it was beyond question the most important ever held in the United States to that date and, one might add, to the present. It offered in its overwhelming size a carefully considered if somewhat makeshift exposition of the history of what we still call "Modern Art"—from Goya, Ingres, and Delacroix through the Impressionists, Post-Impressionists, Fauves, and Cubists. Although the most recent European developments from Cézanne on had occasionally been seen in small shows at Alfred Stieglitz's pioneering Photo-Secession Gallery at 291 Fifth Avenue, this was their first massive presentation to the American public; and coming as they did, telescoped into a single display, the impact was intensified to the level of shock.

This radical new art that people had been hearing about for so long a time was imbedded in a large mass of American art which only in a few cases had even the remotest connection with it. And although some American critics found balm in the sanity of American art in contrast to European decadence, it was the European contingent and the most advanced of those that stole the show. In spite of ridicule and vituperation, the sweep of artistic history could not be impeded by either ignorance or eloquence; American art was never the same again. The impact upon the younger artists was immediate. Complacency was shattered. The Academy was dead, both esthetically and institutionally. The most vital artists in the United States were allied with the AAPS, and they had done what the National Academy of Design had always maintained was impossible without public support, that is, put on an exciting exhibition of monster proportions. It didn't matter that it would never be done again and that the AAPS had shot its bolt; the one shot was enough. The Academy never again played any significant role on the American artistic stage. The younger generation would no longer even seek Academy recognition.

As far as the press and public were concerned, the Show was a circus, full of freaks and clowns, but also of life and color. The press had never had such an opportunity before, an art show that exuded copy by the ream. In the first place, the New York press was down on the Academy because of the latter's earlier campaign to raise money and public support for a new building in Central Park, which most newspapers had fought as an encroachment on public property by a private institution. For a long time the Academy had been blaming most of its ills on the lack of space, and when the AAPS, consisting of but twenty-five artists, through private means, individual initiative, and without public support had given New York an eighteen-room circus, the press was jubilant.

The Armory Show was hailed as "sensational," "magnificent," and "unquestionably the most important ever held in New York." The AAPS was congratulated and commended and the Academy lectured and ridiculed in news stories, reviews, and editorials. The early press reactions were mostly favorable and from an editorial point of view remained so to a very great extent. It was only after the largely conservative critical fraternity began to whip up an esthetic witch hunt and the know-nothing yellow press found in some of the exhibits a source of low humor that the tide began to turn and the public came to gape, snicker, and jeer. These jibes were sometimes good-humored, sometimes tinged with philistine nastiness, and frequently inept, but the critical attacks were hysterically vicious. At the end, in the public mind the immensity and importance of the Exhibition may have been lost in an image of freakish madness, but the younger generation of artists who had seen it had been stirred.

The idea of the Armory Show had taken a long time to mature. Its earliest glimmers go back to late 1911, and in some ways even beyond, with the meeting of four young artists—Jerome Myers, Elmer MacRae, Walt Kuhn, and Henry Fitch Taylor. What eventually took place must have made the preliminary meetings seem in retrospect to have had a more conscious direction than they actually did, and, depending on the person involved, memories of the first encounter vary. What is clear is that these four talked about the problems of the American artist, about the difficulties of showing their work either within or outside the framework of the Academy, about forming an organization through which they might work to improve exhibition conditions, and also about the general problem of getting American art out of its rut.

These first talks and meetings occurred at the Madison Gallery at 305 Madison Avenue and at the nearby studio of Jerome Myers in the McHugh Building, 7 West 42nd Street. The Madison Gallery was part of a decorator's establishment, the Coventry Stu-

Elmer L. MacRae.

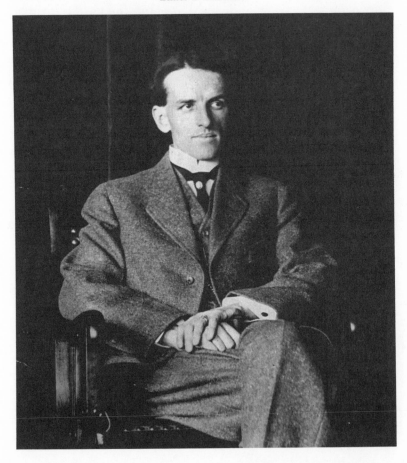

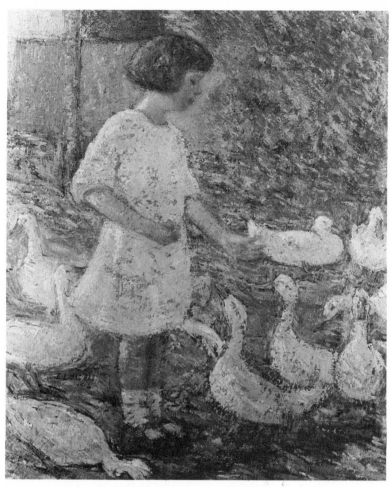

Elmer L. MacRae (1875–1955). *Feeding the Ducks,* 1912.
Oil on canvas, 32 × 26 in.
Location unknown.

dios, run by Clara S. Davidge with, it is said, the backing of
Gertrude Vanderbilt Whitney. The gallery, which exhibited the
work of the more progressive young artists of the period, was
managed by Henry Fitch Taylor, a landscape painter and protégé
of Mrs. Davidge, who was deeply sympathetic with creative
activity (her other protégé at the time was the poet Edwin
Arlington Robinson).

It was early in December of 1911 that the Madison Gallery had an exhibition of the Pastellists, a small group of artists interested in fostering that medium, in which Myers and MacRae were active and in which they and Kuhn were represented. During the usual exhibition doldrums, the four men got together and talked about the difficulties of exhibiting. The talks continued at the gallery and in Myers' studio and they finally decided to take some action. The historic meeting is recorded in the official minutes book of the Association: "On December 14th, 1911 the following men: Messrs. Henry Fitch Taylor, Jerome Myers, Elmer Mac-Rae and Walt Kuhn, met to discuss the possibilities of organizing a society for the purpose of exhibiting the works of progressive and live painters, both American and foreign—favoring such work usually neglected by current shows and especially interesting and instructive to the public."*

The next few days were spent in recruiting the sixteen artists they had decided to invite as charter members of the society. All of them were essentially anti-Academy in outlook, in either an artistic or an organizational sense. Many of them had been involved earlier in the abortive Independent Artists Exhibition held in April, 1910, in a loft at 29 West 35th Street, and in many ways the AAPS was a continuation of that original group. Some of them had participated in the MacDowell Club exhibitions under the aegis of Robert Henri, who had championed the principle of "no jury—no prizes" and favored the practice of small groups of congenial artists exhibiting together. "The Eight," whose exhibition at the Macbeth Galleries in 1908 had created a major stir in American art, all became members of the Association, with the exception of Everett Shinn, who was invited to join but never did. As a matter of fact, all of these three older groups had an interlocking personnel.

The first official meeting of this new society took place at the invitation of Henry Fitch Taylor at the Madison Gallery

---

* In the Kuhn letters given to the Archives of American Art by Brenda Kuhn in February 1965, there is evidence that Kuhn was contemplating the formation of a "new society" as early as December 9, 1911. Kuhn's description of the idea as his own in a letter of December 12 does not accord with his later account in *The Story of the Armory Show.*

on December 19. Although according to an entry in MacRae's diary the original four had met to choose sixteen additional artists as charter members and Kuhn has written that by December 16 there were sixteen members, at that first meeting thirteen artists were present—D. Putnam Brinley, Gutzon Borglum, John Mowbray-Clarke, Arthur B. Davies, Leon Dabo, William J. Glackens, Walt Kuhn, Ernest Lawson, Jonas Lie, George B. Luks, Elmer MacRae, Jerome Myers, and Taylor—and by proxy Karl Anderson, James E. Fraser, Allen Tucker, and J. Alden Weir. The minutes of the meeting along with that of January 2, 1912, exist in a notebook in the Kuhn Papers. Taylor opened the meeting with the following words:

You have been asked to meet here this evening to take active steps toward the formation of a national association of painters and sculptors—an association of live and progressive men and women who shall lead the public taste in art rather than follow it.

The National Academy of Design is not expected to lead the public taste. It never did and never will, and as no such organization as the one contemplated exists in this country today, we must all, I think, admit the very positive need of forming one.

Recognizing, then, the need for such an organization, the only effective way of meeting that need is to set to work and form it. The matter is now before you and open for discussion; and we shall be pleased to listen to any gentleman present who has anything to say either for or against the movement.

After this short welcoming speech, Taylor was elected temporary chairman and Kuhn, temporary secretary. The first order of business was the drafting of a platform, and in the simple and forthright one-sentence statement of principle is the foundation of the organization and the Armory Show itself. Proposed by Borglum and seconded by MacRae, the following was accepted as the Society's platform: "For the purpose of developing a broad interest in American art activities, by holding exhibitions of the best contemporary work that can be secured, representative of American and foreign art."

Considering the later charges by some members that the original conception of the organization was to present American art exclusively and that it was subverted by Davies and his clique into the espousal of foreign art, it should be noted at this point

49

that in the original document not only was foreign art included, but "foreign" was written first, erased and replaced by "American." The intention of the Association was from the very beginning to exhibit art, both American and foreign.

The next order of business was the selection of a name for the group, and after the rejection of "National Association of Painters and Sculptors," "American Painters and Sculptors" was accepted. It became officially the Association of American Painters and Sculptors when the society was incorporated. Kuhn was appointed spokesman for the organization. Borglum proposed the joint and equal membership in office and committees of painters and sculptors. This was later to cause a good deal of trouble since the painters far outnumbered the sculptors and the artificial imposition of numerical equality was not feasible. A Constitutional Committee consisting of Borglum, Davies, and Mowbray-Clarke was elected and directed to draw up a constitution by the next meeting. Luks introduced and Myers seconded a proposal that the nonjury principle be considered for the constitution. The election of officers followed and Weir, who was not present then nor at any subsequent meetings, was elected president; Gutzon Borglum, vice-president; Kuhn, secretary; and MacRae, treasurer. Taylor was elected chairman of a Committee of the Whole, and Myers, Dabo, and Fraser were appointed to an Executive Committee. The membership voted to assess themselves $5 a head for current expenses; the next meeting was set for January 2 at 8 P.M.; and, after Taylor had offered the gallery as a temporary meeting place and was duly thanked, the meeting was adjourned.

Thus began the official history of the Association of American Painters and Sculptors. Certainly none of them envisaged the great adventure they were beginning. But they were an aggressive bunch, determined to do something. From the very outset they made a point of getting their activities before the eyes of the public through the press. They were, after all, a very distinguished group of artists.

Weir, though an academician, was one of the illustrious "Ten," highly regarded as a fine Impressionist painter of the older generation. A genial man, modest, and liberal in his esthetic outlook, he often allied himself with the younger generation and they used him, as in this case, as a symbol of respectability. Gutzon

Borglum was perhaps the best-known artist in America, partly because of his many important public commissions, but mostly because of his flamboyant and pugnacious personality. He was always in the news, for one reason or another, and he loved a fight and usually kept the press informed of his side of the affair through blow-by-blow letters or interviews. Although essentially an academic sculptor, he was one of the first to exhibit a strong Rodin influence in his work and could not abide his more timid and conservative colleagues at the Academy. He had been one of the leaders in the public fight against granting the Academy land in Central Park on which to erect a new building, and his eagerness to join the new group and accept leadership within it was, perhaps, in a large measure the result of a continuing desire to pursue his personal vendetta with the Academy. Arthur B. Davies, of whom I will have more to say later, was looked upon by the more progressive elements in American art, both artists and critics, as the greatest living American painter.

The rest were younger artists who had achieved some measure of recognition, either as members of The Eight and the "Ash Can School," or more modestly in exhibitions like those at the MacDowell Club or the Independents. As a matter of fact, of the twenty-five members who finally formed the roster of the Association, seven were members of the National Academy of Design. Weir and Henri were full members and George Bellows, Glackens, Lie, Lawson, and Mahonri Young were associates. These were, then, not primarily the dispossessed or the incompetents of the art world, but practitioners well known within their profession, interested in showing their works under more congenial circumstances than those offered by the Academy, without the dead weight of that institution's standardized mediocrity, and in stirring the American public to an awareness of the vitality of art as a living experience. From the very beginning they received an excellent press and managed to use that reservoir of sympathy effectively.

The next two weeks must have been full of discussion, of planning for the next meeting, and of instilling in each other the fervor necessary to get the project off the ground. In the early days of the group it was the younger men, the original four especially, who generated most of the enthusiasm. Myers and MacRae were old and close friends as well as colleagues in the Pastellists, where they had amassed a good deal of experience in keeping an organization alive; MacRae was its secretary-treasurer. As a matter of fact, Kuhn had first approached them because he admired their success with that group. The MacRae diary notes some of the activity that went on. He records two meetings, one with Myers, Davies, and Luks, and the other a lunch meeting with Myers and Mowbray-Clarke, with the notation, "meeting about APS." On December 26, Robert Henri, the dean of the Ash Can School and long a rallying point of reform on the American art scene, accepted an invitation in a note to Walt Kuhn: "Success to the young society. May its growth have a long life! Will be there with pleasure Jan. 2 at 8 P.M."

Although the official minutes of the December 19 meeting make no mention of the fact, the MacRae diary notes: "elected Henri charter member." The Constitutional Committee, consisting of Borglum, Davies, and Mowbray-Clarke, must have met several times during those days, working out a set of bylaws which would embody their basic principles and intentions. In a letter dated December 29 they submitted a draft of the constitution to Weir.

The second meeting of the AAPS was held as scheduled. The minutes note that fourteen members were present, but do not list them. Weir, according to his own statement, was not present. After the minutes of the previous meeting were read and accepted, the constitution was read and discussed. There seems to have been some disagreement and it was referred back to the committee. Henri suggested increasing the membership of the AAPS and Borglum then proposed a list of sculptors who were obviously intended to balance the preponderance of painters, for at that time he, Mowbray-Clarke, and Fraser were the only sculptors. He proposed his brother Solon, Andrew O'Connor, Paul Bartlett, Frederick C. R. Roth, and George Grey Barnard, all of whom were elected to membership although none of them ever accepted the honor.

Of the painters proposed and elected, George Bellows, Maurice B. Prendergast, Edward Adam Kramer, John Sloan, and Everett Shinn were proposed by Myers; Guy Pène du Bois and Frank A. Nankivell by Kuhn; Bryson Burroughs by Luks; Childe

Hassam by Taylor; Henry Reuterdahl by Henri; and Bruce Porter by Davies. There was some discussion as to whether Burroughs as curator of painting at the Metropolitan Museum of Art would be able to accept, and it was suggested that he be asked. Hassam declined in a graceful note, but the records show no reply from Reuterdahl or Shinn. One would have expected Shinn to join since he had been so intimately connected with many of the members, but it may be that by that time he was too deeply involved in interior and theatrical decoration and too far removed from their problems and from his earlier allegiance. His occupation with the execution of the mural decoration for the Trenton, New Jersey, City Hall may also have had something to do with his absence.

The final make-up of the organization included also Jo Davidson, Sherry E. Fry, and Mahonri Young, all sculptors, who had probably been invited by the board of directors after the entire slate proposed by Borglum had declined election. Fraser disappears from the lists from this time forth and there is actually no evidence that he ever attended a meeting. Fry accepted the invitation on April 25, 1912, but seems never to have been active in the society. In a letter of resignation dated May 14, 1914, he complained that a resignation tendered a year previously had been ignored. A polite letter of refusal from A. Stirling Calder, dated January 3, 1912, is a little puzzling since there is no record of his being elected to membership. In view of all these facts it must be assumed that either the records of the meetings are incomplete or that the organization was not overly concerned with the letter of the bylaws in inviting participants.

The meeting of January 2 lasted until after midnight but New York's morning newspapers carried the story of the new organization, evidence at the very outset of their ability to handle the press. Kuhn had obviously prepared a press release, since all the dailies printed essentially the same story or parts of it. The fundamental principle of the association was quoted, but it was also stressed that the AAPS was opposed to the Academy, that its purpose was to afford exhibition facilities to artists out of sympathy with the Academy and under conditions of greater dignity, and that it was not dominated by any school or clique. Mention was also made of a plan for a new building in competition with

53

the proposed $200,000 Academy project. This building plan was a curious item. It was mentioned in many of the stories and obviously was not a fabrication, but there are no records or even hints in any of the other available sources that this was ever seriously considered, nor was it ever mentioned again.

Unfortunately, the emphasis of the newspaper accounts on the anti-Academy attitude of the new society precipitated the immediate resignation of the newly elected president, J. Alden Weir. As a matter of fact, he had hardly heard of his election before he was writing an open letter to the *Times*:

I was greatly surprised to find in your columns this morning the statement that I am the president of a new society "openly at war with the Academy of Design." I have been a loyal member of the Academy for more than twenty-five years, and I am now a member of its Council. I believe (under the able leadership of its President, Mr. Alexander) it to be doing everything in its power for the promotion of art in this country, and it would be impossible for me to take such a position as that which the new society is said to occupy.

I have attended no meetings of this society, and was told only that it was formed to provide further facilities for the exhibition of such worthy work, particularly by younger artists, as is, unfortunately, sometimes crowded out of the Academy exhibitions by lack of adequate gallery space, and that it had no intention of antagonizing the older institution. As I am always interested in any movement for the betterment of artistic conditions, I reluctantly accepted the office. . . .

The account of the aims of the new society given to your representative has convinced me that I have no business *dans cette galère*, and I have formally declined the presidency and the membership tendered me.

Trusting that you will give this statement the same publicity as that which you have already printed, I remain, yours truly,

J. Alden Weir
471 Park Avenue, New York, Jan. 3, 1911.

Weir also sent a shorter and more formal note to Henry Fitch Taylor in which he broke off all connections with the association:

When you told me I had been elected President of a new society formed for the exhibition of works of art by our younger artists, I consented to serve in that capacity on the distinct understanding that no opposition to the National Academy of Design was intended. The publication this morning of an account of the aims of the new society entirely changes the situation, and I am made to lend my name to an attack on the Academy and on my friend, John W. Alexander, its President.

I must therefore peremptorily decline to allow any further use of my name as either President or member of the society you are engaged in forming.

An immediate reply was forthcoming from Borglum, who was never loath to speak for publication. In an interview with a *Times* reporter, he expressed amazement that Weir did not know the new society was out of sympathy with the National Academy and stated:

The present urgency for the organization was the full realization that the Academy was on the point of taking steps that would make it impossible to have a non-partisan building in New York. The understanding of this was so clear and it was so freely discussed that no one could possibly have been unaware of its meaning.

I believe Mr. Weir was asked to join in this movement in the same way that I was asked to join it. I joined because the movement was so timely and so necessary. The movement would have gone on and formed itself without Mr. Weir and without me. You may be sure that it will go on. We will find the best painter we can for President in Mr. Weir's place. We will need to find a man that is willing to lead a fight.

In spite of Borglum's strongly stated views, it is probable that the members of the group were not as unanimously anti-Academy as he would have it, and it is entirely possible that that aspect of the group's intentions was never expressed to Weir. At any rate the AAPS, hardly under way, had lost its president and was embroiled in a public dispute with the Academy. But some of its leading members were not ready to see the organization flounder without leadership or dissipate its energies in fruitless debate over the evils of the Academy. The first order of business was the election of a new president. The choice was obviously between Henri and Davies, the oldest and most established of the painters. There must have been a good deal of discussion and maneuvering among adherents of both. The Henri supporters were strong within the organization, but there was probably some feeling that he was too clearly identified with the Ash Can

55

School and previous controversial causes to make the best leader for an organization which desired to present a nonpartisan image to the art world and the public.

The published statements of both Kuhn and Myers, although in disagreement, have created the impression that Davies was pulled out of a hat like a rabbit. The fact is that Davies, as I have already noted, was one of the original members of the society and a member of its Constitutional Committee. It has also been the general feeling that Davies was selected because the members felt that he was the only one who had financial connections which

Arthur B. Davies.

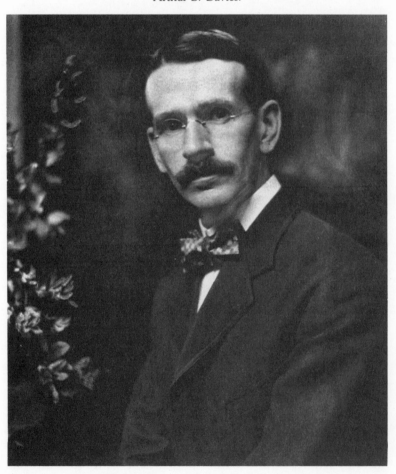

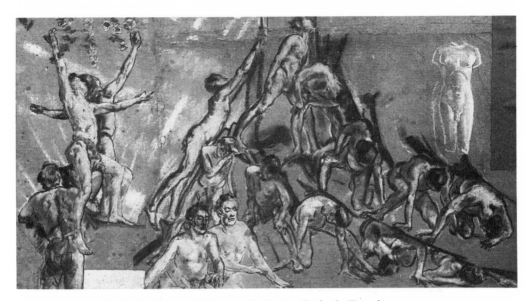

Arthur B. Davies (1862–1928). *Design, Birth of a Tragedy,* 1912.
Pastel on paper, 18 × 34½ in. Colby College Museum of Art, Waterville, Maine;
Gift of Mrs. Joseph M. Kaplan.

would make the Armory Show possible, but what should be remembered is that at the time that dream had not as yet been con-
ceived. It would seem more reasonable to assume that he was selected because he was the logical choice. His reputation was
unassailable, his art was unique and unconnected with any of
the more recognizable tendencies in American art, and he stood
aloof from cliques, yet was identified with liberal artistic movements. The problem seems to have been to convince this essentially retiring and apparently unaggressive individual to accept
the job. And it may have been that a good many of the members
thought they were getting a new figurehead to replace Weir and
that they could then simply go ahead with their own plans. Subsequent events led many to regret the choice, for they had picked
a tiger. This man of fastidiously aristocratic bearing, a painter of
poetic sensitivity bordering on the ephemeral, this shy, reticent,
and coolly formal person, whom his closest co-workers continued
always to call Mr. Davies or "the chief," turned out to be a creature of driving energy, incisive command, organizational ability,

and authoritarian attitude. Once in the seat, he drove with unswerving directness and amazing control. His was truly a hand of steel in a suede glove.

Many years later, writing with some bitterness and a rankling memory of the dissolution of the Association, Guy Pène du Bois recalled the moment:

> When Davies was made president of the society sponsoring the Armory Show, he underwent an amazing metamorphosis. He had been a rather perfervid dweller in the land of romance, an invention of his or of his Welsh blood, in which attenuated nudes walked in rhythmic strides borrowed from the languors of lovers. This was a moody and not too healthy world. Women adored it. Davies, keeping himself inviolate, lived a secret life from which he would sometimes emerge, nervous, furtive, apparently incapable of making the contacts of the real world. He would escape from a gallery which contained more than two or three visitors. That many annoyances, he told me once, defeated his enjoyment of the picture. Another time an invitation to see his work in progress was qualified with the condition that the address of his studio must afterward be forgotten. At meetings of artists he would be the most reserved and quiet one present. His presidency produced a dictator, severe, arrogant, implacable. The isolationist strode out in the open, governed with something equivalent to the terrible Ivan's rod of iron.

However, this "dragon evolved from that very gentle cocoon," as du Bois described Davies, was not everything he appeared on the surface. In spite of his eminence as an artist, he remained enigmatic as a person. Information about his life, suppressed for so many years, which came to my attention during the writing of this book, throws new light on his personality and his actions.

Although Davies was married and had a wife and two sons living in Congers, New York, he was leading and continued to lead until his death a secret, though entirely domestic, existence in New York City with another woman, Edna Potter, who was soon to give birth to his daughter. He kept this part of his life as David A. Owen so well hidden that even his closest associates were unaware of it. His daughter did not learn that her father was Arthur B. Davies until after his death. The "mystery" surrounding his death in Florence is apparently no mystery at all, but simply a fabrication to hide the fact that he died of a heart attack while traveling abroad with his little family, Edna and their young daughter, Ronnie. A good deal of the secrecy of his life and actions must have been the result of an effort to hide his double identity. One wonders how he ever managed to live the life of an artist, and a well-known one, be active in artistic affairs, manipulate a whole circle of devoted women art patrons, visit his family in Congers, and keep a domestic fire burning on East 52nd Street. The man, in spite of his "schoolteacher" look and reticent airs, was a good deal more than he seemed, as his colleagues were soon to discover.

At that time, however, the problem was to get him to accept the presidency. It seems that Myers and MacRae were instrumental in finally convincing him to accept the position, perhaps by assuring him that there would be no opposition to his election. The entries in MacRae's diary for the early days of 1912 are indicative of the concerted activities of these two men who were out to get the membership committed to Davies. It is sometimes difficult to know from the notations whether MacRae was doing things alone or together with Myers. One can assume, however, that the activity was mutually planned and shared. On January 4, Glackens, who was very close to Henri, was won over and consented to Davies' election. The next day Myers and MacRae called on Davies who, after declining at first, accepted. Then followed the feverish activity of convincing the others, perhaps best re-created by the short entries in MacRae's diary:

Jan 5—Called on Davies consent for president—Mad[ison] Gallery Lawson Luks—Myers at Studio—DuBois at Myers—Dabo Myers at Mad[ison] Gal[lery]—
[Jan 6]—Myers family at Cos Cob—Virginia [Myers' daughter] danced—Sunday [Jan 7] Myers and I called at Borglum—Stamford
Jan 8—Brinley—Called up Tucker—Dabo twice—Clark Kuhn Myers for lunch—Borglum at Mad[ison] Gal[lery]

After this preparation, the members met on Tuesday evening, January 9, and elected Davies to replace Weir. They also voted a constitution and elected a board of trustees and a committee to speak for the organization. Henry Fitch Taylor, as chairman of this committee, issued a statement of purpose and policy:

59

The Association of American Painters and Sculptors have organized for the purpose of holding exhibitions of their work and the best examples procurable of contemporary art, without relation to school, size, medium or nationality. It is called American because we are an American organization; beyond that we are not drawing the line of nationality or locality upon art. We shall have among our members such men in the world of the fine arts as believe that sincerity, reverence and individuality are characteristics worthy of fostering.

We have organized to help and to do. We shall push consistently and persistently our constructive policy. We shall make our exhibitions as interesting as they will be representative (do not forget nor lose sight of that word representative) of American or European art activities.

We have no canons except honesty and the ability to express one's self. We do not believe that any artist has discovered or ever will discover the only way to create beauty. That agreed, we make no apology for our existence; and by that same principle we find no fault with others who seek their way in their way.

Exhibition is the purpose of our uniting. How to exhibit and protect the producer against the indefinable tyranny every institution sooner or later exerts is our great problem. That is the one thing we mean to solve if it can be done.

We are ready to help any unselfish plan that may be proposed which admits of development and public exhibition of art productions on the above lines.

If the above principles are antagonistic to the Academy and offend, that, of course, we deplore. That such principles should offend is sufficient proof that generosity, public spirit, a desire to "let live" is not a canon in the creed of our sister organization.

The eight men elected to form the first board of trustees reflected a conscious attempt to embrace the variety of artistic tendencies represented in the Association and included Davies, Borglum, Kuhn, MacRae, Mowbray-Clarke, Myers, Henri, and Taylor.

Some aspects of the constitution accepted at the meeting and released to the press were of unusual interest. In the first place, there were to be no juries for Association exhibitions. Only invited works would be shown. And then there was a novel provision that any member could invite a participant and if the recommendation did not meet with favor, the member could surrender any part or the whole of his allotted space to the artist he had invited. In the heat of the Armory Show, the only exhibition ever held by the AAPS, these carefully considered provisions were completely ignored.

And so, after one false start the Association of American Painters and Sculptors was launched with a flurry of publicity and a round of applause from the press in editorial comment. The new association was welcomed, its statement of principles praised, and the hope was expressed that it would not fall into the trap of institutional rigidity, although there were some misgivings that, though its members were distinguished, it might not be strong enough to buck the entrenched power of the Academy.

Dedicated as it was to exhibition, the Association's first problem was to get a place to show. But this was no simple assignment. After all, the complaint of the Academy had been that New York had no adequate exhibition building for a large show. The earlier Independent Show had been a failure partly because of the inadequacy of the rented loft in which it was presented. The members debated the problem, but none of the proposals seemed feasible. Madison Square Garden was rejected as too large and expensive, and everything else was too small and unattractive. Someone suggested an armory as a possibility. Kuhn visited several of them and in April began negotiations for the use of the new Armory of the 69th Regiment, National Guard, New York, called "The Fighting Irish," on Lexington Avenue between 25th and 26th streets. Negotiations were carried on between the AAPS and Colonel Louis D. Conley, Commanding Officer, and on April 19, Col. Conley wrote Kuhn, as secretary, a letter setting forth the terms. The rent was $5,000 plus $500 for janitorial service and the available dates were February 1 or 15 to March 1 or 15. That was a lot of money and obviously beyond the means of a small group of artists. A good deal of soul- and pocket-searching must have gone on, and one can imagine that the outlook was not very encouraging. But Davies had sources he could go to. He never said who they were, but he made the necessary arrangements and underwrote the adventure. As almost the sole source of support, he took over the reins more firmly, and from then on it would be difficult to question his actions. On May 6, Col. Conley agreed to the lease and option with provisions for the payment of $1,500 on signing the lease before May 25 and an

61

additional $3,500 before February 1, 1913, at which date the $500 for janitorial services was also to be paid. The next day Davies closed the deal with a check for $50 and on the last day of the option the AAPS met the terms of the agreement by depositing checks of $1,000 from Davies and $500 from Borglum.

The official signing of the contract had to await the incorporation of the society, which involved a certain amount of red tape, and although John Quinn, acting as legal representative, tried to hurry things along, it was not until July 1 that the Board of Directors of the newly incorporated Association of American Painters and Sculptors held its first meeting. Present were Davies, MacRae, Myers, Taylor, Mowbray-Clarke, and Kuhn. They went through the necessary formalities of electing officers and notifying members, and empowered a committee consisting of Davies, Borglum, and Kuhn to complete the contract with the Armory. The first step had been taken, but what loomed ahead must have been fairly frightening. This immense and cavernous interior had to be adapted for an exhibition and the art had to be assembled. All the details of invitation, transportation, insurance, storage, publicity, and the many still unguessed tasks would have been enough to give pause to the seasoned staff of a museum or academy, let alone a handful of impractical artists. And here they were, $1,500 in debt and without any answers.

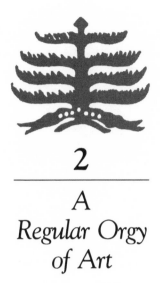

2

A
Regular Orgy
of Art

U nfortunately, the following months are the ones
about which we have the
least information. There are records covering the printing of sta-
tionery and extracts from the constitution. There is even some
indication that invitations to exhibit had been issued to American artists. A letter from Morton L. Schamberg to Walter Pach,
then abroad, is of special interest because it is the only evidence
we have that such invitations had already been circulated. The
following is an extract from that letter, dated August 23, 1912,
and now in the Pach Papers:

Did you know there's to be an exhibition in N.Y. this winter of
American painters and sculptors (a new organization as far as I know).
The president is Arthur B. Davies. I got an invitation to exhibit with

them the other day. It is rather funny as I have just gotten to the point where I don't care whether anyone sees my pictures for years to come. I don't expect to sell and don't need to if the photography goes and while I am glad to show them to anyone who is interested, I can say to hell with the exhibitions and dealers. However this thing sounds as though it might be worth while. We'll see. The MacDowell Club sounded fairly good at first too. . . . I'll surely get over during that show as they promise to have some Cézannes etc.

Doubtless there were proposals, discussions, and counter-proposals about the nature of the Exhibition, yet we have no inkling as to what kind of exhibition the membership wanted or imagined, except for a later statement by Myers that he had always expected it to be a show of American art. However, from the very beginning it was clear that the Association expected to include European art in its exhibitions, probably to increase their appeal. But what kind of European art? It is difficult to know how many of the members were aware of the radical art movements abroad. The truth is that they were largely American-oriented, perhaps radical in a local sense, but essentially insular in outlook. Of the younger American artists who were later to lead American art into the realm of modernism and had experienced the new movements at first hand while studying abroad, none were members of the AAPS. My guess would be that the only ones who had any consciousness of what was going on in Paris were Davies and Prendergast, and the latter was not yet a part of the active group within the society.

The die was cast sometime late that summer when Davies saw a catalogue of the Cologne Sonderbund Show, officially the Internationale Kunstausstellung des Sonderbundes Westdeutscher Kunstfreunde und Künstler, or the International Art Exhibition of the Federation of West German Art-Lovers (Patrons) and Artists. He apparently recognized immediately that this was the kind of show that they needed or, at least, that he wanted. It was large, spectacular, varied, inclusive, and was concerned with presenting contemporary innovations in conjunction with their historical antecedents. There has always been some question why Davies did not go himself to Cologne. The recent birth of a daughter may have made a junket abroad at that time inconvenient, but acting with decision and dispatch he sent the cata-

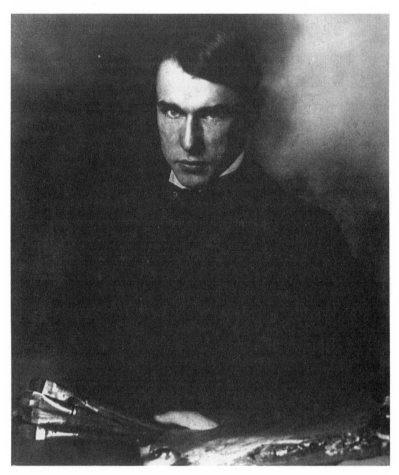

Walt Kuhn.

logue to Kuhn, who was on a painting trip in Nova Scotia. Although there is no documentary evidence, my guess would be that Davies hoped to get the core of that show without its local German flavor as the basis of the European contingent at the Armory Show. According to Kuhn, the catalogue came with a short note saying, "I wish we could have a show like this."

Continuing in Kuhn's own words: "In a flash I was decided. I wired him to secure steamer reservations for me; there was just time to catch the boat which would make it possible to reach Cologne before the close of the show. Davies saw me off at the dock. His parting words at the dock were, 'Go ahead, you can do it.'"

Kuhn reached Cologne late in the evening before September 30, the last day of the exhibition. In the turmoil of the closing, he could get little attention, but he was allowed to wander around while it was being dismantled. The show was a stunner. One can imagine that Kuhn was shaken and excited by the experience. It included an overwhelming collection of 125 works by Van Gogh as the *pièce de résistance,* 26 paintings by Cézanne, 25 by Gauguin, 17 by the Pointillist Henri Edmond Cross and 18 by his colleague Paul Signac, 16 by the new artistic meteor Pablo Picasso, and 32 by Edvard Munch. He saw also some of the leading Fauves and most of the German Expressionists, as well as one painting which he probably did not notice by Piet Mondrian. He met Wilhelm Lehmbruck and arranged to have his works shown in New York. He says that he secured the works of Munch for the

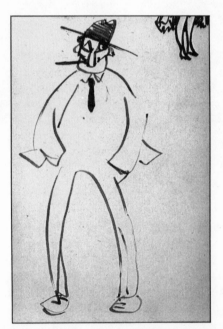

Walt Kuhn (1877–1949). *Untitled (Girl Watched).*
Hirshhorn Museum and Sculpture Garden,
Smithsonian Institution, Washington, D.C.;
Gift of Joseph H. Hirshhorn Foundation, 1966.

Armory Show, but the Munchs in the New York Exhibition were prints which arrived at the last moment.

However, the conception of the Armory Show was set. The problem was now to collect the works, if not to reproduce the Sonderbund, to duplicate, emulate, or rival it. Kuhn visited in rapid succession The Hague, October 5; Amsterdam, October 7; Berlin, October 8; and Munich, October 13. At The Hague he saw for the first time a collection of paintings and pastels by Odilon Redon, who was still little known and not widely appreciated. He was captivated by their uniqueness as well as by their opulence of color and was sure that he had made a momentous discovery. With great enthusiasm he began negotiations with the firm of Artz & de Bois to bring a large representation of Redon's art to America. He also arranged with them for a group of Van Goghs. In Berlin he made contact with the dealer Hans Goltz and in Munich with Heinrich Thannhauser, and to a large extent the German contingent eventually exhibited at the Armory Show was limited to the men handled by these dealers. He had printed a circular in German, announcing the Exhibition and the conditions of participation, which was distributed to German artists.

The Paris of 1912 which awaited him was a rich layer cake of cultural activity. There were many new sensations, insurgent movements in all the arts, a general ebullience of creativity which would be difficult to miss if one were intellectually alive. One could see the Diaghileff ballet or hear the music of Stravinsky and Schoenberg. The world of the visual arts was in constant ferment and new eruptions were occurring almost daily. The Fauve movement, led by Matisse and begun around 1903, had already passed its peak, and many of its adherents were going their own individual ways. The Cubism of Picasso and Braque had by this time attracted a large array of French and foreign disciples: Albert Gleizes, Jean Metzinger, Fernand Léger, Juan Gris, Louis Marcoussis, Roger de La Fresnaye, Marcel Duchamp, Raymond Duchamp-Villon, Jacques Villon, and André Lhote and in sculpture Alexander Archipenko and Ossip Zadkine. André Derain had moved over into the Cubist orbit, and Robert Delaunay and Duchamp were already showing the influence of the Futurists, who had exhibited in Paris in February, 1912, for the first time.

67

Marc Chagall and Giorgio de Chirico were at work in Paris, as were Constantin Brancusi and Amadeo Modigliani.

When Kuhn arrived in Paris on October 25 he looked up some of the American artists then resident, including Alfred Maurer, Jo Davidson, and Walter Pach, all of whom proved helpful. He visited dealers, spread the word about a mammoth American showing of the new art, told each dealer that the others had promised to cooperate, painted a picture of an American market ready to accept the latest word, and must have convinced them all that the AAPS was as solid as the Federal Reserve System. The whole affair began to mushroom beyond his expectations and, struck by the magnitude of the undertaking, he cabled Davies late in October that he needed help. Davies booked passage almost immediately on the S.S. *Minnehaha,* sailing October 26, and he arrived in Paris on November 6. Then began the job of tying up the ends. Kuhn's enthusiasm for Redon was seconded

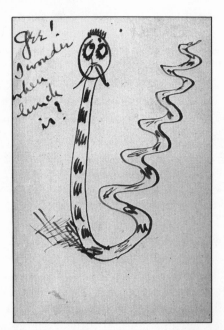

Walt Kuhn (1877–1949). *Gee! I Wonder Where Lunch Is?*
(Walter Pach). Hirshhorn Museum and Sculpture Garden,
Smithsonian Institution, Washington, D.C.;
Gift of Joseph H. Hirshhorn Foundation, 1966.

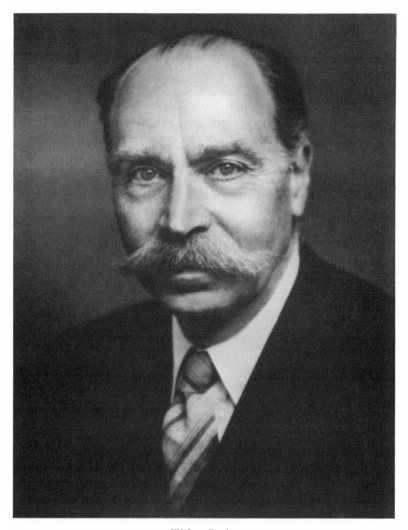

Walter Pach.

by Davies, whose own art had much in common with that of the
French master, and they decided to feature him.

Davies and Kuhn, shepherded by Pach, spent a frantic ten
days trying to round up the best and most advanced art they
could find. Without Pach they certainly could not have accomplished what they did. Pach had been living in Paris for some
time, working at his painting and writing about the new art. He

had a wide acquaintance among artists, dealers, and collectors, and knew what was going on. He has written that he had known Davies since 1909 and had translated articles about recent artistic developments for him. He has also stated that when he heard of the proposed exhibition he wrote to Davies offering "to aid in obtaining a worthy representation of the men" for whom they were looking, and "he [Davies] sent me Kuhn." He introduced them to the avant-garde collection of the Steins, and he tells in his book, A Queer Thing, Painting, how impressed Davies was by it and how he tipped his hat and bowed to the door on the rue Madame after they left, in homage to those pioneer collectors. He took them also to the studio of the Duchamp-Villons, where Davies was greatly moved by the work of all three brothers but especially by that of Marcel Duchamp. "That's the strongest expression I've seen yet!" was his comment.

Their visit to Brancusi was memorable. Davies' admiration for Brancusi was immediate and profound. His statement to Pach—"That's the kind of man I'm giving the show for!"—reveals not only the character of his taste but something of his proprietary relationship to the Armory Show. Before they left he bought the marble *Torse*, which was later in the Armory Show. Davies had confidence in his taste and the courage to back it by purchase for himself or a patron, as witness the occurrence when they went to Redon's studio in connection with the Show. Here again Davies saw something he liked, the *Roger and Angelica* (color plate 7), and in an aside to Pach, Davies said, "That's sold; don't tell him so." It was sold at the Armory Show to Lillie P. Bliss, for whom Davies acted as artistic adviser. Always the gentleman, Davies never would have said to Pach, "It's bought; don't tell her so."

It was also largely through Pach that they added to the French contingent the sculptors Antoine Bourdelle and Archipenko, and the Americans Patrick Henry Bruce, Morgan Russell, and Elie Nadelman. They arranged to show Delaunay and the Cubists Gleizes, de La Fresnaye, Francis Picabia, and Léger. They got to the Fauves Matisse (through the Steins) and Raoul Dufy, as well as to the less radical of the younger French artists like Georges Léon Dufrenoy, Othon Freisz, Marie Laurencin, and André Dunoyer de Segonzac. And several of the leading French dealers, although some were a bit doubtful, agreed, with a hopeful eye on the American market, to round out the selection, despite the fact that it meant immobilizing merchandise for close to six months. Ambroise Vollard, a shrewd operator, to whom Kuhn had been introduced by Maurer, was also friendly with Pach. At the outset he was very cooperative, offering an important group of Cézannes and Gauguins while making a deal to sell his books and lithographs by Cézanne, Gauguin, Bonnard, Vuillard, Redon, Denis, and Renoir. However, he became less helpful when he learned that they had gotten the Cézanne *Femme au chapelet* (*An Old Woman with a Rosary*, color plate 4) from Emile Druet. Bernheim-Jeune let them have a variety of works: Sig-

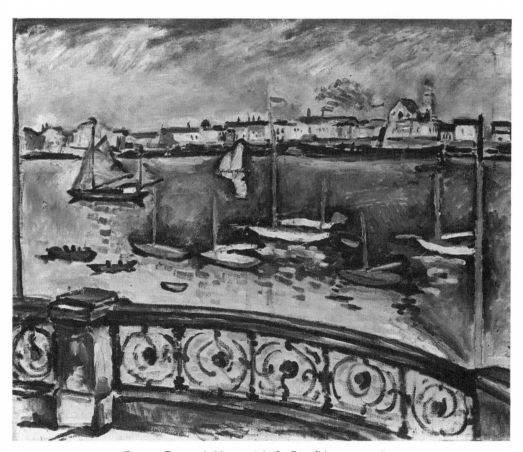

Georges Braque (1882–1963). *Le Port d'Anvers*, 1906.
Oil on canvas, 19⅝ × 24 in. National Gallery of Canada, Ottawa.

nac, Toulouse-Lautrec, Bonnard, Vuillard, and Matisse. From Durand-Ruel they obtained a group of Impressionist paintings by Monet, Renoir, Pissarro, and Sisley. The largest loan of all came from the Galerie Emile Druet, well over a hundred works, a good collection of Post-Impressionist French painting in itself, including works by the Pointillists Seurat, Signac, and Cross; the three great Post-Impressionist masters, Cézanne, Van Gogh, and Gauguin; Toulouse-Lautrec, Félix Vallotton, and Denis; the Fauves Matisse, Albert Marquet, and Georges Rouault; and a selection of the less radical contemporary young French painters, as well as sculpture and drawings by Aristide Maillol. The Redon collection was increased by loans from Joseph Hessel, Marcel Kapferer, and Wilhelm Uhde. Henry Kahnweiler helped strengthen the contemporary list with contributions from Derain and Maurice de Vlaminck, Picasso and Braque, and the Spanish sculptor Manolo.

What Davies, Kuhn, and Pach had accomplished was amazing by any standards, but when we consider the time in which it was done, it seems an unbelievable feat. Davies was in Paris for only a little more than a week, so most of the preliminaries must have been handled by the other two. It is highly improbable that Kuhn could have done this without Pach's intimate knowledge of current Parisian art tendencies or his connections.

Those must have been remarkably hectic weeks. Kuhn's recently discovered letters convey the excitement of the period, while the official correspondence with dealers in Holland, Germany, and Paris records the Armory Show plans, asking for cooperation, arranging for loans, shipping, and insurance. During this time Kuhn was introduced by Davidson to Arthur T. Aldis, a Chicago lawyer and an influential patron of the Art Institute, who wanted the Show for that city. After a meeting with Davies apparently some verbal agreement was made, for Kuhn in his letters to dealers announced as an added inducement that the Exhibition would go on to Chicago. With all the basic commitments made and only details to be settled, Pach was appointed European representative of the AAPS and Davies and Kuhn left for London on November 12 to see the Grafton Show.

The Second Grafton Show, officially the Second Post-Impressionist Exhibition, was organized by Roger Fry, the English critic and esthetician, former curator of painting at the Metropolitan Museum of Art and one of the early proselytizers for modern art. This exhibition, which had opened on October 25 and was due to run until the end of the year, was a sequel to an earlier exhibition also arranged by Fry and shown at the Grafton Galleries from November 8, 1910, to January 15, 1911. The First Grafton Show was officially called Manet and the Post-Impressionists, a designation formulated by Fry which was used here for the first time to describe the French painters who followed and broke from Impressionism. Fry, a perceptive and knowledgeable connoisseur of art and its contemporary manifestations, had in the first show already grouped together the major figures of the movement two years before the Armory Show. Both Grafton shows were small but well selected. The first was limited to French painting, though not French painters, and covered the sequence from Manet to Cubism. The second did not include any of the older men except Cézanne and added English and Russian sections. Matisse was the major figure of this exhibition, with forty-one works in painting, sculpture, watercolor, and drawing, plus a group of unlisted lithographs. Second only to Matisse was Picasso, represented by sixteen examples.

When Davies and Kuhn, freshly arrived in London, visited the exhibition on Saturday afternoon, November 16, they were not greatly impressed and therefore were greatly heartened. Kuhn, writing to Pach, was exuberant: "We are going to put it *all over* it with our proposition." In spite of the brilliant representation of Matisse, the show was not a strong one. It had not the scale nor scope of the Sonderbund nor the coherence of the First Grafton. The "old masters" were missing and in their place was a large array of minor French, English, and Russian examples. However, the show was doing well financially and Kuhn, with his excitement showing, wrote, "Can't you see what is going to happen in New York?"

In spite of their reservations about the show, they were impressed by some of the works they saw. Vollard's two Cézannes, which they had expected would come to New York, they thought the best things in the show, "head and shoulders over everything else." Matisse made so strong an impression that they ordered Pach to get anything he could. They advised him to ask the

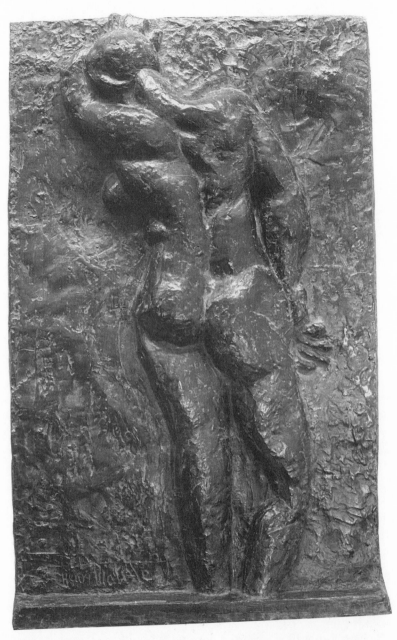

74

Henri Matisse (1869–1954). *The Back, I*, 1909. Bronze, 74⅜ × 44½ × 6½ in.
Collection, The Museum of Modern Art, New York;
Mrs. Simon Guggenheim Fund.

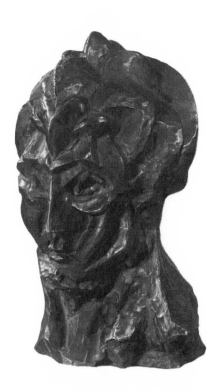

Pablo Picasso (1881–1973).
Head of a Woman, 1909.
Bronze, 16¼ × 9 in.
The Art Institute of Chicago;
Alfred Stieglitz Collection.

Steins to intercede with Matisse to let them have his Grafton exhibits and they urged him to visit Matisse's studio to see whether he would lend others. The Steins were cooperative and so was Matisse. As a result the Armory Show had a really brilliant collection of his work, including the plaster bas-relief of a female nude, *Le Dos* (*The Back I,* page 74), which Davies and Kuhn had wanted more than anything else. They were also much taken with Rousseau, but Léonce Rosenberg refused to lend the *Scène de forêt* from the Grafton Show, and they asked Pach to see if he could find two smaller "subject pictures" to go with the *Centennaire,* which had been promised by Alfred Flechtheim, the German dealer. Among the other requests were that Pach work on Kahnweiler; they were anxious to have strong representations of Braque, Derain, and, especially, Picasso. They also gave him instructions about a number of artists—Eugene Zak, Auguste Elisée Chabaud, Pierre Girieud, Archipenko, and Amadéo de Sousa-Cardoza—and they warned him to get plasters rather than bronzes to avoid endangering the insurance agreement they had with Lloyd's. After final arrangements had been made for the packing and shipment of works promised them from the Grafton Show, they were ready to leave for home. There were still many details to be handled and problems were bound to arise, but they felt confident in Pach's ability to manage.

When Davies and Kuhn boarded the S.S. *Celtic* at Liverpool on November 21 they were in a jubilant mood. The major part of the dream had been accomplished. It was not only the success of their negotiations, but the excitement of the art itself and the expectations of its effect on New York which kept Kuhn, at least, spinning in high. He dashed off a last long letter to Pach, mailed when they put in at Queenstown, which was full of elation and instructions. They were sure of success, couldn't wait to get home and get things rolling and, he added, "We vote you a brick of the best cubist make." But a sea voyage cannot be hurried and there was plenty of time to discuss, to plan, and to dream. Kuhn's mind teemed with ideas for publicity and publication. They found time to plan a series of pamphlets for the Show and Kuhn translated Gauguin's *Noa-Noa*, which was published, and a series of Van Gogh letters that he dictated to Davies, which was not. The first phase of the project had been completed, but they were already thinking and planning ahead. One can only wonder at the optimism and energy of these men.

3

The
Ball Is On
Now

When Davies and Kuhn got back to New York on November 30, they knew they had something big, but as yet it was only a grandiose project, completely enmeshed in commitments and uncertainties, with only one thing they could count on—a deadline sometime in February. But it did not seem to bother them much. Their enthusiasm spilled over. On December 12, Kuhn wrote to Pach, conveying his excitement and hopes:

I should have written you before this but Davies and myself have been on the jump every minute since we landed. Today I gave the papers the list of European stuff which we know of definitely. It will be like a bombshell, the first news since our arrival. You have no idea how eager everybody is about this thing and the tremendous success it's going to be. Everybody is electrified when we quote the names, etc. The outlook is great, and after having figured up the likely income we stand to come out ahead of the game as far as money goes. The articles appearing from now on will increase the desire to help by the moneyed "classes." We owe you a tremendous lot for your indispensable help and advice, but you know that we are all in the same boat for this great chance to make the American think. I feel as though I had crowded an entire art education into those few weeks. Chicago has officially asked for the show, and of course we accepted. . . .

I have planned a press campaign to run from now right through the show and then some. . . .

We are going to feature Redon big (BIG!). You see, the fact that he is so little known will mean a still bigger success in publicity.

John Quinn, our lawyer and biggest booster, is strong for plenty of publicity. He says the New Yorkers are worse than rubes, and must be told. All this is not to my personal taste, I'd rather stay home and work at my pictures, shoving in some of the things I have learned, but we are still in deep water now and have got to paddle . . . our show must be talked about all over the U.S. before the doors open. . . .

The ball is on now and there will be lots doing. We have a great opportunity in this show, and must try to make it truly wonderful and get all the people there, which owing to the extremely short duration of the show is very hard, and can only be done through the press. So don't ignore my plea for minor information; it may be undignified but it brings the desired result. We want this old show of ours to mark the starting point of the new spirit in art, at least as far as America is concerned. I feel it will show its effect even further and make the big wheel turn over both hemispheres. I suppose you are thinking, "There he goes again;" but I guess it's better to say "there he goes" than "doesn't he look natural," as Tad says.

Guy du Bois is on Arts and Crafts (off the Journal) and will devote a whole issue to the show; he's in strong I hear. I expect to see him tomorrow.

The business end of this thing is enormous. I expect to give practically all my time to it, but do it gladly if we can really do what we hope to do.

Had supper in Child's tonight. Oh you Laperousse.

Later that month he also wrote to his friend Henry G. Keller in Cleveland, urging him to send his "most serious and noncommercial" works to the Exhibition, and adding, "This is America's opportunity and an absolutely unselfish matter—the success will be enormous." And in a similar vein, he wrote to Prendergast, bringing him up to date: "Davies and I have had a great time abroad, in fact a regular orgy of art. . . . It is hardly possible to grasp the enormity of the undertaking, and we feel that it will be many years before a show of like import will be gotten together. As you notice [he had included two newspaper clippings] we are taking hold of this thing in a rather modern way, which we trust will aid in bringing the people into the building."

There had been earlier rumors and hints that Davies and Kuhn were abroad collecting works for the Armory Show, and there may even have been some trepidation among the membership as to what was going on, but even before an official meeting of the AAPS was held, a press release was issued on December 12 announcing that a "Sub-Committee of the American Painters and Sculptors" had secured for an exhibition in February, 1913, 399 paintings and 21 sculptures by the leading men of the "new movement in art." It was added that with these would be shown a group of works by the Futurists. The intention was to have separate rooms for Cézanne, Redon, Gauguin, Van Gogh, Matisse, the Cubists, and the Futurists. The selection of the Americans was still in progress and would be announced later.

From the list included in the press release it would seem that the European collection was already set. A few men like Metzinger and Herbin did not come through, but other important figures were later added; among the older ones Adolphe Monticelli and Munch, and among the younger Jacob Epstein and Ernst Ludwig Kirchner and the French painters Delaunay, Léger, Picabia, and de La Fresnaye. The Association must have had some original commitment from the Futurists, for it continued to announce their participation. It was later said that the Futurists would not show because they insisted on exhibiting as a group. Since the AAPS had announced that they would be presented in that way, that hardly could have been the reason for their defection. The Futurists may have been committed to European exhibitions during that time. At any rate, it was a distinct loss that they were not finally included in the Show.

The tempo of activity was becoming almost feverish. European dealers and shippers were sending lists of works, announcing shipments ready to go when notified, and demanding guarantees on insurance; increasing numbers of European artists were asking or consenting to participate; and the Chicago Art Institute was beginning to dicker for the Exhibition. It was obvious that the Association needed an office and a staff to take care of details. Davies and MacRae had looked for quarters before the former left for Europe, but nothing had been settled. Now Davies and Kuhn went out and rented a small office in the Camera Building at 122 East 25th Street, near the Armory, for $25 a month. They had a telephone installed, bought some secondhand furniture, had the place painted and the door lettered, and then they got down to work.

As expenses began to mount, Davies again came to the fore with a check for $2,500, source unspecified. For the next few months the active members had very little time for anything but the Exhibition. They gave their time, their energy, and their en-

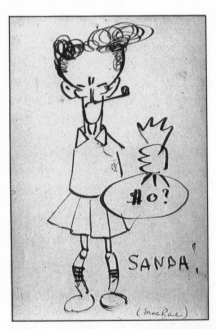

Walt Kuhn (1877–1949). *Sanda* (Elmer L. MacRae).
Hirshhorn Museum and Sculpture Garden,
Smithsonian Institution, Washington, D.C.;
Gift of Joseph H. Hirshhorn Foundation, 1966.

thusiasm without remuneration. Only MacRae, who had to handle so many of the financial details, and perhaps because he needed the money, was later paid $500 and Prendergast $40 for expenses in coming to New York to help select the American works and hang the Exhibition. Walter Pach, who was hired to act as European representative and later as sales manager, and Frederick James Gregg, a newspaperman who served as public relations representative, both were paid $1,200. It would be difficult to find in the annals of art another instance in which men gave of themselves so unstintingly and worked with such dedication. As MacRae wrote later: "Davies, Kuhn, Pach, Gregg and myself gave up a whole year—Taylor and Tucker part of this time—A great deal of this was office work, most of us poorly fitted for it—With all this hard work, we had the time of our lives—so many thrills, so much excitement. It was a great privilege for me to work side by side, day by day, with such men.

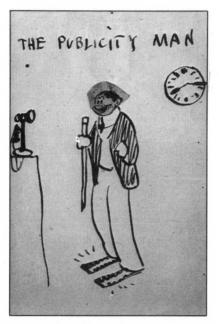

Walt Kuhn (1877–1949). *The Publicity Man*
(Frederick J. Gregg). Hirshhorn Museum and Sculpture Garden,
Smithsonian Institution, Washington, D.C.;
Gift of Joseph H. Hirshhorn Foundation, 1966.

There were anxious moments before the Show opened, we had bitten off a lot financially for artists."

On December 17, the membership of the AAPS met at the office to hear a report from Davies. He described their mission as an unqualified success that would open the eyes of the American public. The presentation of this *fait accompli* was no doubt disturbing to some, though many of the members still had no notion of exactly what was in store for them. However, the smell of success was in the air and no one at that time was ready to cavil, at least not openly, over the direction the Exhibition was taking. After all, there was going to be a larger American section and they would all be part of that.

It may appear from the account so far that the AAPS was being run in a dictatorial manner and that the membership had no voice in its own affairs. It is true that Davies ran things as he saw fit, although he consulted some of his associates, listened on occasion to advice, and acted with arrogance only when provoked and never erratically. However, the very constitution of the society, which had set up a board of directors, placed authority in the hands of this group. The fact that this board was behind their president and that he was getting the bills footed gave him almost unlimited power to call the turns. And it should be said that his direction was clear, decisive, and knowing. He had the capacity for delegating authority and trusting his aides, fading into the background as they accepted the limelight, acting always diplomatically and with grace, working hard behind the scenes, and being able to concentrate on the minutest detail. According to Jerome Myers, Davies made small watercolor sketches of each of the rooms in the Armory Show with all the paintings in place, and there is evidence that he made a complete plan for the hanging of the Chicago Show. It was Kuhn, MacRae, Pach, and Gregg who handled most of the day-to-day activity, but no one will ever know the amount of labor put in by Davies, not only to raise money, for which he has always been given credit with the sometimes condescending addition that "he knew a lot of rich old ladies," but in understanding and supervising every single aspect of the Exhibition from planning to hanging. Without him it never would have happened.

After the membership had been brought up to date, Davies

82

delegated to a series of committees the many tasks that had to be done. To examine those lists carefully is to see with what understanding of the personal qualities of the members Davies operated, and with what awareness of diplomatic necessity in handling them. To the General Executive Committee, which would have charge of the Exhibition and which would include ex officio the officers of the Association, he appointed Myers (chairman), Bellows, du Bois, Fry, Kramer, Luks, and Taylor. He appointed to the Committee on Domestic Exhibits, Glackens (chairman), Brinley, Mowbray-Clarke, Nankivell, Prendergast, Taylor, Tucker, and Fry. The Committee on Foreign Exhibits included MacRae (chairman), Borglum, Dabo, Davidson, Henri, Kuhn, Lie, Lawson, and Prendergast. The Reception and Publicity Committee had as chairman Borglum, and its members were Anderson, Brinley, Bellows, Dabo, du Bois, Lie, and Sloan. The Catalogue and General Printing Committee consisted of Kuhn (chairman), MacRae, Sloan, Taylor, Tucker, and du Bois. And the Committee on Publications, which was actually the publicity committee, was composed simply of Gregg, who had been hired for the job, and du Bois, who was an art critic as well as a painter, and worked for the magazine *Arts and Decoration.* This is a very carefully considered list and shrewdly contrived.

83

Aside from the fact that everyone got on something and people were put on committees where they could function best, they were also kept off those in which they might cause harm or be disruptive. Without going into this too deeply, it is interesting, for instance, to note the diplomatic gesture to Myers, one of the original founders of the society, but unlike Kuhn and MacRae not a member of the inner circle and not sympathetic to the new art, who was given the chairmanship of the major committee. Borglum, who had little real esthetic identity with the rest of the group, was carefully placed on a variety of committees without permitting him any policy-making role. The most important subcommittee, since the foreign exhibits were already chosen, was the Domestic Committee. Here Davies packed the rolls with artists who would be sympathetic to the more progressive aspects of American art and excluded Henri and the Realist group. It should be remembered that by this date Glackens, the chairman, had abandoned the Ash Can tradition for Renoir.

All sorts of things had to be considered—transformation of the Armory into an exhibition gallery; times of opening; admission charge; printing of tickets; policing the Show; reception of guests; method of hanging, since time was so short; hiring of help for the handling of works as well as people; printing the catalogue, posters, booklets, and post cards; advertising; handling the press; and invitations to the opening. In all the fragments of minutes, notes, and diaries nothing is said of raising money. That apparently was the province of the president and his mysterious exchequer. All the other duties were parceled out to various committees. These got to work immediately on the seemingly endless details which included such diverse matters as hiring guards, letting the concession to the cloakroom, renting fire-extinguishers and turnstiles, arranging for a band to play on opening night, and printing buttons.

By the end of the year all the committees were in full swing. And picking his time with care, Davies issued a statement to the press which received extensive and favorable coverage. By this time the publicity about the Exhibition had spawned a rash of rumors that the newspapers were not loath to spread. There seemed to be a feeling that the AAPS was trying to subvert American art by introducing the "mad" and "degenerate" new tendencies from Europe and that they had some esthetic ax to grind. Davies' statement was intended to lay such fears to rest not only among the public but in the art world, and perhaps also to reassure American artists who were being invited to exhibit that they were not being used as a blind for some sort of nefarious artistic propaganda:

On behalf of the Executive Committee, I desire to explain the general attitude of the Association in regard to the International Exhibition to be held in this city in February and March. This is not an institution but an association. It is composed of persons of varying tastes and predilections, who are agreed on one thing, that the time has arrived for giving the public here the opportunity to see the results of new influences at work in other countries in an art way. In getting together the works of the European moderns the society has embarked on no propaganda. It proposes to enter on no controversy with any institution. Its sole object is to put the paintings, sculptures, and so on, on exhibition so that the intelligent may judge for themselves by themselves. Of course controversies will arise, just as they have arisen under similar circumstances in France, Italy, Germany and England. But they will not be the result of any stand taken by this Association as such; on the other hand we are perfectly willing to assume full responsibility for providing the opportunity to those who may take one side or the other. Any individual expression of opinion contrary to the above is at variance with the official resolutions of the Association.

On December 20, the Executive Committee had its first meeting, at which Myers, Kramer, Kuhn, MacRae, Luks, Taylor, Borglum, and Gregg, who had been asked to attend, were present. They considered a variety of matters including admission tickets and prices, engraved invitations, the hiring of help, and handling of shipping. It was at this meeting that the opening date was finally set for February 17. The proposed plans for the Armory Show were accepted and a sub-committee consisting of Borglum, Taylor, Luks, and MacRae was appointed to investigate bids on construction. MacRae was also appointed chairman of a committee on all sales.

In order to solicit financial support, the AAPS also sent out a rather pretentious and somewhat incoherent formal statement printed on fine paper, in elegant type, and with a profusion of capital letters, which they hoped would be impressive.

The American Painters and Sculptors will give an International Exhibition of Contemporary Art, in the City of New York, from February 15th to March 15th, 1913.

A council of the Association will have charge of the management, and of selecting for the exhibition. The aim will be to choose, from all created Beauty of this epoch, that which best reveals the individual or group among creative workers, or the contributions of a race.

The organizing of such exhibitions, the revelation to this great productive community of that which makes the wealth of nations in the highest sense, must appeal alike to love of Art and love of Country.

To specify as to the Character of work to be shown. We wish to present at first hand the work of our artists, and that of artists in foreign countries which best give this permanent valuation of the awakening of a spontaneous individuality to a new use of art forms: the Classicists, Romanticists, Impressionists, Post-Impressionists, Cubists, Futurists, wherever we find Beauty or its Indication.

In France, Degas, Monet, Renoir, Cézanne, Gauguin, Rodin, Maillol.

In England, Stevens, George Clausen, John.

In Ireland, Nathaniel Hone, George Russell, Jack Yeats.

Scotland, Holland, Germany, Norway, Switzerland, Italy, Spain, America, mutually unite the Faith of the Time.

That the plan may stimulate to good results it is desirable to have your cooperation.

Appended to this announcement was a subscription blank asking for pledges in support of the Exhibition, to be sent to Mrs. M. C. Davidge, honorary treasurer.

The Domestic Committee was faced with the staggering task of handling the American contingent. It had already sent invitations to artists asking them to take part in the "First International Exhibition." Artists were advised that there was no limitation as to medium of expression, to submit a list of works numbered according to preference, but that the committee could guarantee to hang only two examples. Lists were to be submitted by January 1; entry blanks, which would be forwarded later, were to be returned by February 5, and works would be received and unpacked at the Armory on February 13 and 14. The AAPS agreed to insure all works, to collect them free within the city, and to pay the expenses of repacking and returning all out-of-town entries. A short statement at the end of the invitation is interesting as an indication of the desire to break through the deadly conformity of the standard exhibition and to discover talents and tendencies unknown, perhaps with the vain hope of matching the revolutionary character of the European section:

The Association particularly desires to encourage all art work that is produced for the pleasure that the producer finds in carrying it out. In this way the Association feels that it may encourage non-professional, as well as professional artists, to exhibit the result of any self-expression in any medium that may come most naturally to the individual.

For instance, a man may be a painter and amuse himself at wood-carving, which he might never intend to exhibit, and yet the wood-carving may be the most valuable as a natural expression of the artist's talent. You may come in contact with someone who is not a professional artist and yet produces original designs in needlework of art value.

The Association would like to be informed of such cases and, through the medium of one of its members, become familiar with the output of such individuals.

Everyone was well aware that the excitement of the European display would be difficult to match and the notion that the national art had been sold down the river seemed already to have created some uneasiness. There is a cryptic entry in MacRae's diary of January 17: "Henri long talk—has come around," which may refer to such dissatisfaction, although it is also possible that

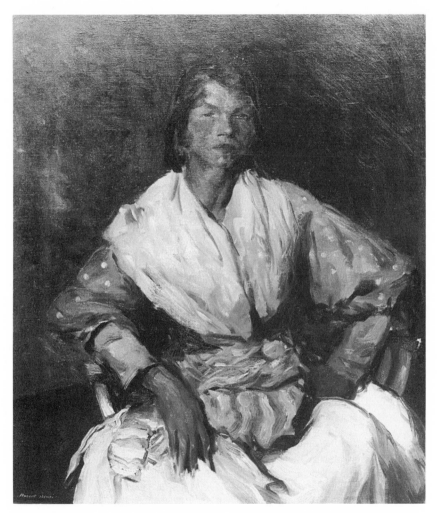

Robert Henri (1865–1929). *The Spanish Gypsy*, n.d. Oil on canvas, 40¾ × 33 in. The Metropolitan Museum of Art, New York; Arthur Hoppock Hearn Fund, 1914.

Henri had been sulking for quite a long time because Davies was running the Show without his advice and was interested in making the Exhibition something more than a display of the progressive aspects of American art. A news story in the New York American as far back as June 27, 1912, reported that Henri had refused to become a member of the AAPS board and that he had refused to help select the European works while abroad unless he had sole authority. He added that he considered the AAPS to have become much like the Academy. But whatever the dissatisfaction, the course was set, and the only thing to do was to make the American section as interesting as possible. This meant avoiding the rather pat formulas of even the progressive circles. The formality of exhibition still had an inhibiting effect on the American artist, and in an effort to break through this barrier, the Domestic Committee on January 4 addressed a plea to some of the men they had invited:

In the forthcoming International Exhibition of Modern Art, the dominant feature of the foreign exhibit is not so much its novelty as its distinct individuality of expression and forceful manifestation of creative power. For this reason it is held to be the more desirable that our home exhibit be equally conspicuous in like feature. The Domestic Exhibition Committee is therefore addressing this note to such artists on its list of invited exhibitors as it deems most essential to be represented, with the request that the prospective exhibitor expose works in which the personal note is distinctly sounded.

The original intention of the Association was to show only invited works from here and abroad. The American list was obviously compiled by the members of the group from the ranks of the more progressive artists largely outside academic circles. Many of them had appeared earlier in the Independents Show of 1910, the National Arts Club Exhibition of 1911, and the Mac-Dowell Shows. It was something of a mixed bag because of the composition of the Association itself, but on the whole it emphasized the tendency toward exploration and experimentation within the still rather narrow limits of American art. It included The Eight, the younger Realists, and unaffiliated artists who were trying to outgrow the set formulas of academic art, as well as the more radical artists connected with Stieglitz who had made con-

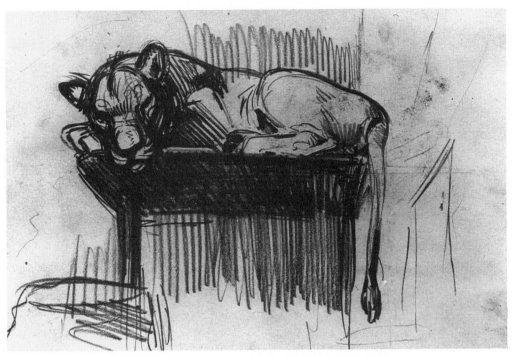

George B. Luks (1867–1933). *Bronx Zoo Study, Lion,* 1904.
Crayon on paper, 7 × 10 in. Addison Gallery of American Art,
Phillips Academy, Andover, Massachusetts.

tact with the new European movements, such as John Marin,
Alfred Maurer, Marsden Hartley, Samuel Halpert, and Abraham
Walkowitz. Max Weber was not included because he withdrew
the two works of his that had been selected, for reasons to be
discussed later.

The Domestic Committee in charge of this end of the Show
was later maligned through innuendo, largely from more conservative quarters, for favoritism in its selections, and the Association members for pre-empting too much space for themselves.
However, the committee seems to have acted in an entirely
honorable manner and one cannot really blame the Association
members for the slight favoritism they showed to themselves and
their friends, since it was after all their show and their effort
which made it possible. The fact is that none of them was blatantly over-represented, some even scantily, and several of the

American loan form.

critics felt that Davies had consciously and mistakenly kept his own selection too modest.

Publicity about the Show led many uninvited artists to request inclusion in the Exhibition. The demand became so great that it was finally decided to liberalize procedures by abandoning one of the basic tenets of the Association and permitting artists to submit works to the Domestic Committee for inspection from January 20 to 26, inclusive. Acting as a jury, the committee examined several hundred examples, mostly by younger and unknown artists. In retrospect one can find little fault with their selections. As a matter of fact, the judgments they made are very close to those of history. Out of the mass of works, they accepted examples by Oscar Bluemner, Maurice Becker, Glenn O. Coleman, Stuart Davis, Andrew Dasburg, Edward Hopper, Bernard Karfiol, Joseph Stella, and Margaret and William Zorach. Charles Sheeler submitted five paintings, but this seems to have been through error. He was apparently invited to exhibit along with his friend Morton L. Schamberg, and a penciled comment in the Domestic Committee record book notes, "taken care of by Kuhn." Only the rejection of Louis Eilshemius can be questioned, but then the taste for the "primitive" had not yet developed. They had missed at least one "personal note distinctly sounded."

But the selection of works to be shown was only the beginning through the month of December and accelerating during January, affairs were coming to a head. So much had to be done and there were so few people to do it. And yet they planned on a scale and with a scope that seems both foolhardy and magnificent. Publicity was a major concern. Kuhn especially was intent on getting not only New York but the whole United States to know about the Show. He issued press releases and wrote to editors throughout the nation, offering photographs and stories. Posters were printed and sent all over the country, to museums, art schools, libraries, and colleges. They ordered 50,000 four-color post cards reproducing the official poster with the pine-tree flag. These were sent out free in small packets of ten with a covering card asking people to use them for ordinary correspondence and requesting names of people who might be "sufficiently interested in the cause to make good use of a like quantity of similar cards." They even investigated the cost of an electric sign in Times Square. One firm offered them the low price of $900 for six weeks because "a member of the company was so interested in the cause," but nothing came of it.

Kuhn kept up a constant correspondence with artists in different parts of the country, urging them to spread the word. He sent them material and information. He wrote to newspapers and magazine editors and critics, assuring them that the Show would be a huge success. To his painter friend Henry Keller in Cleveland he sent a batch of fifty posters to "spread all over town" and wrote, "Things are booming along and a great success is assured." He kept up a barrage of instructions and material to another artist friend, James E. Lamb, who lived near Baltimore and was actively engaged in getting the word around. Kuhn begged him not to miss the Exhibition when it opened and assured him that it would be "worth a two-month trip abroad." And to the Berlin art critic Paul Mahlberg, he wrote that the Show would be "*bahn brechend*" and to "whoop it up among your colleagues." Pressing for publicity, he told his friend Edward Gewey of the Kansas City *Post*, "We are doing this according to American methods and have already spent a good deal of money on advertising. . . . Give me an idea of what sort of photographs you can use. I suppose they will not stand for nudes." As a result there were many stories and picture spreads planted in newspapers and magazines, all of which whetted the public curiosity and interest.

The Armory Show was not only the most dramatic in our history but unquestionably the best publicized. The drumbeating was almost worthy of a Barnum, and the circus atmosphere was eventually abetted, when the Show opened, by the spectacular nature of the new art. But as Kuhn commented to a reporter at the end of the Show, "All the advertising in the world and all the press-agenting will do no good if there is nothing for the public to see when it comes."

The publication plans of the Association were grandiose enough to match the Exhibition itself. A first order for 50,000 catalogues is enough to make one boggle even today. Such audacity sets one to marvel and wonder; were they so confident or was it simply irresponsible fantasy? But an agreement was made on February 3 to publish that number for $4,400. That did not leave much time, and the Catalogue Committee, headed by Allen Tucker, worked frantically down to the wire. Printing conditions must have been somewhat different in those days. The dummy was submitted finally on February 13, a Thursday, and they had the completed catalogue, errors and all, by opening day, the following Tuesday. Considering the circumstances, the errors were not so numerous: misspellings, mostly in the foreign names and titles, works promised but not sent, and works substituted for those promised. However, since entries continued to come in until the last moment, a supplement was printed containing the added works, a list of corrections including errors and works not received, and an index to the Exhibition. As the notice in the catalogue supplement stated, "The catalogue had to be made while the temporary rooms were going up, and before the pictures were hung." It was no doubt an unwieldy system, but, given the conditions, perhaps the only possible solution. As a result, the catalogue was numbered consecutively, and though works by a single artist were generally grouped together, artists were not listed alphabetically or by room, and the index was a necessity. As a matter of fact there were two indexes: at the back of the catalogue, an alphabetical list of artists and numbered works; and in the supplement, a numerical listing of works with appropriate room locations. One can criticize the catalogue for its unwieldiness, its errors, and more than anything else, its tantalizing reticence; but the amazing thing is that there *was* a catalogue.

Intent on proselytizing for the new movement and on educating the American public, the Association also undertook the publication of four small pamphlets, and with characteristic optimism they ordered 5,000 copies of each. These were a 76-page pamphlet *Cézanne* by Elie Faure, translated by Walter Pach; *Odilon Redon* by Walter Pach, of 15 pages; extracts from *Noa-Noa* by Paul Gauguin, translated by Walt Kuhn, 38 pages; and a 21-page brochure by Walter Pach called *A Sculptor's Architecture*, dealing with Raymond Duchamp-Villon's *Architectural Façade*, which was included in the Exhibition. As part of the general intent to educate, although they served also as a source of revenue, were the halftone post cards of objects in the Exhibition. There were 57 in all, including a view of the installation, the only one ever reproduced. There were two other photographs of the American section and one of the exterior of the Armory which now exist only in the Kuhn Papers. One of the truly incredible facts is that in all the years since, no one has ever turned up another photograph of the Armory Show. Only recently and almost by accident a series of photographs of the Chicago installation has come to light. It would seem that with so many thousands of visitors, some camera bug would have taken a picture or the newspapers would have sent a photographer. But newspaper photographers were then not as omnipresent as they are today and newspapers were content to accept photographic handouts. The amateur photographer was also apparently not as ubiquitous then as he is today, and conditions of indoor shooting with flash powder were much more difficult then than now.

The 57 post cards for sale at the Show sold in thousands of copies and were a source of some artistic influence. To artists in other cities they were exciting messages of new discoveries, and for years people in remote areas had only these cards as a source of study. The 57 were equally divided among American and foreign artists, emphasizing the more radical tendencies, and in the American group rather obviously favoring the Association members; post cards of works by Childe Hassam, Robert Chanler, Van Dearing Perrine, and Andrew Dasburg were the only exceptions.

Meanwhile, the Construction Committee was at work arranging for the erection of the scaffolding necessary to transform the Armory into an exhibition hall. The plan called for eighteen oc-

93

tagonal rooms in an ingenious web covering the entire floor of the great space. On January 3, the Committee, consisting of Borglum, Taylor, and MacRae, met with the architect and visited the Armory to inspect the layout. Three days later they met again with the architect and the builder, David Morison, to go over the details. It was agreed to build 12-foot walls on the outside and 10-foot partitions on the interior to be covered by burlap which was to be fireproofed, the total cost of which came to about $3,000.

Throughout January the tempo of activity steadily increased. Shipments of works from Europe were on their way. Expenses for shipping, insurance, printing, and construction kept mounting and money had to be raised. Davies could always manage to find some money, and Mowbray-Clarke got $100 from Alice Lewisohn. But it was Clara Davidge who then began her great crusade to raise money for the cause among her socially prominent and wealthy friends. Clara Sydney Potter was the eldest daughter of Bishop Henry Codman Potter; after the death of her husband, Mason Chichester Davidge, in the late nineties, she had drifted into antiques and decoration. Her early interest in this field led to her fame as "the first interior decorator."

Mabel Dodge has a delightfully malicious account of the Davidge ménage in the old red-brick mansion La Tourette, on Staten Island, and of Clara's efforts to cure Henry Fitch Taylor and Edwin Arlington Robinson of drink. As Mable Dodge described her: "Clarissa Davidge was the unconventional one of the family. She was middle-aged and partially crippled so she walked with a limp, and she had a fringe like ruffled brown feathers and the brightest of brown eyes. Animated, eccentric, rattle-brained Clarissa! Always dressed like the doll of any little girl of ten who has had recourse to the family ragbag and secured bits of gay silk, fur and lace, she was warmhearted, rather bad-tempered, and fond of expressing herself in a loud, high-pitched voice in a language rich with her own variations." Mabel Dodge's describing someone else as "rattle-brained" is a gem of kettle-calling.

The fact is that in spite of Clara's bohemian tastes and sometimes eccentric enthusiasms, she had tremendous energy and a dedication to "creativity." And the Armory Show was her newest cause. She rang many doorbells in her campaign. She wangled donations from William Salomon, Stephen C. Clark, and Mrs. John J. Chapman. With Gregg, she visited Mrs. Edwin Shurrill Dodge, better known as Mabel Dodge, and enlisted her support. Mabel raised $500 from her mother and later gave $200 of her own for decorations for the Armory. Then Clara got $1,000 from Mrs. Harry Payne Whitney, also for decorations, and another $1,000 from Mrs. Whitney's sister-in-law, Dorothy Whitney Straight. From unspecified sources Davies raised another $1,400, and Mowbray-Clarke $800. Mrs. Davidge continued to work diligently even during the Show itself, collecting small as well as large donations, and on March 1, adding $5 of her own to make it a round sum, she turned over another $1,100.

The total of contributions to get the Exhibition under way and keep it going until admission fees and sales commissions could get the operation into the black was $10,050. Some of the credit must go to this woman who was one of the unsung heroes of the Armory Show.

By the beginning of the year, most of the European shipments which had been waiting instructions were on their way to New York. A consignment of photographs and reproductions from Druet and Vollard arrived on January 5 but was held up at Customs because of tariff regulations, and the next week was spent in getting them released. The first shipment of art works due on the 6th was delayed by heavy storms at sea and the S.S. *Mexico* carrying them did not dock until the following week, January 13. To handle this group of objects and the ones to come, as well as the expected increase of official business, the Association on January 15 rented larger office quarters, a store in the Camera Building in which they had the small office, and a stable to store the art at 28 East 32nd Street. The latter was set up immediately to receive the works as they arrived. On January 16, the S.S. *Chicago* with another shipment of foreign art made port and the bulk of the European contingent was in. At that time there was a tariff duty on works of art less than one hundred years old and, since all the works imported for the Exhibition fell within that category, the Association had to post a bond covering the assessed Customs duty. As works were sold during the Exhibition, the duty was paid and they were removed from the bonded list. The accounts with the Customs service dragged on for a long time after the Exhibition and were not finally settled until 1916.

With most of the foreign works already here, the pace of activity became even more frantic. A committee inspected the Armory to plan the hanging of the Exhibition. Delegations from the Chicago Art Institute and the Boston Copley Society came to town to arrange for showing the Exhibition in their respective cities. Loans had to be negotiated from collectors and dealers on this side of the Atlantic to fill in the gaps in the collection. Many of the loans the Association had hoped to get were refused. Davies cabled Pach to increase his efforts abroad, since he was "disappointed by withdrawals here." They had counted on the loan of Manet's *Girl with a Guitar* from a Boston collector, but that fell through; and a request to borrow two Manets from Hugo Reisinger met with an especially annoying refusal in which he wrote, "Unfortunately I cannot lend you the two pictures because Mrs. Reisinger will not allow me to take any pictures out of the parlors, where these pictures are hanging now, and I really cannot blame her because this is the season when we entertain and must have our house in order." The terse pencil notation on the letter, "So helpful!" expresses the frustration Davies must have felt at a refusal accompanied by such an excuse.

But many collectors were more cooperative. Their loans serve also as indications of the level of collecting in the United States at that time. The Manets were not very strong and the work of pre-Manet painters was even less impressive. The bulk of the Impressionist examples came from Durand-Ruel, but the historical section was rounded out with loans from American sources. William R. Ladd lent a Delacroix; Alexander Morten, a Courbet, Daumier, and three Degases; James G. Shepherd, two Corots, four works by Matthew Maris, and a Daumier; Alexander W. Drake, a Daumier; Mrs. B. S. Guinness, a Manet; and Frank Jewett Mather, Jr., art historian and critic, also lent his small Manet, about whose authenticity he later had doubts.

It is somewhat surprising to discover that in America there were collectors, even if few in number, who had heard of the Post-Impressionists and even bought them. John Quinn lent works by Cézanne, Van Gogh, Gauguin, and a large group by Puvis de Chavannes, along with a mass of English and Irish art, featuring Augustus John. Martin A. Ryerson, the Chicago collector, also lent a Puvis as well as a Manet; and Walter L. Taylor, a Puvis and a Sickert. Mrs. J. Montgomery Sears, of Boston, lent a small Cézanne flower piece; Prof. John O. Sumner, also of Boston, lent another Cézanne; Mrs. Emily Crane Chadbourne, the Chicago collector, lent four Gauguin drawings and watercolors, which usually hung in her Paris apartment, and a Redon pastel; and Mrs. Alexander Tison also lent a Gauguin. Katherine S. Dreier lent her small Van Gogh; F. R. Lillie, a Redon; and Gertrude Kasebier, the photographer, six Rodin drawings. Through Stephan Bourgeois, Sir William Van Horne, the great Canadian collector, agreed to lend a Cézanne and two Toulouse-Lautrecs, but he did renege on sending his Cézanne landscape. Although Bourgeois was a dealer, he lent to the Exhibition as a collector (except for one Toulouse-Lautrec with a price tag), providing a Manet, a Renoir, a Cézanne, a Van Gogh, and a Monticelli.

Naturally enough, examples of work by radical contemporary artists were even rarer in this country. Only the Cone sisters, Dr. Claribel and Etta, were quietly collecting Matisse and Picasso, but their slowly accumulating treasure trove in Baltimore was completely unknown then and was only publicly exhibited for the first time in 1930. The Cone sisters were introduced to modern art by their friends the Steins (Gertrude, Leo, Michael, and Sarah), the trail-blazing collectors who had, of course, agreed to lend to the Armory Show when Davies, Kuhn, and Pach had come to see them in 1912. Leo lent a Matisse and two Picassos, and Michael and Sarah two Matisses. Two other Matisses were lent to the Show by American collectors: Mrs. Howard Gans sent a flower piece and George F. Of, painter and frame maker, a *Study*, now called *Nude in a Wood*, which is considered by Alfred H. Barr, Jr., to be the first Matisse to have come to the United States. Alfred Stieglitz, who had shown the work of these men at "291," owned some work by them and lent several Matisse drawings—only one of which was hung—and a Picasso drawing and bronze bust. Paul Haviland, close friend and associate of Stieglitz, lent three small Manolo bronzes. Henri Rousseau was almost unknown here, but Max Weber, who had met and grown friendly with him while in Paris, lent seven small pieces that he had; and Robert J. Coady lent another.

97

The American section of the Armory Show contained a historical survey which was intended to parallel that of the European. It was much smaller and revealed a limited understanding of the native tradition. But since they were looking for equivalents of the modern European developments, it is not strange that they should overlook painters like Homer and Eakins and discover as sources such artists as Whistler, Albert Pinkham Ryder, and the two American Impressionists Theodore Robinson and John Twachtman. Ryder, long ignored by the public, was an important "discovery" of the Armory Show and very well represented in it. There were Ryders lent by John Gellatly, Alexander Morten, J. R. Andrews, and Mrs. Lloyd Williams. Gellatly also lent a Robinson and a Twachtman; Morten, a Robinson; and Mrs. Herbert Pratt, a Whistler. American collectors had, naturally enough, not provided the core of the Exhibition, which was intended to revolutionize American taste, but some did provide the stuffing to fill the chinks.

With affairs rapidly coming to a head, a membership meeting of the Association was called for January 22. Late on that Wednesday afternoon the members voted final and formal approval of their president's policy. It is a pity that the terse sentence in the minutes of that meeting says no more. There obviously was some opposition or dissatisfaction, otherwise why the need for a formal resolution or a vote of confidence. And how many of the members voted affirmatively because there was really nothing much that could be done at that stage without dissociating oneself from what promised to be a smashing success? Also accepted was Davies' "plan of arrangement and policy of distribution of works." This is not absolutely clear, but it probably refers to the layout of rooms in the Armory, for whose construction the contract had already been signed two weeks before, and the general plan of distribution of works in historical sequence and grouping by nation and medium. A plan was approved to hang the works by groups under the direction of "section bosses," subject to the approval of the president. What remained now was the final selection of the American works and the availability of the Armory for the hanging. The selection of the submitted works was completed, according to the schedule, on January 26, and the final decision on invited art was made on January 31.

4

Borglum
Shyly Raises
His Veil

Unfortunately, early in February the deliberations of the Sculpture Committee precipitated a major crisis in the Association. Gutzon Borglum, vice-president of the society and chairman of its Sculpture Committee, considered the action of that committee and the Association high-handed and resigned. The presence of Borglum in the organization had always been an anomaly. From an esthetic point of view, he had never been in sympathy with the other members of the Association. His longstanding feud with the Academy had led him to make common cause with this group of younger radical artists while, for their part, he served as a symbol of status and respectability. However, from the very beginning he had fought for the equality of sculpture in a society that was overwhelmingly representative of painting.

It was unfortunate that American sculpture at that time was even more academic than painting, and although Borglum was an organizational maverick his artistic attitudes were essentially conservative. The list of sculptors he submitted for inclusion in the Association was indicative of his allegiance. They were all men of recognized academic standing, successful executors of monumental public commissions, without interest in radical causes, and naturally enough, all of them had refused election to the Association, election which had obviously been motivated by a desire to please Borglum. The fact is that in 1913 an American sculptor was considered radical if he showed an influence from Rodin.

The innate conflict between Borglum and the leaders of the AAPS became apparent in the course of selecting sculpture to be included in the Exhibition. The committee empowered to choose these works consisted of Borglum, Mowbray-Clarke, and Davies. Since sculpture, unlike painting, could be shipped only at great expense, the committee took upon itself the task of visiting the studios of sculptors and examining their works. Faced by the monumental machines of the famous sculptors recommended by Borglum, the other two were in a quandary. They were looking for the new and "personal note distinctly sounded," but found instead a nightmare of sculptured rhetoric. Although Borglum accused them of high-handed arrogance, it would seem that these two elegant gentlemen were more concerned with how to phrase a polite refusal, and were led by embarrassment to accept smaller, tentative works or sketches which seemed more personal and alive, and, incidentally, which would not overwhelm their neighbors by scale alone. A gallery full of such whited-marble sepulchres would have stunted the Exhibition. To have turned down Daniel Chester French, taken one small piece from Janet Scudder, and selected only a minor group of firemen from among 39 pieces by Anna Coleman Ladd was obviously an affront to Borglum, but it does show courage and dedication to an ideal on the part of Mowbray-Clarke and Davies. Considering that these sculptors were long-time colleagues and friends, Borglum had no alternative but to protest and his reaction was characteristically violent. He gathered his grievances and on February 1 wrote a long letter of resignation from the Sculpture Committee:

I have received the minutes of the board meeting held recently, during my absence from the city, in which I find that a resolution adopted previously by the same gentlemen, sitting as executive committee, in response to my plea that sculpture be adequately represented at the exhibition had been revoked, and I feel that I cannot continue to hold the farcical position of head of the sculpture department.

As chairman of the committee on constitution, a committee still in being for the purpose of completing the by-laws, I am acquainted with the principles that made us an association. We are a dual association of painters and sculptors, sharing and enjoying equal rights and responsibilities, and every safe-guard was introduced to protect the freedom and authority of each. We united on principles of fairness, and unprejudiced attitude toward all art, and the generous exhibition of all sincere work wherever found. These are principles to which I gave my support; we have built upon these principles. We have solicited public interest upon these principles and employed them to break down the prevalent

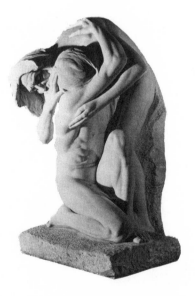

George Grey Barnard (1863–1938). *The Prodigal Son and His Father*, 1904. Marble, 81¼ × 54 × 60½ in. The J. B. Speed Art Museum, Louisville, Kentucky.

distrust of us; we have solicited financial help and secured it and exhibits through publication of these principles. I meant everything I wrote in that constitution. I support everything that was written into it by other members of the committee, reported by us unanimously and adopted by the Association.

What has been done? Hardly a tenet of our constitution that has not been broken, in letter and principle, and in the face of this several members of the executive committee exclaim: "We don't care for the Constitution, we are paying no attention to it, we are getting up an exhibition!" That constitution was created scarcely a year ago to govern our exhibitions and to maintain the Association's attitude toward art through its committees.

This state of mind has created a condition wholly at variance with our pretended services to and position in American art.

The sculpture committee had never been completed, and seeing the unauthorized gathering of work unknown to the committee as a whole and the unwarranted rejection everywhere of splendid work, I asked that my committee be given the same standing under the Constitution as other committees. That was done—only to be revoked *in my absence.*

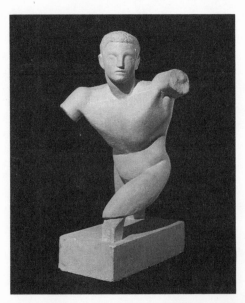

Raymond Duchamp-Villon (1876–1918). *Torso of a Young Man,* 1910.
Plaster, 23⅞ × 13¼ × 13⅛ in. Hirshhorn Museum and Sculpture Garden,
Smithsonian Institution, Washington, D.C.; Gift of
Joseph H. Hirshhorn, 1966.

I have too much regard for many of the members I have had the pleasure of knowing in forming our association to hold all responsible or to blame them for the unconstitutional revoking of the request of the head of the department of sculpture for aid necessary to elevate and secure an exhibition, fair and representative, of the American sculptors, for the real situation was and is unknown to them, and I know they are as earnestly opposed to this spirit of unfairness as I am. Neither will I comment further on the work that has been admitted by the other two members of my committee, but I do say that we violate the very principles of our association of honesty and fairness when we select as we have and reject as we have, and are open to the gravest public and art-world censure by so doing—a censure that cannot but close all further opportunity for consequential exhibition by us.

I cannot consider these things lightly. This may be a color orgy, "getting the best of the Academy!" "putting one over"—whom? It ought to be a great large spirited movement bulwarked by sincerity and unselfishness, or else it is a fake and a masquerade. We have led the public to expect something, and we are fooling them, deceiving them. We have got their interest on false pretenses.

Sculpture as it really exists in America will not be shown, because it has not been given a chance, not a fair chance.

I have personally kept a record of the committee's authorized work as a committee. I am not referring to the sculpture Messrs. Davies and Clarke have, without the authority of the whole committee, invited, nor to date even reported to the committee for approval. *I* have made no such selections; no member has the authority to do so without surrendering his own space or receiving the committee's approval or authority, and excepting three or four able men, who have consented to exhibit, as they state, through my assurance that they would be fairly dealt with, there will not be an exhibition honestly representative of America's ability in sculpture. I protest against this, and shall continue to protest against it with all the ability I have.

I must, painful as this is to me, herewith resign from the chairmanship of the department of sculpture and membership on the committee, which is a farcical position, and decline all responsibility as such for the character of that department of the exhibition or the use of my name published. Nor can I exhibit while good men and good work are ignored. They are excluded while miserable work and favorites are surreptitiously invited, without knowledge of the committee.

In many respects the Borglum charges were well founded. At an Executive Committee meeting of January 13 the question of space to be given to sculpture at the Exhibition and the size of the Sculpture Committee was debated. It was decided on Borglum's motion to add three members to the committee. However, at the January 18 meeting of the Board of Directors, this stand was reversed. The composition of the Executive Committee in charge of the Exhibition which met on the 13th was identical with that of the Board of Directors of the Association which met on the 18th except for Bellows, Brinley, and Glackens. Borglum was absent from the latter meeting, as he states, but had given his proxy to Kuhn.

It is obvious that for reasons one can only guess, the leaders of the Association had changed their minds about the sculpture situation and voted full approval of the "Sculpture Committee as it stands." To nail down this decision and forestall any further discussion or disagreement, they voted three other resolutions: "that any special action taken by a sub-committee will be subject to the ratification of the Board of Directors at the earliest convenient occasion," "that the confidence of the Directors is extended to those whom it has placed in charge of important details," and "that in case of certain unfinished work being pursued by a committee, a report should not be insisted upon by the Board until such work has reached a state of completion."

With all the legalistic verbiage removed, this simply meant that the Board did not want the Sculpture Committee increased in membership for fear that Borglum might be able to fill the Show with academic sculpture; it gave the Board immediate control of any action that committee might take; it asserted its confidence in the committee on which Davies and Mowbray-Clarke were the majority; and it gave them carte blanche to continue selecting without interference until completion of the selection, thus forestalling any direct objection from Borglum as the minority. Borglum might complain that this was high-handed, but it was legal. Whether it was unconstitutional is a question which was never pursued. That is how matters stood and Borglum had no recourse except to take his case to the membership.

Borglum did not attend the January 22 membership meeting, either because he was still out of town or because he had decided that his was a lost cause. His resignation from the Sculpture Committee on February 1 elicited no immediate response from the Association, and on the 4th he wrote requesting the return of all photographs of his work and forbidding their reproduction. On the next day Kuhn, as secretary, formally acknowledged his resignation from the Sculpture Committee. Borglum recognized his isolation within the Association, but he was not one to take defeat gracefully or quietly, and on February 6 he resigned from the Association and simultaneously released the news of his departure to the press:

I have gone more carefully into the records of your Association, and I feel that what I had hoped would be unnecessary I am compelled to do, that is to resign entirely from the organization. The utter disregard of the common agreement that we drew up together, and the arbitrary abuse and misuse of the public confidence we had established, compels me to repudiate the three or four men that pretend to be the Association.

I think you know me well enough to feel sure that I would not do this if I had not the amplest ground for the protest I am making.

Forced to make a public response, though they would have much preferred a quiet resignation and a heartfelt sigh of good-riddance, Davies and Kuhn issued a bitter and personal answer, also released to the press:

We deny our Constitution has been broken. We deny your pretense that the Sculpture Committee has never been completed. You made no such claim until a week ago, after the work of that committee had been substantially completed, and only when you had evidently become dissatisfied regarding selection of work you seemingly favored. You now complain of the committee's selections and rejections when, in fact, you, with the other two members of that committee, unanimously approved its decisions. We deny utterly your absurd assertion that sculpture as it exists in America will not be adequately shown, or that what you call American sculpture has not been given a fair chance.

But above all, we denounce and condemn the absurd charge that there has been abuse and misuse of public confidence. The work of our association in organizing this great exhibition of modern art will speak for itself. By that we will be judged. Your excitement and hurt vanity cannot change that verdict.

Borglum's resignation and blast did the Association no real harm. Borglum had a reputation for public controversy and the newspapers either reported the story straight or favored the Association editorially. The *Sun* thought his letter of resignation "pompous" and added that "the Association is powerful enough without Mr. Borglum's countenance." The *Globe* felt that it was all something of a tempest in a teapot and found Borglum's excursions into controversy becoming stale:

Every now and then Mr. Gutzon Borglum shyly raises his veil and reveals features working with strong emotion. Or else he steps forward out of the shadow and is seen in the act of righting a wrong. His sympathies, if we understand him rightly, predispose him to attack those who sit in the seats of authority, to defend the weak, to uplift the fallen. . . . Sometimes, when . . . one of these Borglum controversies happens to break out, we wish Mr. Borglum walked to the battlefield upon ankles not quite so thick, and touched his adversary with a lighter hand. . . . For then, whenever Mr. Borglum started something, the public would be sure of a little harmless pleasure.

Borglum got very little sympathy except from the artistic know-nothing fringe which saw an opportunity to get in a few licks of their own. The *American Art News* had consistently implied nefarious intentions or organizational irregularities in the AAPS and now took the opportunity to hint at behind-the-scenes shenanigans; and Charles Vezin, president of the Art Students League, who remained for years one of the stalwarts of anti-modernism, wrote a letter to the New York *Tribune* congratulating Borglum on his resignation and reminding him that "The hatred for the academic makes strange bedfellows. There rest under the same blanket (or rather, toss feverishly) anarchists, terrorists, degenerates, rowdies, scavengers, dreamers, poets, liberators and patriots." One wonders to whom each of these descriptive adjectives applies, but whatever Borglum was, he was obviously well out of that bed.

Actually, this public altercation did not hurt either the Association or the Exhibition. The attendant publicity only helped build up a head of steam for the final sprint down to the opening. That last week was hectic. Late works were coming in. Last-minute arrangements were being made. The Post Office agreed to install a temporary mailbox so people could mail their post cards from the Show. The cloakroom concession was rented. Posters were sent out to schools and colleges in the city. And Mowbray-Clarke was quietly elected to take Borglum's place as vice-president of the AAPS.

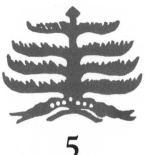

5

American
Art Will Never Be
the Same
Again

On February 13, the invited American works began to arrive and the hanging began. It is difficult to imagine how it all was done, but the entries in MacRae's diary note that the work began at 10:30 [A.M. or P.M.?] on the 13th and was "pretty nearly finished" on the next day. Approximately 1,300 works hung and mounted inside two days! It all seems incredible.

The amount of preliminary planning and organization necessary to accomplish this staggers the imagination. After all, this was a group of artists usually thought of as incompetent in the ways of the world. But wherever they learned it, they knew how to put on a show. A story in the New York *Sun* of January 26 describes the planning of the Exhibition. Just five days before the opening, work would commence according to a prearranged plan. One hundred and fifty men would be involved in the building of the rooms and the hanging of the Show. A partition wall was constructed on casters, pictures would be hung on it, and it would be moved around to test the lighting. Twenty-four hundred running feet of wall had to be hung with paintings; and the sculpture, including such large figures as the plasters of Wilhelm Lehmbruck and the marbles of George Grey Barnard, placed on pedestals. Arrangements had to be made for the decorations, consisting of streamers of cloth suspended from the ceiling, forming a dome, with bunting and greenery adorning the sides of the Armory and the partitions. A system of arc lighting to illuminate the interior was also devised. Only dedicated men working for a single purpose could have done it. And if we did not have the historical evidence that the Armory Show opened on time and the photographs to prove that it happened, it would be hard to believe.

But it did take place. It happened exactly as planned. The preview for the press was held on Sunday afternoon, February 16, and Elmer MacRae, the modest but fanatical treasurer of the Association, who had given so much of his time and energy to the Show, records that it was "a great success." But can we trust the testimony of a man who adds that he sold $6.75 in post cards (perhaps that is really a lot considering that it was a newspaper crowd on the cuff) and that he dined with Uncle Moody? His testimony is, however, substantiated by the newspaper stories that appeared the next day and especially after the official opening on Monday evening.

Whatever one might think of the art exhibited—"freakish," "mad," or "inane"—the Show itself was an unquestioned success. The New York *Sun* wrote that the AAPS "has wrought something very like a miracle," the Show was "sensational," "an event not on any account to be missed." The New York *American*—which found that the original idea of showing the development of the independent spirit in art over the last hundred years was lost in excessive size, mass advertising, and circus atmosphere, and that the selection of works was uninformed, unequal, and unfortunately the selection of a single man, Arthur B.

Davies—still had to admit rather reluctantly and sadly that it was "going to prove a bomb shell." The Exhibition made the point, according to that reporter, that the United States was twenty-five years behind the times and that "when we have digested this exhibition we shall be less stolidly complacent over the achievements of our painters."

The *Evening Post* called it an exciting show, honest and noncommercial, a job well done. "The American public will not be compelled from now on to judge certain initiators through the columns of the comic supplement," it added.

The *Times* felt that "no one within reach of it can afford to ignore it," and the *Press* reported that it had made a profound impression on sophisticated press viewers.

Joseph Edgar Chamberlin, reviewer for the New York *Evening Mail*, reported: "The AAPS has triumphed over all formal restrictions . . . academic prejudices and conventional cowardice. . . . It was a privilege to get out of the artistic strait jacket." Even Royal Cortissoz, who was the rigid backbone of conservatism and thought that the Exhibition included "some of the most stupidly ugly pictures in the world and a few pieces of sculpture to match," found it a "fine and stirring exhibition." He had only praise for its purpose and tone, was so impressed with the feat of converting the Armory into a spectacular gallery that he threw a verbal rock at the Academy, and even went so far as to clear a large proportion of the exhibits by assuring his readers that they were not "subversive."

The AAPS received accolades from all sides for its magnificent Show. The fight against superhuman odds, the successful achievement of the impossible—all without calling for public assistance—pleased the press and of course the public. The little, neglected, artistic underdog, the AAPS, had licked the rich-kid Academy, and all fairminded, one hundred per cent American art lovers were happy until they caught on to what the kids from the other side of the tracks had done. The *Globe* informed its readers, "American art will never be the same again."

After the glittering success of the opening, some of the organizers like Kuhn felt a little let down that the doors were not stormed every day; he wrote later about his disappointment at the "dribbling attendance" of the next two weeks. But, judging from his letter on March 3 to his friend Rudolph Dirks—the comic-strip artist of the Katzenjammer Kids, who was then in Europe and who had several paintings at the Armory—his mood was entirely different.

You haven't any idea how this confounded thing has developed; every afternoon Lexington Avenue and the side streets are jammed with private automobiles, old-fashioned horse equipages, taxi cabs and what not. To give you an idea of what a hit the show has made, I might merely state that the receipts for admission and catalogues last Saturday amounted to $2000 (two thousand dollars). That's going some, isn't it? The newspapers have treated the thing royally and over ninety works have been sold since the opening; it's all like a dream but the unexpected has happened, that is unexpected as far as the public is concerned. You know what I have always thought of it; the expenses of the show will amount to about $30,000, and at that we expect to make money. All foreigners who have seen European shows concede that this is greater than any ever held anywhere on earth. The stranglers of art have retired to their holes and concede in a feeble whisper that "we must admit it is a fine show"; of course my being in the midst of it prevents a clear perspective; it will take at least two years for me to realize what this thing really means . . . you were an awful chump that you did not come back in time to see the show, for there is no doubt that this marks the beginning of "doings" in America.

Except for the Joaquin Sorolla exhibition at the Hispanic Society in 1910, such a response had never even been approached. Arthur Hoeber in the *Globe* described the crush on the outside as resembling opening night at the opera, with a uniformed attendant in a gold-lettered cap using a megaphone to call the chauffeured automobiles. Inside, the visitors milled around in rooms thronged by thousands, "like a great fair," mostly in front of the strange and incomprehensible works of the European moderns.

What was the Armory Show really like?

The Armory Show displayed about 1,300 works of art, of which approximately one-third were foreign. Walter Pach estimated the total, including lithographs which were not in the Exhibition proper, at 1,600. The original catalogue lists 1,046 items and the supplement brings the number to 1,112; however, some of the entries patently included more than one work, as for instance #397, 15 *Aquarelles* by Signac. These, of course, can be

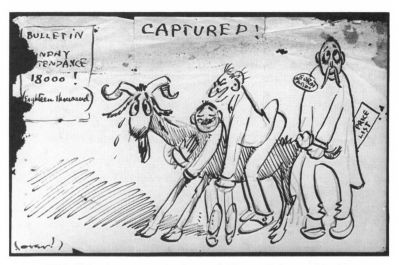

Walt Kuhn (1877–1949). *Captured* (Gregg, Kuhn, and Pach).
Hirshhorn Museum and Sculpture Garden, Smithsonian Institution,
Washington, D.C.; Gift of Joseph H. Hirshhorn Foundation, 1966.

tallied, but there are also entries like *#933, Drawings* by Art
Young, where the number exhibited is plural but undetermined.
By adding the determinable multiple exhibits to the recorded
total and subtracting those listed in the supplement as having
been "catalogued but not received," we come up with a total of
1,275, although I would not like to take an oath on it. That
leaves us with some additional items which we know to be plural
but indeterminate, and a few works that were added at the last
moment and went uncatalogued, such as *La Douleur* by Jo Davidson. There seems to be a current notion that there were a great
many works in this latter category, perhaps fostered by artists
who in retrospect would like to have been in the Armory Show
but were not. My own opinion, after careful study of all the existing records, newspaper reports, and the annotated and priced
catalogues of both Kuhn and MacRae, is that very few works
were added, not more than a dozen.

The number of works in the Show was impressive, but it was
not this which lent it excitement and importance. In spite of
efforts by the critics to find the American section better, and if
not better, at least saner than the foreign, it was the European

section which drew the crowds and created the discussion. Whatever the circus aspects of the Armory Show, the serious and comprehensive display of the latest manifestations of European contemporary art gave it its true significance. Davies' intention was not simply to collect examples of the new movements in art, but to display them in a way that would make them understandable to the public. In short, this was a supreme effort to educate American taste.

The guiding principle behind this presentation was a coherent explanation of the development of modern art, and although Americans had been given the opportunity previously to see isolated aspects of the new in the small exhibitions superbly mounted at Stieglitz's "291," the Armory Show was the first major display in this country of a comprehensive survey covering the entire history of what we call "Modern Art." It is in this that the strength and failings of the Armory Show are to be seen. Its underlying philosophy was that art must be alive, that life presupposes change, and that the new may at first appear strange but will eventually be accepted and become the old; thus the inevitability of revolution and the continuity of tradition. This apparent paradox the conservatives could never accept even in the face of historical evidence, but it was this doctrine that Davies was intent on demonstrating. He wanted to document the continuity of creative tradition in art from Goya, Ingres, and Delacroix to Cubism. He presented the history of French nineteenth-century painting in a fairly conventional manner as a continuous development from Ingres and Delacroix, through Courbet and Realism, Impressionism and Post-Impressionism—insisting, however, that each of the successive steps was a revolutionary break from the previous style, eventually supplanting it. In each case the change was at first inimical to reigning standards of taste, but with time was understood and accepted. The present situation, then, was simply another in this line of artistic revolutions which the public did not comprehend but would one day welcome. The inevitable gap between the revolutionary creator and the conservative spectator demanded on the part of the latter an effort at learning and a reservation of judgment.

In the March issue of *Arts and Decoration*, entirely given over to the Armory Show and including a series of articles and state-

ments by Davies, du Bois, Quinn, Glackens, Gregg, Jo Davidson, Mabel Dodge, and William M. Fisher, there was a chart by
Davies outlining the chronological development of "Modern
Art." Here he divides the painters of the nineteenth and early
twentieth centuries into three categories: Classicists, Realists,
and Romanticists. If one is willing to accept this classification,
his listings, except for several questionable designations, are generally accurate. Among the Classicists he includes Ingres, Corot,
Puvis de Chavannes, Degas, and Charles Serret. Why Corot is
not clear. Degas is understandable, at least in part, because of his
relation to Ingres as a draughtsman, though one could argue for
his inclusion among his Impressionist colleagues with the Realists. Serret is a curious addition, first, because he was unimportant, and second, because he was represented by only three
drawings, which, incidentally, belonged to Davies. The line
continues through Cézanne, Gauguin, Matisse, and the Post-
Impressionists to the Cubists and Picasso. Cézanne's connection
with the Classic tradition is obvious, but one would have to guess
that Gauguin and Matisse are included in this category because
of their insistence on line, which from the time of Ingres was an
attitude identified with Classicism. But exactly what Davies
meant by Post-Impressionists is not at all clear, since Cézanne,
Van Gogh, and Gauguin are listed separately, as are Toulouse-
Lautrec and Redon, and Matisse is placed earlier in time. The
Realists comprise Courbet, Manet, Monet, Sisley, Pissarro, Signac, Cassatt, Toulouse-Lautrec, and Morisot; and if one accepts
the Impressionists as a continuation of Realism, as is generally
done, then one cannot quibble with this list. Nor would I argue
with his inclusion of Cézanne, appearing for the second time,
among the Realists; but the designation in this same category of
the Futurists as "feeble realists" is confusing, to say the least.
Among the Romanticists, he placed Delacroix, Daumier, Redon, Renoir, Van Gogh, and Gauguin.

The article that appears after the chart is an extension of it in
argument. It was written by Guy Pène du Bois, but is probably a
paraphrase of Davies' explanation of the chart and his personal
understanding of the modern movement. It is a rather gener-
alized, poetic, and emotional statement, which characterizes
Classicism as seeking the "order of life," Realism the "power of

life," and Romanticism the "sensuous delight of life." In its predilection for Classicism one can recognize Davies' own identification with Cubism. And in this light one can also understand certain distortions in the listing of artists in the Classic line and Davies' personal failure to appreciate either the Expressionists or the Futurists.

In the hanging of the Exhibition, Davies clearly tried to present this argument to the public, but the exigencies of space and circulation partially obscured the underlying theme. As has already

Gallery A, American sculpture and decorative art.

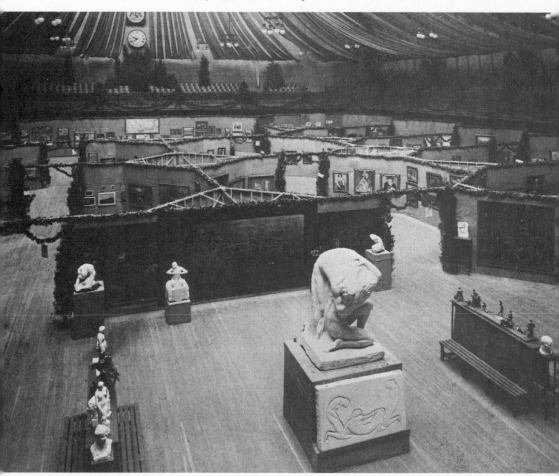

been noted, the Armory was divided into eighteen octagonal rooms, with circulation directed down the center rooms from one end to the other, or circularly around the Armory. There was no lateral connection between the file of rooms on the north or south sides and the center.

As one came into the gallery space from Lexington Avenue, through the entrance flanked on either side by a tall pine, the large central room (A) housed American sculpture and decorative arts, mainly white marble and plaster statuary dominated

Plan of exhibition floor.

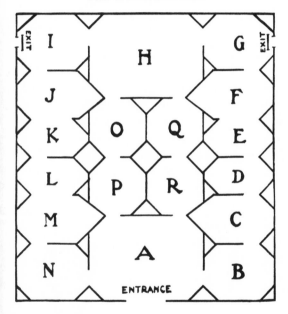

Gallery A.   American Sculpture and Decorative Art

Gallery B.   American Paintings and Sculpture

Gallery C.   American Paintings

Gallery D.   American Paintings

Gallery E.   American Paintings

Gallery F.   American Paintings

Gallery G.   English, Irish and German Paintings and Drawings

Gallery H.   French Paintings and Sculpture

Gallery I.   French Paintings and Sculpture

Gallery J.   French Paintings, Water Colors and Drawings

Gallery K.   French and American Water Colors, Drawings, etc.

Gallery L.   American Water Colors, Drawings, etc.

Gallery M.   American Paintings

Gallery N.   American Paintings and Sculpture

Gallery O.   French Paintings

Gallery P.   French, English, Dutch and American Paintings

Gallery Q.   French Paintings

Gallery R.   French, English and Swiss Paintings

American Art Will Never Be the Same Again

by Barnard's *The Prodigal Son and His Father* (page 101). It certainly was fitting that the first room be assigned to American art, but it threw the idea of the Exhibition a little off-center. If one turned right, toward the north, one entered a row of rooms (B through F) devoted entirely to American art, mostly painting. Once one entered this row, there was no egress except by retracing one's steps. The last room (G) on the north side was reserved for English, Irish, and German painting, including the Kandinsky and the Kirchner, and two Vlamincks which had overflowed from an adjoining room. Turning to the left, unless one wanted to leave the Exhibition by the north exit, one entered the great room (H) at the other end of the Armory, which contained French painting and sculpture. But this sequence obviously has no connection with the theme of the Show. By returning to the entry and turning left or toward the south, the sequence is no better. One entered here a row of rooms matching those on the north side. The first of these (N), like its mate opposite, contained American paintings and such sculpture as overflowed from the large sculpture gallery. Then followed in order a room of American painting (M); American watercolors, drawings, etc. (L); American and foreign watercolors, drawings, and prints (K); French painting, watercolors, and prints, dominated by the 38 Redons (J); and, lastly, the Show's major attraction, the Cubist room (I).

It was in the central section of the Armory, in the area between the two great rooms at either end, divided into four rooms, that the historical background of modern art and its "old masters" were presented. The first of these (P), on the left, contained a variety of American and foreign nineteenth-century paintings. Beginning with a miniature by Goya, it presented pre-Impressionist French painting by examples of the work of Delacroix, Corot, Daumier, Courbet, and Manet, plus Puvis de Chavannes, Monticelli, and Henri Rousseau, as well as a late-entry Renoir, which probably did not fit into the adjacent room (O) assigned to the Impressionists. Room P also included a group of American "old masters": Whistler, the Impressionists Theodore Robinson and John Twachtman, and a large collection of paintings by Ryder, here treated for the first time as an important forerunner of modern American painting. The Impressionist room had paintings by

Manet, Degas, Monet, Renoir, Pissarro, Sisley, Cassatt, Seurat, and Toulouse-Lautrec.

One had to go out into the large hall and double back to get to Room Q, which housed the paintings of Cézanne and Van Gogh, or starting again from the sculpture court go through Room R, which held a grab bag of paintings, including Manet, Puvis de Chavannes, Gauguin, Hodler, Matisse, Picasso, and Augustus John. The carefully planned presentation was dissipated to a certain extent by the physical limitations of the layout as well as by the accepted exhibition custom of separating works in different media. This latter practice lessened the impact of some artists, as for instance Picasso.

However, in spite of these difficulties, one could get the general idea by moving down the center aisle and fanning out to both right and left if one were not too compulsive about absolute sequence, and I imagine most people were not, since this was long before the tyranny of display which leads one through a space funnel devised by someone who knows what is best for one. As a matter of fact, most of the critics grasped the idea and commented upon it very favorably. The plan managed to present the foreign section as a development of modern art climaxed by the most recent examples, but at the same time separated the Americans from the Europeans by relegating them to the large entrance hall and the flanking rooms on either side of the Armory.

Up to the time of the Show's opening, the entire operation had been financed with borrowed or donated funds, but the Association had always at least hoped that the enterprise would eventually pay its way; and some, like Kuhn, even dreamt of financial success. The major source of expected revenue was admission fees. The printing and sale of catalogues, pamphlets, post cards, and photographs was probably intended as an educational service rather than a profitmaking venture, just as the sale of works for which they took a commission was seen essentially as a service to the artists.

The Exhibition was open from 10 A.M. to 10 P.M. on weekdays and Saturday; from 2 P.M. to 10 P.M. on Sunday. Admission was 25 cents except for weekday mornings until noon, when the entry fee was $1. An unlimited admissions card could be bought for $5, but very few of those were sold. In spite of wide newspaper coverage and really very favorable publicity, early attendance during the week was disappointing, although three thousand people paid to see the Show on the first Saturday. This was apparently fewer than had been expected. There was no appreciable improvement for the next two weeks, but toward the end of the third week attendance began to increase and built steadily during the last week to a climax of an estimated ten thousand visitors on the last day. Receipts from admissions on that Saturday were $2,300.

It is impossible to be precise about the number of people who saw the Armory Show, for a variety of reasons. Among the MacRae Papers is a tally sheet which records the daily receipts from admissions and sales. There are also four cashbooks in which the girls at the several booths entered daily totals as well as numbers of admissions. Unfortunately, the figures in these books do not always jibe with those on the tally sheet. By breaking down the entries in the cashbooks, which are admittedly incomplete, we have a total of 62,102 paid admissions. Total receipts from admissions on the tally sheet are given as $18,905.70, an obvious arithmetical error. A summary financial statement in MacRae's handwriting among the same papers lists the paid admissions as 75,620. This figure was apparently arrived at by the simple expedient of dividing the total receipts by four and ignoring the extra 70 cents. The actual number of paid admissions must therefore be somewhere between the incomplete tally of 62,102 and the inaccurate estimate of 75,620. To complicate matters further is the fact of free admissions. MacRae estimated this number as approximately 1,000 at the press view, 5,000 at the opening reception, 1,000 complimentary passes, and 5,000 free tickets. The overall total is then given as 87,620, which is as close to the truth as we ever will or need to get. Subsequent estimates have tended to increase the total, Pach, for instance, raising it to a quarter of a million, almost as if the importance of the Show were thereby bolstered. The approximately seventy thousand visitors who paid cold cash to look at an art exhibit is testimony enough to the success of the venture.

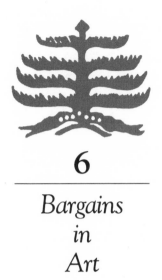

6

Bargains
in
Art

Another indication of the success of the Armory Show, and one which carried great weight with both press and public, was the sales record. From the very time art became a commodity for sale in an open market, prices have had an unusual fascination for the public, which has as much difficulty understanding why great works cost as much as they do as that works they do not understand sell at all. In a money economy, hard cash can transform naïve merriment into troubled wonder, and when many of the most radical works were sold people either had to take a second look or become morally indignant, for hardly anything can incite more moral fervor than the expenditure of money. During its exhibition in New York and the subsequent travels of the Armory Show to Chicago and Boston, 174 works of art were sold, of which 123 were by foreign artists and 51 by American. Approximately 90 prints which were not actually on display were also sold. Kuhn's totals are somewhat at variance with these figures, which are based on the financial records of the Association in the MacRae Papers. Kuhn's figures of 130 foreign and 35 American works sold are certainly approximate and obviously do not include the Vollard prints. The total sales amounted to $44,148.75. The records indicate sales of $30,491.25 for foreign works and $13,657.50 for American. According to notations by both Kuhn and MacRae, $11,625 was finally paid by the Association to American artists and $12,886 to foreign. The difference between receipts and disbursements reflects the sales commission charged by the Association as well as transportation and Customs fees, which were deducted in the case of foreign works.

From the outset, the Association planned to act as agent and expected or at least hoped to make sales. All their negotiations with artists and dealers abroad emphasized the possibility of sales in an untried market, and it was probably this very hope which led to the cooperation of the latter with the project. Walter Pach arrived home in time to assume the post of sales manager in charge of several assistants selling works on commission. The honor of the first purchase at the Armory Show goes to Daniel H. Morgan, who bought three Redon paintings on February 19. On the next day two very perceptive men, Arthur B. Davies and Alfred Stieglitz, made interesting though not expensive purchases; the former bought *Danseurs*, a plaster by Duchamp-Villon, and the latter, *Chula*, a sculpture by Manolo. It is one of those minor coincidences with no significance that both were priced at $67.50. The ice was broken, and on the 22nd two of the major collectors of the time, who in quite different ways left an indelible mark on the history of American collecting, Lillie P. Bliss and John Quinn, made the first of their many purchases at the Armory Show. Miss Bliss began rather tentatively with two Redon lithographs, but Quinn, as betokened his adventurous nature, plunged right in with three Villon paintings and one each by Redon and Zak.

The influence of Davies and Kuhn is apparent here. The two men who had the most to do with the Exhibition each convinced the collector with whom he was most closely connected that this was the time to make a move. One may safely assume that both were acting not without personal interest, since the success of the Exhibition depended upon public acceptance, and nothing reveals this as clearly as sales. It seems almost as if each one was bringing up his big gun to break the jam. That both Miss Bliss and Quinn decided to act on the same day is probably pure coincidence.

Among the coterie of wealthy women interested in art who looked upon Arthur B. Davies as mentor and friend, Lillie Bliss was the most important. The artistic alliance between these two did much to establish modern art in this country. Under the guidance of Davies (and, after his death, Kuhn), Miss Bliss accumulated a magnificent collection of modern masterpieces, including 26 Cézannes, which eventually became the nucleus of the Museum of Modern Art in New York. It was certainly the urging of Davies which led her to take her first steps in that direction at the Armory Show. Although these first steps were tentative and conservative, they must have seemed daring to herself and friends. She bought in all two Redons and 18 assorted prints. Her major development as a collector of modern art came only later, but it was at the Armory Show that it began.

Of entirely different background, temperament, and intent was John Quinn, the brilliant lawyer who found his most creative expression in supporting art, either as patron or collector. Aline Saarinen in her fascinating book *The Proud Possessors* calls him "the twentieth century's most important patron of living literature and art." As a friend of Walt Kuhn, Quinn was in on the Armory Show almost from the very beginning. He acted without fee as the Association's legal adviser and singlehandedly carried their case against the duty on living art to the Congress and eventually won its repeal. He was an honorary member of the Association, acted often as its front, and delivered the welcoming address at the opening of the Show. He had already collected works by such artists as Cézanne, Van Gogh, and Gauguin, but Kuhn now convinced him (with some difficulty, for though Quinn took advice he did not take easily to direction) that now was the time to fish or cut bait. Quinn came back again and again, even following the Show to Chicago and buying there.

121

Quinn spent $5,808.75 at the Armory Show for works by Alexandre Blanchet, Derain, Duchamp-Villon, Girieud, Manolo, Pascin, Redon, Segonzac, Signac, Villon, and Zak. He showed his personal loyalty to Kuhn by buying both of his paintings in the Show, and his gallantry by keeping two watercolors by Edith Dimock, the wife of William Glackens, even though he had changed his mind about them. Included also were a number of prints and Vollard lithographs, which he probably distributed as gifts. It was a varied selection, which reflects no deep commitment to the more experimental phases of contemporary art. The Armory Show gave added impetus and direction to his later collecting, which evolved into that superb and almost legendary accumulation of modern masterpieces for which he is remembered.

Next to Quinn the largest buyer at the Armory Show, and in this case an even more adventurous one, was the Chicago lawyer Arthur Jerome Eddy. One wonders whether it is purely accident

122

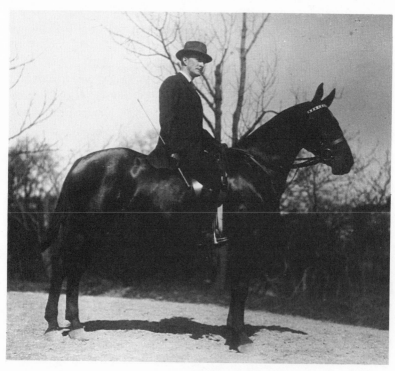

John Quinn.

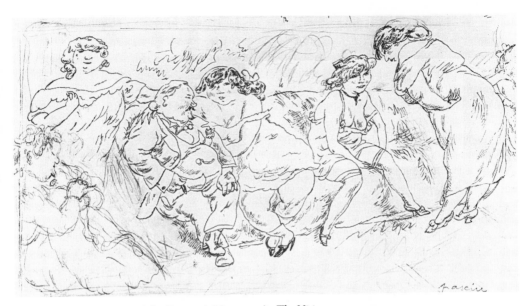

Jules Pascin (1885–1930). *The Visit*, c. 1904–5.
Pen, ink, and pencil on paper, 8¼ × 11⅛ in. Collection,
The Museum of Modern Art, New York; Gift of A. Conger Goodyear.

that three of our most daring and individualistic of twentieth-century collectors were lawyers—Quinn, Eddy, and John G. Johnson. According to Kuhn, Eddy heard of the Quinn purchases and, not to be outdone, came to New York to enter the competition. The fact is that Eddy, like Quinn, was a man of great energy, audacious and individualistic. He had always been fascinated by the unusual and especially the new. He is reputed to have been the first to ride a bicycle in Chicago and the first to own an automobile. Like Quinn and Johnson, he found the practice of law less than enthralling and sought expression in a variety of fields. He wrote on economic theory, esthetics, criticism, and even tried his hand at fiction. He also collected; one of the first works he bought was Manet's *Philosopher* at a time when Manet was still not very well known to American collectors. He was an early admirer of Whistler, had his portrait painted by him, and wrote a critical essay on him. Anything which had the promise of excitement and controversy was sure to interest Eddy, and the Armory Show promised plenty of both.

The Show had already been earmarked for Chicago, but Eddy could not wait. He came to New York to see it and became a convert almost overnight. His first purchases on Thursday, February 27, were not unusual—Chabaud's *Le Laboureur* and Zak's *Berger*—but he was back again on Saturday and this time he went for broke. He bought five pictures that day—two by Segonzac, Villon's *Jeune Femme* (*Young Girl*, page 125), Duchamp's *Portrait de joueurs d'échecs*, and Gleizes' *L'Homme au balcon*. Like a man in a fever, he was back the next day, Sunday, to buy four more of the most advanced paintings in the Exhibition—Picabia's *La Danse à la source* (*Dances at the Spring*, color plate 10), Duchamp's *Le Roi et la reine entourés des nus vites*, Derain's *La Forêt à Martigues*, and Vlaminck's *Rueil* (*Village*, page 126). He made further purchases in New York and later in Chicago, where he acquired three paintings by the Portuguese Sousa-Cardoza. These latter, unimportant and only superficially modernist, are an anti-climax to the daring of his earlier selections and seem almost the expression of uncertainty. Perhaps he was momentarily overwhelmed by his own rashness and had his moments of doubt. As a matter of fact, as we shall see later, Eddy had what appeared to be a temporary change of heart when the Show came to Chicago. His vacillation was short-lived and he was soon back in the race not only buying the latest manifestations of contemporary art but fighting for its recognition. His *Cubists and Post-Impressionism*, published in 1914, is one of the earliest books to appear in America on the subject of modern art. The collection of 18 paintings and 7 lithographs bought from the Armory Show, which led Eddy along the high road of artistic adventure, cost him $4,888.50, a mere pittance.

None of the other collectors bought as widely and intensely as did Quinn and Eddy, but many of the names later famous in the annals of American patronage are on the roster of buyers, and their selections are an interesting indication of the state of their taste at that time. Most of the buyers belonged naturally enough to the younger generation of collectors rather than to that select group of titans who were committed to the old masters, solid values, and high prices. As a matter of fact, some of the established dealers in masterpieces were uneasy about the effect that this invasion might have on the art market. The *American Art News*,

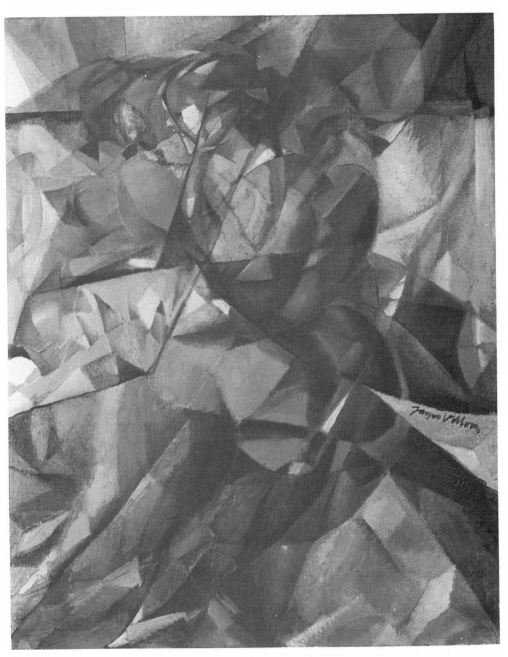

Jacques Villon (1875–1963). *Young Girl,* 1912. Oil on canvas, 57¾ × 45⅛ in.
Philadelphia Museum of Art; Louise and Walter Arensberg Collection.

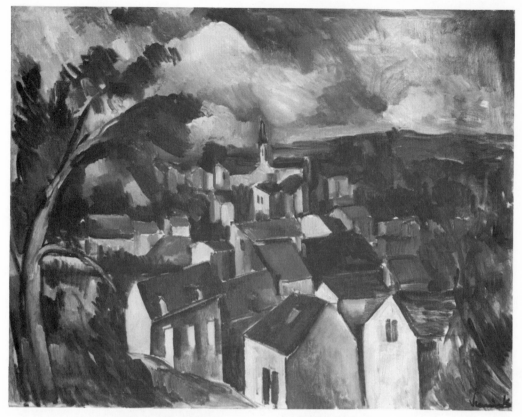

Maurice de Vlaminck (1876–1958). *Village (Rueil)*, c. 1912.
Oil on canvas, 29 × 36¼ in. The Art Institute of Chicago;
Arthur Jerome Eddy Memorial Collection.

which was not much more than a shill for art dealers, did its
worst to ridicule the Show and discredit it through innuendo.
One of New York's leading art galleries, Knoedler's, refused to
advertise in the Armory Show catalogue because it felt the Association was fostering "radical tendencies in modern art." Some of
the great collectors of that era may have come to the Exhibition,
but only one of them made a purchase—and a rather curious
one. Henry C. Frick bought a small painting by Pach, *Flowers*,
for $87.50. Pach himself, who was in charge of sales, has written
that Frick was interested in an important picture which was already sold and, also, "had it not been for the adept handling of

the dealer who came with him, Mr. Frick would almost certainly have bought" the great Cézanne *Femme au chapelet* (*An Old Woman with a Rosary*, color plate 4). It is fascinating to speculate what such a purchase at that time would have meant for the Frick Collection and the history of American collecting.

Of the younger collectors, Dr. Albert C. Barnes, Walter C. Arensberg, A. E. Gallatin, Stephen C. Clark, Edward W. Root, and Hamilton Easter Field bought from the Show and must have been influenced by what they saw. The "terrible-tempered" Dr. Barnes, who had made a fortune in Argyrol and had recently turned to collecting modern art under the urging of William Glackens, turned up and, it is said, announced that he had better stuff. His purchase of Vlaminck's *Figues*, for which, incidentally, he took an unconscionably long time to pay, is an indication of the state of his taste at that time as well as his attitude toward money. It is interesting, considering his later predilection for the art of Matisse (he eventually amassed the largest collection of Matisses in this country), that he did not respond to any of the important works by that master at the Armory Show. And for a bargain hunter, the prices should have been enticing: $4,050 for the famous *Panneau rouge* (*Red Studio*), $1,350 for the *Jeune Marin*, and the same price for *Le Luxe*. Barnes could never understand Cubism, but at that time he was not even up to Matisse. Eliza G. Radeke, autocrat of the Rhode Island School of Design Museum, with no pretensions to being a collector of modern art but with much greater acumen, bought a Matisse drawing for $67.50 and two small Signac watercolors for $65.

Walter Arensberg came down from Boston in the last days of the Exhibition, procrastinated and lost out on a Rodin drawing which had already been bought by W. R. Valentiner, then with the Metropolitan Museum's Department of Decorative Arts, and settled rather meagerly for a Vuillard lithograph. He may have brooded over his loss for a while, but the seeds of a life-long occupation with modern art were then planted. They took some time to mature, for Arensberg was introspective, tenacious, and even his most esoteric tendencies were never rash; and it was not until the last day of the Show in Boston, before it was dismantled for good, that he returned the Vuillard lithograph and bought the last and smallest of the Villons, one of the Puteaux studies.

With this began his long and lasting interest in Villon and his brother, Marcel Duchamp, whose close friend he later became. It was not long after, with his mind finally set, that he began an assiduous search to assemble all those works he had missed the first time around. The Louise and Walter Arensberg Collection now at the Philadelphia Museum of Art contains three of the Duchamps which were at the Show, including the notorious *Nu descendant un escalier* (*Nude Descending a Staircase*, color plate 9) and two of the Villons, among a great many other works by the brothers which were not in the Exhibition. Slow to start, he

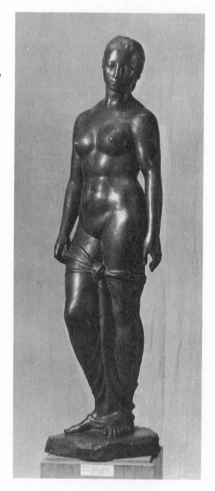

Wilhelm Lehmbruck (1881–1919).
Standing Woman, 1910.
Cast in New York, 1916–17,
from an original plaster.
Bronze, 75⅛ × 20½ in. Collection,
The Museum of Modern Art,
New York; Given anonymously.

128

eventually accumulated a unique, completely personal, and very important collection of modern art.

Katherine Sophie Dreier, who exhibited two small paintings at the Armory Show, was still a long way from her later impassioned espousal of the most radical aspects of modern art, as her purchases at the Show indicate—one Gauguin and one Redon lithograph. She already owned a small Van Gogh which she lent to the Exhibition, but it was only after she met Marcel Duchamp that she began her collecting and proselytizing for the new movements and formed the Société Anonyme, Inc., the forerunner of the present Museum of Modern Art.

A. E. Gallatin was still a decade short of succumbing to the taste for modernism. Loyal to the Ash Can tradition, he bought a chalk drawing by Boardman Robinson. Edward Root, whose commitment was, and remained, to American art, had lent some Luks drawings to the Armory Show and during the first week bought a large oil, *Landscape with Figures* (color plate 19), by Maurice Prendergast, an American artist who was among the closest in affinity to the modern movement abroad. Stephen Clark showed an early interest in the new art by his financial contribution to the Show and his purchase of a small Marquet drawing and the *Jeune Femme* (*Standing Woman*, page 128) by Lehmbruck, for which he paid $1,620, the highest price paid for a piece of sculpture at the Exhibition. Hamilton Field, as always, with sensitivity and discrimination selected a single work, one of the studies of Puteaux by Villon.

Some of the most perspicacious of buyers were not primarily collectors. Of these the most notable were Davies and Stieglitz, whose selections reflect a refinement of taste and knowledge of contemporary art. Davies bought the Duchamp-Villon terracotta *Danseurs*, the Manolo statuette *Femme nu debout*, the Villon *Arbres en fleur*, and the Picasso *Les Arbres*, all four for $648, an excellent example of shortness of means making for careful choice. Stieglitz showed the same shrewdness in selection as well as price. He picked five drawings by Archipenko for $135, a Davies drawing for $65, a Manolo statuette for $67.50, and one of the most audacious purchases, the only Kandinsky in the Exhibition, the large *Improvisation #27* (color plate 8), now in the Metropolitan Museum of Art, for $500. Anyone with a drop of

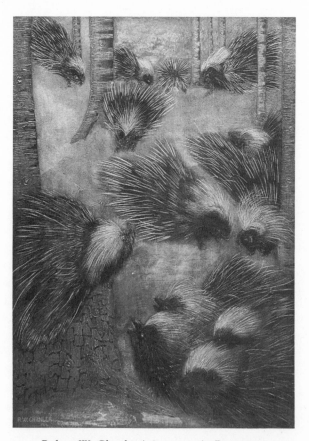

Robert W. Chanler (1872–1930). *Porcupines*
(variation of the work exhibited at the Armory Show), 1914.
Painted screen, 69½ × 48¼ in.
The Metropolitan Museum of Art, New York;
Gift of Mrs. Jay Chapman, 1927.

collector's blood in his veins must develop a retrospective itch to
have been there and had the same chance at prescience.

Other artists besides Davies also bought from the Show, although modestly; Edith Dimock acquired a Kuhn drawing; Kuhn,
a Cézanne lithograph; MacRae, a Renoir lithograph; Pach, a
Gauguin lithograph; and Allen Tucker, a Gauguin lithograph.
Robert Chanler, the flamboyant scion of the Whitney clan,
whose marriage to the notoriously temperamental operatic diva
Lina Cavalieri was one of the juicier news items of the day, had

achieved resounding acclaim for his decorative screens at the Armory Show. He sold one of them to George F. Porter in Chicago for $1,500 and reinvested some of it in purchases. He bought two paintings by Amadéo Sousa-Cardoza, the Portuguese painter whose style was similar to his own and who was, like Chanler, one of the unexpected hits of the Exhibition; two Redon lithographs; and—one of the canniest selections of all—a bronze version of the *Mlle. Pogany* by Brancusi, for which he paid $550.

The Duchamp *Nude*, which had been the most talked of work in the Show, was bought, sight unseen, by Frederic C. Torrey of the San Francisco firm of art dealers and decorators Vickery, Atkins and Torrey, for the sum of $324. There were many subsequent offers for the painting, but Torrey turned them down and exhibited the picture on the West Coast until its sale to Klaus Spreckels, who eventually sold it to Walter Arensberg in 1927. The highest price for a work of art at the Armory Show and one of the most important sales was the $6,700 paid by the Metropolitan Museum of Art for Cézanne's *Colline des pauvres*, the first painting by that artist to enter an American museum collection.

The sales at the Armory Show are a clear indication of the profound effect which the Exhibition had on collectors and on American taste. It led many young collectors into the domain of modern art and forced others to re-examine their tastes. With this first important breach in the solid wall of the "old master" market a new era in American collecting was opened. If people were willing to buy, there were soon dealers ready to sell modern art, and in the next few years a whole new group of art dealers was in business to sell the very latest in contemporary art. This movement was aided in no small measure by the repeal of the duty on contemporary art, in which struggle the Association had taken a leading role.

The American art world was not ready for the Armory Show. It was entirely unaware except through vague rumors of unusual artistic happenings abroad. The last major revolutionary movement to come from Europe was Impressionism, which had invaded America in the eighties and had by now been absorbed into the academic hierarchy of values. The Ash Can revolt had upset the gentility of American taste much more by its "vulgarity" of subject matter than by any innovations of style. The

131

untroubled surface of complacency was rudely shattered by the presentation in one mass of the insurgent art of Europe created during the preceding thirty years. America saw cheek by jowl the work of Cézanne and Picasso, the Post-Impressionists and the Cubists. The public had not had a generation to get used to the older revolution, which might have prepared it for the new; it got everything at once and it is no wonder that the total was indigestible.

The Armory Show was the first opportunity America had to see a collection of works by the Post-Impressionists Cézanne, Gauguin, and Van Gogh, who were already in the "old master" ranks on the European market. This was, however, still a fairly recent phenomenon; the recognition of Cézanne dates from the Cézanne Memorial Exhibition at the Salon d'Automne of 1907, Van Gogh from the Memorial Exhibition at Bernheim-Jeune in 1901, and Gauguin from the Gauguin Memorial Exhibition at the First Salon d'Automne of 1903. But by 1913 their prices were already phenomenally high, at least by American standards. It seems almost incredible that the *Femme au chapelet* at the Armory had a price tag of $48,600, but it is listed in a ledger in the MacRae Papers for 180,000 francs (a franc was then worth 27 cents), and it was insured for 120,000 francs. Equally surprising is the price of $40,500 for the Gauguin *Fleurs sur un fond jaune*. As a matter of fact, this seemed so far out of line that it was listed in the priced catalogues of both MacRae and Kuhn for sale at $4,050. The ledger again shows a valuation of 150,000 francs. None of the Van Goghs were of that quality or price but the *Montmartre*, lent by Artz & de Bois, was offered for $26,000. It is obvious that American collectors, hardly aware of the existence of such artists, would not be ready to pay such prices. One wonders what the reaction of the press would have been had such figures been made public. The roughly sixfold inflation of the dollar since that time would bring the price of the Cézanne close to $300,000.

7

The
Rude Descending a
Staircase

133

It was difficult to know in advance what would attract the public's attention in an exhibition of this kind, and although some of the reaction could have been predicted on the basis of shock value, some of it came as a surprise. It was naturally enough the colorful and novel examples of the avant-garde from Post-Impressionism to Cubism which captured public interest and received most of the critical comment. The public was especially attracted by the non-representational character of Cubism (which was a totally new experience), repelled by the revolutionary color and distortion of Matisse, and highly amused by the startling simplifications of

Brancusi. However, critical comment and sales indicate an acceptance of at least some aspects of the new movement.

As Davies and Kuhn had hoped, Redon went over big. Of all the avant-garde artists he was accorded the most favorable reception in the press. The esoteric symbolism and strange forms of his art did not seem to disturb the critics and he was hailed as a great master. The ravishing quality of his color, the poetic and mystical content of his art appealed to a taste conditioned by Whistler and Davies. One could overlook its involved personal symbolism,

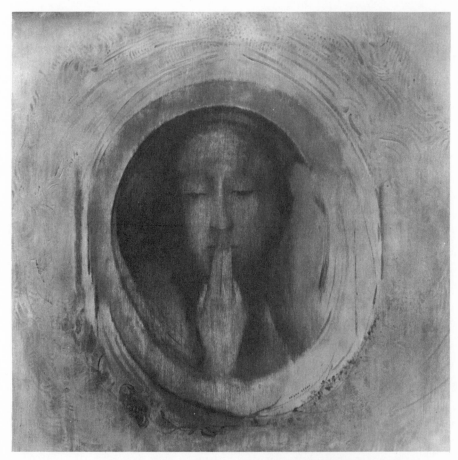

Odilon Redon (1840–1916). *Silence,* c. 1911.
Oil on gesso on paper, 21 ¼ × 21 ½ in. Collection,
The Museum of Modern Art, New York; Lillie P. Bliss Collection.

since it appeared to reflect legitimate artistic license and philosophical profundity. Redon was by far the most successful of the exhibitors and the phenomenal acceptance of his work came while he was still alive. Thirteen of his paintings and pastels and twenty prints were sold from the Armory Show.

Lehmbruck also received a measure of critical acclaim; one reviewer characterized his work as having "singular and penetrating power." But the Duchamp-Villon brothers proved the most successful in sales after Redon, even though their critical reception was not favorable. Raymond Duchamp-Villon sold three of his four sculptures in the Exhibition, Marcel Duchamp sold all four of his paintings, and Jacques Villon all nine of his. Such amazing success is hard to explain, considering the fact that although all three were not unknown in Paris they had not achieved anything near the reputation of Picasso or Braque. This unexpected triumph in America may have been due in part to the publicity given to them in the press as a family of avant-garde artists; pictures of them in their garden at Puteaux were the only photographs of contemporary European artists distributed by the Association to newspapers and were used in stories and Sunday supplements.

Although all of these artists were men who later achieved even greater recognition, there were several others who found unanticipated acceptance but are today almost unknown. Both the American Robert Chanler and the Portuguese Amadéo Sousa-Cardoza appeared modern without being too extreme, and the public found that half-way station more comfortable than the uncompromising radicalism of the Fauves and Cubists. The colorful decorative screens of Chanler won instant popularity although only one of them was sold. Sousa-Cardoza's mannered stylization of form, quite similar to that of Chanler, also had popular appeal and, perhaps because they were so reasonably priced, seven of his paintings were purchased, all but one of those exhibited. Curiously, although Edward Adam Kramer, one of the Association members, was not very well known and not especially noted in reviews, he was the most successful among the American artists in sales. This may have been due partly to the size of his representation, 14 paintings and pastels, which gave his art added impact. Kramer sold five works for $1,525, the top amount for an American artist at the Show, and it was without doubt the most important event in his career.

Whatever the considered opinion of the critics or their efforts to support the American section, whatever the judgment of collectors expressed in their purchases, the public was irresistibly drawn to the most talked of works of the European insurgents. There was usually such a crowd before the Duchamp *Nude Descending a Staircase* (color plate 9) that it was difficult to see. The buzz of excitement was exhilarating. Some tried to understand, others tried to explain, the great majority either laughed or were infuriated. It could be seen as a symbol of the ultimate in moral degeneracy or as a mad and irresponsible joke. People generally do not like to become too involved with art, probably because they do not know how; it is much easier to cover one's insecurity with laughter. And there was a good deal of laughter, especially in the "Chamber of Horrors," as the Cubist room was called. Because of a certain incongruity in its title and the puzzle which it presented, the *Nude* became the focal point of the Exhibition. One could come and see the joke and forget to be troubled by revolutions. It was the butt of humorous jibes, the object of verse, a puzzle to be deciphered. The search for the nude was on, as if discovery would reveal some great secret. The *American Art News* offered a $10 prize for the best solution. The winning entry was a poem called "It's Only a Man:"

> You've tried to find her,
> And you've looked in vain
> Up the picture and down again,
> You've tried to fashion her of broken bits,
> And you've worked yourself into seventeen fits;
> The reason you've failed to tell you I can,
> It isn't a lady but only a man.

This is not even immortal doggerel, but it is less disturbing than Arthur Jerome Eddy's serious search for and discovery of the nude, which was published in the Chicago *Tribune*, complete with diagram. There were also cartoon take-offs, the best of which was one by J. F. Griswold in the *Evening Sun* called "The rude descending a staircase (Rush hour at the subway)."

The *Nude* was variously described as "a lot of disused golf clubs

136

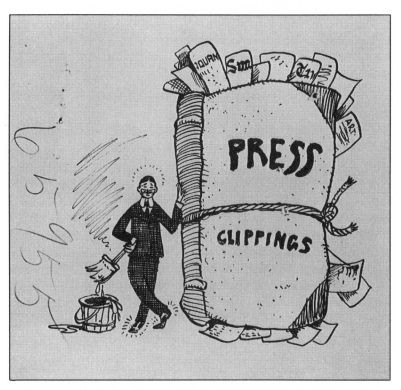

Walt Kuhn. Printer's proof of drawing, probably for press-clipping scrapbook.
Hirshhorn Museum and Sculpture Garden, Smithsonian Institution,
Washington, D.C.; Gift of the Joseph H. Hirshhorn Foundation, 1966.

and bags," "an assortment of half-made leather saddles," an
"elevated railroad stairway in ruins after an earthquake," a "dyna-
mited suit of Japanese armor," a "pack of brown cards in a
nightmare," an "orderly heap of broken violins," or an "academic painting of an artichoke." The most popular description,
"an explosion in a shingle factory," was used by Julian Street
in *Everybody's,* but it was also attributed to Joel E. Spingarn.
Gutzon Borglum renamed it "A staircase descending a nude."
Many of these descriptions intended as humor are rather more
descriptive than humorous. But most of the jibes directed at the
avant-garde art, either in cartoons, jokes, or jingles, were neither good nor funny. As one editorial writer pointed out, you
can't spoof what you don't understand.

There were, however, occasional verses which had at least the virtues of good humor and metric felicity. One contributed to the *Sun*, March 8, by Maurice L. Ahern, was called "A Post Impression" and read:

> Awful lack of technique
> Awful lot of paint
> Makes a Cubist picture
> Look like what it ain't.

The Chicago *Tribune* column "A line o' type or two" offered some of the better examples of verse. The February 9 issue carried a longish poem with a few good lines:

> I do not say that Futurism
> May merely be astigmatism.
> I do not urge the Futurist
> To hasten to an oculist;
> If this or that I can't divine,
> It's eight to five the fault is mine.

And the February 8 issue had a lively quatrain:

> I called the canvas *Cow with cud*
> And hung it on the line,
> Altho' to me 'twas vague as mud,
> 'Twas clear to Gertrude Stein.

Maurice Morris did a series of poems on various exhibits, published in the *Sun* of February 23, which were somewhat above the general level of the poetic parodies current at the time:

> To Ingres and Cézanne
>
> Ingres, a heavy burden must you bear!
> And you, Cézanne, an even greater sinner!
> Futurist, Cubist, Spherist, all declare
> You led them to the Essence of the Inner.

> Picabia's "Procession, Seville"
>
> Of fair Sevilla's towers
> I gain a faint impression,
> But still am several hours
> In rear of that "procession."

"Nude Lady Descending Staircase"

O lady fair,
As down the stair
You trip, your air
Enthralls my being!
Ah, could you wis
The sense of mys-
Tery, the bliss
With which I'm seeing!

The face unguessed,
The form repressed,
And all the rest
Unseen, I'm chanting

Each curlicue
And whirl of you,
Each splotch and hue
But leaves me panting.

A tear unbid
From 'neath each lid
Has downward slid.
Ah, depth of woe! You
Upon the street
Suppose I meet;
I cannot greet
You. I won't know you!

Most of the running gags about the Armory Show were not exactly witty. They were usually of the Joe Miller Joke Book variety, like the one about Braque's *Violon*, which included the names Kubelik and Mozart. Two men were looking at the painting and one said, "Braque is the painter who put cube in Kubelik." "No," said the other, "he put art in Mozart." And then there was the one about the anonymous punster who was overheard saying, "It is a long step from Ingres to Matisse, but it is only a short one from Matisse to anger."

As might be expected, Brancusi's *Mlle. Pogany*, which was described by one critic as "a hardboiled egg balanced on a cube of sugar," was a favorite subject of jokesters. A long poem called "Lines to a Lady Egg" was printed in the *Evening Sun*. The last stanza of this metrically erratic but impassioned avowal of undying devotion went as follows:

> Ladies builded like a bottle,
> Carrot, beet or sweet potato—
> Quaint designs that Aristotle
> Idly drew to tickle Plato—
> Ladies sculptured thus, I beg
> You will save your tense emotion;
> I am constant in devotion,
> O my egg!

The naïve doggerel, the sophomoric satires, the puerile jokes at least reflected a certain amount of amiability, but there were a great many people who were seriously disturbed by the new art. A sense of outrage underlay the hysterical vituperation of many spectators and critics.

Americans have always had a strong aversion to pomposity and sham, and perhaps because of it our humor has been especially trenchant in puncturing pretension. At the same time we have a less endearing trait of lampooning things which we simply do not understand. The one expresses a healthy skepticism, the other a philistine ignorance; unfortunately, the two are much too frequently confused. There were several lampoons of the Armory Show even while it was current. These seem, on the whole, to have substituted high spirits for wit and the bludgeon for the rapier. The only thing they had in common with good satire was malice.

The Architectural League held a smoker on March 11 at the Fine Arts Building, 215 West 57th Street, at which many of the leading academic artists took pot shots at the new menaces. A competition for lead medals was held on the theme of the "Three Foolish Virgins" in which four teams participated: Futurists led by Edwin H. Blashfield, Cubists by Taber Sears, Post-Impressionists by George W. Breck, and Classicists by Francis Jones. It is to be assumed that a gay time was had by all, although the description of the festivities in the next morning's newspapers seems a little flat. At 11:30 P.M. a call was put in for an ambulance and Dr. Blashfield pronounced Futurism dead as a result of the activities of the members.

The sixth annual meeting of "Les Anciens de l'Académie Julian," held at the old Brevoort House, was transformed into a burlesque of the new art movements. These former habitués of that most popular of Parisian studios among American artists gathered on March 17 in their blue smocks and corduroy pants for their yearly bow to nostalgia. The invitation to the affair had been accompanied by a bit of verse which set the tone of the evening:

> We'll likewise hold in gay review
> The fads in art that now are new;
> Impressions, oval, cubic, post.
> We'll analyze and mayhap roast,
> And prove by showing sketch and skit
> That everybody's doing it.

Many of the artists brought mock modernist works done for the exhibition to be held the following Saturday for the Lighthouse for the Blind and hung them around the walls of the dining room. The prizes were a "gold dust medal" for the best figure study, "linear or cubic," and a "silver polish medal" for the best landscape "never previously seen in nature." The success of the evening was Benjamin A. Francke, who exhibited as "the first, the original, and only octagonalist." The general feeling was strong that the burlesque had really not come off because the parodies were too sane and that hung at the Armory Show they never would have been detected. As one of the "Anciens" said to a reporter: "No matter how wild we grew, no matter how preposterous we made these things, we couldn't really attain a burlesque. The originals were always worse. To paint a real, genuine cubist painting you have to be genuinely and unquestionably mad."

The newspapers also announced the "First Annual Vanishing Day" of the "Academy of Misapplied Arts" to be held on March 22 for the benefit of the Lighthouse of the New York Association for the Blind. It was advertised as the "Post Mortem Impressionist Exhibition," in which the "most distinguished artists of the Cubistic, Post-Impressionist, Futuristic, Neurotic, Psychotic, and Paretic Schools" including the "Ten Mattewan Muralists and other nutty groups" would participate. Again those involved comprised most of the leading members of the National Academy of Design—John White Alexander (its president), Blashfield, Kenyon Cox, and among others, George Bellows, one of the members of the AAPS. One artist took a pot shot at two targets by titling his work *Cubist Painting, Cubist Painting, Cubist Painting.* There were at least two burlesques of the *Nude*, one called *Nude Ascending a Staircase* and a still life called *Food Descending a Staircase.* The reporter for the *Globe and Commercial Advertiser* on the following day declared that Enrico Caruso's cubistic self-portrait had "Picasso looking like an amateur" and he personally awarded first prize to a painting by a ten-year-old, Nanette Turcas, with the comment, "That she cannot draw matters not the least, neither does Matisse."

Burlesquing the extremists was a natural. Many mock exhibitions and publications have vanished from memory or crumbled into oblivion, and one recalls them now only as mildly diverting footnotes to history. A search in the yellowed and disintegrating pages of old newspapers would turn up many more examples, but it should suffice to note a few. The students of the National Academy of Design and the Pennsylvania Academy of the Fine Arts had their fling at parody exhibitions. The Society of American Fakirs, a jolly group of artists connected with the Art Students League, took a few swipes at the new isms by word and picture in "The Futurist Fakirs in India," an issue of its magazine, and G. P. Putnam's Sons brought out a burlesque children's book, "The Cubies' ABC," by Mary and Earl Lyall. Echoes of laughter were heard as far north as Hartford, Connecticut, where the Arts and Crafts Club put on a "fake" Cubist-Futurist exhibition.

142

8

But
Don't Do It
Again

Duringthe month that the Show was at the Armory it became the talk of the town. There were almost daily stories about it in the press and critical coverage of one sort or another, including picture spreads in the Sunday editions. The galleries were full of people who came once to gape, artists who came often to study or deride, and celebrities who came as much to be seen as to see. It was taken up by New York society and became one of the things to do. Mrs. Astor came every morning after breakfast and the galleries were usually dotted with elegantly dressed ladies. John Quinn came whenever he could find the time. And Frank Crowninshield, a devoted advocate of the new art, was in frequent attendance, expiating his guilt. As editor of the *Century* magazine, he had been caught in a dilemma about which he expressed his embarrassment and very real concern in a letter to Kuhn on January 15:

I am worried about the article by Mr. Cortissoz. Here are the facts: You have been most kind and have given us just what we wanted. Furthermore, you have refused to let us pay for the photographs. As you know, Mr. Whittle and I are both keen about the movement—but—and here is the trouble—I have just called up Mr. Cortissoz to speak to him about our choice of illustrations, and he tells me that the article he is writing is (1) not an article on your show alone, but an article on the whole movement in general, (2) the article will, on the whole, line the author up as opposed to the movement. He says he will be critical and impartial but that he will never be a wholehearted enthusiast about the movement. No one has read his article. It is not finished, even, but I cannot accept these photographs, and your friendly offices in loaning them to us, until I make the matter perfectly plain. If you feel that, under the circumstances, Cortissoz should not be aided by you, I will at once return the photographs or try to secure them elsewhere. If not, won't you let us pay for them and, in that way, ease our consciences a little?

I abide wholly by your better judgment.

P.S. Perhaps you can look at it in the following light: e.g. Cortissoz is not enthusiastic about our movement, but, what we want, after all, is serious discussion—for and against—and with Cortissoz writing in the Century, even writing adversely, we shall attain serious consideration for our subject.

Cortissoz's article was naturally adverse and Crowninshield insisted on clearing his conscience with a check for $52, the only payment for the use of photographs on the Armory Show books.

Enrico Caruso, the great singing star of the Metropolitan Opera, turned up one Saturday afternoon and thrilled the crowds by doing caricatures of the paintings on Armory Show post cards and distributing them as souvenirs. The scion of the Morgan family was outraged that he had to pay 25 cents to see such trash. Another banker, James A. Stillman, who did not permit money to cloud his vision, made a classic comment: "Something is wrong with the world. These men know." Few showed the tolerance of the old genre painter Edward Lamson Henry, who, after being shown through the Exhibition by Jerome Myers, said, "Mr.

144

Myers, they told me there was a lot of crazy wild art here, but I really found it wonderfully interesting and I am very glad to have seen it."

Former President Teddy Roosevelt picked March 4, appropriately enough, to visit the Armory Show while President-elect Woodrow Wilson was taking the oath of office. He was shown around the galleries by Davies, Kuhn, Chanler, and Gregg. He was "most gracious, though noncommittal," but he observed carefully and keenly, and his article "A Layman's View of an Art Exhibition," which appeared in the *Outlook,* was both canny and ignorant. Like a good politician, he came out for fair play but disassociated himself from any connection with radicalism.

"The exhibitors are quite right as to the need of showing to our people in this manner the art forces in Europe, forces which can not be ignored. This does not mean that I in the least accept the view that these men take of the European extremists whose pictures are here exhibited." He said, "A glance at this [American] work must convince anyone of the real good that is coming out of the new movements." He went on to praise the spirit of change: "There was one note entirely missing from the exhibition, and that was the note of the commonplace. There was not a touch of simpering, self-satisfied conventionality. . . . There was no stunting or dwarfing, no requirement that a man whose gift lay in new directions should measure up or down to stereotyped and fossilized standards." This was praise for the Americans, who may have been sincere but were not very radical. He found the real proponents of change a bit hard to take:

145

But this does not in the least mean that the extremists . . . are entitled to any praise, save, perhaps, that they have helped to break fetters. Probably in any reform movement, any progressive movement, in any field of life, the penalty for avoiding the commonplace is a liability to extravagance. It is vitally necessary to move forward and to shake off the dead hand of the reactionaries; and yet we have to face the fact that there is apt to be a lunatic fringe among the votaries of any forward movement. In this recent exhibition the lunatic fringe was fully in evidence, especially in the rooms devoted to the Cubists and the Futurists, or Near-Impressionists.

His comments on the more radical art revealed the essential ignorance and prejudice which he shared with the majority of "our people." He felt that the "Cubists are entitled to the serious attention of all who find enjoyment in the colored puzzle pictures of the Sunday newspapers." He compared the *Nude Descending a Staircase* (color plate 9) with a Navajo rug, to the advantage of the latter. Before the Lehmbruck *Kneeling Woman*, he was impelled to the ex-cathedra dictum that "though obviously mammalian it is not especially human. . . . One might as well speak of the 'lyric grace' of a praying mantis, which adopts much the same attitude; and why a deformed pelvis should be called 'sincere,' or a tibia of a giraffe-like length 'precious,' is a question of pathological rather than artistic significance."

All sorts of incidents and newspaper stories kept the publicity pot boiling. A report of the attempted theft of a Rousseau drawing led one newspaper to comment that if this kind of art were worth stealing, someone might consider it worth buying. One short newspaper item, revealing an ignorance of both French and art, inadvertently got off one of the *bon mots* of the Exhibition in describing the Rousseau still life (*nature morte*) as "La morte de nature." A number of newspapers ran a story along with a photograph showing a donkey painting a picture with its tail. The incident concerned an artist who had set up a situation in which a donkey painted a picture by swishing paint on a canvas with its tail. It was alleged that the result was exhibited without detection and with great acclaim among works of the avantgarde. The whole thing was obviously a hoax and not a new one. The same story is reputed to have been used to ridicule the Impressionists many years earlier. It is apparently still current and credible in some circles. Khrushchev once resurrected it, perhaps in the guise of a Russian folk saying, to discredit his own avantgardists; and during a newspaper strike in New York during the early 1960s, I managed to catch a straight-faced repeat of the same story complete with picture in the Newark *Star Ledger*. The newspapers played it straight, out of either naïveté or malice, but the public was no doubt convinced that this was the ultimate rebuttal to modern art.

Solon Borglum, shortly after the opening, decided that he wanted no part of the Exhibition, not because of any solidarity with his brother but because of the radical character of the art shown, and requested that his sculpture be removed. This led to charges and countercharges. Gutzon Borglum took this opportunity to get back into the fray with a statement that Rodin had refused to lend to the Exhibition, although there is no evidence that he was asked. Solon Borglum's statuary remained and the pot kept perking.

The next blast came from a much more serious source. The *Tribune* of March 2 carried a long story concerning a demand by Robert Delaunay, the French painter, that all his works be removed from the Exhibition. Samuel Halpert, the American painter and friend of Delaunay, had appeared at the Armory Show armed with a telegram authorizing him to remove the Delaunay paintings. Another, from Patrick Henry Bruce, the American painter then working in Paris, requested the removal of his own works as a gesture of disapproval of the treatment accorded Delaunay. The withdrawn pictures of both artists were then to be exhibited privately in opposition to the Armory Show. The reason for Delaunay's annoyance was that Davies had gone back on his word and refused to hang his large painting, *Ville de Paris*. Delaunay had originally asked Halpert to stretch and hang the picture when it arrived because its size, 12 by 9 feet, required that it be shipped rolled. Halpert stated that he had been requested by Davies to do so but that when he appeared at the Armory he was told that it had been decided not to hang the painting.

Davies, Kuhn, and Pach had visited Delaunay in Paris and arranged for a representation of his work at the Armory. A series of communications between Delaunay and Pach exists in the archives and indicates some uncertainty about what would be shown. Delaunay was then rapidly moving from Cubism through Futurism to Orphism, and the *Ville de Paris* seems to have been a last-minute entry. Pach, in discussing the matter with the *Tribune* reporter, charged that Delaunay had "foisted the big one upon us." At any rate the painting had arrived, had been listed in the catalogue, but at the last moment, probably because of its size, had not been stretched and hung; instead it was described in the supplement as "catalogued but not received." This was not cricket and Delaunay had a legitimate complaint, but Davies must have felt that the dominance of so large a canvas would jeopardize the balance of the Exhibition.

147

When Halpert tried to have the works of Delaunay and Bruce removed, Davies, Kuhn, and Pach after consultation refused on the grounds that all loans had been made without restriction and that they would have to remain. Halpert told the press that Bruce was "the only American painter at all considered by French artists" and that "Delaunay is more important than Villon and all the other painters of the revolutionary school put together." He also advised the reporter that "Max Weber, who was not represented in the Show although he had loaned a number of his Rousseaus, was the pioneer post-Impressionist in this country" and had been so badly treated that he had withdrawn all his works. When interviewed, Weber concurred with Halpert's opinion that he was the most important Post-Impressionist in the United States and explained that he had pulled out of the Armory Show because only two of his works were accepted, whereas he had insisted on at least equal representation with artists whom he considered less important. He had demanded that eight or ten of his paintings be included but had been refused.

There was some repercussion in Paris as a result of this contretemps. According to a *Times* news story datelined Paris, March 22, a new art magazine, *Montjoie,* had carried an editorial attacking the Armory Show, which was quoted in part:

Young painters on this side were invited to send canvases to be shown at a certain exhibition of French art now being held in New York. The news, however, has just reached here that this exhibition is merely a pretext for giving prominent display to the pictures of certain bad American painters, who are among the organizers.

The works of the French artists are scattered and badly hung, serving only as bait for the public. A large canvas by de Launay called *Ville de Paris,* has not even been hung, while, as Picasso's canvases are not grouped together, no idea can be formed of this artist's talent. The same treatment is given to the works sent by Mlle. Laurencin, Derain, etc.

Several young American painters, aware of the injustice offered their French confrères, whose talent possesses real importance in contemporary art, have decided to withdraw their canvases, this ought already to have been done.

"The New Spirit" is the motto of this exhibition. It appears that this boasted "new spirit," however, is a very old one—namely, the spirit of business.

Although the works of Delaunay and Bruce stayed on in New York for the duration of the Show, they were not sent to Chicago or Boston. As an aftermath, the *Ville de Paris* was damaged on its return journey and a long hassle ensued, with the Association finally settling for $61.79 on November 5, 1913.

One of the major surprises of the Armory Show was the attention paid to Picabia. He did not have the international reputation of Picasso or Braque, but his paintings at the Exhibition were more striking in both size and color, so that to an American audience with no experience in Cubism, he could appear as the major figure in this movement. He was often treated in critical reviews as the leading representative of the style, an impression which Picabia was not interested in dispelling. Added to this was the fact that Picabia was the only foreign artist represented at the Show who was in America at the time. He was not averse to publicity, and the press carried interviews in which he explained the modern movement and described himself as one of its leading and most successful members. His availability and articulateness added color to the Exhibition, although his explanations of modern art were not entirely comprehensible to the uninitiated, and the American public was decidedly uninitiated. It should be remembered that this was the first contact the public had had with radical esthetic theory, which is at best fairly complex and often rather turgid. At times presented straight and without comment, at others vigorously assailed with equally serious logic, Picabia's esthetic formulations also lent themselves to obvious spoofing. The *Sunday World* printed a long statement by Picabia and offered as a prize for the best 150-word explanation of its meaning one original "cubist" drawing by a member of the newspaper's art staff.

Flushed with success, the Association threw a beefsteak party for its "friends and enemies" of the press at Healy's Restaurant, 66th Street and Columbus Avenue. The critics may have been rough, but the artists picked up the $234 tab without complaint because the press, for or against, had made the whole thing possible. All the art critics had been invited: Royal Cortissoz of the *Tribune*; Arthur Hoeber of the *Globe*; Roy L. McCardell of the *World*; Byron Stephenson of the *Post*; Samuel Swift, Henry McBride, and Charles Fitzgerald of the *Sun*; William B. McCor-

149

mick of the *Press;* James B. Townsend of *American Art News;* Guy Pène du Bois of *Arts and Decoration,* who was also a member of the Association; and his boss, Thomas E. Ashwell. Also invited were such special friends as John Quinn, Bryson Burroughs, Joel E. Spingarn, and Alfred Stieglitz. Davies sat at the head of the horseshoe table, flanked by Gregg, who acted as master of ceremonies (the *American Art News,* which was usually wrong, reported that it was Quinn), and Kuhn on his right, with Quinn, Pach, Mowbray-Clarke, and Cortissoz on his left. It was a gay party and the food and drink was served by waitresses who according to accounts "sang and danced." The participants, not to be outdone, also sang and danced. Sometime during the festivities, speeches were made. Gregg had a speech all prepared

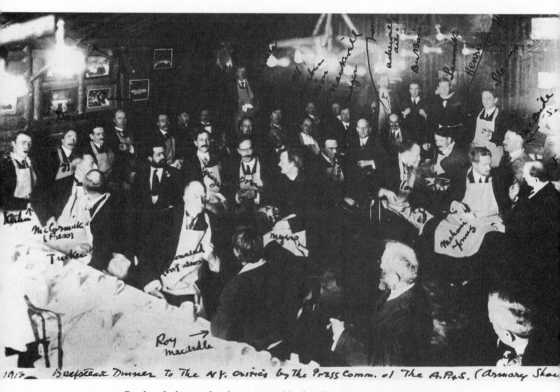

Beefsteak dinner for the press at Healy's Restaurant, March 8, 1913.
Seated at head table, l. to r.: Kuhn, Gregg, Davies, Quinn,
Pach, Mowbray-Clarke, Cortissoz.

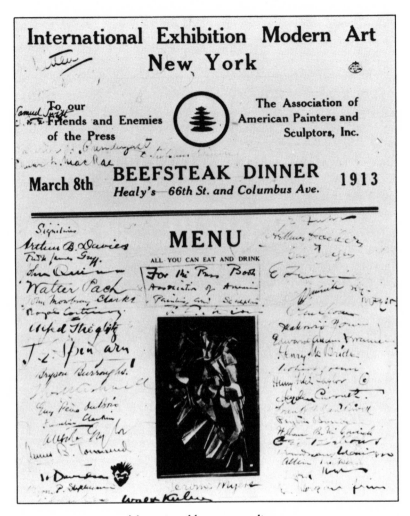

Menu signed by guests at dinner
for the press.

and left over from the opening which he now proceeded to deliver. Cortissoz, speaking for the critics, and referring to the invitation, said: "Gentlemen, you have no enemies in the press; you have only friends. Don't you remember the words that Pete Dunn gave to Mr. Dooley at the time of the Boer War? 'I tell ye, it's a terrible thing, Hennessey, when ye come into camp of an evening, and have to scrape what's left of your best friend off the side of your breeches.'" Cortissoz closed his remarks with a word of praise and admonition, "It was a good show, but don't do it again."

The *World*'s Roy McCardell and the cartoonist Hy Mayer were reported to have been humorous, but their words were not recorded. Quinn repeated most of what he had said at the opening in praise of the Association. The toastmaster, whoever he was, read a series of telegrams composed by Walt Kuhn, which were of that after-dinner variety of intramural humor always received with hilarity. They included a burlesque of Gertrude Stein's literary style, a compliment to Gregg for his great job on publicity, and a jibe at Mayor Gaynor and the recurrent police scandal. The purported telegram from George Luks, referring to his penchant for either the bottle or goldbricking, read: "Regret can not be with you tonight. Have not been able to get around since I got through hanging my own pictures at the exhibition."

The one from Roger Fry—"Have not seen your exhibition but am sure it does not amount to much"—was obviously a reference to Fry's annoyance with the AAPS for having cut short his Grafton Show by insisting on delivery of the works which had been promised for the Armory. There was also one from the California Consolidated Ostrich Farm Co.: "Reserve for us replica of Brancusi's Madame [sic] Pogany as nest egg for our hatchery. Answer at once." After a while one gets the feeling that no one was writing good jokes in those days. Then a doddering old man with a long white beard and a Lincoln stovepipe hat came in to announce, amid great laughter and applause, that he was the representative of the National Academy of Design. The party became more boisterous as the irrepressible D. Putnam Brinley, almost seven feet tall, led the apparition in a wild turkey trot. Once started, Brinley was hard to stop, and he won a high-kicking contest, which he probably instigated, through sheer physical advantage. A rousing time was had by all, but the high spirits, the gallantry, and the good humor hid a basic incompatibility. It was a pleasant but very temporary truce.

9

Blague
in a Loud
Voice

While public and press found the Armory Show provocative and amusing in a superficial sense, the professional critics of newspapers and magazines faced up to the situation in a conscientious and serious manner. Taking into account the fact that most of them were unprepared for the startling revelations of the Exhibition, the results were in some cases, whether pro or con, surprisingly considerate and intelligent, in spite of the almost hysterical reactions of others.

The critic's role is not enviable, although it seems to be an increasingly necessary or at least common one in our society. No one likes the critic, least of all the artist, yet we not only tolerate but even exaggerate his importance. The deep-seated human aversion to criticism has been reinforced by the description of the critic as someone who cannot do what he presumes to judge. He is therefore not only vulnerable to this most obvious of *ad hominem* arguments, but since he operates in an even more exposed position than the creator, he is essentially a sitting duck. The saving grace of opinion, which is by its very nature fallible, is that it is easily and quietly changeable, except for the critic who is inevitably and permanently saddled with his failures and too rarely cited for his successes. One wonders why anyone should want to be a critic. But whatever his personal motivations and the hazards of his vocation, our communications-dominated culture simply requires the critic and criticism. And the public, even when it would like to disassociate itself from the "unclean" act as it does in the case of the hangman and the butcher, still identifies with the critic as an extension of its own intellectual life. Criticism is, after all, along with creativity, a fundamental function of the human intelligence. The critics of the Armory Show performed their duties sometimes haltingly, sometimes stupidly and even maliciously, but they were on the whole expressing public opinion.

Critical evaluation of the Armory Show was mixed, more con than pro. There was general praise for the Association for the purely physical aspects of the Exhibition, as has already been mentioned, and for its presentation of the new art to the American public even though they were not favorably impressed by it. There was also a great deal of applause for the sanity of the American section in contrast to the wildness of the radical Europeans. Earlier nineteenth-century French painting had, of course, already achieved recognition although there were still some mossbacks who found difficulty in accepting Manet; but the Post-Impressionist "masters," Cézanne, Van Gogh, and Gauguin, received mixed reviews. Considering the fact that the critics did not show any wide acquaintance with the subject, it is rather surprising to find the recurring criticism that these men were not well represented. And since this was to some extent a valid observation, one can only guess that someone had passed the word around. The most violent attacks naturally enough were against the newest manifestations of revolution, Fauvism and Cubism, with the major shafts aimed at Matisse.

The controversy over modern art, which has continued in varying although fundamentally similar forms down to the present day, had its first full-scale performance in connection with the Armory Show. There had been earlier dress rehearsals as a result of the small exhibitions of advanced art at "291," but it now took center stage and proceeded to tear opinion to tatters. The majority of New York reviewers may have been sympathetic to the aims of the Association but they were hostile to the revolution in art. There were really two elements involved—the laudable intention of the Association in presenting the new and attempting to revitalize American art, which most critics and editorial writers applauded, and the challenge of the art itself, which most of them found too much to take. Royal Cortissoz of the *Tribune*, William B. McCormick of the *Press*, Joseph Edgar Chamberlin of the *Mail*, Arthur Hoeber of the *Globe*, Roy L. McCardell and Charles Henry Dorr of the *World*, and Byron Stephenson of the *Post* were in varying degrees opposed. The *Times*, which was as staunchly conservative as the rest, did not use bylines on its art criticism unless it was by an invited critic like Kenyon Cox, but one can assume that the thumbs-down opinions in the *Times* were those of Elizabeth Luther Carey.

155

On the other hand, the *Sun*, which followed the same policy of critical anonymity, had an art staff which was largely sympathetic and throughout the history of the Association acted as its champion. Gregg had been an editorial writer for the *Sun* before he became drumbeater for the Association and was a close friend of its critic Charles Fitzgerald, one of the first to defend the Ash Can painters. Also on the *Sun* were Samuel Swift and Henry McBride, who had just begun his long connection with that paper, during which he remained a consistent defender of modern art. Charles H. Caffin, who had recently come to the *American*, was also favorably disposed to the new movements, partly because they were new; and Harriet Monroe, writing for the Chicago *Tribune*, blew hot and cold before finally settling down to an espousal of the avant-garde. The weight of published opinion was thus clearly on the side of the antis.

Although the affirmative team picked up some strength among the free-lance magazine critics, two of the negative's big guns, Kenyon Cox and Frank Jewett Mather, Jr., also wrote articles for magazines. The former was a contributor to the *Century* and *Scribner's*, while the latter served as art critic for the *Nation*. Christian Brinton and J. Nilsen Laurvik, free-lance writers, were both knowledgeable and, although they had serious reservations about latter-day developments in modern art, played a role in the explanation and defense of the new movements. *Arts and Decoration*, under the editorship of Guy Pène du Bois, acted for a short time at least as the official spokesman for the Association. The *American Art News*, with James B. Townsend as editor, was on the other hand continually sniping at the Association, although the modernists received more sympathetic treatment in its columns from James Britton. There was some informed opinion on both sides, and critical writing was, at its best, serious and well-intentioned, but it was far from profound and rarely even informative, while, at its worst, it sank to abysmal levels of ignorance and philistinism.

First reactions to the Armory Show, perhaps because it was so impressive, were generally fair appraisals with little antagonism. One of the staunchest defenders of the past was Royal Cortissoz, yet he wrote in the *Tribune* after attending the press viewing that the Exhibition was an expression of "healthy independence" rather than "freakish violence," which he had apparently been expecting. The *Post* also felt that it would be unfair to overemphasize the radical aspects of the Exhibition because there really was so much that was beautiful in it. And Charles Henry Dorr in the *World* had only praise for the Association and the Exhibition, even though he found nothing good to say about modernism. It is a little strange that Charles H. Caffin, whom one would have expected to defend the Exhibition, attacked it strongly in the *American*, even before it opened, perhaps to demonstrate his own familiarity with the subject. He claimed that the Association's aim of showing the independent artistic spirit of the last hundred years, which he found commendable, was lost somewhere in the size, the commercialism of the advertising, and the circus atmosphere of the whole. He criticized the selection as being uninformed and unequal, and the work of one man, Arthur B. Davies. He seemed most upset that the "major figures"—Cézanne and Van Gogh—were not well represented, and it may have been here that the idea was planted; that only the *Femme au chapelet* (*An Old Woman with a Rosary*, color plate 4) was first-rate among all the Cézannes; that there were no good Van Goghs; and that Gauguin, whom he did not recognize as on the level of the other two, was disappointing. Only Matisse was adequately shown and, unfortunately, his work was dispersed. Caffin felt that the public had been bilked; it had been offered sensationalism instead of education.

America had never had a full-scale presentation of the great triumvirate of modern art—Cézanne, Van Gogh, and Gauguin—but many of the critics had at least heard of their growing reputations and made a serious effort to understand their importance. Harriet Monroe, writing for the Chicago *Tribune* of February 23, granted their stature, whereas several days earlier, on February 16, in a preview of the coming Show, she had characterized Cézanne as "the shabby French vagabond," Van Gogh as "the half-insane Flemish recluse and suicide," and Gauguin as "the disreputable world wanderer." Adept at picking up the opinions of her peers, she was well enough informed in the later article to note that they were not well represented. William Howe Downes, of the Boston *Transcript*, was generally restrained and paid tribute to the older generation of French painters while castigating the contemporaries. He thought Cézanne a serious artist though not especially revolutionary and added, again, that he was not well represented. Van Gogh appeared to be crude but expressive and Gauguin unexpectedly interesting. Speaking for Philadelphia, the *Inquirer* critic reported that the Cézannes were inferior except for the *Femme au chapelet* and that Van Gogh was not forceful enough.

It is a little strange that although the journeymen critics occasionally found something worthwhile in these great masters of French painting, the paladins of the craft, like Cortissoz, Cox, and Mather, saw little or nothing in them. Royal Cortissoz was the bellwether of the nay-sayers, and while his invective was frequently caustic it always wore the guise of rational probity and moral rectitude. He never became hysterical or rabid, but he had difficulty masking his gentlemanly annoyance at what he called the squalor and crudeness of modern art, while reluctantly recognizing its earnestness and vigor. He was just a little frightened of these "foolish terrorists" who wanted "to turn the world upside

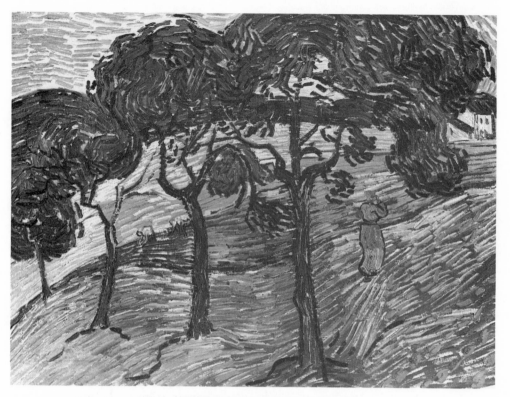

Vincent van Gogh (1853–1890).
Landscape with Figures, 1889.
Oil on canvas, 19 ⅝ × 25 ¾ in.
The Baltimore Museum of Art; The Cone Collection,
formed by Dr. Claribel Cone and Miss Etta Cone of Baltimore, Maryland.

down" and whose art seemed to deny what he considered fundamental principles. But when he went in search of principles,
they seemed to evaporate and he was left with the rather bare
bones of skill and taste. For a man who believed that "the function of the artist is to learn his trade and then produce beautiful
pictures," the new art could be disturbing, for nothing interested
the modernists less. It is not strange then that he should with
some magnanimity characterize Cézanne as a "sincere amateur"
who "simply did not know his trade," a "second-rate Impressionist who had now and then the fair luck in painting a moderately
good picture," and someone "not unaccustomed to paint non-

sense." In his opinion Van Gogh, whom he thought unbalanced, was nothing more than "a moderately competent Impressionist who was heavy-handed, had little if any sense of beauty and spoiled a lot of canvas with crude, quite unimportant pictures." This is the sort of thing that can come back to haunt a critic eternally. In another place he was even less generous to Van Gogh and described his art as "incompetence suffused with egotism." As for Gauguin, Cortissoz dismissed him with the assurance that he was a "mediocre technician, trying to do something he cannot accomplish," and he used as corroborative witnesses John Singer Sargent and John La Farge. Cortissoz concluded with the pronouncement, "The common sense view is that these men painted poorly."

Kenyon Cox admitted that as an artist after forty years of study he had a distinct prejudice against modernism. Although he complimented the Association for bringing this art before the American public, he wrote in *Harper's Weekly*, "This thing is not amusing; it is heart rending and sickening." Cox leveled his major attack upon the contemporary movements, but he saw the whole history of modern art, going back to Manet, as the result of a social dislocation. He explained that both Manet and Whistler had suffered from a lack of training and a disruption of normal relations with their public, and that, in spite of the undeniable beauty of some of their work, it was ineffectual and fragmentary. As for Cézanne, he was "absolutely without talent and absolutely cut off from tradition." Van Gogh he found "too unskilled to give quality to an evenly laid coat of paint," and Gauguin a "decorator tainted with insanity." He had rather more violent opinions of the avant-garde, but some of his observations about members of the intermediary generation were also not without venom. He described Rousseau as "perfectly innocent, entirely inept" and his art as "resembling the productions, on a larger scale, of a child of seven." Maurice Denis struck him as an "amiable caricature of Puvis de Chavannes." And he summed up his credo by saying, "Believing, as I do, that there are still commandments in art as in morals, and still laws in art as in physics, I have no fear that this kind of art will prevail, or even that it can long endure. But it may do a great deal of harm while it lasts." His advice to the public was, "If your stomach revolts against this rubbish it is because it is not fit for human food. Let no man persuade you to stuff yourself with it."

Frank Jewett Mather as an art historian was more knowledgeable than the critic Cortissoz or the artist Cox, but his judgments, if somewhat more reasoned and restrained, were historically no more valid. He found Post-Impressionism a "gaudy and ill-favored plant" which he tried to account for in art-historical as well as social terms. He felt along with Cox that it was all due to a dislocation in society resulting in an overemphasis on personal as opposed to social aims. According to him, the revolutionary insistence of the Post-Impressionists on what he called the "isolated ecstatic state" had led art away from the classic conception of the picture as a composite, reflective, and intellectual statement. The limits of his own taste are indicated in his statement that "the great painters of the last century, Corot, Constable, Millet, Rousseau, Puvis, stand singularly apart from this progress." He described the retrospective section of the Armory

Paul Gauguin (1848–1903). *Faa Iheihe*, 1898. Oil on canvas, 21¼ × 66¾ in. Reproduced by courtesy of the Trustees of the Tate Gallery, London.

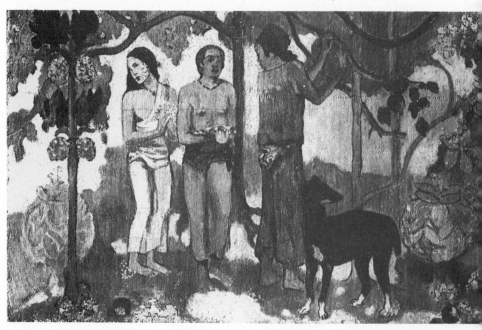

THE STORY OF THE ARMORY SHOW

Show as not notable and criticized the absence of Théodore Chassériau and Gustave Moreau. Most of his remarks were directed at the more recent developments and he had relatively little to say about the older men. He did feel, however, that the representations of Cézanne, Van Gogh, and Gauguin were inadequate. Of Cézanne he wrote that "reseen [he] hardly measures up to the impressive figure of fifteen years ago" and that "his paler landscapes have for me the exquisite balance of John Twachtman's—the same economy of means." He maintained that inasmuch as Post-Impressionism was based on a desperate struggle for originality and a false theory of emotions, it was a "negligible eccentricity" which would soon run its course, but that it was "setting hundreds of young painters to coddling their sacred impulses, so far as it accentuates an already exaggerated cult of the individual, it will work nothing but harm."

As part of the campaign of defamation, the almost mythological facts concerning the lives of the three masters of modern art were usually included in the newspaper stories. Cézanne as the misanthropic banker-recluse, Van Gogh the insane preacher-

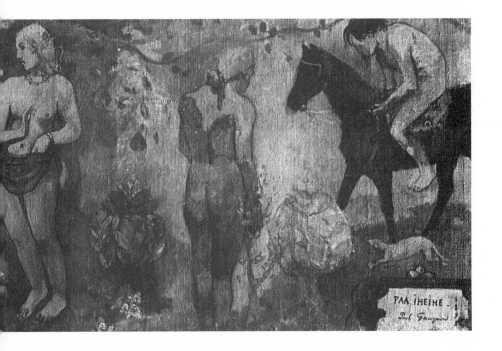

painter who cut his ear off and committed suicide, and Gauguin the stockbroker who deserted his wife and family for art and then went to live with the natives in Tahiti—all this was romantic color that the newspapers delighted in. The Chicago *Inter Ocean* had as its critical hatchetman an assistant professor, presumably of art history from the University of Chicago, a certain George B. Zug, who handled the situation with proper authority and dispatch. He assured his readers that Van Gogh had only meager training and insufficient knowledge, that Gauguin was inept, and that both had "apparently never learned to paint"—but only after recounting the lurid details of their hapless existence.

Innuendoes of moral turpitude and mental instability as well as outright charges of incompetence directed against the older generation of insurgent artists were as nothing in comparison with the execration of their artistic descendants. From ridicule to vituperation, the stops were out, and one must admit that wrongheaded as most of it was, it did have passion and sometimes even style. The radicals—the Fauves, Cubists, and Futurists—were accused of many things. They inherited from their esthetic antecedents the smell of decadence and the stigma of incompetence to which were added a whole set of vices of their own. Of course their decadence was more profound and their incompetence more obvious. The former reached the level of moral depravity and the latter became so patent that it could be explained only as a hoax. Although the older men were treated as misguided they were usually thought of as sincere. Only Gauguin was suspect, perhaps because it was inconceivable that anyone would give up a good job and security for art.

The younger men, on the other hand, were consistently charged with insincerity, charlatanry, and trickery. The things they exhibited appeared so obviously inept and weird that one was led to assume they had been done for some ulterior motive. In a world of shifting values, the only thing the layman felt sure of, and unfortunately without foundation, was skill. But his very conception of skill made these objects incomprehensible. Harriet Monroe, still fighting off the inevitable conversion, wrote that Matisse seemed to her "fundamentally insincere" and that he talked "blague in a loud voice." The critic of the Boston *Transcript* found Matisse and the Cubists "playing a game of mystification." Mather gave his readers a choice: Cubism was either "a clever hoax or a negligible pedantry." Cox, not to be outdone, offered "sheer insanity or triumphant charlatanry." In an attack on the Armory Show in the *Times* of March 22, he stated bluntly that up to the time of Matisse the artistic revolutionaries had at least been sincere, they had committed suicide or died in madhouses, but now they were making insanity pay.

And so, if they were not fakers they were insane. Many critics preferred the latter explanation. Gutzon Borglum had an opportunity to speak his mind again in a lecture at Cooper Union in which he charged that the whole affair was a "farcical and foolish exhibition made up largely of paranoiacs," which had been blown up out of all proportion by the press. The *Evening World* of February 22 carried a story by someone called Nixola Greeley-Smith, no doubt a pseudonym with humorous intent, but the article itself was not humorous at all. "No imagination," the author contended, "outside the psychopathic ward of Bellevue or the confines of Mattewan can conceive without actually seeing it what a cubist picture is. . . . Cubism must have originated in the brain of a professor of mathematics stricken with paresis." Cox had a similar reaction after having seen the Armory Show; he felt that he had "passed through a pathological museum where the layman has no right to go" and that he had "seen not an exhibition but an exposure." Mather, in the *Nation* of March 6, joined him in finding an analogy between the new art and insanity: "On all hands I hear in the show the statement, 'At any rate, this new art is very living and interesting.' So much may be said for much of the Post-Impressionist and Cubist work; and something like that might be one's feeling on first visiting a lunatic asylum. The inmates might well seem more vivid and fascinating than the everyday companions of home and office." The Brooklyn *Life*, whatever that might have been, produced a blistering tirade which labeled the Armory Show as a "temporary lunatic asylum" and described the paintings as "blear-eyed daubs and phantasmagorias of the insane."

Although one may be able to understand if not sympathize with the accusations of incompetence, fakery, and insanity, since they are attitudes still with us, it is more difficult to comprehend the concern people then had with the immorality of modern art.

163

There actually was nothing in the Show which from a contemporary point of view might be called immoral, perhaps because we naïvely equate immorality in art with lewdness or pornography. In those days, any attack on established standards of beauty in general and especially of the female body (which was usually referred to, almost as a single word, as the "female form divine") was suspect as subversive and immoral. And one must admit that the f.f.d. did receive short shrift from the modernists. One could hardly accuse them of taking sensuous delight in nudity; quite the contrary, they seemed to take an almost sadistic pleasure in destroying any vestiges of divinity still residing in the age-old academic clichés of the female nude. But years of concerted effort on the part of the artistic community to establish in the Puritan mind the notion that the depiction of nudity had sanction because the human body was the work of God had left its mark. Any attempt to tamper with God's will in the form of the academic nude was considered a sacrilege. Writing in the Boston *Transcript*, Downes, in referring to Matisse, complained, "It is impossible to accept such offensive presentations of the human form divine as those which appear in *La Coiffeuse* and the *Panneau rouge* and the *Portrait of Marguerite*." The New York *Review* showed the same concern because the modernists, according to its correspondent, "Distort the human form divine until it becomes a nauseating monstrosity."

Whether from puritanism, provincialism, or chauvinism, there was a rather strong feeling in America that European culture was decadent. It is still an attitude which is too common among us. The image of America as youthful and Europe as aged is a persistent bromide that still hangs on. Many Americans of 1913, and one would hope fewer now, found the radical art movements an expression not only of the decadence but of the degeneracy of European culture in an intellectual, moral, and political sense, and therefore dangerous to the virile wholesomeness of our own. This callow view of European cultural sophistication led to statements permeated by either panic or bad manners. Even before the Exhibition, the *Press* of January 26 revealed an uneasiness about the art which was being brought over. "Some critics," the story went, "see in this general movement nothing but European intellectual degeneracy carried to its lowest depths." From the wide open spaces of the West came an echo: Caryl B. Storr, writing in the Minneapolis *Tribune*, April 6, described modern art as an expression of the "crazy theories of decadent or perverted zealots" capable of inducing, at least in her case, "physical nausea."

The implication, frequently explicitly stated, was that such things would undermine American spiritual health and that they were a direct assault on moral standards. It is difficult to understand the rationale behind all of this, but there is no question that many saw modern art as morally dangerous. Apparently the Puritan tradition can accept art only on the premise that it is capable of spiritual uplift, and the underlying distrust of sensuous experience immediately comes to the surface whenever the forms of art become disturbing in themselves. In this case the guardians of morality literally exploded in a fury of fulmination. Quotes from publications of the day sound positively hysterical. Some may be the expressions of a lunatic fringe, but many were published in respectable journals. Mather in the *Independent* of March 6 let his flock know that "the layman may well dismiss on moral grounds an art that lives in the miasma of morbid hallucination or sterile experimentation, and denies in the name of individualism values which are those of society and of life itself." One of the outstanding screeds of the time was a diatribe in the New York *Review* of March 22. The author began by anathemizing the avant-garde as the "degenerates of art" and added that "the propaganda of the Cubist, Futurist and Post-Impressionist painters is not only a menace to art, but a grave danger to public morals." He described their work as the expression of "minds which, according to that eminent psychiatrist Krafft-Ebing, would be classed as hopelessly diseased" and that the "wildest imaginings of the victims of Sadism . . . are not more viciously degenerate." He summed it all up by calling to task a valiant ally who had fallen asleep at his post. "Mr. Anthony Comstock," he wrote, "hitherto our only art censor, seems to have ignored his opportunities." He expressed the fervent hope that if the Show were ever repeated, "St. Anthony or some other guardian of public morals will be on the job."

Writing for a female audience in the *Journal* of March 3, Margaret Hubbard Ayer quoted a lady poet, Mrs. Carey Sheffield, whom she described as young and not narrow-minded. Mrs. Sheffield's comments were on the shrill side, but they exhibited a flair for calumny. She began with the rather sober warning that "pictures like this are a menace to morals," but she was soon off in flights of sheer invective—"excrescence of art," "disgorging of a curdled imagination," "disorders of a feverish brain," "degrading, degenerate and an evil influence," "bilious and lurid canvases of decomposed flesh." However, she pulled herself together, took a deep breath, smiled brightly, and closed with a reassuring thought: "One of the best signs of the day is that these pictures evoke laughter instead of fear, mystery, desire, or any of the other sentiments they were expected to inspire. I am thankful to say that I have seen each woman burst into laughter or grow indignant or uncomfortable as she looked at certain of the lurid pictures. . . ." With a sigh of relief, Mrs. Carey Sheffield knew that American womanhood was safe. And to prove that the crisis was over and cool logic was in control again, she offered this closing observation: "Have you noticed that the futurist ladies have no back to their heads and the men no foreheads?"

There was a strong, if misguided, feeling that innate American sanity, expressing itself in laughter, would see us through. The *American Art News* of March 1 was sure that "New York's laugh will bury these new apostles of art in oblivion." Harriet Monroe, still not certain of her stand, wrote in the Chicago *Tribune* of February 23, "If these groups of theorists have any other significance than to increase the gayety of nations your correspondent confessed herself unaware of it." *Town Topics* advised its readers to see the Armory Show for laughs, and its art columnist, The Gilder, found it even better than the zoo: "I can guarantee you won't get as many laughs there as to watch these international reformers disporting themselves on their tails."

Some might feel that laughter was shield enough, but there were others who took a dimmer view and identified modern art with revolution in a political as well as a social sense. It was Mather who said that Post-Impressionism was a "harbinger of universal anarchy," and Cox who wrote, "There is only one word for this denial of all law, this insurrection against all custom and tradition, this assertion of individual license without discipline and without restraint; and that word is 'anarchy.'" Cox elsewhere characterized the modernists as being "as truly anarchistic as those who would overthrow all social laws." Cortissoz also had misgivings that the modernists were dangerous and that "their cue [was] to turn the world upside down." Expressions of shock and outrage found their way to the letters-to-the-editors columns of newspapers and in them the modernists were reviled as the "Huns of the art world" or "anarchic hordes." An editorial comment in the *Times* on the day after the Show's closing summed up by agreeing with Kenyon Cox and saying:

It should be borne in mind that this movement is surely a part of the general movement, discernible all over the world, to disrupt and degrade, if not to destroy, not only art, but literature and society, too. There is a kind of insanity extant which has its remote origin, it must be said, in the earlier developments of the democratic spirit. Its kinship to true democracy and to real freedom in thought, action, or expression, however, is slight and indefinite, but the cubists and futurists are own cousins to the anarchists in politics, the poets who defy syntax and decency, and all would-be destroyers who with the pretense of trying to regenerate the world are really trying to block the wheels of progress in every direction.

Leila Mechlin, editor of *Art and Progress*, issued a warning call to all defenders of civilization in the April number of that magazine. "In a well organized civilization," she wrote in the lead editorial, "overt individualism is held in check by law—the profligate is debarred from society, the bomb thrower is imprisoned, the defamer and lunatic is confined, not for the good of the individual, but for the protection of the many who might be harmed. Why then, may we ask ourselves, do we so blithely tolerate these same crimes in art."

All this waving of the red herring may seem a little ludicrous today, but the equating of artistic insurgence with political radicalism can be traced back to the branding of the Impressionists with the *spectre rouge* during the 1870's. And it is interesting to note that the left-wing press of 1913 accepted with just as little understanding the implications of political revolution in the new art movements. The New York *Daily People*, although somewhat confused and not at all sure that the avant-garde artists were not madmen, charlatans, or degenerates, still ventured the guess that art forms might be outworn and that, perhaps, abstraction was the answer. Their allegiance to political revolution seems to have given them an empathy for revolution in other forms. The Socialist *Call*, out of sheer solidarity, urged its readers to suspend judgment until more was known. The *Independent* for April was much clearer in its position and actually picked up the gauntlet thrown down by the "capitalist" press in the following statement: "Papers like the New York *Times* fulminated against the Show as though it had been a triumphant advance of the revolutionists. The instinct of these hostile critics is correct. The art does come, as Syndicalism comes in an industry, as Free Thought comes in religion, as new standards come in sex, to supplant and transform the old." The lines were then at least sharply drawn, and if they have with time become obscured, it is perhaps because the same art has been just as violently attacked by the "official" revolution, but as "bourgeois decadence."

Unquestionably the leading target of the American critics was Matisse. No one else suffered the lacerating critical assault that he did. Cubism appeared so strange that it could be ridiculed, but there was absolutely no humor in the disparagement of Matisse; it was angry, vicious, and almost psychotic in its ferocity. It is a little difficult to understand today, but there were reasons. In the first place, Matisse was the most completely represented of all the contemporary artists; the selection shown included some of his greatest works, so that the impact of his art was especially strong. But beyond that, his style exhibited a distortion of form and an erratic use of color which was incomprehensible. Fauvism in its emotional violence was completely foreign to American taste. Whereas Cubism started from entirely new premises and produced an unrecognizable art which could be simply ignored or rationally discussed and found wanting, and one could even see in it evidences of intellectual speculation, technical proficiency, and neatness, Matisse was blatantly undermining all the accepted and recognizable forms of art: the nude, the still life, the portrait, genre, or symbolic themes. And what he did with them was a caution. When one adds to this the fact that he had a reputation as an accomplished painter and draughtsman, it is no wonder that his works appeared to American eyes as unaccountable and willful impertinence.

Matisse's art was so uncompromising that most critics could

168

not even recognize what we consider his most obvious qualities. It is true that a few caught a glimmer of his magical sense of color and some grudgingly admitted a certain linear fluency, but on the whole his art seemed a complete denial of all esthetic standards. Cortissoz, whose gods were Sargent and Giovanni Boldini, could not fathom this new and alien divinity. He wrote therefore in irritation: "It is I believe a matter of history that he has learned how to draw. But whatever his ability may be it is swamped in

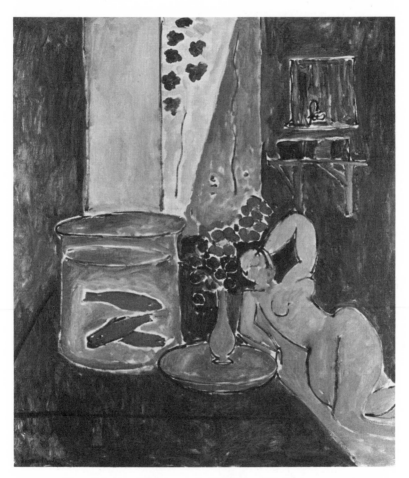

Henri Matisse (1869–1954). *Goldfish and Sculpture,* 1911.
Oil on canvas, 46 × 39⅝ in. Collection, The Museum of Modern Art, New York; Gift of Mr. and Mrs. John Hay Whitney.

the contortions of his misshapen figures. . . . If Matisse were the demigod he is assumed to be, there would be at least some hints of an Olympian quality breathed through his gauche puerilities." Cox, conservative even by academic standards, naturally considered Matisse an out-and-out charlatan and angrily dismissed his art. "It is not madness that stares at you from his canvases," he wrote, "but leering effrontery." He described the draughtsmanship of Matisse as the "exaltation to the walls of a gallery of the drawings of a nasty boy," and found their "professed indecency absolutely shocking." Cox's parting shot was again an intimation of quackery: Matisse "paints with tongue in cheek and an eye on his pocket."

Mather, on the other hand, admitted that Matisse was an "original and talented draughtsman" although he found his "pictorial ideas . . . either trivial, monstrous or totally lacking." "It is an art essentially epileptic," he wrote. "Sincere it may be, but its sincerity simply doesn't matter, except as it is pitiful to find a really talented draughtsman the organizer of a teapot tempest." Cox disputed the idea that Matisse was a great talent gone awry. He maintained that Matisse had never had any talent, could not make his way in the art world, and had decided to shock it into attention. How did he do it? He took the "ugliest models, poses them in the most grotesque and indecent poses and draws them as would a savage or depraved child."

It was clear enough, even to American critics, that Matisse was trying to achieve a "childlike" or "primitive" vision, but this was in itself upsetting. European art had revolted against the sophistication and "decadence" of the late nineteenth century, and was searching for "fundamentals," while American esthetic thought was still naïvely sold on "progress." There were some critics who recognized the conscious effort of the modern artist to recapture the conceptual vision of primitive, archaic, or Eastern art as legitimate, but for the majority who accepted the Western tradition of representation as the ultimate goal, this effort appeared to be a regression. This attitude was clearly expressed by Adeline Adams in "The Secret of Life," an article which appeared in the April issue of Art and Progress. "The childlike attitude as an idée fixe shows degeneration in viewpoint," she wrote. "It is as if man, having by ages of effort learned to walk upright, should petulantly conclude, perhaps after all, he would better achieve his adventures on all fours." For the author of an article about the Armory Show in the Harrisburg *Independent*, there was no question that the ultimate in art was representation and what he had seen aroused his indignation. Centuries of civilization, knowledge, and technique had been thrown out and we were back to the time of Cortez. It was obvious to him at least that twentieth-century man had nothing to learn from aboriginal art. To accept modern art was to permit the accumulation of the ages to disappear down the drain, with all those years between, from an Aztec idol to a portrait by John White Alexander, lost.

Critics in general, just like the public, were hard put to understand how a sophisticated artist could turn his back on tradition and try to see like a primitive or a child. William Howe Downes, writing in the Boston *Transcript* for February 17, expressed the feeling of most when he said: "Matisse is deliberately mystifying the public. . . . Among all these painters there is none whose work appears as perfectly childish, crude and amateurish. . . . I know no more offensive form of affectation than this pose of intentional naïveté. It is impossible to take Matisse seriously." Cortissoz agreed that Matisse's art did not express the "naïveté of a child" but of an "adult playing a trick" and was thus the "negation of all that true art implies." The *Globe* described it as "unbelievable childishness" and the Brooklyn *Life* critic decided that the *Red Studio* reminded him of a "sampler done by an imbecile at the age of eight." Even Caffin of the *American*, who had many favorable things to say about modern art, found the Fauve search for the primitive false. Most critics, if they understood the problem at all, agreed with their colleagues at the *Times* and the *Evening Sun* that it was not worth all the trouble.

Matisse was shocking largely because of the apparent crudity of his technique and his willful distortion of form. He was the "apostle of ugliness." And it was difficult to understand why someone who obviously knew better, or at least was supposed to know better, should want to create ugliness. The critic for the *Times* on February 23, even though crediting him with a revitalization of color, was led to complain that "his pictures are ugly . . . they are coarse . . . they are narrow . . . they are revolting in their inhumanity." And Cortissoz brushed them off as "wanton ugliness." After describing Matisse as an "unmitigated bore," Harriet Monroe in the Chicago *Tribune* of February 23 described his paintings as "the most hideous monstrosities ever perpetrated in the name of long suffering art." Chicago, which far outdid New York in spleen, was also more susceptible it would seem to boredom. Prof. George B. Zug, whose erudition in the March 6 article for the Chicago *Inter Ocean* is underlined by his description of "Paul" Picasso as an Italian, echoed Miss Monroe in the statement, "His work is so crude that after the first shock at its effrontery one is only bored by it." On the other hand, the critic for the Newark *Evening News* remained incensed: "Where Matisse violates all laws of beauty and replaces this lack by nothing except an apparently coarse and insolent self-insistence, one has greater difficulty in keeping the silence of discretion." Before the reader becomes too complacent in his superiority to the benighted viewers of an earlier day, he should be reminded that what they saw was not the delightful sensuousness of Matisse's later years which has become so popular, but the harshly iconoclastic works of his more revolutionary youth.

While Matisse provoked anger, the Cubists created bewilderment. The American public in its innocence lumped Cubism and Futurism together, and for a long time afterward the term *Futurism* or *Futuristic* remained the generic term for modern art, possibly because it was more evocative than *Cubism*. Part of the confusion was certainly due to the fact that the Futurists had been originally advertised as participating in the Show. Although no members of the Futurist movement were represented, Duchamp's *Nude* and the paintings of Picabia were closer to Futurism than to Analytical Cubism, and it is not difficult to understand how critics and public with no clear notion of either movement should confuse them and treat them as one. Unlike Matisse, that "genius of disorder and destruction," who was assailing the fortress of tradition, the Cubists seemed to have created a totally new world and one which was not without visual analogies to contemporary industrial life. As a result, Cubism received, if not acceptance, at least more tolerant treatment.

Caffin, who was the staunchest journalistic defender of the new art, had praise for Picasso and Picabia and attempted to analyze and explain their art in the March 3 issue of the *American*. It was a rather involved and not always convincing argument, already mired in the jargon of modernist esthetics, but there is no question of his sympathies. But even a conservative like McCormick on the *Press* could find the Cubists competent artists. If I quote at some length from his article of February 23, it is because I think it reveals something of the fundamental American artistic bias at that time for the intellectual as opposed to the emotional, a bias that made it so difficult for Americans to understand and accept expressionism in art.

Frankly, much of this Post-Impressionism seems to us so much artistic rubbish. But when it comes to the Cubists and Futurists one may at least take comfort in the fact that strange as their drawing and composition are, when looked at from the viewpoint of the old standards, they at least can draw them accurately, arrange them in at least the normalities of a kaleidoscope, and paint them smoothly and with admirable color. Picabia's *Procession in Seville* may be nothing but a queer jumble of the forms known to the science of angles, and may have some approximation to a musical composition, as he says it does, but at least the color is lovely and the forms truly represented. And so it is with the Cubist Villon in his *Fille au piano* in which the dimly made out form of the young woman is more beautiful to the normal eye than are the ugly feminine figures that dot so abominably the creations of the Post-Impressionist Gauguin.

It is strange to hear these men defined as "feeble realists," but whatever the classification, in the old sense, these Cubists and Futurists fall under dogmatically, it is a pleasure to see in their work good, sound painting and drawing, elements that seem to be quite unknown by Matisse et Cie. At present its success is merely that of amused curiosity; but we do not believe it is rubbish by any means. For it has the highly important qualification of arousing thought. . . .

173

The obvious intellectual control and technical precision of the Cubist paintings prevented the indictment of incompetence usually directed against the Post-Impressionists and Fauves. It even led in some cases to the criticism of overintellectuality and mechanical rendering. Mather, for instance, in two articles, one for the *Nation* and the other for the *Independent*, referred to the Cubists as no better than mechanical draughtsmen.

To the majority of critics and public, however, Cubism was

just a little too revolutionary for either comfort or understanding. Cox as usual was at the head of the cohorts of conservatism and brooking no nonsense he stated flatly, "The real meaning of this Cubist movement is nothing else than the total destruction of the art of painting." In a somewhat more reflective mood, though no more forgiving, he explained that the Cubists had invented a new language, which was unintelligible and therefore worthless. Most writers, like Downes of the Boston *Transcript,* were completely bewildered by the Cubists and felt they were "playing a game of mystification." Francis J. Ziegler of the Philadelphia *Record* admitted that he could make nothing of Cubism and added that in comparison Matisse was at least understandable even if not acceptable. Cortissoz, who had meticulously dissected and relegated to oblivion the other exponents of modernism, found Cubism simply beneath argument and proposed to ignore it:

When we bid farewell to Matisse, whose nudes, preposterous as they are, yet suggest the forms of men and women, we find ourselves in the company of "revolutionaries" who are not dealing with form as we understand it at all. With them a man begins to look like something else, preferably like some mass of faceted or curved little bodies thrown together in a heap. The Cubist steps in and gives us not pictures but so many square yards of canvas, treated as though they were so many square yards of wallpaper. But the Cubist wants to eat his cake and have it, too. He paints you his riddle of line and color, and then, as in the case of M. Marcel Duchamp, calls it "Nude Descending a Staircase." In other words, he has the effrontery to assert that his picture bears some relation to human life. Who shall argue with him? For our own part we flatly refuse to offer him the flattery of argument. According to the Spanish proverb it is a waste of lather to shave an ass, and that criticism of the Cubists is thrown away which does not deny at the outset their right to serious consideration. Are we to be at great pains to explain that a chunk of marble is not a statue? Are we elaborately to demonstrate that a battered tin can is not in the same category with a goblet fashioned by Cellini? Are we to accept these Cubists as painters of pictures because they have covered the canvas with paint? Are they indeed "forces which cannot be ignored because they have had results?" These "results" have nothing to do with art. Why should they not be ignored?

The Baltimore *Sun,* in announcing that the city would not get

174

the Armory Show, reported that most artists were not sorry and that Cubism was only a passing fancy after all. The imminent demise of Cubism was a frequent prediction. Cox, in an interview with a New York *Sun* reporter on the day of the Show's closing, reassured America, "The public is sure to find out sooner or

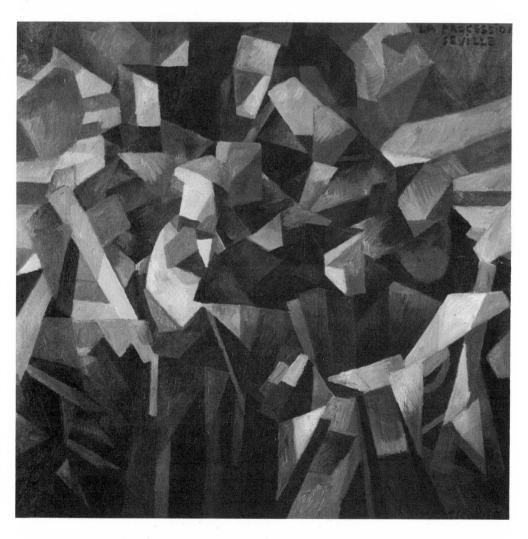

Francis Picabia (1879–1953). *The Procession, Seville*, 1912.
Oil on canvas, 48 × 48 in. Private collection.

Blague in a Loud Voice

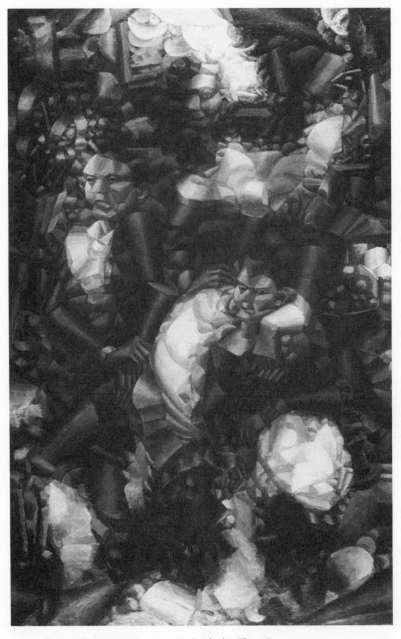

Fernand Léger (1881–1955). *Study for Three Portraits*, 1910–11.
Oil on canvas, 76¾ × 45⅞ in.
Milwaukee Art Museum; Anonymous gift.

later that anyone can do Cubism . . . and when the public finds out it will be the end of the movement." As a matter of fact, by March 24 the New York *Post* was already passing on the good news that Cubism and Futurism had long been dead in Paris without our knowing it and that "Orphism" was the *dernier cri.*

Curiously enough, one of the most frequently repeated criticisms of Cubism showed some sophistication. It was argued most eruditely by Mather that Cubism was excessively literary, symbolic, and programmatic. This is somewhat confusing, since Cubism in its search for "pure form" pretended an opposition to those elements. It should be remembered that American artistic taste already influenced by Whistler had reached its own level of poetic purity in art which was antithetical to the same "literary" elements. The very intellectualism of Cubism and Futurism therefore seemed a retrogression to symbolic art. In his article "Newest Tendencies in Art," for the *Independent* of March 6, Mather wrote:

> In short, so far as Post-Impressionism and Cubism are not mere sham they seem to me an insidious rebirth of the literary picture. Only the models have changed. The mid-Victorian literary picture was nourished on harmless anecdote. The Post-Impressionist or Cubist picture is spawned from the morbid intimations of symbolist poetry and distorted Bergsonian philosophy. In fact the unwholesomeness of the new pictures is their most striking and immediate condemnation. . . . The critic notes a forced and hectic mixing of pictorial and literary values.

The same charge is to be found in many newspaper reviews of the Armory Show. The New York *Evening Sun* of February 18 labeled Cubism programmatic painting; the *Times* of the 23rd also called it programmatic and found fault with the "literary" character of its titles, as did the Chicago *Tribune* and the Philadelphia *Inquirer* of the same date.

And finally, the ignominy of boredom was charged to the Cubists as it was to Matisse. Cortissoz assured his readers that after examining all of the Cubist works in the Show, all he could say was that they were "such a bore." And a fairly intelligent anonymous review in the Springfield *Republican*, after a considered and very favorable account, could say, "Picasso fails to impress."

It is easy enough with hindsight to ridicule the errors of judgment that the New York art critics of that day perpetrated. When the Exhibition went to Chicago, their local colleagues outdid them in both ignorance and outrage. But it should be said for the critics that there were many among them who were not unintelligent, that most of them took their work seriously, made an honest effort to understand, and according to their lights acted fairly. Their lack of prescience is a normal human condition, even among present-day art critics.

The critics for the defense could not base their case on accepted standards of artistic judgment. They had to prepare the ground by establishing a whole new set of values. The process of indoctrination begun then has continued down to our own day, often using the same catechisms. Newspapermen writing about art, without much formal knowledge of art history or deep involvement with the subject, depended on handouts from the Association, prepared by Gregg on the basis of information and argument supplied by Pach and Davies. Pach at least had an understanding of what was happening and could supply the facts as well as the standard premises of the new art which, although fairly current abroad, were not well known here, except in the Stieglitz circle. The only previous discussion of such ideas in this country had occurred in Stieglitz's pioneering publication, *Camera Work*. Aside from that there had been neither books nor articles to prepare the American public and art world for so serious a revision of esthetic attitudes.

The major argument for the defense and the one calculated to have the widest appeal was the validity of change. This was sometimes presented, especially by the radical elements, as revolution, unfortunately a disturbing word which identified the new art with anarchy and bomb-throwing. Much more acceptable was the notion of change as progress, which in the United States had an almost magical charm for both conservative and radical. Arguing against progress was equivalent to trampling on the flag, and any espousal of it was calculated to elicit a *nolo contendere*, except that the interpretation of progress was debatable. The conservatives here maintained that the new art was not progressive but retrogressive, as witness the conscious return by some modernists to the primitive and the childlike. Progress to the conservative was the accumulation of lessons from the past, the careful addition of new experience to tested formulas, and the extension of techniques and skills. To the radicals, the very nature of change was revolutionary and therefore progressive, from Ingres to Delacroix, to Courbet, to Impressionism, to Post-Impressionism, to Fauvism, to Cubism—on *ad infinitum*, onward and upward with the arts.

Still another conception of change was its equation with inexorable biological processes, thus establishing it as a law of life. This proposition was extremely popular in that period of general optimistic liberalism. It received spirited support from people like Stieglitz and Hutchins Hapgood, who tended to call on "life forces" in almost any situation. For them the moral standards of good and evil were replaced by new moral standards of life and death. Hapgood, who regularly contributed a rather lush column of positive thinking in the *Globe*, greeted the opening of the Armory Show with a piece which achieved some currency and received a good deal of comment both pro and con; it was called "Life at the Armory" and was a rather wordy sermon on the life force of art. But the tone had been set for this kind of defense by an article contributed by Stieglitz to the *Sunday Times* of January 26, in which he wrote:

The dry bones of a dead art are rattling as they never rattled before. The hopeful birth of a new art that is intensely alive is doing it. A score or more of painters and sculptors who decline to go on doing merely what the camera does better, have united in a demonstration of independence—an exhibition of what they see and dare express in their own way—that will wring shrieks of indignation from every ordained copyist of "old masters" on two continents and their adjacent islands.

This glorious affair is coming off during the month of February at the Sixty-ninth Regiment Armory in New York. Don't miss it. If you still belong to the respectable old first primer class in art, you will see there stranger things than you ever dreamed were on land or sea—and you'll hear a battle cry of freedom without any soft pedal on it. . . . If a name is necessary in writing about these live ones, call them "Revitalizers." That's what they are, the whole bunch. They're breathing the breath of life into an art that is long since dead, but won't believe it. . . . Individual independence, both in expression and in acceptance or rejection of whatever is expressed—that is the first principle of those who are trying to inject some life into the decaying corpse of art.

But once one got beyond the general and philosophical argument for either the virtue or the inevitability of change, the defense became more difficult. It was obvious that the art of Matisse was predicated on totally different assumptions from that of George de Forest Brush. As long as the public accepted the faithful representation of nature as the ultimate in artistic goals, it could not possibly understand the new art. However, the fact that even for someone like Cortissoz a faithful reproduction of reality was not enough, that some sort of interpretation, transformation, or emotional expressiveness was necessary, was a wedge by which the older conceptions could be moved. The basic argument that art was not representation but expression was repeated even by antagonistic critics as an explanation of what the avant-garde artists were attempting to achieve. It was the emotional reaction to a thing or an event, rather than its representation, which was the objective. In that sense there was not much distinction made among any of the various tendencies. A Van Gogh and a Picasso were both seen as expressions of subjective experience. This is fairly primitive esthetics, but it seems to have satisfied a good many critics even in conservative circles, at least as an explanation. It was so current that an editorial writer for the *Tribune* used it in an attack on national financial policies, characterizing them in terms of the new art as "not what things are but the expression of introspection." However, it was the ultimate subjectivity of expression carried beyond the point of comprehensibility which the conservatives found impossible to accept. What appeared as anarchism, narcissism, or sheer self-indulgence to them was, on the other hand, accepted by the defenders as the expression of individuality, the untouchable core of the creative artist.

Individualism is one of the sacred cows in the American hierarchy of values, which is rather strange for a people who, at least in the twentieth century, have been so intolerant of its expression. As we become less individualistic in fact, we pay greater homage to this symbol of an earlier independence of spirit. It is always a good bet in a debate; it is just as unassailable as babies. However, the artist, the last truly individualistic man in our society, is treated with suspicion. The excuse for this is that he exercises too much or not the right kind of individuality. Modernism was attacked on such grounds. The defense maintained the essential and central importance of individuality in art and offered it as a justification. The artist had the right to express himself, to experiment and to change. The very act of creativity, the very nature of genius were tied to individuality.

Obviously related to expression, emotion, and individuality was the concept of the instinctive as fundamental in art. The return to the wellsprings of instinctive behavior was a moth-eaten Romantic notion which had been revitalized by Freud in psychiatry and Bergson in philosophy, and if those who professed it knew of neither man it made no difference; they could get it regularly in the art pages of the New York *American* from Charles Caffin, something of an equivalent in art criticism to Hutchins Hapgood, who had carte blanche to wander through all the fields of culture. Caffin had difficulty restraining his *Weltanschauung* in an article in the *American* of February 23 where, after lauding the Armory Show for the stimulation of thought and discussion that could signify the liberation of American art, and after agreeing with Hapgood in his views of life and art, he staged a full-scale attack on the limitations of American culture, its sentimentality, prudishness, and sexual inhibitions. Modern art in its courageous search for fundamental human experience, he argued, had a great deal to teach us. His description of modern art as a seeking for instinctive perception of form and abstract expression was not bad for those days. He was among the few who appreciated the work of Brancusi and he said of him that he "stripped away the partial disguise of natural accident and revealed . . . the naked, essential facts of structure." Although this is well within the tradition of writing on modern art, Caffin was not an especially predictable thinker. By the end of the article he was decrying the Fauves because they were lacking in intellectuality, since he had some muddled idea about modern man being basically intellectual, and was finding "primitivism" retrogressive. Like most Americans, Caffin was willing to go along just so far but no further. The extreme, at least in thought, is not an American trait.

The idea that modern art was alive and vital, that it had tapped some elemental force of the human psyche was in some ways even accepted by the opposition. A writer for the Toronto

Globe described modern art as expressing a youthful and courageous animalism. Anna Page Scott in the *Post Express* felt that in comparison with Academy exhibitions the Armory Show was full of life and animation. And Mather even in derogation could say, "Unquestionably, Matisse is more exciting than, say, George de Forest Brush; it doesn't at all follow that Matisse is the better artist." The general impression remained that the modernists had uncovered some new source of energy to which one was forced, in spite of preconceived notions and prejudices, to respond. On March 15, when the Armory Show closed and the Academy Show opened, the *Globe* summed up the former by reporting: "A crowd has been made to come, not only once, but several times, laughing at first, perhaps, less protesting afterward, and finally profoundly interested. . . . It has made men stop and think, made the public wonder if, after all, there was not something really worth their while in this courageous departure from convention. They have set New York and its artists by the ears." And the *Herald* reporter at the Academy opening was forced to admit: "The walls are monotonous in their representation of picture after picture painted by the half dozen recognized formulas that have grown to constitute American art. . . . Most of them are well painted but few of them present either ideas or emotions that stir the spectator." The recognition that a well-painted picture was not the ultimate in art was revolution enough for America.

But for Joel E. Spingarn, professor of philosophy at Columbia and staunch advocate of the intellectual revolution, the new art represented something more than mere vitality. In a letter to Mowbray-Clarke, which was reprinted in the *Evening Post* of February 25, he eulogized the recapturing of the "essential madness" of art:

The opening night of the International Exhibition seemed to me one of the most exciting adventures I have experienced, and this sense of excitement was shared by almost everyone who was present. It was not merely the stimulus of color, or the riot of sensuous appeal, or the elation that is born of a successful venture, or the feeling that one has shared, however humbly, in an historical occasion. For my own part, and I can only speak for myself, what moved me so strongly was this: I felt for the first time that art was recapturing its own essential madness at last, that the modern painter and sculptor had won for himself a title of courage that was lacking in all the other fields of art.

For all that, though it needs repeating in every civilization, madness and courage are the very life of all art. From the days of Plato and Aristotle, who both shared the Greek conception of genius as a form of madness, . . . all who have ever given any real thought to art or beauty have recognized this essential truth. The virtue of an industrial society is that it is always more or less sane. The virtue of all art is that it is always more or less mad. All the greater is our American need of art's tonic loveliness, and all the more difficult is it for us to recapture the inherent madness without which she cannot speak or breathe.

But here was madness, and here was courage that did not fear to be mad. I confess that when I left the exhibition my feeling was not merely one of excitement; but mingled with it was a real depression at the thought that no other artists shared this courage of the painters of our time. How timid seemed our poetry and our drama and our prose fiction; how conventional and pusillanimous our literary and dramatic criticism; how faded and academic and anemic every other form of artistic expression. But these painters and sculptors had really dared to express themselves. Wrong-headed, mistaken, capricious, they may all turn out to be for all I care; but at least they have the *sine qua non* of art, the courage to express themselves without equivocating with their souls.

The defense of modernism was thus based not so much on esthetic as broadly philosophical grounds. Hardly anywhere in the mass of newspaper and magazine criticism is there an indication that the esthetic arguments for Fauvism, Cubism, or Futurism were known. Picabia's attempt to explain his art in a widely reprinted interview was the first taste America had of the rationale of modernism. Although in the next several years the contributions to esthetic discussion by Eddy, Willard Huntington Wright, and Leo Stein raised the level of criticism, the only exceptions at that time to the general naïveté of American critical thinking were J. Nilsen Laurvik and Christian Brinton. Not that they were especially perceptive or cogent critics, but they did have a knowledge of the field in its various ramifications. They could be precise about the various movements and personnel and were capable of distinguishing among objectives. The weakness in both their cases was an attempt to reduce the diversity to some basic philosophical generalization.

Brinton's critical orientation, like that of the arch-reactionary Kenyon Cox, was based on a sociological analysis of the development of modern art and was expressed most clearly several years later, in 1916, when he wrote *Impressions of the Art at the Panama-Pacific Exposition*. Democracy, he contended, had liberated the artist from the older conditions of patronage and, in setting him free, had created the condition for which the artist was "paying the penalty of isolation." The social consciousness of the artist on the other hand had increased insofar as "painting was no longer content to minister modestly unto life; it had learned to echo in theme and treatment the social, political, and intellectual complexion of the age." Writing at the time of the Armory Show, he characterized the new art as presaging "a profound spiritual rebirth in the province of esthetic endeavor" which was bound to benefit American art if we had the courage to grasp the opportunity.

Brinton did not agree with the accepted notion that modern art was revolutionary, which he explained as the result of a lack of knowledge. Modern art was, instead, a return to the older synthetic vision of primitive man and Oriental art, a departure in Western art from the more recent traditions of objective reality to subjective synthesis. This search for spirit rather than substance had led to the "primal spontaneity of untutored effort," a mixture of sophistication and voluntary savagery as in the art of Matisse. Of Picasso and the Cubists he wrote: "Sublime elementalism herewith gives place to divine geometrizing, with the result that we are at last freed from all taint of nature imitation and watch unfolding before us a world of visual imagery existing of and for itself alone. . . . Call it optical music, emotional mathematics . . . they lead us . . . into a realm where subjectivity reigns supreme, and no one can hold that they have not done something toward establishing a purely abstract language of form and color."

Brinton had a wide acquaintance with developments in other cultural fields, but no one writing at that time in America showed as complete an understanding of current art movements abroad. He was the only critic to point with precision to the incompleteness of the Armory Show as a cross-section of contemporary art, noting the absence of the Dresdener Brücke, the Berliner

184

Neue Sezession, the Münchener Neue Vereinigung, the Stockholm Eight, and the Futurists. He had apparently not yet heard of the newly formed Blaue Reiter group, but he called attention to the absence of artists like Franz Marc, Iran Meštrovič, George Minne, David Burliuk, and Kees van Dongen. The fact is that the Association had politely refused the request of the Berliner Neue Sezession and the Dresdener Brücke to participate in the Armory Show, with the excuse that the rolls were closed, when in actuality the inquiries had arrived early enough for them to be included had Davies and Kuhn felt that German contemporary art was worth inclusion. Brinton was also the only critic to question the ballyhoo for Redon, and he was the only one conversant enough with events to compare the Armory Show with the London Grafton Show, which he described as more concentrated, and the Cologne Sonderbund, which he found more inclusive. His comment on the state of American art in relation to European influences in "Evolution not Revolution in Art," published in the April 1913 issue of *International Studio,* is both perceptive and accurate:

185

> Separated from Europe by that shining stretch of sea which has always clearly conditioned our development—social, intellectual and esthetic—we get only the results of Continental cultural endeavor. We take no part in the preliminary struggles which lead up to these achievements. They come to our shores as finished products, appearing suddenly before us in all their salutary freshness and variety. The awakening of the American public to the appreciation of things artistic has, in brief, been accomplished by a series of shocks from the outside rather than through intensive effort, observation or participation.

Laurvik was neither as knowledgeable nor as sympathetic to modern art as Brinton, although he defended its earlier developments and attempted to explain the general evolution of styles. He agreed with Brinton that modernism was no revolution but a return to a synthetic vision. This fact he could understand and explain, but it did not make him very happy, since he felt that the more recent movements had perverted the great nineteenth-century evolution of "scientific realism" from Courbet to Cézanne. He considered Picasso and the other followers of Cézanne, as he described them, to be the creators of an introverted art, a turning away from realism to metaphysics. He regretted the "pseudo-primitivism" of the modernists as a conscious regression to lower forms of art and in the balance felt that they had fallen short of the greatness of Cézanne and Gauguin.

The strain of "progress" is clearly visible in both Brinton and Laurvik and it was the element in their thinking which kept them from a full acceptance of the most recent art. They were never apologists for modernism, but they not only helped in the defense of some of its aspects, they also played a role in the general education of the public to the significance of what was going on. They helped American criticism take its first steps out of the fog of uninformed opinion.

186

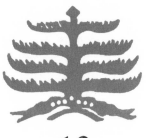

10

It's
a Rube
Town!

Interest in the Armory Show, promoted by the continuing press comment and controversy, kept mounting and reached a triumphant climax on the last day, Saturday, March 15. All day long and into the evening a steady stream of spectators surged through the galleries. The surrounding streets were clogged by automobiles and carriages, people had to line up and wait to get in, and from two to four during the afternoon the doors had to be closed because the Armory was filled to capacity. Newspaper estimates of attendance printed the following day ranged from ten to twelve thousand, and it was reported that many visitors had been turned away.

Jerome Myers, recalling that night years later, wrote with fond nostalgia:

It was the wildest, maddest, most intensely excited crowd that ever broke decorum in any scene I have witnessed. The huge Armory was packed with the elite of New York—and many not so elite. The celebrities were too numerous to register. Everyone came to witness the close, and the audience created a show equally as phenomenal as the exhibition itself. Millionaires, art collectors, society people, all were packed in like sardines. Fortunately the huge sculptures bore the strain of the surging crowd without casualties. More interesting to me than all this mob, the millionaires, celebrities, and all the Grade B people, was the figure of William M. Chase, with his immaculate high hat and his Sargentesque appearance—an artist whose work was not included in the exhibition and who had every reason to feel the indignity of having been slighted.

Crowds still filled the hall, with spectators packed tight in front of the *Nude* at the witching hour. At 10 P.M. the guards began to urge the last visitors to leave. The next morning the *Sun* carried the story under the head, "Cubists Migrate: Thousands Mourn." But when the doors closed that evening there was a jubilant celebration with members and guests, guards, ticket sellers, guides, and members of the 69th Regiment, who had come to the closing, all participating. An impromptu snake dance led by the regimental fife-and-drum corps got under way with D. Putnam Brinley, his lanky height topped by a bearskin hat, acting as drum major; and, as it swept through each of the galleries in turn amid songs, shouts, and buoyant laughter, the participants saluted the artists past and present who had made it all possible.

The party picked up in pace when the champagne arrived, allegedly supplied by John Quinn. As the band played and corks popped, the artists, exhilarated by success as much as by wine, whirled the girls who had worked in the office and sold tickets at the Armory around the floor in dance. One artist, carried away by the celebration, shouted above the din, "To the Academy!" It is doubtful that anyone was interested in anything but continuing the party, but Quinn shouted back: "No, no! Don't you remember Captain John Philip of the *Texas?* When his guns sank a Spanish ship at Santiago, he said, 'Don't cheer, boys, the poor devils are dying!'" The Association had emerged triumphant, and even a more gallant gesture would only have been a gesture, for the Academy was irretrievably dead.

What was left of the night was spent in dismantling the Exhibition. Kuhn reports that he stayed with the workmen, and that at 10 o'clock on the morning of St. Patrick's Day the 69th Regiment Band marched into an empty hall to salute the memory of the Armory Show with the playing of "Garry Owen." The first and major phase of the great project was finished; its echoes in Chicago and Boston, whatever they might be, could not change the verdict of success.

There was hardly time to enjoy the victory, for the Exhibition had to be prepared for its scheduled opening in Chicago on March 24, exactly one week away. Negotiations to present the Show in the second city had begun long before, when Arthur T. Aldis, the Chicago lawyer, art collector, and influential member of the Art Institute, was introduced to Kuhn by Jo Davidson while in Paris; later he met with Davies early in November of 1912. Aldis had already heard of what was afoot and was eager to bring the new art to his home city. Although a legal agreement or an official statement was still premature, a gentlemen's understanding was arrived at. What Davies could tentatively promise Aldis was apparently satisfactory, but the latter had the problem of convincing the members of the board of trustees and the officials of the museum to be as daring as New York. Chicago's civic pride can usually be taunted into emulating its older and more cosmopolitan rival, but it often takes a lot of doing.

Even though Aldis had many friends on the board on whom he relied, he anticipated that others—including the museum's director, William M. R. French—would not be overjoyed at the prospect of an exhibition of works by some wild foreign artists. He was not wrong, for French, without being openly antagonistic, dragged his feet and anything else available during all the negotiations. Until overridden by board pressure, he pleaded that it was too late to revise the museum's exhibition schedule, that the space available was insufficient, and that the problems of rehanging were too great. When everything else failed he quietly got out from under by leaving on vacation before the opening. But the insistence of Aldis and his friends who wanted the show for Chicago was too great. French conceded as gracefully as possible and carried on negotiations with the Association as punctiliously and correctly as was to be expected. Aldis, who knew his man and his sentiments, acted diplomatically, but kept his hand in by communicating directly with Kuhn.

189

Early in December of 1912, after Aldis had returned from abroad and got the wheels in motion, French wrote to Borglum asking him to act in behalf of the Institute in getting the Armory Show for Chicago. He mentioned the fact that there might be trouble about finances, but hoped that arrangements could be worked out. One must assume throughout that behind the scenes his hand was being forced. On December 13, he wrote to Davies, alluding to the Paris meeting, and officially requested the Armory Show for the Chicago Art Institute. Davies answered after the December 17 meeting of the Association that a committee had been appointed to negotiate arrangements. On the same day, December 19, Kuhn communicated directly with Aldis, advising him of developments. French wrote Kuhn on December 26 asking clarification of several matters, and on Friday, January 10, he had lunch with Davies and Kuhn in New York to discuss details. On the following Tuesday, French reported to Davies that he had met with the president of the board, Charles L. Hutchinson, who had called a meeting of the Art Committee for Thursday, and he was sure that permission would be granted to unhang the temporary galleries to make room for the Armory Show. He could not resist complaining that previous commitments would make it all very difficult, but he also advised Davies that the Art Institute was prepared to assume all expenses of the Exhibition, including transportation, insurance, etc., and suggested March 25 as the best date for the opening. Obviously, whether French liked it or not, the Art Institute was committed to underwriting the revolution.

At that point, the Association, buried to its eyes in its own problems, did not get around to clinching the deal. After waiting for two weeks, French wrote to Kuhn asking if any action had been taken on the contract and prodding him to get on with it. Another week went by before Kuhn answered with the suggestion that they wait until the Show opened in New York, after which French could come to see it and they could then settle all the details. Kuhn assured him that the Association was operating with such efficiency that there would be absolutely no problem with details. He also promised that Chicago would get a representative selection of the New York Exhibition. French had done his duty, and perhaps he even hoped that after the Show opened and they had seen it, his board might get cold feet. At any rate, he accepted the suggestion and promised to come on March 1.

Meanwhile, Aldis had received word that a similar deal had been arranged with the Copley Society to send the Exhibition to Boston. Afraid that the works would be split between the two cities, he wrote Kuhn on February 17 reminding him of Chicago's priority and asking that they not be slighted in the division. He took the opportunity to warn Kuhn that French might be difficult since he was reluctant to dismantle the necessary galleries. He also suggested cannily that the Association, rather than French, select the works to come to Chicago. Kuhn answered immediately that there was nothing to worry about, Chicago would get a "square deal." He also advised Aldis that French was in town and in the hands of Davies. Kuhn seemed supremely confident that if anyone could handle the director, Davies was the man. Apparently his faith was not misplaced, for a memorandum of agreement was arrived at and on February 22 Kuhn sent Aldis a copy. Aldis, who had a rather fearful eye peeled in the direction of French, had already written Kuhn on the 20th that he and George F. Porter were planning to come to New York to see the Armory Show and that, if any help was needed, to get in touch with him at the Ritz-Carlton. But Davies had managed French without difficulty.

The agreement provided for a payment of $2,500 from the Art Institute to secure the Show; the Institute would pay for transportation and insurance from New York to Chicago and return; each would properly pack and box the collection at its end; and they both would share equally the "net receipts" (this later caused some difficulty) from the sale of catalogues, photographs, reproductions, and prints of works exhibited. All admission fees were to go to the Institute and all receipts and commissions from the sale of works of art were to go to the Association. From an artistic point of view the major provision was that Davies would select the works to be sent to Chicago, subject to final approval by French. Other details were covered in the agreement, including a pledge by both parties to do all they could "to make the exhibition in Chicago as valuable and profitable to each other and the public as possible."

The signed contract finally embodied these provisions, but on

March 3 and 4 a flurry of telegrams revealed a temporary disagreement. The Institute trustees raised objections to the flat fee
of $2,500 and proposed, instead, splitting the profit from the
catalogues and reproductions sold. The Association refused on
the grounds that the agreement had already been made, and the
Institute backed down. They insisted, however, that the catalogue be printed in Chicago, since costs of printing in New York
were too high and they could do better locally. Throughout, the
Chicago administration made its feeling very clear that the Association was rather inept in financial matters. French also requested, interestingly enough, that the Chicago catalogue be all
in English—no foreign titles. On March 5 Kuhn sent a telegram
to Quinn, the Association's legal adviser: "Chicago accepts all
conditions."

With negotiations out of the way, the actual business of trans-
porting the Exhibition to Chicago could proceed. French advised
Davies that the Institute had decided that what it wanted was
the most novel part of the Show—the European section, and the
most radical of that. He suggested omission of the historical segment, examples of which were available in the museum. He also
expressed a desire to limit the American representatives to one
work per artist, although he diplomatically excepted Davies and
was willing to accept a representative selection of his works. Because of costs, the Institute had decided to omit all the American
sculpture and accept about fifteen outstanding examples by foreign sculptors. French also felt that the representation of Augustus John was too extensive and should be cut, but he was
especially anxious to have a full quota of Chanler screens to serve
as entrance decorations.

Kuhn, writing for the Association, acknowledged receipt of
the contract and asked immediately for plans of the hanging area
so that they could get to work on designing the Exhibition. He
notified the Institute that he was sending the cuts for the poster
and a package of advertising post cards. He had also ordered
photographs from Hagelstein, the Armory Show's official photographer, and suggested Gregg for publicity. He added that both
he and Gregg were already at work publicizing the Chicago Show.

The Chicago staff was showing its professional mettle and on
the next day, March 7, had a measured plan of the hanging space

in the mail. At this point Newton H. Carpenter, secretary of the Art Institute, who was to take over the task of handling exhibition affairs when French left, entered the picture and immediately got down to details. He wrote Kuhn asking for Gregg to come and begin the publicity build-up. He also wanted to know what he would have to sell and how much profit there would be on each item. With an accountant's persistence he was henceforth constantly badgering the Association to act like respectable merchants. Of course the Armory Show was still in progress and the Association had more immediate problems, but Kuhn wrote to Carpenter that he would send all the material for sale as soon as the Show closed in New York, that Gregg was arranging to come to Chicago in a few days, and that he, Kuhn, planned to be in Chicago when the Exhibition arrived. He also reassured Carpenter that Davies was at work on the selection and plan of the Show.

Preparations for sending the Exhibition had already begun. Permission had to be obtained from lenders to extend their loans to cover the Chicago and Boston Exhibitions and not all were amenable. Foreign dealers especially were beginning to clamor for results. Their merchandise had been abroad on consignment for three months and they did not know whether any sales had been made. Demanding and threatening cablegrams arrived. But the Association promised, cajoled, or simply sat tight. Davies played it fast and cool and, in spite of transoceanic Morse-code screams, he managed to hold most of the Exhibition together until the course was run. He mollified lenders and convinced buyers not to pull their works out of the Chicago and Boston Exhibitions, so that both cities eventually got representative collections. It is very possible that many a museum director could have taken lessons from Arthur B. Davies and his gang.

Carpenter, however, was after action. He had a job to do and he was out to do it. His letters are full of requests, details, complaints, and impatience, and it was Kuhn's job to keep him at bay—which he did fairly well. Of course he had all the cards, or at least all the works of art, and he, or perhaps Davies, just would not be rushed. On March 13, Carpenter wrote Kuhn that people were beginning to react to the coming Show. He had so much to do and wanted information about sales, advertising, shipment, etc. A letter from Davies to French which crossed Carpenter's letter in transit outlined the entire Exhibition, gallery by gallery, with the admonition not to break the format in order to retain the maximum impact. He explained that he was sending the French modern section almost intact and reducing the American, English, Irish, and German contingents. French's answer was something of a surprise. He thought the Davies plan excellent, but more than that, he admitted an earlier uneasiness about the Exhibition and confessed that he had originally hoped to take only a few of the more radical works, but his attitude had changed and he now realized that covering the ground thoroughly was a better idea. And so, in spite of some earlier antagonism, the two sides were now reconciled and Chicago was going to get the heart of the Armory Show with the body pared to a minimum. The controversial foreign core was to remain almost intact.

As the day approached, excitement increased, especially among the Chicagoans. In his next letter Carpenter, sensing a great smash, became enthusiastic and cooperative, even extending the hope that more room would be made available. Arthur Jerome Eddy, back home, was having second thoughts. He demanded of Davies that the American as well as foreign works he had bought be included in the Chicago display, since he wanted to avoid any misunderstanding about his attitude toward art. It is difficult to know whether he was concerned that Chicagoans might question his patriotism or his taste. At any rate, the inclusion of his American purchases would prove his support of native art as well as blunt the impression of radicalism that his foreign purchases might engender. Aldis also wrote asking, at the suggestion of George Porter, that a Childe Hassam and a J. Frank Currier be included, with the hope that the Friends of American Art might purchase them for the museum.

By March 18, Carpenter was getting jittery, for, as he wrote Kuhn, French was preparing to leave on vacation and the Exhibition would then be his baby. He bombarded the New York office with letters and telegrams increasingly frantic in tone as the opening day approached. One can understand his nervousness as he waited for an exhibition that might not arrive in time. He kept reminding Kuhn that time was short, the catalogue had not come, and he had no indication as to when the works would appear. He was also worried about certain financial arrangements: he complained that the cost of photographs was too high and he preferred to have the work done in Chicago; he also felt that the insurance rates were out of line and that the Institute could arrange a better deal. With no specific information and only assurances from New York, his panic increased.

He telegraphed again on Wednesday, the 19th, reminding Kuhn that the Exhibition was scheduled to open on Monday afternoon and as yet there was no sign of either the catalogue or the Exhibition, nor any indication of who was going to come and help hang the Show. But in spite of mounting anxiety, one part of his brain could still continue to concern itself with insurance, printing, and photograph rates. His fears seem to have infected Eddy, who on the same day sent a telegram to Pach: "Wire personally conditions of packing and catalogue. Worried by delay. Invitations for Monday afternoon and evening receptions out." The answer, dated the 20th, is a masterpiece of nonchalance. It must have hidden a titanic sigh of relief. "One car left today, balance tomorrow, catalogue mailed tonight. Everything on schedule. No occasion to worry."

By the evening of the 20th there was nothing much left to worry about, except perhaps a train wreck, but the five days since the closing of the New York Show must have been filled with a fury of activity. The nearly 650 works to be sent had to be selected, packed, boxed, and shipped. The catalogue listing had to be made and translated. Pamphlets, post cards, and photographs also had to be packed and shipped. This does not include all the paperwork involved in arranging for the extension of the Exhibition, all of which had been started much earlier. Through it all, Davies never panicked. He handled the situation with firmness, never permitting the Chicago administration to wrest control of the Exhibition from the Association. It remained the kind of show the Association wanted and on its terms. He rejected Chicago proposals in relation to insurance and photographs, and rebuffed every effort to minimize the role of the Association or cheapen the Exhibition.

Gregg had already left for Chicago to handle publicity, and on the 19th he held a press conference in which he was somewhat roughly treated. As he wired Kuhn, "Had a time handling a press

195

crowd today." And the Chicago *Inter Ocean* reported him as saying: "It is too bad. Chicago has failed to appreciate. It has laughed." All this before the Show had even arrived. Gregg at first and later Kuhn and Pach were to discover that Chicago was not New York. It was not only more provincial, but it suffered from a badly concealed sense of inferiority and its press took a decided show-me attitude to what had set New York agog. The situation was also quite different from that in New York before the Armory Show opening. Chicago knew much more clearly what to expect, had heard all the jokes and denunciations, was aware of all the innuendos and rumors, but rather than learn from New York's experience, it decided instead not to be taken in. No wonder Kuhn scrawled across the top of a letter written to MacRae, "It's a Rube Town!"

On the evening of March 20, with the first shipment on its way, Kuhn and Pach boarded the *Twentieth Century Limited* at 8:30 P.M., in order to be on hand when the shipment arrived. The director of the Institute had quietly and, one assumes, happily slipped out of town even before the works came in from New York. He was off with his wife on a vacation to California. He confided to a reporter from the *Record Herald* before boarding his train that he couldn't stand the stuff. Chicago would have to face its test without him.

After all the preliminary frenzy, the actual event of hanging the Show was an anticlimax of administrative and mechanical efficiency. The works of art, Kuhn, and Pach all appeared on schedule. The cases were opened in the presence of Customs inspectors and the entire Exhibition was hung in less than one day. There is no question that the museum staff was efficient and cooperative, but it was the preliminary planning and sense of purpose which made the problem in logistics manageable. Davies and Company had done it again.

There were exactly 634 works exhibited in Chicago, including 312 oil paintings, 57 watercolors, 120 prints, 115 drawings, and 30 sculptures. The entrance to the Exhibition, on the landing below and above the double staircase, was decorated with eight colorful Chanler screens. On the upper landing, among the screens, sculptures by Bourdelle, Maillol, Bernard, Matisse, and others were displayed. The first room off the landing, the East

Gallery, contained works by Matisse, Denis, and the other non-Cubist French painters, as well as sculpture by Lehmbruck and Archipenko. Then in sequence came a selection of English, Irish, German, and some American paintings in gallery 51; Cézanne, Van Gogh, and Gauguin in gallery 52; the Cubists in gallery 53; the Americans in gallery 54—the Southeast Gallery; and Redon in the last, gallery 26. The Institute was concurrently housing the annual exhibition of the Watercolor Society, a collection of portraits by Pauline Potter, and an exhibit of the Hor-

First-floor landing—sculpture and Chanler screens, Chicago.

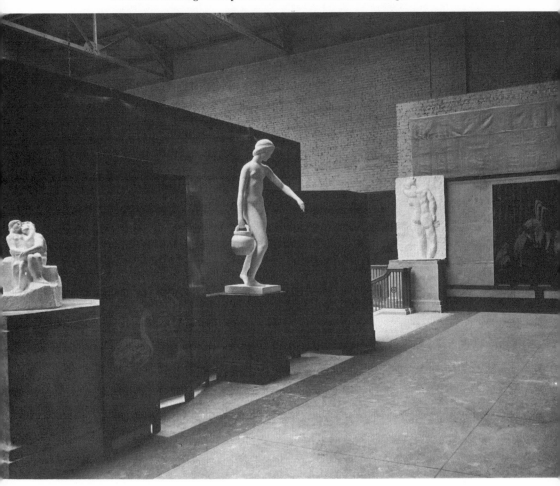

It's a Rube Town!

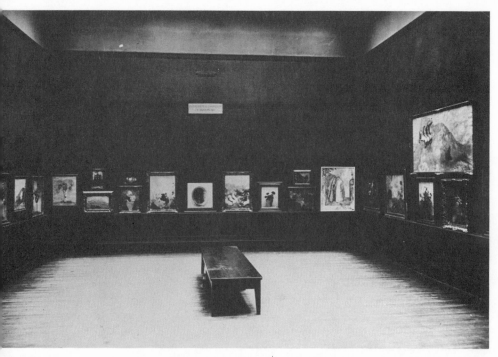

Gallery 26, Redon room, Chicago.

Gallery 51, German, English, Irish, and American works, Chicago.

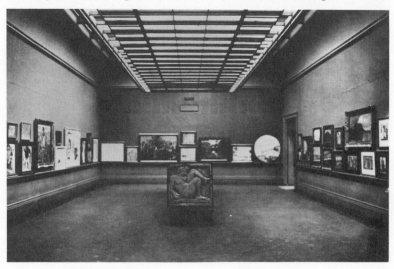

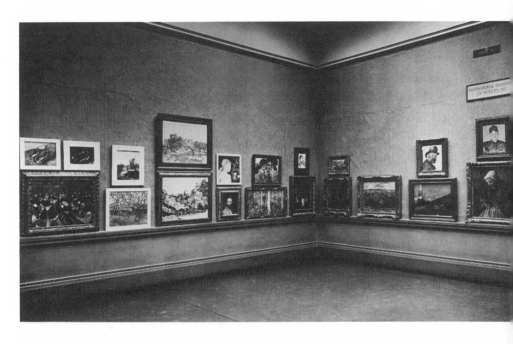

Gallery 52, Cézanne, Van Gogh, and Gauguin (2 views), Chicago.

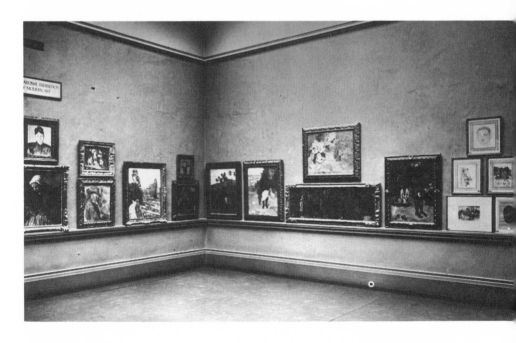

It's a Rube Town!

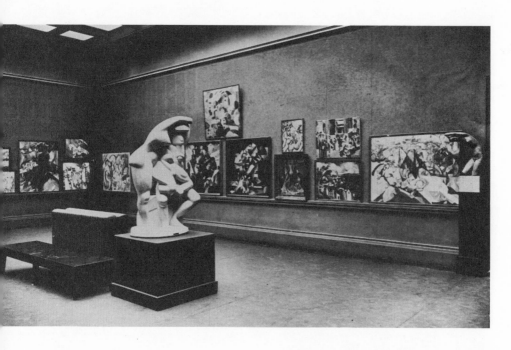

Gallery 53, Cubist room (2 views), Chicago.

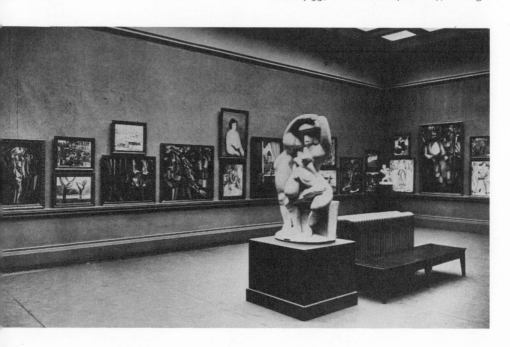

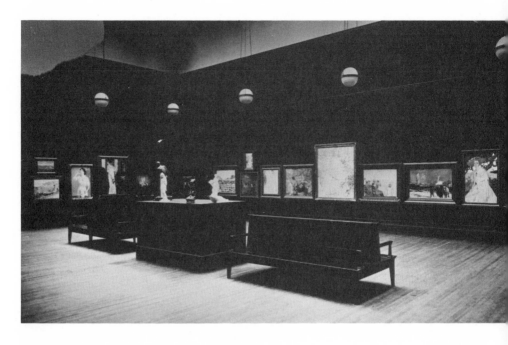

Gallery 54, American room (2 views), Chicago.

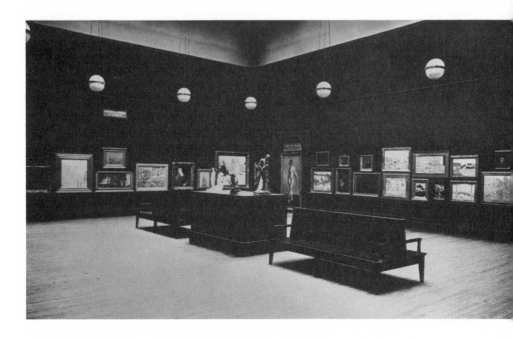

It's a Rube Town!

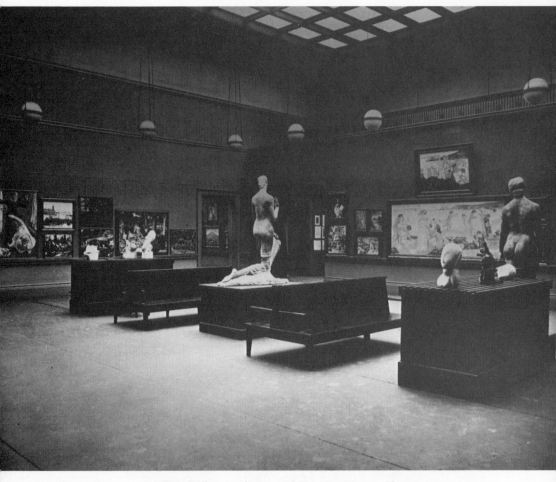

East Gallery, sculpture and French painting, Chicago.

ticultural Society, which incidentally refused to permit any of its flower arrangements to be placed in the Cubist gallery, thereby keeping itself untainted by any subversive, foreign, or decadent tendencies that might be abroad.

The Exhibition was ready for all Chicago to see. The Show opened on Monday, March 24, first with an afternoon reception for members of the Institute and a gala in the evening for the benefit of the Municipal Art League with an admission fee of one dollar, to which all of Chicago society came dressed to the teeth and ready for anything. Kuhn, Pach, and Gregg were joined at the afternoon affair by Robert Chanler and Jo Davidson, who had arrived in Chicago for the opening, and they all did their best to explain modern art to anyone who would listen. The *Inter Ocean* reported next day that "Walt Kuhn . . . bore the brunt of the battle and bore it bravely. But 'bore' isn't just the right word, perhaps, for Mr. Kuhn is an artist and chivalrous gentleman. He might have been bored but he strove hard against giving any outward sign of the fact." The *Examiner* found Chanler similarly occupied as a cicerone. But most of the stories, strangely enough, dealt not with the art, except in a cursory and mocking manner, but mostly with the color and the crowd. Many of the newspapers sent their society reporters along with the newsmen, and their stories were printed side by side, color and gags along with society and fashion notes.

Walt Kuhn has left a record of his impressions in a letter he wrote to MacRae:

Last night was the opening reception, they charged a dollar a head admission to come in and see the "circus" as they call it. We were very delicately informed that our presence was not positively necessary. It was "cleverly" done and we had no come-back, but truthfully speaking we were not sorry. They did root up Pach about 10 P.M. to have him give a lecture. By the way, all the artistic lights in town are lecturing on cubism. Carpenter is all right and we pull fine with him. I see no trouble ahead, and (considering the free days) Chicago ought to run up to 200,000 attendance. Today it is blowing a gale of rain and sleet and the place is comfortably full although it's a pay day. Guess we'll pull out O.K. . . . I shall be *god-damned* glad to get through here and back to N.Y.

And to Davies he wrote: "The Cubist room looks simply great. The room is larger and well lighted. I also think we have a luckier arrangement. . . . There is no doubt in my mind that the only way to show modern art is the 'armory way.' Only now do I realize what a dandy show we had in N.Y."

Although Kuhn was repelled by the provincialism of the city and by the reaction of the press and public and although he felt that the show would have no effect on Chicago art, people came in great numbers. Due partly to free admission days, attendance surpassed that of New York. In the three and a half weeks,

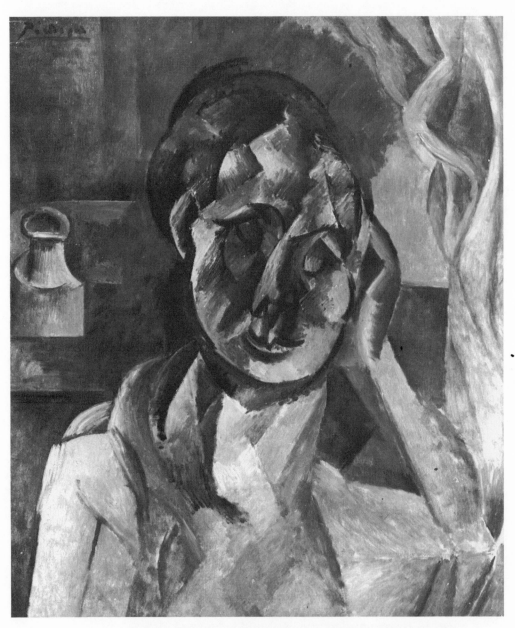

Pablo Picasso (1881–1973). *Woman with Mustard Pot*, 1910.
Oil on canvas, 28¾ × 23⅝ in.
Haags Gemeentemuseum, The Hague,
The Netherlands.

the Show attracted 188,650 visitors and sold almost 12,000 catalogues.

The atmosphere in Chicago was decidedly different from that of New York. The serious intent of the Exhibition was somewhat lost in the "circus" atmosphere heightened by an unexpected epidemic of "morals" rumors and charges. The carnival spirit had been abetted by a press that was intent on highlighting the freakish even before the Show came to Chicago. Every hint of abnormality had already been reported, and a large segment of the public must have come simply to check. The level of news-paper comment, as Kuhn rightly complained, was unusually low. Compared with Herman Landon of the *Record Herald*, Professor Zug, who kept the readers of the *Inter Ocean* moderately ill-informed, was a paragon of accuracy. Landon, in a story an-nouncing the arrival of the Show, obviously without having seen it, described Brancusi's *Mlle. Pogany* as a painting; ascribed Picasso's *Femme au pot de moutarde* (*Woman with Mustard Pot*, page 204) to Kahnweiler, the dealer; confused Picabia with Gino Severini, who was not represented in the Exhibition; and, per-haps because he had an old press release, closed with a long dis-cussion of Futurism, which he must have felt would be helpful to his readers. On the day of the opening, the Chicago *Tribune* pub-lished Eddy's discovery of the nude in Duchamp's *Nu descendant un escalier* (*Nude Descending a Staircase*, color plate 9) with a dia-gram, possibly as a public service.

The morals binge in Chicago was compounded by a sequence of events. Shortly before the arrival of the Show, defenders of public morals had forced the removal from a dealer's window of a reproduction of Paul Chabas' *September Morn*, a typical French academic example of simpering nudity, and a Fraestad barnyard scene from the Art Institute. The situation was ripe for a crusade. "A clergyman," according to Walter Pach, "wrote to the news-papers that he had been obliged to turn back his flock of Sunday school children at the head of the stairs . . . [when] he saw from the door that the rooms were filled with the degeneracies of Paris; he demanded that the public be protected from them as he had protected his children." A high-school teacher announced that the Exhibition was "nasty, lewd, immoral and indecent." When questioned, the superintendent of schools let it be known that he was considering declaring the Show off-limits for school children. A party of women had discovered some lewd scratchings on Archipenko's *Le Repos* and threatened to report it to the police. H. Effa Webster, writing in the Chicago *Examiner* of April 1, built up a full head of outrage:

Our splendid Art Institute is being desecrated. This has been going on for a week. It is likely to continue two weeks more. This blasphemous innovation in our museum is taking place in some of the galleries occupied by the International Exhibition of Modern Art, under the auspices of the Association of American Painters and Sculptors. This pollution is materialized in several paintings of the nude; portrayals that unite in an insult to the great, self-respecting public of Chicago.

Just who is responsible for this showing of dishonor to sensitive great art that finds expression in the chaste and beautiful painting of the human figure in the nude in our Institute?

Paul Gauguin's "The Spirit of Evil" [*Words of the Devil,* color plate 2] is as obscene as it is vile. The nude woman is profanely suggestive, even the face is detestable in its evil leer.

"The body is the temple of God," said Charles Francis Browne to a ladies' group in Evanston, "and the cubists have profaned the temple." Arthur Burrage Farwell, president of the Chicago Law and Order League, warned: "It is a grave mistake to permit these pictures to hang either here or elsewhere. Why, the saloons could not hang these pictures! There is a law prohibiting it. The idea that some people can gaze at this sort of thing without its hurting them is all bosh. This exhibition ought to be suppressed."

Through sheer coincidence the Illinois legislature was in the midst of its annual gesture toward the investigation of vice—specifically, prostitution, one of the perennial problems of wideopen Chicago. M. Blair Coan, investigator for the Senatorial Vice Commission, popularly known as the "white slave commission," wasted no time in announcing that, in response to many complaints, he was instituting a personal and "thorough investigation" of the Exhibition. He later advised the press that, after having visited the Show and inspected the works, he found Futurist art immoral, that every girl in Chicago was gazing at examples of distorted art, and that one of the women in Matisse's *Le Luxe* had four toes.

It turned out, however, that a secret agent, Mrs. Maud J. Coan Josephare, sister of Mr. Coan and a member of the Plastic Club of Philadelphia, was the expert source of the investigator's opinion. Revealing her activity to the press, she said, "I found pictures at the exhibition that are simply lewd and others that are lewd only to artists." Mr. Coan informed reporters that an artist, Jens Haelstrom, had been subpoenaed to appear before the Commission and that its chairman, Senator Woodward, would also make a personal inspection of the Exhibition. The Senator did indeed appear and was taken around by Pach, who later wrote that the Senator was most interested in a soberly symbolic painting of two fully clothed figures by Henry Fitch Taylor called *Prostitution* and the famous Duchamp *Nude*, in neither of which he could find anything salacious. The entire affair was permitted to expire in a legislative debate during which a variety of Senators rehashed the by then standard repertoire of modern art jokes, including the one about an animal being able to paint just as good a picture with its tail. No indication of any action was reported.

Kuhn related some of this madness to Davies: "I wired you that our pamphlet 'Noa-Noa' was withdrawn by the directors on moral grounds. There have been several kicks regarding Gauguin's 'Spirit of Evil,' also Seurat's 'Models,' but I think we would make an issue on those. All in all we have the situation pretty well in hand." And several days later he added another item: "Gregg and I have been after one of the local papers for printing an article which reflected on the personal morals of one of our exhibitors. We called on the city editor and had a real rough-neck time. It's the finest bit of excitement we have had." All of this naturally attracted attention, and according to Pach, many people normally not interested in art came to look for the "dirty pictures." Some who were disappointed that the promised indecencies did not materialize among the modern works found more satisfying examples among the antique casts in the basement.

At the same time interest in the new art on a more intellectual level was satisfied by the controversies which raged around the work of the modernists. Charles Francis Browne, president of the Society of Western Artists, lectured at the Institute to a packed house in Fullerton Hall the day after the opening and castigated the Cubists, characterizing their art as a "toss-up between madness and humbug" and quoting French as saying, "How shall these artists have the admiration of sensible people?" The Chicago *Tribune*'s story on Browne's talk carried an announcement that Eddy would also attack the new art in a lecture the next afternoon, March 27. This appears at first glance as a misprint since Eddy had bought some of the most radical of the works exhibited at the Armory Show. But in a letter to MacRae, Kuhn had written on the day after the opening: "It's very hard to write you now. The entire situation is entirely different from N.Y. So far the best man here is still Aldis, his motives are unselfish. Carpenter has turned out O.K. too, but Eddy has been a source of annoyance. It's a lucky thing that we insisted on our preface and emblem in the catalogue otherwise this Chicago bunch would have claimed all. It was only by strong team work of our trio [Kuhn, Pach, and Gregg] that we prevented all kinds of cheap deals."

And writing to Davies on the following evening he expressed his anger more openly: "Well the show is on—the town is on its ear and very curious, but I fear very much that the show will leave but a scant impression upon the development of Chicago art. This applies to the 'high as well as the low brows.' The very sponsors with the possible exception of Aldis look upon this thing in the usual 'Porky' parvenu manner. Eddy and [Ira N.] Morris are about the worst." But writing to Davies again on Saturday night, March 29, he added: "Since I started to write this note Mr. Eddy has changed his tune. He gave a lecture Friday to about a thousand people in Fullerton Hall, endorsing the Association and asking fair play for the exhibitors. This is the direct result of our asserting our rights to him at last Sunday's seance. This Chicago business looked a bit difficult at first, but we have the situation well in hand." Whatever the reason for the disagreement, Eddy was back in the fold and defending modern art. The attendance at these lectures was so great that Eddy repeated his on April 3, Browne his on April 10, and Gregg gave one on April 8.

Interest was high, and since the Show was not getting a very good press, Gregg and Kuhn decided to issue a little pamphlet containing pieces about the Exhibition, both for and against, so that Chicago viewers could have the kind of background material which had been available to the New York audience but was not being supplied by the Chicago press. Edited by Gregg, it was called *For and Against* and dubbed the "Red Pamphlet" because of the color of its cover. It was an interesting compilation of diverse material among which were the reprint of an article by Gregg from *Harper's Weekly*, "Letting in the Light"; two short pieces by Walter Pach, "Hindsight and Foresight" and "The Cubist Room"; "Cubism by a Cubist," a statement by Picabia; and for the prosecution, Kenyon Cox, "The New Art," reprinted from the *New York Times,* and Frank Jewett Mather, Jr., "Old and New Art," reprinted from the *Nation.* Between the two camps stood an article from the Chicago *Evening Post,* "The Great Confusion," an equitable though not enthusiastic defense of the Exhibition. In their optimism they printed 5,000 copies, but did not do badly in selling 1,668 at 25 cents apiece.

It was reported in the *Record Herald* of April 2 that the artists of the "Cliff Dwellers" club had arranged a burlesque exhibition in its headquarters in Orchestra Hall, but one of the major centers of opposition to the new art and a constant source of annoyance to Kuhn and his fellows was the student body of the Institute's art school and its academically oriented faculty, who egged the youngsters on. Angered by the arrogance and, perhaps even more, by the provincialism of students and teachers, in contrast to the reaction of at least a good many students and artists in New York, Kuhn poured out his feeling of resentment in a letter to Davies:

The art students and public are a lot of rowdy rough-necks. You would get sick at heart if you were here. Gregg and I are not over popular because we refuse to surrender our goats and meet the most vicious attacks with the usual smile. The press here is what I would expect at Paducah, Kentucky. All the instructors at the Institute are mad through, one even went so far as to take a big class of the students into the French room and threw a virtual fit condemning Matisse. We three stood in the hall and laughed at him. However, I had this stopped and after this the lecturing will be done outside the exhibition rooms.

As a climax, the students planned to celebrate the April 16 closing of the Exhibition with a hanging in effigy of Matisse, Brancusi, and Walter Pach. The intended lampoon of the Show did not come off as planned, first, because some of the members of the Chicago Art Students League were not willing to go along with the prank, and also, because Elmer MacRae, in town to help close out the affairs of the Exhibition, lodged a complaint with Carpenter. The news account in the *Examiner* of the following day explained that, in spite of the injunction against hanging any of the Cubist artists in effigy and a police restriction that the ceremonies be confined to the Museum terrace, the students as individuals and not as representatives of the League staged a mock trial of one, Henri Hairmattress, who was accused and convicted of a long list of crimes, then stabbed, pummeled, and dragged about the terrace to the edification of a large crowd on Michigan Avenue. Imitations of Matisse's *Le Luxe* and *La Femme bleue* (*Blue Nude*, color plate 6) were burned and, according to the newspaper, "A sort of May frolic dance followed the ceremonies, and then a cubist song was sung under the direction of the league band." An official of the Institute, unofficially of course, praised the students for their display of sanity.

Just as there were students who would not subscribe to the intent of the horseplay, there were voices in Chicago raised against philistinism and in defense, if not of the new art movements, at least of intellectual tolerance. Under the heading "Fair Play for Insurgent Art," the Chicago *Evening Post* ran a chiding editorial on the eve of the Show's opening:

Chicago ought to give to "the greatest exhibition of insurgent art ever held" a fair hearing and a serious consideration.

The Exhibition of International Art which will have its opening tomorrow at the Art Institute has already impelled many of us to arm ourselves against its novelty with weapons of ridicule. We have heard it attacked in New York as a crazy, revolutionary, impudent circus and we have shown a preliminary disposition to receive it in a spirit of humorous hostility. Some of us have even gone so far as to sound the alarum and summon all the true friends of art to repel boarders.

Now it is more than probable that most of us will bear away from the exhibition something of the contemptuous or vengeful feeling which the critics of the schools hold toward the post-impressionistic impulse. This is no more than the reaction of natural conservatism. Those who are consistent philistines will undoubtedly have "the time of their lives" over the cubist extremists. Others who are conscientious artists will find themselves wrenchingly throwing their verdict to the same side. A few will "get" the message which the strange canvases contain; more, perhaps, will yield to the temptation to pretend to do so, for the sake of being in the current fashion.

But however our verdict may run after we have seen the exhibition, it is but fair that we should approach it with our minds and feelings as unprejudiced as possible. This is all that is asked either by the artists themselves or by Messrs. Arthur B. Davies and Walt Kuhn. . . . We cannot laugh this new post-impressionistic, cubist, spherist, exceptionalist—or whatever else it may be called—movement out of court. It is too deeply and widely grounded in the great art centers of the world. Right or wrong, ugly or beautiful, sincere or impertinent, it has projected an immense influence into modern art. And however incomprehensible its methods may be, it at least embodies a spirit of individualistic revolt that ever wins the respect of men. This spirit American art can least of all afford to reject. We need it keenly right here in the art schools of Chicago.

Harriet Monroe, whose position had been equivocal, now added her voice to the cause of tolerance and understanding in an article for the Chicago *Sunday Tribune* of April 6:

A number of protests against the present international exhibition have been printed in the newspapers or received by the directors of the Art Institute. Some of these object to the show itself, others to the fact that it receives the hospitality of the Institute.

The present critic, being one of those who, after seeing the exhibition in New York, strongly advised its being shown in Chicago, believes these protests to be ill-advised. The exhibition represents certain phases of European art, phases which have been recognized abroad by critics and students and which have enthusiastic admirers among well-known connoisseurs. Under these circumstances, why should we not acquaint ourselves with the facts, learn what is going on?

One might construct a syllogism. Either these pictures are good or they are not. If they are good, they will make their way in spite of objections; if not, they will perish without the aid of objections. Meantime, all of us, conservatives and radicals, Philistines and anarchists, Republicans, Progressives, and middle of the road Populists, have the pleasure and benefit of intellectual exercise. We are discussing, even to the point of excitement, a question which has nothing to do with money, floods, reforms, clothes, or any of the usual trials and occupations of our little corner of the world. We are fighting one of those battles of the intellect—those of us who have any—which are common enough in Paris, but altogether too rare in our provincially shortsighted and self-satisfied community.

It is to be deplored that our discussion is not always quite urbane. One objector, for example, states in print that the exhibition is a "mercenary affair, which has been cunningly devised and shrewdly exploited." If he had taken the trouble to inform himself he would have discovered that no group of men was ever less mercenary than the handful of artists who, a year ago, formed the new Association of American Painters and Sculptors, and decided to give one international modern show as a protest against the tiresomely narrow and exclusive conservatism of the National Academy of Design and other societies which run most of the annuals in this country.

He would find that Arthur B. Davies, the association's president, is not only one of our finest, most idealistic artists, but a man of exalted sincerity and disinterestedness, incapable of any but the most generous motives. He would discover that Mr. Davies has given up almost a year of his valuable time to the gathering of this exhibition, that the foreign part of it represents his choice of works from whatever groups seemed to him vital and significant in modern European art, while the American part represents the choice of a somewhat radical but entirely competent jury. And our inquirer would find also that the request for the transfer of part of the show to Chicago came not from Mr. Davies or his staff but from directors of the Art Institute.

Moreover, these artists and directors are right. American art, under conservative management, is getting too pallid, nerveless, coldly correct, photographic. Better the wildest extravagances of the cubists than the vapid works of certain artists who ridicule them. Better the most remote and mysterious symbolism than a cameralike fidelity to appearances. We are in an anaemic condition which requires strong medicine, and it will do us good to take it without kicks and wry faces.

Also in a profound sense these radical artists are right. They represent the revolt of the imagination against nineteenth century realism, they represent disgust with the camera, outrage over superficial smoothness which covers up weakness of structure. They represent a search for new beauty, impatience with formulae, a reaching out toward the inexpressible, a longing for new versions of truth.

Revolt is rarely sweetly reasonable; it goes usually to extremes, even absurdities. But when revolutionary feeling pervades a whole society or its expression in the arts, when the world seems moved by strange motives and disturbing ideals, then the wise statesman, the true philosopher, is in no haste to condemn his age. On the contrary, he watches in all humility the most extreme manifestation of the new spirit, eager to discover the deeper meaning in them.

Harriet Monroe had made her peace with the future.

If the Chicago Show was a *succès de scandale*, it was not a great financial success. The Institute had driven a hard bargain and there was even some dispute at the end as to the division of the receipts. Elmer MacRae had come to Chicago on the 14th to close out the Show along with Pach and settle financial accounts with Carpenter. The negotiations got a little heated, and after the first session MacRae wired Kuhn: "Had to take firm stand. I am on to his curves. Tried to put it over on me but got left. Expect more trouble tomorrow. Will be delayed." The final settlement left the Association with only $1,585.28 outside the $2,500 guarantee, and it did not include a variety of expenses which had to be paid by the Association. Nor had the sale of pictures been any better.

Chicago collectors apparently preferred to make their art purchases where the women selected their wardrobes, in New York or Paris. Eddy, Aldis, Porter, and Morris had come to see the Armory Show in New York and bought from it then. In Chicago only a limited number of works were sold. Eddy had a minor splurge and bought three more Sousa-Cardozas plus four Vuillard and three Denis lithographs. Manierre Dawson, a young architect friend of Eddy's, bought a Sousa-Cardoza and Duchamp's *Nu*; W. Clyde Jones purchased Kate T. Cory's *Arizona Desert*; Dr. D. D. Vandergrift bought *The Big Wave* by Chester Beach; and George F. Porter reserved a Chanler screen which he had in his home for a while and finally purchased in May. John Quinn bought a Gauguin print for a friend, Miss Coates; and Walter Pach, who was busy trying to sell art, bought a Gauguin print for himself. Also sold in Chicago were a Mayrshofer drawing to Mrs. A. L. Farwell and a Redon lithograph to Harriet Monroe. All told, this was not an impressive showing. Chicago collectors had not been stirred.

Attendance at the Exhibition tapered off in the last days after a record-breaking weekend in which more than 20,000 visitors jammed the Institute on both Saturday and Sunday. With the closing of the Exhibition on the 16th, the second chapter in the

213

story of the Armory Show was ended. Kuhn had left Chicago on April 4 and Gregg on the 8th. Pach and MacRae were left to handle dismantling and shipping for the final stage, Boston. Again, the logistics were carefully planned. Kuhn dispatched lists dividing the collection into three sections, one to go on to Boston, another to go directly to the foreign shipping agent in New York for transportation abroad, and a third to the Association warehouse for distribution in America. By noon on the day after the closing the Show was down. The Institute staff had everything packed in short order; the consignment for New York left on the 20th and that for Boston on the 22nd.

In some ways the Chicago Exhibition was a disappointment to the Association, financially and in terms of artistic impact, but there was no denying the public excitement it had aroused. It had been a publicity success, perhaps for the wrong reasons, but attendance figures of close to 200,000 were some solace for a failure to communicate the message of modern art.

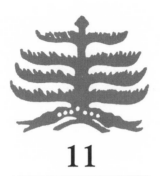

11

We'll Chop It Off with Boston

It is a pity that one must end the story of the Armory Show with Boston, which proved a disappointment and an anticlimax. The Exhibition never did catch on there. The Brahmin mind was not capable as was Chicago philistinism of raucous jeering, but it also was not moved to either intellectual indignation or, as was feared, moral outrage. Boston simply ignored the intellectual and esthetic challenge of the Exhibition and, perhaps because it had arrived under so distinguished an aegis as the Copley Society, had the good manners not to question its decency. However, the Exhibition was far from a total failure; the Show was handsome, attendance was not bad, and the Association made a profit.

The Copley Society, late in January, in a letter from J. F.

Coolidge to Walt Kuhn, had requested the Show which Coolidge, incidentally, referred to as "the exhibition of Futurists." Kuhn answered that the Exhibition had already been scheduled for Chicago but that arrangements could be made to have it go on to Boston and that an agreement could be worked out on a percentage basis. The terms were acceptable to the Society, and Holker Abbot, its president, wrote Kuhn on February 11 that a representative would come to see the Exhibition when it opened in New York and consult with the Association. Thus matters stood until March 13, when a telegram announced, "Four of our committee will meet you at the exhibition Friday." John Osborne Sumner, who had lent a small Cézanne to the Armory Show, was with the delegation and a satisfactory agreement was reached. A contract was immediately drawn and forwarded to Boston, and the tentative dates of April 23 to May 14 were set for the Exhibition.

Late in March a series of communications between the Association's contingent in Chicago and the New York headquarters debated the advisability of using Copley Hall, which was considered too small. Mechanics Hall was suggested by Kuhn, who continued to think in terms of "doing things big." Perhaps others were tired, but not he. In a telegram from Chicago to Davies, he argued: "Copley Hall too small for good showing. Suggest they secure Mechanics Hall and do it rich." However, Mechanics Hall was unavailable. A proposal of the dealers Doll and Richards that the Exhibition be split, with the foreign works in Copley Hall and an American section selected by Macbeth in their galleries, did not meet with approval. On April 1, a joint telegram from Davies, MacRae, Taylor, and Mowbray-Clarke in New York to Kuhn, Pach, and Gregg in Chicago advised that Mechanics Hall was out and that Copley Hall was large enough to handle a good show. It had already been decided to send Taylor to Boston to make final arrangements. Since the Boston opening had been set back to the 28th it was thought advisable to extend the Chicago Exhibition through the weekend to the 19th, giving them nine days to get the Show to Boston. However, the Institute was not interested in extending the Exhibition.

Henry Fitch Taylor, one of the original organizers of the Association, and Clara S. Davidge, in whose gallery it had all begun, were married on March 20, and someone had the delightful idea

216

of sending the newlyweds on a honeymoon to Boston to arrange details. Taylor reported to Kuhn from Boston on April 7 that he thought the entire Chicago Exhibition could be hung in Copley Hall, but the final decision was to send only the foreign contingent. At the same time the Copley Society proposed a revision of the contract to provide for sharing of admission fees rather than a flat-sum payment. This was accepted by the Association with the proviso that the entrance charge be 50 cents with free admission only to members of both organizations. Finally, the Association agreed to reduce the entrance fee to 25 cents on Sundays.

In the introduction to the Boston catalogue, Gregg wrote: "No works by Americans are shown in the Boston Exhibition because of lack of space. The members of the Association preferred to withdraw all of their own paintings and sculptures rather than make a choice, or have themselves represented when other American exhibitors were not. They considered that the most important thing of all was to display the European section of the International Exhibition to the greatest possible advantage."

There were 244 numbered items shown in Boston with a possible total of nearly 300 works of European modern art. The appearance of the Boston Show must have been quite different from the shows in New York and Chicago. It was completely stripped of both the historical and the large American sections. Kuhn commented on it in an enthusiastic letter to Art Young: "The New York show was a great demonstration, but the Boston one excels as an art exhibition; it is a wonder." And to William F. Tuttle, the assistant secretary of the Art Institute, he wrote that the Boston exhibition was an even greater success than the New York or Chicago version. This was not literally true and was perhaps intended to needle the Chicago crowd, especially since Kuhn seems not to have got to Boston to see it. The cumulative impact of the avant-garde art was, unfortunately, wasted on the Athens of America.

A total of 12,676 paid admissions for Boston was far from spectacular, but considering the size of the city, and the admission fee, certainly not disastrous. In fact, on May 2, Kuhn had occasion to write Gregg in Boston, "Hurrah for the attendance." An unseasonal heat wave which had settled over the Eastern seaboard was blamed for some of the slackness in attendance, but Kuhn, ever the cheerleader, urged Gregg to "Whoop her up so that we will have a good hot finish."

Sales also fell far below expectations. Although Pach, writing many years later, stated that fifty works were sold in Chicago and Boston, the records show that only half that number were, and only five in Boston. In spite of Kuhn's admonition to Gregg to "keep after the sales-booth people," the buyers did not materialize. As has already been mentioned, Walter Arensberg came back several times and bought the last of the Villon Puteaux studies and two lithographs, and Thomas W. Bowers acquired a Mayrshofer drawing and a Vuillard lithograph. This meager list constituted the total of sales in Boston, and both buyers were from Cambridge.

Boston was difficult to whip into any semblance of enthusiasm. As Pach recalls, the museum crowd was even afraid to be seen visiting the Show. Kuhn's optimistic belief that a new shipment of Augustus Johns would make a stir was unfounded. Even the Laurvik incident, which would have meant headlines in Chicago, hardly ruffled the surface. J. Nilsen Laurvik had written a small pamphlet called *Is It Art?*, which he hired some newsboys to hawk outside the hall. Gregg got the police to stop them and that was the end of it. There was nothing to halt the ebbing tide. Declining curiosity in the Show after three months of newspaper coverage and the waning interest of Association members themselves all indicated the approaching end. Kuhn's zeal could do nothing to counteract the obvious inertia which was beginning to stall the caravan. And in the end even he was willing to bow to the inevitable. There were many requests for the Exhibition, in whole or in part, from St. Louis, Milwaukee, Kansas City, Baltimore, Washington, and even Toronto, but the decision was made not to dissipate the impact of the Exhibition by dribbles. As Kuhn announced in a letter to Gregg: "Nothing doing! We'll chop it off with Boston." And so they did. The Show ended rather too quietly considering the excitement at its birth.

The dénouement of the Boston Show left a bitter aftertaste. A dispute over the division of receipts arose between the two societies, based on a difference in interpretation of the contract terms. The wrangling went on for more than a year until it

218

was settled by arbitration in July, 1914, with the payment of $4,230.47, which was actually better than the Association had done in Chicago, if one excepts the commissions from sales.

There were still many things to do and many days to pass before the physical entity of the Armory Show ceased to exist. But one approaches the telling of that story with reluctance. Only the storyteller can say, "And so he died" or "They lived happily ever after," and draw the curtain on time. In reality even heroes die of hardening of the arteries and beautiful damsels may have to spend their last years surrounded by dozens of uninterested grandchildren. These are all details of little pertinence to the story. It might matter that the Association had trouble with Delaunay and his rolled-up canvas, the *Ville de Paris*, since it was part of the life of the Exhibition, but how unimportant it is that there was in the dispersal of the exhibits a long hassle over damages to the painting which took months to settle. If the truth forces us to tidy the scene, let us at least hurriedly sweep most of the debris under the carpet.

The Boston Show had to be taken down and the works sent to New York for shipment back to Europe, where they again had to be distributed to their owners. Settlements had to be made with dealers and artists; insurance claims and Customs duties paid; even the gas, electricity, and telephone had to be shut off. The mechanics of this total operation went on until August, 1916, when the final account with the U.S. Customs Office was closed. By that time Europe was at war and the Armory Show was a vague memory slowly sinking into the past until the time would arrive for it to be recalled as a legend.

The Armory Show had been a large operation and closing out its accounts was a long and tedious job. Some members of the Association, certainly Davies, Kuhn, and MacRae, had given a year or more of their lives almost exclusively to it and were anxious to get back to their art. As Kuhn had written to Pach long ago, "I'd rather stay home and work at my pictures, shoving in some of the things I have learned." But there were so many things that still had to be done, which they, in the name of the Association, were liable for, legally as well as morally. Although Davies carried most of the responsibility, his closest co-workers remained loyal.

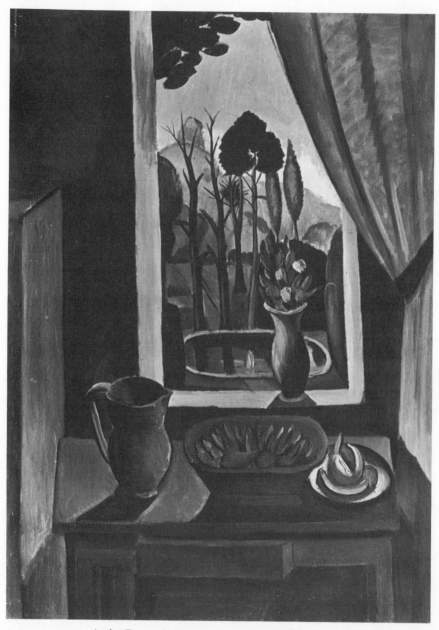

André Derain (1880–1954). *Window at Vers*, 1912.
Oil on canvas, 51½ × 35¼ in. Collection,
The Museum of Modern Art, New York; Abby Aldrich Rockefeller Fund,
purchased in memory of Mrs. Cornelius J. Sullivan.

Works of art dispatched to their original senders strayed and had to be searched for; others had been damaged, especially the plaster sculptures; frames were chipped and paintings scratched; and claims had to be filed and fought. The warehouse was closed at the end of April and the office vacated on July 1. The office furniture was sold and the accumulation of catalogues, pamphlets, and post cards had to be disposed of. Efforts were made to sell these to booksellers and department stores but without success. It must have been something of a wrench to have to sell them for waste. Some 12,000 catalogues and 60,000 post cards were first offered on consignment to George E. Newcombe and Co., but there are no records of any receipts from the sale of copies, and the catalogues were finally sold as waste paper for $7.80. Perhaps this amount also covered the post cards, for no other accounting is given. Approximately 19,000 pamphlets also were consigned to G. P. Putman's Sons, but here again no indication of what happened to them exists. At least no money was ever paid to the Association for them.

Payment was made to all the artists and dealers whose works had been sold; and although there were occasional difficulties, all accounts were finally settled. Of the dealers, Vollard, mostly through the sale of Cézanne's *Colline des pauvres*, received the largest amount, $6,441.27; Druet, $2,314.25; Artz & de Bois, $1,894.20; Kahnweiler, $1,314.64; Kapferer, $967.98; Uhde, $821.88; Goltz, $290.40; and Thannhauser, $55.45. These constituted the total of sales less commissions, expenses, and Customs duty charges. They were not figures to enthuse the European dealer about prospects of a new and lucrative American market. A letter from Stephan Bourgeois, written on June 10 from Paris to Walter Pach, presents a picture of the American art market as it appeared to a European dealer who had lent to the Exhibition and been here during it:

Thank you very much for your kind letter and the return of my Cézanne and the two Van Goghs. I am happy to learn that your efforts in introducing modern art to the United States have been crowned with success.

Only, what astonishes me is that the great French impressionist masters have not received the attention which is due them. Finally, I believe that it is only a question of time before they will achieve it; it will come some day as it did in Germany, which has for several years been buying everything that is best in France. Unfortunately, Americans will begin to form interesting collections of modern art when the prices will have become exorbitant, a situation which in my opinion is not far off; while today a collector of limited means can still manage to assemble a collection of the first quality.

I tell you frankly that I was basically very disappointed by the lack of public interest in Cézanne and Van Gogh who are like giants among all the other painters represented at your exhibition; but the good will always be good and what is not understood today, will be tomorrow.

If our effort, yours in that magnificent exhibition and mine in business, has not found its merited reward, we are convinced that our opinion will prevail someday and because of that I try always to add continually to my small collection. I just again recently bought a magnificent landscape by Van Gogh, a vegetable garden in all its morning freshness, and I hope I will soon have the pleasure of showing it to you here in Paris as well as all the other things I have had the luck to find. [Translated by the author.]

American collectors were obviously not ready for avant-garde contemporary art and it was not until well after the First World War that they began to buy in this field. The John Quinn Sale in 1927 indicated that Paris was still held to be a better market than New York.

12

Not
an Institution
but
an Association

The Association of American Painters and Sculptors, like the salmon or the butterfly which lives only to give birth, brought forth the Armory Show and expired. It is almost as if the very process of creation had consumed all its energies. The Association had not been intended as a one-shot or temporary organization. The care with which the constitution was drafted indicated a concern with permanence. When Davies announced in an official statement that it was "not an institution but an association," he was attacking the academic idea of self-perpetuation with all its concomitant baggage of hierarchy, honors, and exclusions. These men wanted no part of the artistic establishment. They saw themselves as a voluntary association of like-minded artists joined for the purpose of exhibition, which did not preclude an interest in continuity. It was simply that circumstances would not have it so.

In retrospect the demise of the Association may seem a distinct loss to American art, but the day of the artistic institution in its academic form was past, and while destroying the power of the Academy, the Association was itself doomed. This situation had developed earlier in France, but it had finally come here as well, and from then on no artists' organization has had any importance in American art. For good or ill, the centers of power have moved elsewhere. One would have preferred, perhaps, that the death of the Association had been more dramatic or graceful, but in looking back one can see that it was inevitable.

The success of the Armory Show had given everyone the feeling that an important new institution had been born. But even before the first flush of victory had paled there were already misgivings among some members of the Association. Discord within the society can be traced to two sources, one personal, the other artistic, although they were both intricately related. Baldly stated, if one were against Davies—and he was the pivotal figure—it was because of personal *and* artistic reasons.

In the first place, there was an antagonism between those who, with Davies, were in control of the organization and those who were outside the group. This was intensified by the fact that the out crowd, looking to Henri for guidance, was substantially the old Ash Can School or the New York Realist group, who up to then had been the leaders of the Independent movement: Henri, Luks, Sloan, Bellows, and Myers. Since they had been cut out of most of the important activity in arranging the Exhibition, it is not strange that they should have begun to look at the Davies group as a clique. The additional fact that Davies ran the Show out of his hat did not help matters. The very nature of the constitution gave him the power (as long as he had the board of directors on his side, which he did to the very end) to make decisions and have them carried out. The only thing that could have stopped such high-handed procedure would have been a failure of financial resources, in which case he would have had to have gone to the membership for help and they might have questioned his policies. But as long as he could pay for his commitments, he had a practically free hand and very loyal support from Kuhn, MacRae, Taylor, and Mowbray-Clarke.

Although the attack against this "clique" was made on the basis of its dictatorial actions, the truth is that a more fundamental disagreement on artistic matters was accentuated by the Armory Show. The Ash Can School had been fortuitously and temporarily joined with Davies, Prendergast, and Lawson in the exhibition of The Eight. It was never a marriage, only a liaison of convenience which today appears incongruous. Although in no sense chauvinistic, the Realists were interested in American art and not simply in the American artist. Davies and his group, on the other hand, were primarily concerned with art aside from its relevance to American life. The Realists saw themselves as expressing American life; the others saw themselves as expressing fundamental artistic impulses, whatever they might be. They all had a common ground since American artists had particular difficulties in exhibiting; and in the broad prospectus of the organization there at first appeared no antagonism. It is clear that the Realists envisaged the Armory Show as an exhibition of American art which would stir the country to a recognition of its artistic resources; Davies wanted to shake American complacency by demonstrating its retardation and insularity.

Word of what Davies and Kuhn had found abroad produced the first twinges of uneasiness. Myers recalls Dabo's saying at that time: "This man Davies has started something. I'm afraid it may be more of a calamity than a blessing, though it's a damn good show." And he also remembers Davies' telling him, "Myers, you will weep when you see what we've brought over." Myers' reaction must have been typical of many of the members. "And when I did see the pictures for the first time," he writes, "my mind was more troubled than my eyes, for Davies had unlocked the door to foreign art and thrown the key away. Our land of opportunity was thrown wide open to foreign art, unrestricted and triumphant; more than ever before, our great country had become an art colony; more than ever before we had become provincials."

Henri was badly shaken by these newest revelations. To have lived a life and built an image as a leader of the progressive forces in American art, as the jouster against reaction and the defender of the new, and then to discover that a revolution much more

225

profound had been going on without his knowledge, was a shattering experience. The shock to the others of the Realist group must have been just as profound. Luks never thought much, but Sloan and Bellows showed the effects even if somewhat delayed. At any rate, we can observe Bellows' confusion and his attempt to understand even at a time when he was participating in the high jinks of the Architectural League. His comment to the reporter of the *Sun* who did a wrap-up on the closing of the Show is revealing: "In my humble 'American' opinion the Cubists are merely laying bare a principle of construction which is contained within the great works of art which have gone before. By isolating 'measure,' both of form and color, and by realizing the intimacy between music, as 'measured sound,' and color and form, as 'measured sight,' they have arrived on the borderland of possible technical discoveries which may or may not be new and which may nor may not be valuable."

As the French modernists continued to capture the lion's share of publicity and sales, even though the critics defended the Americans against the intruders, the bewilderment among these men increased. For them the great success was a hollow victory. All the cheering was for a job well done, for attendance and sales, but they were not misled; they understood that the real victor was modernism. Perhaps they were not consciously aware of the new generation waiting in the wings to supplant them as the new revolutionary force in American art—Marin, Weber, Maurer, Hartley, and others. They were still faced with that older generation led by Davies which was using the Armory Show to subvert American art. The excursion of the Exhibition to Chicago and Boston, with which they had nothing to do and in which American art was successively reduced until it disappeared, alienated them completely and finally from the Association.

With the dismantling and dispersal of the Exhibition continuing into the summer, Davies and Company were so immersed in detail that they gave no thought to the organization as such. The summer months also saw the usual exodus of artists from the city. Kuhn was vacationing with Quinn in the North Woods country at Tupper Lake, and MacRae was at Cos Cob, back at his pastels. Davies remained in New York, working and handling whatever details turned up and, as he wrote to MacRae, seeing an occasional baseball game. In that same letter he added, "As soon as Kuhn gets back we must go over all outstanding unfinished business."

But it was not until November 12 that a directors' meeting was held. Davies congratulated the society for the success of the Armory Show. MacRae submitted a treasurer's report, explaining that only the Boston account was still open; but since it was still incomplete, he asked that it be put over until the next regular annual membership meeting. It was then voted, in view of the great energy that had gone into the Armory Show and the lateness of the date, that no annual show be given during the coming season. Kuhn, Taylor, and Myers were appointed to revise the by-laws of the Association. It was decided to hold a membership meeting and elections in January, 1914. Davies closed the meeting by congratulating the society on the successful completion of the fight for duty-free art; he cited Quinn for his devotion to this project which he had carried through on his own, filing the briefs and assuming all the expenses during an eight-month campaign.

Although from a legal point of view there was nothing irregular in not calling a membership meeting at that time, it would seem that the same report of success could have been made to the membership as a whole. There may have been some feeling on the part of Davies and his group that the presentation of an incomplete financial report would have opened too many avenues for questioning and that only a final financial statement of unqualified success would silence objections or induce some of the members to forget that the original intention of the Exhibition had been subverted. Myers was the only member of the opposition on the governing board and he may have raised some objections, but there are no minutes of the meeting and the official letter reporting it, which went out to the membership, makes no mention of debate on any of the items.

The membership meeting scheduled for January was never held. By this time Davies had probably already lost interest in the Association as an organization. Unlike Henri (by nature a joiner, who had been a member of the Society of American Artists, had become a member of the National Academy of Design when the Society amalgamated with it, and had never resigned from the Academy even in the heat of his disputes with its policies), Davies was not interested in institutions. The job he had wanted done had been accomplished and he was ready to move on. On April 15, in answer to Myers' proddings about a membership meeting, he expressed his feelings: "Your note was received yesterday afternoon. I have forwarded it to Kuhn with a request from me to arrange for a meeting of the Association of Painters and Sculptors at once. It is important to hold a meeting of the members and your request is the first received as I have wished all along for a meeting and relief from any future business of the Association." In response to Davies' suggestion, Kuhn wrote to Myers on April 23: "What do you say to having a directors' meeting some day next week? I wonder if we can impose on you to the extent of using your studio for the purpose. We can then arrange for a general meeting, which we ought to have before the end of the month. How about Wednesday afternoon? Write me as soon as you can."

On April 29 a directors' meeting was held at Davies' studio, 337 East 57th Street. The succinct minutes of that meeting record that all members were present, the minutes of the last meeting were read and accepted, and the postponed membership meeting was scheduled for May 18.

This meeting, held at the Hotel Manhattan, marked the effective end of the Association. Although the organization continued beyond that date for two years, it existed on paper only to clear up the last lingering details of the Armory Show. Twenty-four men were recorded as present, but six were there only by proxy—Porter and Prendergast to Davies, Anderson to Mowbray-Clarke, Davidson to Kuhn, Tucker to MacRae, and Lawson to Glackens. All six proxies were, therefore, in the hands of the Davies group, since Glackens had consistently been siding with Davies against his former colleagues of the Realist group. The only one of the members to leave an account of the historic encounter was Jerome Myers in *Artist in Manhattan*. The following is the statement in question in its entirety:

After this great success [the Armory Show] it was natural that they [the members of the Association] should have some curiosity about the financial results; and accordingly, by their constituted authority, they called a meeting, to hear the secretary's report. What ensued at that

228

session, held at the Manhattan Hotel, threw a characteristic light on the differences between the artist and the business man while facing the firing line. When the report was duly laid on the table, a silent drama took place. Guy du Bois was the first to look at it. Shrugging his shoulders, he said simply, "I resign." Robert Henri followed, with the same procedure and conclusion; then likewise George Bellows, Mahonri Young and several others, including myself. It was rather a marvelous demonstration of the fact that artists are not especially business-like in the acceptance of an unsatisfactory situation. Dignity rode high, as one by one the members left in silence.

Written many years after the fact, the statement includes, naturally enough, some vagueness, some error, and perhaps a desire to forget the incident.

Both Kuhn and du Bois, who committed their memories to print, seem to have wanted to forget the meeting and make no mention of it. Nor are there any minutes of this meeting among the Kuhn Papers, but there is a series of proxies, ballots, and tally sheets which indicates the transaction of other business besides a consideration of the "secretary's report" or, perhaps, a treasurer's report on which MacRae had been working. It would appear then that elections were held before the report was presented, since all the members voted. The tally sheets are countersigned by Nankivell and Kramer, who acted as tellers. The vote was a clear-cut victory for Davies, who did not run for office but remained as a director. He received 23 votes; Myers, 22; Taylor, 15; Kuhn, MacRae, and Prendergast, 13; and Mowbray-Clarke, 12. This slate was, except for the addition of Prendergast, the old board of directors. Henri and du Bois, with 10 each, polled the highest vote among the dissident group, except of course, for Myers, who still remained a member of the board. Actually, the vote for Myers was a courtesy gesture; when officers of the Association were voted on, his candidacy for president and vice-president was effectively blocked. Prendergast was elected president with 13 votes as against Myers with 11, and Mowbray-Clarke was elected vice-president with 10 votes as against 7 for Taylor and 5 for Myers. Taylor was elected secretary with 19 votes, and MacRae, a glutton for punishment, treasurer again with 18. The Henri group had obviously made an effort, but had failed to unseat the incumbents.

It is possibly at this point, with the show of power complete, that the report was made. It was certainly prefaced by a description of the success of the Exhibition, but the financial report, still incomplete because the Boston matter had not been settled, was the excuse for the resignation of the opposition. At that particular point in Association affairs the books show an income of approximately $87,000 and expenditures of $84,000, although here again, considering the nature of the financial records, I would not like to take an accountant's oath on the exactness of these figures. Two facts should be noted: the report was incomplete and the figures indicated a profit, though not a very large profit; as a matter of fact, it was rather disappointing, considering the volume of business. Although there was eventually a good deal of acrimony on both sides, I doubt that anyone seriously questioned anyone else's honesty. Any examination of the books, and I have spent endless hours with them, mostly because I don't know anything about bookkeeping, would show that, although the members of the Association also knew very little about bookkeeping, they were scrupulously honest and had nothing to hide.

What set off the revolt was the realization that after so much effort, and what to some was a betrayal of the Association's intentions, the cupboard was still so bare. My guess is that if they had turned up with a substantial nest egg insuring the continuation and success of the society, things might have been different; but as things stood, the inevitable act was one of resignation, not in the philosophic but in the legal sense. And resign they did, as Myers reports with some inaccuracy. Before they left each wrote out his resignation, all of which are in the files, and Mahonri Young was not among them. Seven men resigned at that time: Henri, Luks, Sloan, Bellows, du Bois, Lie, and Dabo. Myers apparently resigned after they left; his resignation was tabled and then accepted. Sherry Fry had sent in his resignation in answer to the invitation to the meeting, with the reminder that he had resigned a year before. In all, then, eight men walked out on the Association that night. Whatever face might be put on it, the victors had lost.

Hard feelings erupted in charges and countercharges, and the Association was in the news again shortly and for the last time.

The next day du Bois wrote Myers a note, which incidentally indicates that the latter had not resigned with the others:

Very glad to hear that you resigned—considering the way things went. There is less room or reason for catholicism in the society than ever. They have everything their way. As a director you could still be a minority of one. You saw how much they were for you when it came to the election of officers. I, for one, am mighty glad to be out of the mess with clean hands and a clear record. There will be something about the meeting in the Globe this afternoon. I hope Hoeber got the news of your resignation. I got it too late to give it to him. But it is very possible that he read the press this morning.

I am surprised that Young did not resign with us. Also, I imagine that there was some talk among those who remained in the "art room" after we left it. I will try to see you this week. Kramer, I must confess, in his wild desire to remain, no matter the condition, in any organization that might perchance give him an opportunity to exhibit, disgusted me. Brinley's proxy voting for directors was another asinine and ugly bit of business.

But, as a matter of fact, I don't believe that I have had so much fun, so amusing an afternoon in a long time. It was a great sight to see the guilty gloom on the faces of the victors.

The same bitterness was expressed on the other side by Davies, who wrote MacRae a short note on the evening of the very same day: "Yours just rec'd. I tell you sleep *was sweet* last night—the dread of possible treachery had fled. How we did torment Myers, with his guilt running all down his face! his show of manhood [illegible word]."

The account of the dispute in the *American Art News* explained the resignations as a dissatisfaction with the absence of financial reports. It stated that there had been an approximate return of $82,000 from the Exhibition and a balance of $5,000, but that there was no detailed statement of accounts. The resigners charged that the directors had become a self-perpetuating body through their control of proxies. According to this story the split was triggered by the question of Fry's resignation. McCormick's story in the *Press* outlined three reasons for the resignations: 1) The dissidents believed in complete freedom from the jury system, 2) the artistic principles they professed would not be carried out by the society, and 3) the treasurer's report was not ready after eighteen months. There was also some talk of forming a new society on the lines of the MacDowell Club.

Davies was goaded to fury and his answer, published in the press, was less than just and lost the majority a good deal of sympathy. His countercharge was that those who had resigned were motivated by the fear that a change in taste might lead to a loss of popularity and that they were interested primarily in their private merchandise. He accused them of having been the least active in the Association and of having profited as much as anyone from publicity and sales. They had been in disagreement with the aims of the Association from its very beginning and their defection now was no great loss. On the other hand, the present administration had acted in a most conciliatory manner in order to maintain the organization, but the minority had fought to gain control and on failing had resigned. He added also that the Henri group was hostile to the fight for duty-free art because they were more interested in maintaining the trade value of their own products than in the education of the public. Overstated and harsh though this statement was, it clearly revealed the underlying antagonisms.

232

And du Bois' answer in the *Tribune* was not so much a refutation as a reiteration and expansion of the original sources of disagreement. He now charged that there had been irregularities in the financial accounts and intimated that the proxies had been used illegally. He countered the insinuation that the Realists were only interested in sales by observing that the members of the majority had become Post-Impressionists overnight because it was the new fashion. His final complaint illumined the underlying discord. Davies, in selecting the artists to be included in the Montross Gallery exhibition of February, 1914, according to du Bois, had implied that they were the pick of American artists from the Armory Show. Whatever the validity of this accusation, Davies had chosen the men with whom he now identified, and none of the Realists were included; in the list were Davies, Glackens, Kuhn, MacRae, Tucker, Taylor, Pach, Schamberg, Sheeler, Howard Coluzzi, Joseph Stella, George F. Of, and Manierre Dawson. The difference between the two factions was a very real and irreconcilable one, a difference in conception of art and its future in America.

It was not long before the victors had second thoughts on the subject and realized that the Association was through as an effective organization, as their decision to rescind the dues recently collected would indicate. From then on the Association existed only for the purpose of settling the final insurance and Customs claims.

During the next two years, there were occasional meetings about which no information is available except as noted in the financial ledger. Meetings were held on November 2, 1914, at which the long-awaited financial report was given; January 29 and March 1, 1915, for which luncheon bills are listed; October 25, 1915, directors' meeting; November 1, 1915, at which officers were elected, although no records exist; November 29, 1915; and the last recorded meeting, a directors' luncheon on February 9, 1916.

The last entry in the Association records is dated August 23, 1916, and covers the payment of $2,894.35 to the U.S. Customs Office, liquidating the last of the outstanding accounts. With that, the Association, which had quietly dropped out of sight, ceased to exist. The final accounting shows a credit of $93,025.59 and a debit of $93,086.19, and one can assume that the deficit of $60.60 was somehow covered by Arthur B. Davies. According to Kuhn, as noted in closing his *Story of the Armory Show:*

> It took an entire year to close up the affairs of the exhibition, with many disagreeable chores of a minor sort. There were no debts left to embarrass any of us. If anybody was embarrassed, it could only have been Arthur B. Davies and he certainly did not show it. After squaring everything, the bulk of the money left was turned over to him and by him possibly to friends who had supplied it to him in the beginning. All had worked hard, but not one member of the Association accepted a penny as remuneration for his services. Nothing remained now, but to see what effect our great adventure would have on these United States.

233

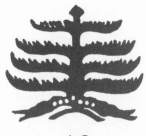

13

The Effect of the Great Adventure

The Armory Show was a major event in American art history, perhaps the single most important one, if importance can be weighed at all. In its favor as candidate for this honor is the fact that it was a pivotal affair around which other occurrences cluster. It was both a culmination and a beginning, an effect as well as a cause; it cannot be understood as an isolated phenomenon, an accident, or a fluke. The Armory Show was the outgrowth of years of experiment, experience, and development among American artists and it served as a stimulus to a new sequence of events. And just because it stands in such direct and structured relation to both the past and the present, it has rightfully achieved the status of a symbolic moment in our artistic history.

Revolutions in art are made by artists through creative activity, but since such developments mean nothing until they are exhibited, we think of change in terms of the spectacular displays which bring them to public view, like the Salon des Refusés of 1863, which introduced the era of Impressionism, and the Salon d'Automne of 1905, which established the Fauves. The process of history is neither as neat nor as obligingly climactic as we expect it to be, but historians are not above forcing facts into logical patterns which are easy to remember. It is quite natural, then, to think of the Armory Show as the turning point in American art of the twentieth century. And if one recognizes the built-in simplification of such a statement, it is not untrue.

It has already been pointed out that there were many important developments which preceded and prepared the arena for the entry of the Armory Show. To recapitulate, there were two major sources from which it emerged: the Independent movement led by Henri and the Realists, and the modernist movement fostered by Stieglitz at "291," movements which were mutually antagonistic but temporarily reconcilable. They united in an attack on the status quo of American art, its institutions, standards, and restrictions, although with varying intentions and in different degrees. It was this community of interest which made it possible for The Eight to form, for the Independent Exhibition of 1910 to be held, and for the Association of American Painters and Sculptors to be organized and to arrange the Armory Show. The difference between them was not as apparent then as it seems today or perhaps the difference was not as intense as it later became as a result of the Show.

If we forget those artists in the Association who had little artistic or historical importance, we are left with two constellations: the Realists—Henri, Sloan, Luks, Bellows, and Myers—and a more radical group: Davies, Prendergast, Glackens, Lawson, and Kuhn. The latter was not, however, the avant-garde of American art at the time; that was the Stieglitz coterie—Weber, Marin, Maurer, Hartley, and Walkowitz. In a sense it was exactly the middle position of the Davies faction which made the transition from the old to the new possible. It is only this group which could have put on an exhibition motivated in part by the reformism of the Realists and leading to the revolution of the modern-

235

ists, with the Armory Show serving as the act of transition itself. You may invent your own metaphorical image to describe the phenomenon—caterpillar transformed into butterfly, a weight added to a balanced scale, a machine transforming something into something else—but in any case the American art world after the Armory Show was not the same as that which preceded it.

The effect the Armory Show had on the men who arranged it was varied. The one among them who could be identified in any way with the new movements was Prendergast, the only authentic "Post-Impressionist" of that generation of American artists. Davies was part of an international Symbolist movement related to Art Nouveau, with similarities to Puvis de Chavannes, Ferdinand Hodler, and Hans van Marées. This may have been considered advanced in American circles, but it was by this time fairly old hat. Lawson was an Impressionist and remained one, Glackens had moved out of the Realist orbit and established an allegiance to Renoir, and Kuhn was still unformed and susceptible to influences from many sources. The Realists were committed to a clearly defined esthetic that could not encompass the new vision of the Post-Impressionists and their progeny.

The Armory Show's impression on all of these men was understandably limited. Prendergast was untouched; he continued to paint as he had before. The Armory Show revealed that he was a major figure in American art, the greatest of his generation. On the other hand, the Armory Show had a profound effect on the man who had been most influential in its formation. Davies made a supreme effort to catch up with history, and although his experiments with Cubism were far from successful, his last landscapes before his death show a new mastery and a personal synthesis based on that experience. Lawson exhibited in his post-Armory landscapes a strong Cézanne influence, and Glackens became more firmly tied to Renoir. For Kuhn it was the beginning of a period of experimentation with both Fauvism and Cubism before he settled down into his own personal idiom. Of the Realists, Bellows was led by the challenge of Cubism to investigate pseudo-scientific alternatives which proved a hindrance rather than a help, and Sloan after many years accepted his own version of the new esthetic as the basis for a radical transformation of his vision. The rest, by and large, turned their backs on modernism and continued unchanged.

To a whole group of artists, the Armory Show was a vindication and a springboard. Those who had exhibited at "291" were aware of modern art. They did not need the Armory Show to reveal the truth to them. After all, what had been a traumatic shock to Henri, Myers, Dabo, and the others was their conviction. One cannot attribute to the Armory Show any strong influence on artists like Weber, Marin, Maurer, Hartley, Halpert, Walkowitz, or Oscar Bluemner, who had discovered the new art while studying abroad or at "291." Then there were the younger men, still unknown, who had had some contact with modernism: Arthur G. Dove, Arthur B. Carles, Joseph Stella, Morton L. Schamberg, and Charles Sheeler. Still others, like Patrick Henry Bruce and the Synchromists Morgan Russell and Stanton Mac-Donald-Wright, were involved with modernism abroad without connection with art in America. To all of these the Armory Show was a substantiation. For the first time the art which they professed and the sources from which it developed were presented in a major exhibition. They became part of the American art scene, and it would not be long before they dominated it.

For a whole generation of artists the Armory Show was the introduction to modern art. Cézanne, Van Gogh, Gauguin, Fauvism, and Cubism struck them all at once, as they did the public; but whereas the public saw the new art as an aberration, it was a relevation to artists. Standards of art that had been long accepted were undermined. Younger artists who had exhibited at the Show, like Stuart Davis, Glenn O. Coleman, and Andrew Dasburg, and others, like Schamberg and Sheeler, who had already taken tentative steps toward modernism, turned their backs on the past and began daring experiments.

The understanding which American artists had of the revolutionary movements was not always clear nor were their own developments consistent, but the basic framework as well as the direction of American art had been altered. It is possible this change would have been more profound and thoroughgoing had not the outbreak of war in Europe and our own subsequent involvement temporarily cut the new artistic tie between America and Europe. The period immediately following the Armory Show saw a general and intensive experimentation in the new

237

forms. Some American artists like Davis, Dove, and Georgia O'Keeffe became involved for the first time with abstract art, but most of them eventually worked their way back toward "reality." For the Americans these new movements were still borrowings, influences that came from the outside and were not part of a normal historical evolution, and as influences they were absorbed. It is interesting that only Bruce and Russell, who remained in France, retained an undeviating commitment to abstract art.

The Armory Show also had its effect upon the art world as well as the artist. The rigid structure of the American art market was shaken. In a very short time a new group of galleries emerged to exhibit European as well as American modern art. Whereas previously it had been extremely difficult for American artists of progressive tendencies to get a hearing, it now became fairly easy. Only Macbeth had earlier had the courage to exhibit The Eight; but in February, 1914, N. E. Montross opened his doors to the moderns and permitted Davies to arrange a series of exhibitions of the more radical Americans, including quite a few unknowns. In December, 1913, the Daniel Gallery, which was to remain for more than fifteen years a haven for the American avant-garde, opened under the unlikely direction of Charles Daniel, a former bartender, and his assistant, Alanson Hartpence.

Macbeth, Daniel, Montross, Folsom, and, of course, "291" were the nucleus of galleries now exhibiting the new art in varying degrees of radicalism, but before long others joined this group in the presentation of both domestic and foreign modernists. The Bourgeois Gallery, for which Walter Pach arranged exhibitions of modern art, made its debut in February, 1914. Within a year after the Armory Show, the *American Art News* was complaining that there were current at that time "six exhibitions devoted to the 'Faddists' . . . in which the artists represented run the gamut from the Botticellian caricaturist Davies, to the eccentric interpreters of dreams and emotions, Marsden Hartley and Joseph Stella. And the procession goes on." The Carroll Gallery, angeled by John Quinn, entered the lists and in March, 1914, exhibited the works of the young American originators of Synchromism: Morgan Russell, who had sold a picture (though not a synchromy) from the Armory Show, and Stanton Mac-Donald-Wright. And in October, 1915, the Modern Gallery, backed by Walter Arensberg and run by Marius de Zayas, caricaturist and critic, opened with an exhibition of Picasso, Picabia, and Braque. The moderns also found easier acceptance in noncommercial galleries like the National Arts Club, which presented a large exhibition by radical Americans in February, 1914, and smaller club galleries, including the Gamut Club, the Liberal Club, the Cosmopolitan Club, and the Thumb Box Gallery.

For some American collectors, the consequences of the Armory Show were direct and immediate. I have already described the relationship to the Show of Quinn, Bliss, Barnes, Eddy, Arensberg, Dreier, Gallatin, and Root. All of them bought from it. Some of them indicated by their purchases an immediate involvement with the new art, while for others the impact was the beginning of a slower process of maturation. There is no question that for all of them the Armory Show was an unforgettable experience and a formative one. This first generation of American collectors of modern art eventually amassed magnificent accumulations of objects, but unlike the tycoons of an older generation who collected the old masters, most of these had in common the uncommon need and desire to proselytize, which they seem to have inherited from the Armory Show itself. This evangelistic activity had a great deal to do with the transformation of taste in the United States during the next two decades.

239

It is one of the tragedies of American art history that the Quinn collection, whose character was decisively changed by the Armory Show, was ultimately dispersed, but the others were institutionalized and became part of our rich artistic heritage. The Bliss collection became the nucleus of the Museum of Modern Art; the Arensberg collection became the Louise and Walter Arensberg Collection of the Philadelphia Museum of Art, which now also houses the Albert E. Gallatin Collection, once called the Gallery of Living Art; Katherine Dreier formed the Collection of the Société Anonyme, now at the Yale University Art Gallery; and much of the Eddy collection became the Arthur Jerome Eddy Memorial Collection of the Chicago Art Institute. How much effect, if any, the Armory Show had on Barnes is hard to say, but most of the other collectors acknowledged the importance of the event on their taste and thinking, Duncan Phillips even admitting his original antipathy.

In summary, it can be said that the Armory Show had a profound effect on artists, collectors, and the art market. It set in motion forces which eventually transformed the character of American art. It would be inaccurate to attribute everything which has happened in the last fifty years to this one show or even to say that it was the most important factor in the development of modernism in the United States. One might even argue that it all would have happened anyway without the Armory Show, but the fact remains that the Armory Show did occur and that its influence was crucial and generative. Like any decisive battle, it served to determine the course of history, though we may continue to argue over its relative significance.

I have left for last a consideration of the effect of the Armory Show on the public and its taste because it is a subject difficult to manage with any preciseness. The public reacted to the Show with a display of interest rare in the annals of art history, a fact which is attributable to publicity and a spectacular presentation, but it is highly debatable whether the public was either profoundly moved or educated. It is more than likely that its unflattering image of the artist was reinforced and its unconcern with art vindicated. It is even doubtful that if re-created in its entirety today the Armory Show would find a more receptive audience among the general public.

The Armory Show was a wedge which helped shift the weight of American taste, but only to a limited extent that of public taste. At most, only a small proportion of the public, the literate and sophisticated, have been affected in any meaningful sense. Museum attendance has increased; more and more expensive coffee-table art books are published; printed and recorded courses in art are disseminated along with illustrations and slides in full and unconvincing color; and popular journals now broadcast the latest experiments in art to the corners of a country apparently hungry for Culture, or is it Status? Modern art is now accepted, at least in some circles, with the same unthinking aplomb as the *Mona Lisa*. But the hard core remains unchanged. I recently took a taxi to the Museum of Modern Art, and as I paid my fare, the driver in aggressive puzzlement asked me, "What do you see in that nutty stuff?" I rarely argue with cab drivers, and I went in to see what the Armory Show had wrought.

CATALOGUE RAISONNE

The following catalogue is a revision of the original catalogue and supplement issued for the Armory Show. It includes a listing with annotations of every work known or supposed to have been exhibited in New York, Chicago, and Boston, based on documentary evidence that has come to light in the Kuhn Papers, the MacRae Papers, and the sales books of Walter Pach.

The items included in all the catalogues have been compiled and arranged in alphabetical order under the artist's name, with the works listed in numerical order. The corresponding Chicago and Boston numbers and titles are given on the line following the New York number and title.

Titles: All typographical and orthographical errors have been corrected; capitalization has been standardized. The original titles often included medium and date, which have been removed and listed in the appropriate place. When the Chicago and Boston titles vary in any important respect from those in New York (often they were translated into English), the alternative title is given after the Chicago and Boston numbers. No notice is taken of minor variations in wording or punctuation unless the variation has some relevance. The English titles in all three shows and all the titles of the Chicago and Boston shows are almost identical except for minor variations, mostly in punctuation. Present and variant titles are also given.

Medium: The original catalogue noted that the medium was assumed to be in oil unless otherwise indicated. Supports such as canvas, panel, board, and paper were not originally given nor are they included here. The catalogue was in error in many cases, and corrections based on documentary evidence from a variety of sources have been made.

Date: The dates given are those included in the original catalogue, listed on the entry blanks that accompanied each work, or determined from other sources. Unfortunately, only the entry blanks of the foreign works, which did not always include the date, are still extant in the Kuhn Papers. The entry blanks of the American works have not as yet come to light.

Lenders: In the original catalogue, groups of works were listed with the name of the lender at the end of each group, which was often confusing. The lenders' names have been checked against the ledger of foreign loans in the MacRae Papers. A comparable listing of American lenders does not exist. Wherever no lender was given in the original catalogue, the assumption is that the work was lent by the artist. The works of contemporary artists in some cases came through dealers, but when no lender was listed in the original catalogue they are entered here as lent by the artist.

Price listed: The original catalogue did not list prices of works for sale. The information included here is compiled from the annotated Armory Show catalogues belonging to Kuhn and MacRae, from notations on the entry blanks, from a variety of correspondence in both the Kuhn and MacRae Papers, and from the prices listed in the foreign ledger of the MacRae Papers.

Buyers and prices paid: The names of buyers and the prices paid for works have been compiled from the official entries in the three ledgers in the MacRae Papers, from the two personal sales books of Pach, who was in charge of sales, and from a variety of other documentary evidence. The discrepancies among them are discussed in notes.

Present collection: Most of the information given here derives from the research done for the Fiftieth Anniversary Exhibition of the Armory Show at the Munson-Williams-Proctor Institute and the Henry Street Settlement. This monumental work of discovery and identification is only partially completed and some of the objects have only tentatively been identified. Collection information has been updated whenever possible. Private collections that could not be verified have nonetheless been retained, with the notation (*1963*) added to indicate that they were accurate as of that date. Those works for which evidence seems inconclusive have not been included, although they may eventually turn out to be authentic. Only versions of sculpture or prints that can be identified as the actual examples exhibited at the Armory Show have been cited.

Added works: Works that were in the Show but not listed in the catalogue have been added at the end of the appropriate artist listing, along with the evidence for each inclusion.

* This sign before the number indicates that the work was reproduced and sold in post card form at the Armory Show.

† This sign following the title indicates that the work was uninvited and accepted after examination by the Domestic Committee.

ABENDSCHEIN, Albert
(1860–n.d.)

27. *Leslie.*
Oil.
Lent by the artist.
Price listed: $550.

28. *Central Valley.*
Oil.
Lent by the artist.
Price listed: $550.

AITKEN, Robert I. (1878–1949)

684. *A Creature of God.*
Marble, 1910.
Lent by the artist.
Price listed: $1,000.
Present collection (1963): Mrs.
Robert I. Aitken, New York.

685. *The Dregs of Love.*
Marble.
Lent by the artist.
Price listed: $1,000.
Present collection: The Berkshire
Museum, Pittsfield, Massachusetts.

686. *George Bellows.*
Plaster.
Lent by the artist.
No price listed.
Present collection: Mrs. John
Hay Whitney.

687. *Study.*
Elsewhere called *Tired Mercury.*
Plaster, 1910.
Lent by the artist.
Price listed: $250.
Present collection (1963): Mrs.
Robert I. Aitken, New York.

ALGER, John H. (1879–n.d.)

750. *Sunlight and Clouds.* †
Chicago, 1.
Oil.
Lent by the artist.
Price listed: $300.

ANDERSON, Karl (1874–1956)

*890. *Woman Drinking Glass*

of Water.
Chicago, 2.
Oil.
Lent by the artist.
Price listed: $600.

891. *Boy Playing with Goat.*
Oil.
Lent by the artist.
Price listed: $800.

892. *The Apple Gatherers.*
Oil, 1912.
Lent by the artist.
Price listed: $1,500.
Present collection: Cleveland
Museum of Art; Bequest of Ralph
King.

1105. *The Sparkler.*
Oil.
Lent by the artist.
No price listed.

1106. *The Naturalist.*
Oil.
Lent by the artist.
No price listed.

Boy and Goat.
This painting was not listed but was
added in the Kuhn catalogue with
the notation "small."
Oil.
Lent by the artist.
Price listed: $500.

ARCHIPENKO, Alexander
(1887–1964)

153. *Drawings, Nos. 1–5.*
Chicago, 7. Boston, 1.
Drawings, dated on entry blank
1912.
Lent by the artist.
Price listed: $27 each. Sold for $135
to Alfred Stieglitz, March 7, 1913.

601. *Négresse.*
Chicago, 3. Boston, 1. *Negress.*
Plaster. According to the artist, this
was a cement cast. Dated on entry
blank 1911.
Lent by the artist.
Price listed: $216.

244

*602. *Le Repos.*
Chicago, 4. *Repose.*
Plaster, dated on entry blank 1912.
Lent by the artist.
Price listed: $216.
Former collection: The artist,
New York.

603. *Salomé.*
Chicago, 5.
Plaster, dated on entry blank 1910.
According to the artist, this was a
cement cast.
Lent by the artist.
Price listed: $540.
Present collection: According to the
artist, this was in a private
collection in Paris in 1963.

*604. *La Vie familiale.*
Chicago, 6. Boston, 2. *Family Life.*
Plaster, dated on entry blank 1912.
Lent by the artist.
Price listed: $2,700.
According to the artist, this work
was destroyed during World War I.

ASHE, Edmund Marion (n.d.)

749. *Spirit of the Pool.* †
Oil.
Lent by the artist.
Price listed: $300.

BARKLEY, Florence Howell
(1880/81–1954)

743. *Landscape over the City.* †
Now called *Jerome Avenue Bridge.*
Oil, 1910–11.
Lent by the artist.
Price listed: $100.
Present collection: Museum of the
City of New York.

BARNARD, George Grey
(1863–1938)

997. *Prodigal Son.*
Now called *The Prodigal Son and His
Father.*
Marble, 1904.
Lent by the artist.

Price listed: $18,000.
Present collection: J. B. Speed Art
Museum, Louisville, Kentucky.

998. *Solitude.*
Marble.
Lent by the artist.
Price listed: $2,000.

999. *Musician Dying.*
Marble.
Lent by Samuel Swift, but not so
listed in catalogue.
Price listed: $2,000.

1000. *The Birth.*
Marble.
Lent by the artist.
Price listed: $2,000.

1001. *The Mystery of Life.*
Marble.
Lent by the artist.
Price listed: $2,000.
Present collection: National
Museum of American Art,
Smithsonian Institution,
Washington, D.C.; Gift of John
Gellatly.

Note: Nos. 998–1001 may be
studies for or replicas taken from
Barnard's monumental *Urn of Life,*
in the collection of the Carnegie
Museum of Art, Pittsburgh.

BEACH, Chester (1881–1956)

653. *Mermaid.*
Marble, 1911.
Lent by the artist.
Price listed: $700.
Present collection (1963): Mrs.
John McLaury, Florida.

654. *The Unveiling of Dawn.*
Marble.
Lent by the artist.
Price listed: $1,000.
Present collection: The
Metropolitan Museum of Art, New
York; Gift of Mr. and Mrs. George
W. Davison.

655. *The Big Wave.*

245

Chicago, 8.
Now called *The Wave*.
Bronze, c. 1912.
Lent by the artist.
Price listed: $600. Sold for $500 to
Dr. D. D. Vandergrift [Van de
Grift], April 15, 1913, Chicago.
Present collection: The Art
Institute of Chicago; Gift of Daniel
Van de Grift.

656. *Frame of Medals.*
Bronze.
Lent by Dr. Christian A. Herter,
Actors Fund.
Not for sale.

BEAL, Gifford (1879–1956)

13. *Here Come the Elephants.*
Oil.
Catalogued but not received.

14. *When the Circus Starts.*
Oil.
Catalogued but not received.

BECHTEJEFF, Wladimir von
(1878–n.d.)

159. *Nausikaa.*
Oil.
Lent by Hans Goltz.
Price listed: $812.50.

BECKER, Maurice (1889–1975)

765. *Sketch, Dog's Head.* †
Drawing, charcoal on newspaper.
Lent by Nessa Cohen.
Not for sale.
Destroyed.

BECKETT, Marion H. (n.d.)

758. *Portrait of Mrs. Charles H.
Beckett.* †
Oil.
Lent by the artist.
Not for sale.

759. *Portrait of Mr. Edward J.
Steichen.* †
Chicago, 9. *Portrait, Edouard J.*

Steichen.
Oil.
Lent by the artist.
Not for sale.

BELLOWS, George (1882–1925)

919. *Circus.*
Oil, 1912.
Lent by the artist.
Price listed: $1,200.
Present collection: Addison Gallery
of American Art, Phillips Academy,
Andover, Massachusetts; Gift of
Elizabeth P. Metcalf.

919A. *Polo Crowd.*
Oil.
Lent by the artist.
Price listed: $1,200.
Present collection: Mrs. John
Hay Whitney.

920. *Portrait, Mrs. Albert Miller.*
Oil.
Lent by the artist.
Not for sale.
Present collection: Columbus
Museum of Art, Columbus, Ohio;
Gift of Mrs. Bartley Arnold.

921. *Docks in Winter.*
Chicago, 10.
Oil.
Lent by the artist.
Price listed: $800.
Present collection (1963): Mrs.
Symington, Baltimore.

922. *Evening Harmony.*
Elsewhere called *Evening Glow*.
Oil, 1912.
Lent by the artist.
Price listed: $150.

1043. *Lightweight Champion of the
World.*
Chicago, 11. *Lightweight Champion*.
Drawing.
Lent by the artist.
No price listed.

1044. *Between Rounds.*
Drawing.

Lent by the artist.
No price listed.
Present collection (1963): Mrs.
Charles S. Payson, Manhasset,
New York.

1045. *Polo Field.*
Now called *Polo at Lakewood.*
Wash drawing, 1910.
No price listed.
Present collection (1963): Winthrop
Taylor, New York.

1046. *Park Parties.*
Chicago, 12. *Luncheon in the Park.*
Now called *Luncheon in the Park.*
Drawing.
Lent by the artist.
No price listed.
Present collection: Albright-Knox
Art Gallery, Buffalo, New York;
George Cary Fund.

Note: An error in the catalogue
listed 1043–46 as oils.

1104. *Four Drawings.*
Lent by the artist.
Price listed: $150 each.

Dancer.
Not listed but added in pencil in
Kuhn catalogue.
Oil.
Lent by the artist.
Not for sale.

BERLIN, H. See Paul Burlin.

BERNARD, Joseph (1866–1931)

187. *Jeune Fille à la cruche.*
Chicago, 13. Boston, 3. *Girl with
Pitcher.*
Plaster, dated on entry blank 1912.
Lent by Musée de Lyon.
Price listed: $4,860 (bronze).

188. *La Tendresse.*
Chicago, 14. *Tenderness.*
Plaster, dated on entry blank 1910.
Lent by Musée de Lyon.
Price listed: $2,160 (bronze);
$4,050 (marble).

BICKFORD, Nelson N.
(1846–1943)

640. *Pelican.* †
Sculpture.
Lent by the artist.
Price listed: $60 (bronze).

641. *Turkey.* †
Sculpture.
Lent by the artist.
Price listed: $50 (bronze).

642. *Leopard.* †
Sculpture.
Lent by the artist.
Price listed: $50 (bronze).

BITTER, Karl (1867–1915)

652. *Bust, Andrew D. White.*
Bronze.
Catalogued but not received.

BJORKMAN, Olaf (1886–1946)

722. *A Vala, Prophetess, Norse
Myth.*
Sculpture.
Lent by the artist.
Price listed: $650.
Present collection (1963): Mrs.
C. Timken.

BLANCHET, Alexandre
(1882–1961)

183. *Deux Amies.*
Chicago, 15. Boston, 4. *The Two
Friends.*
Oil, dated on entry blank 1912.
Lent by the artist.
Price listed: $540. Sold for $540 to
John Quinn, February 26, 1913.
Present collection (1963): Graham
Galleries, New York.

BLUEMNER, Oscar (1867–1938)
801. *South River.* †
Watercolor.
Lent by the artist.
Price listed: $150.

802. *Canal in New Jersey.* †

247

Watercolor.
Lent by the artist.
Price listed: $150.

803. *Hackensack River.* †
Oil, dated on entry blank 1912.
Lent by the artist.
Price listed: $500.

804. *Morning on Long Island.* †
Oil.
Lent by the artist.
Price listed: $500.

805. *Harlem River.* †
Watercolor.
Lent by the artist.
Price listed: $150.

BOLZ, Hans (1887–1918)

197. *Maskenfest.*
Chicago, 16. *Carnival.*
Wood engraving.
Lent by the artist.
Price listed: $13.50.

198. *Bar.*
Chicago, 17.
Wood engraving.
Lent by the artist.
Price listed: $16.20.

199. *Ostende.*
Chicago, 18.
Wood engraving.
Lent by the artist.
Price listed: $13.50.

200. *Eglise St. Nicolas.*
Chicago, 19. *St. Nicolas Church.*
Wood engraving.
Lent by the artist.
Price listed: $10.80.

BONNARD, Pierre (1867–1947)

193. *Conversation Provençale.*
Chicago, 20. *A Provençale
Conversation.*
Elsewhere called *La Sieste.*
Oil, 1911. Reworked 1927.
Lent by Bernheim-Jeune & Cie.
Price listed: $2,700.

Present collection (1963): Galerie
Moderne, Prague, Czechoslovakia.

Lithographs.
Not listed in New York catalogue,
but displayed for sale and order.
Chicago, 21.
From the evidence available it is
impossible to determine which or
how many were exhibited.
Lent by Ambroise Vollard.
Price listed: $12 each. One sold for
$12 to Mrs. Alexander Tison,
March 7, 1913. Four sold for $48 to
Francis L. Pruyn, March 8, 1913.

BORGLUM, Solon (1868–1922)

707. *1.*
Sculpture.
Lent by Theodore B. Starr.
No price listed.

708. *2.*
Sculpture.
Lent by Theodore B. Starr.
No price listed.

709. *3.*
Sculpture.
Lent by Theodore B. Starr.
No price listed.

710. *4.*
Sculpture.
Lent by Theodore B. Starr.
No price listed.

711. *5.*
Sculpture.
Lent by Theodore B. Starr.
No price listed.

712. *6.*
Sculpture.
Lent by Theodore B. Starr.
No price listed.

713. *7.*
Sculpture.
Lent by Theodore B. Starr.
No price listed.

248

BOSS, Homer (1882–1956)

38. *A Study.*
Now called *Land and Sea.*
Oil, 1912.
Lent by the artist.
Price listed: $1,500.
Present collection (1963): Mrs.
Homer Boss, Santa Cruz, New
Mexico.

39. *Portrait.*
Elsewhere called *Girl in Blue and
Gold.*
Oil, 1910.
Lent by the artist.
Price listed: $1,500.
Present collection (1963): Mrs.
Homer Boss, Santa Cruz, New
Mexico.

BOURDELLE, Emile Antoine
(1861–1929)

209. *Portrait.*
Oil.
Lent by the artist.
Price listed: $270.

210. *Observatoire de Meudon.*
Oil, c. 1905.
Lent by the artist.
Price listed: $270.
Present collection: Musée
Bourdelle, Paris.

605. *Tête d'Apollon.*
Bronze, 1900.
Lent by the artist.
Price listed: $540. Sold for $540 to
Sir William Van Horne, March 8,
1913.
Present collection (1963): Mr. and
Mrs. Henry H. Crapo, Boston.

606. *Une Muse.*
Chicago, 23½. A *Muse.*
Plaster bas-relief, dated on entry
blank 1912.
Lent by the artist.
Price listed: Not for sale (plaster);
$1,350 (marble); $1,080 (bronze).

607. *Le Matin.*
Chicago, 22. Morning.
Elsewhere called *Statue de femme.*
Plaster.
Lent by the artist.
Price listed: $270 (bronze).

608. *Heracles.*
Chicago, 23. Boston, 5.
Now called *Herakles Archer.*
The small version of this work was
in the Armory Show.
Bronze, 1908–9.
Lent by the artist.
Price listed: $540 (bronze).

BRANCUSI, Constantin
(1876–1957)

616. *Le Baiser.*
Chicago, 24. Boston, 6. *The Kiss.*
Plaster, 1908.
Lent by the artist.
Price listed: $270 (plaster); $540
(stone).

617. *Muse endormie.*
Chicago, 25. Boston, 7. *Sleeping
Muse.*
Plaster, dated on entry blank 1911.
Lent by the artist.
Price listed: $270 (plaster); $1,350
(marble).

*618. *Une Muse.*
Chicago, 26. Boston, 8. A *Muse.*
Now called *The Muse.*
Plaster, dated on entry blank 1912.
Lent by the artist.
Price listed: $270 (plaster); $810
(marble).
Present collection (marble):
Solomon R. Guggenheim Museum,
New York; Gift of Mrs. Walt Kuhn.

*619. *Mlle. Pogany.*
Chicago, 27. Boston, 9.
Plaster, dated on entry blank 1912.
Lent by the artist.
Price listed: $270 (plaster); $540
(bronze). Bronze sold for $550 to
Robert W. Chanler, June 7, 1913.

249

620. *Torse.*
Marble.
Probably lent by Arthur B. Davies.
Not for sale.

BRAQUE, Georges (1882–1963)

*205. *Le Violon.*
Chicago, 28. Boston, 10. *The Violin.*
Now called *L'Affiche de Kubelick.*
Elsewhere called *Kubelik.*
Oil, dated on entry blank 1912.
Lent by Henry Kahnweiler.
Price listed: $202.50.
Present collection (1963): Andreas Speiser, Basel, Switzerland.

206. *Anvers.*
Now called *Le Port d'Anvers.*
Chicago, 29. Boston, 11. *Antwerp.*
Oil, dated on entry blank 1906.
Lent by Henry Kahnweiler.
Price listed: $202.50.
Present collection: National Gallery of Canada, Ottawa.

207. *La Forêt.*
Chicago, 30. Boston, 12. *The Forest.*
Oil, dated on entry blank 1908.
Lent by Henry Kahnweiler.
Price listed: $216.

BREWER, Bessie Marsh
(1884–1952)

821. *The Furnished Room.* †
Drawing.
Lent by the artist.
Price listed: $25.

822. *Curiosity.* †
Drawing.
Lent by the artist.
Price listed: $25.

823. *Putting Her Monday Name on Her Letterbox.* †
Drawing.
Lent by the artist.
Price listed: $25.

BRINLEY, D. Putnam
(1879–1963)

840. *The Emerald Pool.*
Chicago, 31.
Oil.
Lent by the artist.
Price listed: $1,200.
Present collection (1963): Mrs. Jane D. Terhune, Little Compton, Rhode Island.

841. *The Peony Garden.*
Oil.
Lent by the artist.
Price listed: $400.

*842. *A Walled Garden.*
Oil.
Lent by the artist.
Price listed: $800.

843. *Color Note.*
Oil.
Lent by the artist.
Price listed: $40.

844. *Color Note.*
Oil.
Lent by the artist.
Price listed: $40.

845. *Color Note.*
Oil.
Lent by the artist.
Price listed: $40.

846. *Color Note.*
Oil.
Lent by the artist.
Price listed: $40.

The four *Color Notes*, nos. 843–46, were sold for $115 to Frederic C. Torrey, February 22, 1913.

BROWN, Bolton (1865–1936)

826. *Green Fire.* †
Oil.
Lent by the artist.
Price listed: $600.

BROWN, Fannie Miller (Fannie Wilcox Brown? Born 1882.)

948. *Embroidery.*
Lent by the artist.
Price listed: $225.

BRUCE, Patrick Henry
(1880–1937)

160. *Nature morte* (1).
Oil, dated on entry blank 1910.
Lent by Maurice Feldman.
Price listed: $190.

161. *Nature morte* (2).
Oil, dated on entry blank 1911.
Lent by the artist.
Price listed: $135.

162. *Nature morte* (3).
Oil, dated on entry blank 1910.
Lent by the artist.
Price listed: $135.

163. *Nature morte* (4).
Oil, dated on entry blank 1910.
Lent by the artist.
Price listed: $135.

BURLIN, Paul (1886–1969)

1008. *William Street.*
Drawing.
Lent by the artist.
Price listed: $85.

1009. *Minetta Lane.*
Drawing.
Lent by the artist.
Price listed: $65.

1010. *Remains of Equitable Building.*
Drawing.
Lent by the artist.
Price listed: $85.

1011. *Washington Market District.*
Drawing.
Lent by the artist.
Price listed: $65.

Note: According to the artist, 1008–11 were drawings; they were listed in catalogue as oils.

BURROUGHS, Mrs. Bryson
(Edith Woodman) (1871–1916)

725. *Bust.*
Now called *Portrait of John Bigelow.*
Bronze, c. 1910.
Lent by the artist.
No price listed.
Present collection: Museum of Art, Rhode Island School of Design, Providence; Gift of Caleb Randal Woodhouse.

BUTLER, Theodore Earl
(1876–1937)

1087. *Marine.*
Chicago, 32.
Oil.
Lent by the artist.
No price listed.

1088. *Fourteenth of July, Paris.*
Oil.
Lent by the artist.
No price listed.

1089. *Early Cubist Study, 16th-Century Italian.*
Drawing.
Lent by John Oakman.
No price listed.

Note: An error in the catalogue listed this drawing as by Butler. It was a 16th-century Italian drawing, probably by Luca Cambiaso.

CAMOIN, Charles (1879–1965)

235. *Liseuse.*
Chicago, 33. *The Reader.*
Oil.
Lent by Emile Druet.
Price listed: $162.

236. *Seville.*
Chicago, 34.
Oil.
Lent by Emile Druet.
Price listed: $216. Sold for $216 to Mrs. Randolph Guggenheimer, March 14, 1913.

237. *Collioure.*
Oil.
Lent by Emile Druet.

251

Price listed: $216. Sold for $216 to Dr. Helen C. Loewenstein, February 22, 1913.

238. *Moulin Rouge.*
Oil, dated on entry blank c. 1910.
Lent by Heinrich Thannhauser.
Price listed: $240.75.

CARLES, Arthur Beecher
(1882–1952)

56. *Landscape.*
Now called *The Church/L'Eglise.*
Oil.
Lent by the artist.
No price listed.
Present collection: The Metropolitan Museum of Art, New York.

57. *Landscape.*
Oil.
Lent by the artist.
No price listed.

Chicago, 35. *Interior.*
Oil.
Lent by the artist.
No price listed.

CARR, Mrs. Myra Mussleman
(1880–n.d.)

715. *Electra.*
Statuette.
Lent by the artist.
Price listed: $50 (bronze).

716. *Indian Grinding Corn.*
Statuette.
Lent by the artist.
Price listed: $40 (bronze).
Another work, *Old Woman*, is substituted in the Kuhn catalogue.

CASARINI, Athos (1884–1917)

123. *Crime.*
Pastel.
Lent by the artist.
Price listed: $90.

CASSATT, Mary (1845–1926)

493. *Mère et enfant.*
Oil, 1903.
Lent by Durand-Ruel & Sons.
Price listed: $4,950.

584. *Mère et enfant.*
Watercolor.
Lent by John Quinn.
Not for sale.

CESARE, Oscar E. (1883–1948)

1004. *The Sisyphus of the East.*
Chicago, 36.
Drawing.
Lent by the artist.
Price listed: $100.

1005. *L'Etat c'est moi.*
Drawing.
Lent by the artist.
Price listed: $100.

1006. *Our Friend the Horse.*
Drawing.
Lent by the artist.
Price listed: $100.

1007. *Mors Pasha.*
Drawing.
Lent by the artist.
Price listed: $100.

CEZANNE, Paul (1839–1906)

The number in parenthesis following each title refers to Lionello Venturi, *Cézanne: Son art, son oeuvre*, Paris, 1936, 2 vols.

* **214.** *Femme au chapelet.* (V. 702)
Chicago, 38. Boston, 14. *Woman with Rosary.*
Now called *An Old Woman with a Rosary.*
Oil, 1900–1904. Now dated c. 1896.
Lent by Emile Druet.
Price listed: $48,600.
Present collection: The National Gallery, London.

215. *Portrait de Cézanne.* (V. 579)

252

Chicago, 39. Boston, 15. *Portrait of Cézanne.*
Oil, dated on entry blank 1892.
Lent by Ambroise Vollard.
Price listed: $6,500.
Present collection: Bridgestone Museum, Tokyo.

216. *Baigneuses (No. 1).* (V. 384)
Chicago, 40. Boston, 16. *Bathers.*
Oil, dated on entry blank 1878.
Lent by Ambroise Vollard.
Price listed: $6,500.
Present collection: Paul Haim, Paris.

217. *Colline des pauvres.* (V. 660)
Now called *The Poorhouse on the Hill.*
Oil, c. 1877. Dated on entry blank 1887.
Lent by Ambroise Vollard.
Price listed: $8,000. Sold for $6,700 to The Metropolitan Museum of Art, March 16, 1913.
Present collection: The Metropolitan Museum of Art, New York.

218. *Auvers.* (V. 312)
Chicago, 42. Boston, 17.
Oil, dated on entry blank 1880.
Lent by Ambroise Vollard.
Price listed: $9,500.
Present collection (1963): Basil Goulandris, New York.

219. *Portrait [of Boyer].* (V. 130)
Chicago, 43. Boston, 18.
Oil, 1867.
Lent by Ambroise Vollard.
Price listed: $4,000.
Present collection (1963): Mme. Lecomte, Neuilly-sur-Seine, France.

220. *Melun.* (V. 304)
Chicago, 44. Boston, 19.
Now called *Jas de Bouffan.*
Oil, dated on entry blank 1879.
Lent by Ambroise Vollard.
Price listed: $8,000.
Present collection: National Gallery, Oslo.

580. *Portrait of Madame Cézanne.* (V. 229)
Chicago, 46. Boston, 21.
Oil.
Lent by John Quinn.
Not for sale.
Present collection: Takahata Art Salon, Osaka.

1068. *Flowers.*
Chicago, 47. Boston, 22.
Oil.
Lent by Mrs. J. Montgomery Sears.
No price listed.
Present collection (1963): Private collection, New York.

1069. *Harvesters.* (V. 1517)
Chicago, 48. Boston, 23.
Now called *Les Moissonneurs.*
Oil, 1875–78.
Lent by Prof. John O. Sumner.
No price listed.
Present collection (1963): Private collection, Paris.

1070. *Landscape.* (V. 52)
Chicago, 49. Boston, 24.
Now called *The Road.*
Oil.
Listed in Chicago catalogue but without a lender's name.
No price listed.
Present collection: Mr. and Mrs. William Rosenwald, New York.

1071. *Portrait de Cézanne.* (V. 514)
Chicago, 50. Boston, 25.
Oil, dated on entry blank 1892.
Lent by Stephan Bourgeois.
No price listed.
Present collection: Ny Carlsberg Glyptotek, Copenhagen.

1072. *Portrait of Madame Cézanne.* (V. 520)
Chicago, 51.
Oil.
Lent by Sir William Van Horne.
No price listed.
Present collection: Private collection, Switzerland.

253

1084. *Watercolor.*
Chicago, 45. Boston, 20.
Lent anonymously.
No price listed.
Present collection: John W.
Worrington, Cincinnati.

Lithograph (large).
Not listed in New York catalogue,
but displayed for sale and order.
Chicago, 37. Boston, 13.
Lithographs.
Color lithograph, 1898. This was
probably *Les Baigneurs,* from
Vollard's unpublished third volume
of *L'Album des peintres-graveurs.*
Lent by Ambroise Vollard.
Price listed: $27. One sold for $21
to Arthur B. Davies, March 1,
1913. One sold for $25 to Alfred
Stieglitz, March 5, 1913. One sold
for $40 to Lillie P. Bliss, March 6,
1913 (Present collection: The
Museum of Modern Art, New York;
Lillie P. Bliss Collection). One sold
for $40 to Mrs. Charles C. Rumsey,
March 6, 1913. Two sold for $54 to
John Quinn, March 10, 1913. One
sold for $40 to Walter C.
Arensberg, May 19, 1913.

Lithograph (small).
Not listed in New York catalogue,
but displayed for sale and order.
Chicago, 37. Boston, 13.
Lithographs.
Color lithograph, 1897. This was
probably *Les Baigneurs,* from
Vollard's second published *L'Album
des peintres-graveurs.*
Lent by Ambroise Vollard.
Price listed: $21. One sold for $15
to Arthur B. Davies, March 1,
1913. One sold for $25 to Lillie P.
Bliss, March 6, 1913 (Present
collection: The Museum of Modern
Art, New York; Lillie P. Bliss
Collection). One sold for $25 to
Mrs. Charles C. Rumsey, March 6,
1913. Two sold for $42 to John
Quinn, March 10, 1913. One sold
for $15 to Walt Kuhn, no date.

CHABAUD, Auguste Elisée
(1882–1955)

168. *Le Laboureur.*
Chicago, 53. *The Laborer.*
Oil.
Lent by the artist.
Price listed: $270. Sold for $270 to
Arthur J. Eddy, February 27, 1913.

583. *Le Troupeau sort après la pluie.*
Chicago, 52. Boston, 26. *The Flock
after the Rain.*
Oil, 1912.
Lent by John Quinn.
Not for sale.

CHAFFEE, O. N. (1881–1944)

832. *A Village.* †
Oil.
Lent by the artist.
Price listed: $800.

833. *A Pine Tree.* †
Chicago, 54.
Oil.
Lent by the artist.
Price listed: $800.

834. *Pine Tree.* †
Oil.
Lent by the artist.
Price listed: $800.

CHANLER, Robert W.
(1872–1930)

1023. *Screen. Hopi Snake Dance.*
[Misspelled in catalogue as *Moki
snake dance.*]
Lent by the artist.
Price listed: $5,000.

1024. *Screen. Swan.*
Chicago, 55.
Lent by Mrs. W. A. Delano.
Price listed: $2,000 (original).
Present collection (1963): Mrs.
Edward J. Jorgensen, Syosset, New
York.

1025. *Screen. Fish.*
Chicago, 56. *Fight under the Sea.*
The Chicago screen may have been

254

a different one. It was described in a newspaper account as depicting a scene of crocodiles and devilfish fighting under water, and cited in two newspapers as the "Whitney Screen."
Lent by the Vanderbilt Hotel.
No price listed.

*1026. *Screen. Leopard and Deer.*
Chicago, 57.
Lent by Mrs. [Harry] Payne Whitney.
Price listed: $1,200 (replica).
Present collection: Chanler Chapman, Red Hook, New York.

1027. *Screen. Indian.*
Lent by Mrs. Dalzeal.
No price listed.
Present collection: Mrs. T. Reed Vreeland, New York.

1028. *Screen. Deer.*
Lent by Mrs. Sidney Harris.
No price listed.

*1029. *Screen. Porcupine.*
Chicago, 60.
Lent by Mrs. John Jay Chapman.
Price listed: $2,000.
Present collection: The Metropolitan Museum of Art, New York; Gift of John Jay Chapman.

1030. *Screen. Fantasy; Bamboo and Birds.*
Chicago, 61.
Lent by Henry Clews, Jr.
No price listed.

1031. *Screen. In Red.*
Chicago, 62.
Lent by the artist.
Price listed: $2,000. Sold for $1,500 to George F. Porter, May 3, 1913.

Jungle Screen.
Not listed but added in Kuhn catalogue.
Chicago, 58.
Lent by the artist.
Price listed: $3,500.

Chicago, 59. *Screen. Birds of*

Paradise.
Lent by the artist.
No price listed.

CHARMY, Emilie (1880–n.d.)

169. *Roses.*
Chicago, 63.
Oil.
Lent by Emile Druet.
Price listed: $108.

170. *Paysage.*
Chicago, 64. *Landscape.*
Now called *L'Estaque.*
Oil, c. 1910.
Lent by Emile Druet.
Price listed: $135. Sold for $135 to Arthur J. Eddy, March 4, 1913.
Present collection: The Art Institute of Chicago; Arthur Jerome Eddy Memorial Collection.

171. *Soir.*
Chicago, 65. *Evening.*
Oil.
Lent by Emile Druet.
Price listed: $135.

172. *Ajaccio.*
Oil.
Lent by Emile Druet.
Price listed: $135. Sold for $135 to Dr. Helen C. Loewenstein, March 2, 1913.

CHEW, Amos (n.d.)

718. *Pelf.* †
Plaster.
Lent by the artist.
No price listed.

Portrait.
Not listed but added in Kuhn catalogue.
Lent by the artist.
Price listed: $1,000.

CHURCHILL, Alfred Vance (1864–1949)

831. *Rain Pause.* †
Oil.

Lent by the artist.
Price listed: $500.

CIMIOTTI, Gustave, Jr.
(1875–1969)

60. *The Barrier.*
Oil, 1912.
Lent by the artist.
Price listed: $750.
Present collection (1963):
The artist, New York.

61. *Hillside.*
Chicago, 66.
Oil, 1912.
Lent by the artist.
Price listed: $300.
Present collection (1963):
The artist, New York.

CLYMER, Edwin Swift
(1871–n.d.)

92. *Great Hill.*
Drawing.
Catalogued but not received.

COATE, Harry W. (n.d.)

9. *Portrait.*
Oil.
Lent by the artist.
Price listed: $350.

10. *Portrait.*
Oil.
Lent by the artist.
Price listed: $350.

COHEN, Nessa (1885–n.d.)

659. *Age.*
Plaster.
Lent by the artist.
Price listed: $125.
Former collection:
The artist, New York.

660. *Portrait.*
Plaster.
Lent by the artist.
Price listed: $200 in Kuhn
catalogue; $300 in MacRae

catalogue.
Possibly destroyed.

661. *Sunrise.*
Bronze.
Lent by the artist.
Price listed: $600.
Former collection:
The artist, New York.

COLEMAN, Glenn O.
(1887–1932)

768. *Election Bonfire.* †
Drawing.
Lent by the artist.
Price listed: $100.

769. *Street Scene.* †
Drawing.
Lent by the artist.
Price listed: $100.

770. *The Fleet.* †
Oil.
Lent by the artist.
Price listed: $400.

COLUZZI, Howard (n.d.)

32. *Fresco.*
Catalogued but not received;
perhaps received later.
Price listed: $500.

93. *Drawings.*
Chicago, 67. *Drawing.*
Lent by the artist.
No price listed.

Mahabarata.
Not listed but added in Kuhn
catalogue.
Oil.
Lent by the artist.
Price listed: $300. Sold for $200 to
Mrs. Charles C. Rumsey, March 1,
1913.

CONDER, Charles (1868–1909)

569. *La Belle Antonia.*
Chicago, 68. Boston, 27. *The
Beautiful Antonia.*

Oil, 1902.
Lent by John Quinn.
Not for sale.
Present collection: K. Schneider,
London.

570. *Fantasia.*
Chicago, 69. Boston, 28.
Silk panel.
Lent by John Quinn.
Not for sale.
Present collection: J. S. Mass and
Co. Ltd., London.

571. *Casino de Paris.*
Chicago, 70. Boston, 29.
Painting on silk.
Lent by John Quinn.
Not for sale.

572. *La Toilette.*
Chicago, 71. Boston, 30. *The Toilet.*
Pastel.
Lent by John Quinn.
Not for sale.

573. *The Guitar Player.*
Sanguine drawing, 1904.
Lent by John Quinn.
Not for sale.

1020. *The Crinolines.*
Chicago, 72. Boston, 31.
Oil.
Lent by Mrs. Edwin Shurrill Dodge.
Price listed: $1,000.

1074. *Lithograph in Red.*
Chicago, 74.
Lent by the artist.
No price listed.

1075. *Etching.*
Chicago, 73.
Lent by the artist.
No price listed.

COROT, Jean-Baptiste-Camille
(1796–1875)

594. *La Clairière.*
Oil.
Lent by James G. Shepherd.
Not for sale.

595. *Châtillon.*
Elsewhere called *Châtillon-sur-Seine.*
Oil.
Lent by James G. Shepherd.
Not for sale.

CORY, Kate T. (n.d.)

122. *Arizona Desert.*
Chicago, 75.
Oil.
Lent by the artist.
Price listed: $150. Sold for $150 to
W. Clyde Jones, March 24, 1913.

COURBET, Gustave (1819–1877)

1017. *Blacksmith Shed.*
Oil.
Lent by Alexander Morten.
No price listed.

CRISP, Arthur (1881–n.d.)

792. *Panels for a Dining Room.* †
Oil.
Lent by the artist.
Price listed: $150.

CROSS, Henri Edmond
(1856–1910)

229. *Amandiers en fleurs.*
Chicago, 77. *Flowering Almonds.*
Oil.
Lent by Emile Druet.
Price listed: $1,215.
Present collection (1963): César
de Hauke, Paris.

230. *La Clairière.*
Oil.
Lent by Emile Druet.
Price listed: $4,050.

231. *Aquarelle.*
Chicago, 78. Boston, 32.
Watercolor.
Lent by Emile Druet, #2703.
Price listed: $121.50.

232. *Aquarelle.*
Chicago, 79. Boston, 33.
Watercolor.

257

Lent by Emile Druet, #6428.
Price listed: $189.

CROWLEY, Herbert (n.d.)

88. *Temple of Silence.*
Drawing, pen and ink.
Lent by the artist.
Price listed: $250. Listed as not for
sale in Kuhn catalogue.
Destroyed.

89. *Slander.*
Drawing, pen and ink.
Lent by the artist.
Price listed: $250.

CURRIER, J. Frank (1843–1909)

1096. *Forest Interior.*
Chicago, 76.
Oil.
Lent anonymously.
No price listed.

CUTLER, Carl Gordon
(1873–1945)

989. *China Cupboard.*
Oil.
Lent by the artist.
Price listed: $1,000.

990. *Portrait Study.*
Oil.
Lent by the artist.
No price listed.

DABO, Leon (1868–1960)

850. *Iona Island.*
Oil.
Lent by the artist.
Price listed: $1,000.

851. *Before the Storm.*
Oil.
Lent by the artist.
Price listed: $1,000.

852. *Canadian Night.*
Chicago, 80.
Oil.
Lent by the artist.
Price listed: $1,000.

1092. *Evening North Sierra.*
Oil, 1910.
Lent by the artist.
Price listed: $1,000.
Present collection: Private
collection, New York.

DASBURG, Andrew (1887–1979)

44. *Still Life.*
Oil.
Lent by the artist.
Price listed: $250.

45. *Still Life.*
Oil.
Lent by the artist.
Price listed: $250.

46. *Landscape.*
Chicago, 81.
Oil.
Lent by the artist.
Price listed: $350 in Kuhn
catalogue; $250 in MacRae
catalogue.

*★647.** *Lucifer.*
Plaster.
Lent by the artist.
Price listed: $200.
Destroyed.

DAUMIER, Honoré (1808–1879)

596. *Troisième Classe.*
Now called *Third-Class Carriage.*
Oil.
Lent by James G. Shepherd.
Not for sale.
Present collection (1963):
Private collection, Boston.

597. *Outside Courtroom.*
Oil.
Lent by Alexander W. Drake.
Price listed: Ask for offer.

1018. *Pencil Sketch.*
Lent by Alexander Morten.
No price listed.

DAVEY, Randall (1887–1964)

793. *Girl in Blue.* †

Oil.
Lent by the artist.
Price listed: $600.
Destroyed.

DAVIDSON, Jo (1883–1952)

*677. *Decorative Panel.*
Sculpture.
Lent by the artist.
Price listed: $5,000.
Present collection: Jacques
Davidson, Indre-et-Loire, France.

678. *Yoshinosen.*
Chicago, 82(?).
Bronze.
Lent by the artist.
Price listed: $1,000 (stone); $600
(bronze).
Present collection: Jacques
Davidson, Indre-et-Loire, France.

679. *Yoshinosen.*
Chicago, 82(?).
Bronze.
Lent by the artist.
Price listed: $650.
Present collection: Jacques
Davidson, Indre-et-Loire, France.

680. *Study in Action.*
Sculpture.
Lent by the artist.
No price listed.

681. *Study in Repose.*
Bronze, 1909.
Lent by the artist.
Price listed: $5,000.

682. *Statue.*
Stone.
Lent by the artist.
No price listed.

683. *Torso.*
Bronze.
Lent by the artist.
Price listed: $300.
Present collection: Jacques
Davidson, Indre-et-Loire, France.

1100. *Two Drawings.*
Lent by the artist.

No price listed.

1101. *Eight Drawings.*
Lent by the artist.
No price listed.

La Douleur.
Not listed but added in Kuhn
catalogue.
Stone, 1912.
Lent by the artist.
Price listed: $1,350 in Kuhn
catalogue; $4,000 in MacRae
catalogue.

DAVIES, Arthur Bowen
(1862–1928)

923. *Hill Wind.*
Chicago, 83.
Oil.
Lent by the artist.
Price listed: $2,800.

924. *A Line of Mountains.*
Oil.
Lent by the artist.
Not for sale.
Present collection: Virginia Museum
of Fine Arts, Richmond.

*925. *Seadrift.*
Oil.
Lent by the artist.
Price listed: $1,000.

*926. *Design, Birth of Tragedy.*
Chicago, 84.
Pastel, 1912.
Lent by the artist.
Not for sale.
Present collection: Colby College
Museum of Art, Waterville, Maine;
Gift of Mrs. Joseph M. Kaplan.

927. *Drawing.*
Now called *Reclining Woman.*
Pastel, 1911.
Lent by the artist.
Listed as not for sale, but sold for
$65 to Alfred Stieglitz, February 20,
1913.
Present collection: The
Metropolitan Museum of Art,

259

New York; The Alfred Stieglitz
Collection.

928. *Drawing.*
Lent by the artist.
Not for sale.

Chicago, 84½. *Golden Sea Gardens.*
Now called *Golden Sea Garden.*
Oil.
Lent by George F. Porter.
No price listed.
Present collection: The Art
Institute of Chicago; George F.
Porter Collection.

DAVIS, Charles H. (1856–1933)

104. *L'Allegro.*
Oil.
Lent by the artist.
Price listed: $1,500.

DAVIS, Stuart (1892–1964)

813. *Servant Girls.* †
Watercolor, 1913.
Lent by the artist.
Price listed: $100.
Present collection: Munson-
Williams-Proctor Institute, Utica,
New York.

814. *Dance.* †
Watercolor, 1912.
Lent by the artist.
Price listed: $100.
Former collection: Downtown
Gallery, New York.

815. *The Doctor.* †
Now called *The Doctor* (*Interior*).
Watercolor, 1912.
Lent by the artist.
Price listed: $100.
Present collection: Elvehjem
Museum of Art, University of
Wisconsin, Madison; Gift of
D. Frederick Baker, from the
Baker/Pisano Collection.

816. *Babe La Tour.* †
Watercolor, 1912.
Lent by the artist.

Price listed: $100.
Present collection: National
Museum of American Art,
Smithsonian Institution,
Washington, D.C.; Gift of
Henry M. Ploch.

817. *The Musicians.* †
Watercolor.
Lent by the artist.
Price listed: $100.

DEGAS, Hilaire-Germain-Edgar
(1834–1917)

1012. *Chevaux de course.*
Now called *Racehorses.*
Oil, 1884.
Lent by Alexander Morten.
Not for sale.
Present collection (1963): Mrs.
Allan Shelden, Grosse Pointe
Farms, Michigan.

1013. *La Sortie du bain.*
Now called *After the Bath.*
Pastel, 1885.
Lent by Alexander Morten.
Not for sale.
Present collection (1963): Estate of
Mrs. Charles Suydham Cutting,
Gladstone, New Jersey.

1014. *Femme sur lit.*
Now called *Reclining Girl.*
Pastel.
Lent by Alexander Morten.
Not for sale.
Present collection: North Carolina
Museum of Art, Raleigh.

DELACROIX, Eugène
(1798–1863)

1076. *Christ on Lake of Genezareth.*
Oil, 1853.
Lent by William R. Ladd.
No price listed.
Present collection: Portland Art
Museum, Portland, Oregon.

DELAUNAY, Robert (1885–1941)

255. *Route de Laon.*
Oil, dated on entry blank 1912.
Lent by Monsieur K., Paris.
Price listed: $270.

256. *Les Fenêtres sur la ville.*
Subtitle on entry blank *1ᵉ partie 2ᵉ motif.*
Oil, dated on entry blank 1912.
Lent by Monsieur K., Paris.
Price listed: $540.
Former collection: Sonia Délaunay, Paris; now deceased.

257. *La Ville de Paris.*
Although listed as catalogued but not received, it actually was received but not hung.
Oil, dated on entry blank 1910–12.
Lent by the artist.
Price listed: $5,400.
Present collection: Musée National d'Art Moderne, Paris.

DENIS, Maurice (1870–1943)

311. *Maternité.*
Chicago, 85. *Motherhood.*
Oil.
Lent by Emile Druet.
Price listed: $1,080.

312. *A la fenêtre.*
Chicago, 86. *At the Window.*
Oil.
Lent by Emile Druet.
Price listed: $1,620.

313. *La Plage.*
Chicago, 87. *The Beach.*
Oil, 1903.
Lent by Emile Druet.
Price listed: $8,100.
Present collection: Musée d'Orsay, Paris.

314. *Angélique.*
Chicago, 88. Boston, 34. *Angelica.*
Oil.
Lent by Emile Druet.
Price listed: $1,620.

315. *La Forêt.*
Chicago, 89. Boston, 35. *The Forest.*
Oil.
Lent by Emile Druet.
Price listed: $864.

316. *Maternité.*
Chicago, 90. *Motherhood.*
Oil.
Lent by Emile Druet.
Price listed: $1,080.

317. *Nausicaa.*
Chicago, 91. Boston, 36.
Oil.
Lent by Emile Druet.
Price listed: $5,400.

Lithographs.
Not listed in New York catalogue but displayed for sale and order.
Chicago, 92.
From the evidence available it is impossible to determine which or how many were exhibited.
Lent by Ambroise Vollard.
Price listed: $12 each.
Of the following, all the identified prints are from "Amour," a portfolio of 12 color lithographs published by Vollard, Paris, 1898. Three sold for $36 to Lillie P. Bliss, March 4, 1913: *Les Crépuscules ont une douceur d'ancienne peinture*, plate 6; *Elle était plus belle que les rêves*, plate 7; *Mais c'est le coeur qui bat trop vite*, plate 12 (Present collection: The Museum of Modern Art, New York; Lillie P. Bliss Collection). Two sold for $24 to Gertrude Watson, March 4, 1913. Two sold for $24 to Mrs. Alexander Tison, March 7, 1913; one of these was *Les Attitudes sont faciles et chastes*, plate 2. One sold for $12 to John Quinn, March 7, 1913. One sold for $12 to Mrs. Porter Norton, March 7, 1913. *Sur le canapé d'argent pâle*, plate 10, sold for $12 to Mrs. Richard Sheldrick, March 13, 1913. Two sold for $24 to Zoë

261

Hannah, March 15, 1913. Three sold for $36 to Arthur J. Eddy, April 10, 1913, Chicago.

DERAIN, André (1880–1954)

342. *Le Pot bleu.*
Chicago, 93. Boston, 37. *The Blue Pot.*
Oil.
Lent by Henry Kahnweiler.
Price listed: $202.50.

343. *La Forêt à Martigues.*
Chicago, 94. *The Forest at Martigues.*
Oil, c. 1908–9.
Lent by Henry Kahnweiler.
Price listed: $378. Sold for $378 to Arthur J. Eddy, March 2, 1913.
Present collection: The Art Institute of Chicago; Arthur Jerome Eddy Memorial Collection.

344. *La Fenêtre sur le parc.*
Chicago, 95. Boston, 38. *The Window Overlooking the Park.*
Now called *Window at Vers.*
Oil, 1912.
Lent by Henry Kahnweiler.
Price listed: $486. Sold for $486 to John Quinn, February 26, 1913.
Present collection: The Museum of Modern Art, New York; Abby Aldrich Rockefeller Fund, purchased in memory of Mrs. Cornelius J. Sullivan.

DIMOCK, Edith (1876–1955)

114. *Sweat Shop Girls in the Country.*
Watercolor.
Lent by the artist.
Price listed: $35. Sold for $35 to John Quinn, March 13, 1913.

115. *Mother and Daughter.*
Watercolor.
Lent by the artist.
Price listed: $35. Sold for $35 to John Quinn, March 13, 1913.

116. *Group.*

Watercolor(?).
Lent by the artist.
No price listed.

117. *Group.*
Watercolor(?).
Lent by the artist.
No price listed.

118. *Group.*
Watercolor(?).
Lent by the artist.
No price listed.

119. *Group.*
Watercolor(?).
Lent by the artist.
No price listed.

120. *Group.*
Watercolor(?).
Lent by the artist.
No price listed.

121. *Group.*
Watercolor(?).
Lent by the artist.
No price listed.

All six, nos. 116–21, were sold for $280 to George E. Marcus, February 22, 1913.

Chicago, 96. *Drawings.*
Lent by the artist.
No price listed.

DIRKS, Rudolph (1877–1968)

954. *Cows.*
Now called *Wisconsin Cow Path.*
Oil.
Lent by the artist.
No price listed.
Present collection (1963): Mrs. Mae St. Clair, Washington, D.C.

955. *Landscape.*
Oil.
Lent by the artist.
No price listed.

DOLINSKY, Nathaniel (1889–n.d.)

757. *The Sightless.* †

262

Oil.
Lent by the artist.
Price listed: $600.
Present collection (1963): The artist, Hunter, New York.

DONOHO, G. Ruger
(1857–1916)

124. *A Garden.*
Oil.
Lent by the artist.
Price listed: $2,000.

125. *A Veil of Leaves.*
Oil.
Lent by the artist.
Price listed: $2,000.

126. *Portrait of Self.*
Oil.
Lent by the artist.
Not for sale.

DOUCET, Henri Lucien
(1856–1895)

363. *Torre del greco.*
Chicago, 97.
Watercolor.
Lent by Heinrich Thannhauser, #1620.
Price listed: $26.

364. *Vesuvius.*
Watercolor.
Lent by Heinrich Thannhauser, #1608.
Price listed: $26.

365. *Orsay.*
Chicago, 98.
Watercolor.
Lent by Heinrich Thannhauser, #1616.
Price listed: $26.

366. *Naples.*
Watercolor.
Lent by Heinrich Thannhauser, #1619.
Price listed: $26.

367. *Palms near Naples.*
Watercolor.

Lent by Heinrich Thannhauser, #976.
Price listed: $26.

368. *Palermo.*
Chicago, 99.
Watercolor.
Lent by Heinrich Thannhauser, #1634.
Price listed: $26.

DREIER, Katherine Sophie
(1877–1952)

36. *Blue Bowl.*
Oil.
Lent by the artist.
Price listed: $300.

37. *The Avenue, Holland.*
Oil.
Lent by the artist.
Price listed: $300.

DRESSER, Aileen (n.d.)

788. *Quai de la Tournelle, Paris.* †
Oil.
Lent by the artist.
Price listed: $100.

789. *Madame DuBois.* †
Oil.
Lent by the artist.
Price listed: $100.

790. *Notre Dame, Spring.* †
Chicago, 101.
Oil.
Lent by the artist.
Price listed: $300.

DRESSER, Lawrence Tyler (n.d.)

799. *A Russian Student.* †
Oil.
Lent by the artist.
Price listed: $300.

800. *Mlle. Lucienne.* †
Oil.
Lent by the artist.
Price listed: $300.

DREYFOUS, Florence (n.d.)

811. *A Boy.* †
Watercolor.
Lent by the artist.
Price listed: $200.

812. *Mildred.* †
Watercolor.
Lent by the artist.
Price listed: $150.
Former collection: Carl Sprinchorn, New York; now deceased.

DU BOIS, Guy Pène (1884–1958)

1034. *Waiter.*
Oil.
Lent by the artist.
Price listed: $200.

1035. *Interior.*
Chicago, 102.
Oil, 1912.
Lent by the artist.
Price listed: $300.
Present collection (1963): Mr. and Mrs. Henry Katz, New York.

* **1036.** *Twentieth-Century Youth.*
Oil.
Lent by the artist.
Price listed: $200.
Present collection (1963): Albro C. Gaylor, Sparkhill, New York.

1037. *Cascade, Bois de Boulogne.*
Chicago, 103.
Oil.
Lent by the artist.
Price listed: $200.
Former collection: Mr. and Mrs. Lawrence A. Fleischman, New York.

1038. *Virginia.*
Oil.
Lent by the artist.
Price listed: $200.

1039. *The Politician.*
Chicago, 104.
Oil.
Lent by the artist.
Price listed: $200.

Present collection: Barnes Foundation, Merion, Pennsylvania.

DUCHAMP, Marcel (1887–1968)

* **239.** *Le Roi et la reine entourés des nus vites.*
Chicago, 105. *King and Queen Surrounded by Nudes.*
Now called *The King and Queen Surrounded by Swift Nudes.*
Oil, 1912.
Lent by the artist.
Price listed: $324. Sold for $324 to Arthur J. Eddy, March 2, 1913.
Present collection: Philadelphia Museum of Art; Louise and Walter Arensberg Collection.

240. *Portrait de joueurs d'échecs.*
Chicago, 106. *Chess Players.*
Now called *Portrait of Chess Players.*
Oil, 1911.
Lent by the artist.
Price listed: $162. Sold for $162 to Arthur J. Eddy, March 1, 1913.
Present collection: Philadelphia Museum of Art; Louise and Walter Arensberg Collection.

* **241.** *Nu descendant un escalier.*
Chicago, 107. Boston, 39. *Nude Figure Descending a Staircase.*
Now called *Nude Descending a Staircase, No. 2.*
Oil, 1912.
Lent by the artist.
Price listed: $324. Sold for $324 to Frederic C. Torrey, March 5, 1913.
Present collection: Philadelphia Museum of Art; Louise and Walter Arensberg Collection.

242. *Nu.*
Chicago, 108. Boston, 40. *Sketch of a Nude.*
Now called *Jeune Homme triste dans un train.* Elsewhere called *Nu (esquisse).*
Oil, 1912.
Lent by the artist.
Price listed: $162. Sold for $162 to Manierre Dawson, April 7, 1913,

Chicago.
Present collection: Peggy
Guggenheim Collection, Venice.

DUCHAMP-VILLON, Raymond
(1876–1918)

609. *Façade architecturale.*
Plaster, dated on entry blank 1912.
Lent by the artist.
Price listed: $5,400 (with
reproduction rights).
See no. 1112.

*610. *Torse.*
Chicago, 109. Boston, 41. *Torso.*
Now called *Torso of a Young Man.*
Plaster, dated on the entry blank
1911. Now dated 1910.
Lent by the artist.
Price listed: $54 (plaster); $216
(bronze); $135 (terracotta). Bronze
sold for $216 to John Quinn,
February 26, 1913.
Present collection: Hirshhorn
Museum and Sculpture Garden,
Smithsonian Institution,
Washington, D.C.; Gift of Joseph
H. Hirshhorn, 1966.

611. *Fille des bois.*
Chicago, 110. Boston, 42. *Girl of
the Woods.*
Bronze, dated on entry blank 1910.
Although listed in catalogue as
plaster, it was described as bronze on
entry blank, shipping invoice, and
in ledger.
Lent by the artist.
Price listed: $270. Sold for $270 to
John Quinn, February 26, 1913.

612. *Danseurs.*
Terracotta bas-relief, dated on entry
blank 1911. Listed as terracotta in
ledger, described as bas-relief in
terracotta on entry blank; "plaster"
crossed out in Kuhn catalogue.
Lent by the artist.
Price listed: $67.50 (terracotta).
Sold for $67.50 to Arthur B.
Davies, February 20, 1913.
Present collection: Munson-
Williams-Proctor Institute, Utica,
New York.

613. *Baudelaire.*
Chicago, 111. Boston, 43.
Listed as terracotta in record book
and on entry blank, 1911. Broken
and repaired in Boston.
Lent by the artist.
Price listed: $162, limited edition.

DUFFY, Richard H. (1881–1953)

1021. *Tristesse.*
Plaster.
Lent by the artist.
Price listed: $75.

1022. *Study of Lady.*
Plaster.
Lent by the artist.
Not for sale.

DUFRENOY, Georges Léon
(1870–1944)

261. *Vals et vallons.*
Oil.
Lent by Emile Druet.
Price listed: $540.

262. *Sienne.*
Chicago, 112. *Siena.*
Oil.
Lent by Emile Druet.
Price listed: $540.

DUFY, Raoul (1877–1953)

331. *Leopold Str., Munich.*
Chicago, 113. Boston, 44.
Oil, dated on entry blank 1909.
Lent by the artist.
Price listed: $540.

332. *Regate sur la Manche.*
Chicago, 114. Boston, 45. *Regatta
on the English Channel.*
Oil, dated on entry blank 1909.
Lent by the artist.
Price listed: $540.

EBERLE, Abastenia St. Leger
(1878–1942)

265

672. *Group, Coney Island.*
Sculpture.
Lent by the artist.
Price listed: $500 (bronze only).

673. *White Slave.*
Statuette.
Lent by the artist.
Price listed: $500 (bronze only).

EDDY, Henry B. (1872–1935)

942. *Drawings.*
Lent by the artist.
No price listed.

EELS, Jean (n.d.)

949. *Case of China.*
Decorated china.
Lent by the artist.
Silver Willow Bowl. $50.
Orange Bowl. $25.
Orange Cups (pair). $15.
Ballet Girl Tray. $12.
Golden Glow (cup and saucer). $15.
Dark Blue and Gold (cup and saucer). $15.
Silver Lustre Tea Pot. $15.
White and Gold (cream pitcher). $6 (to order only).
White and Gold (meat platter). $25 (to order only).
White and Gold (dinner plates). $175 dozen (to order only).
Silver Flower (salad plates). $125 dozen (to order only).
Pale Blue (tea cups). $60 dozen (to order only).

ENGLE, Amos W. (n.d.)

775. *Windy Night.* †
Oil.
Lent by the artist.
Price listed: $75.

776. *The Sprint.* †
Oil.
Lent by the artist.
Price listed: $150 in Kuhn catalogue; $95 in MacRae catalogue.

EPSTEIN, Jacob (1880–1959)

589. *Bust of E. L.*
Now called *Euphemia Lamb.*
Bronze, 1908.
Lent by John Quinn.
Not for sale. Copies $1,170 (bronze).

ESTE, Florence (1860–1925/26)

90. *The Village.*
Watercolor.
Lent by the artist.
Price listed: $500 in Kuhn catalogue; $200 in MacRae catalogue.

91. *The First Snow.*
Chicago, 120.
Watercolor.
Lent by the artist.
Price listed: $300 in Kuhn catalogue; not for sale in MacRae catalogue.

EVERETT, Lily (1899–n.d.)

741. *Sunset on the Cottonfields.* †
Oil.
Lent by the artist.
Price listed: $300.

FLANDRIN, Jules (1871–1947)

164. *Coin du village.*
Chicago, 121. *Village Corner.*
Oil.
Lent by Emile Druet.
Price listed: $540.

165. *St. Marc, Venise.*
Oil.
Lent by Emile Druet.
Price listed: $648.

166. *Venise.*
Chicago, 122. *Venice.*
Oil.
Lent by Emile Druet.
Price listed: $1,080.

167. *Vallée Isère.*
Chicago, 123. *Isère Valley.*
Oil.

Lent by Emile Druet.
Price listed: $540.

FOOTE, Mary (1872–1968)

103. *Portrait.*
Chicago, 124.
Now called *Old Lady.*
Oil.
Lent by the artist.
Not for sale. This picture was sold
to the Friends of American Art in
Chicago after the Show. The AAPS
was paid $80 in commission on
November 29, 1913.
Present collection: The Art
Institute of Chicago; Gift of Friends
of American Art.

FRASER, James Earle
(1876–1953)

674. *Frame of Medals.*
Bronze.
Lent by the artist.
No price listed.

675. *Horse.*
Bronze.
Lent by the artist.
No price listed.

676. *Grief.*
Marble.
Lent by the artist.
No price listed.
Present collection (1963): Mrs.
James Earle Fraser, Westport,
Connecticut.

FRAZIER, Kenneth (1867–1949)

33. *Winter Garden.*
Chicago, 125.
Oil.
Lent by the artist.
Price listed: $500.
Present collection (1963): Mrs.
Donald MacInnes, Garrison-on-
Hudson, New York.

34. *The Shade Hat.*
Oil.
Lent by the artist.

Price listed: $500.

35. *Study.*
Oil.
Lent by the artist.
Price listed: $500.
Present collection (1963): Mrs.
Donald MacInnes, Garrison-on-
Hudson, New York.

FREUND, Arthur Ernest
(1890–n.d.)

820. *The Pig.* †
Chicago, 130.
Oil.
Lent by the artist.
Price listed: $150. Sold for $150 to
Mrs. Barend Van Gerbig, March 7,
1913.
Present collection (1963): Avis
Roemer Gardiner, Stamford,
Connecticut.

FRIESZ, Othon (1879–1949)

154. *Paysage.*
Oil.
Lent by Emile Druet.
Price listed: $324.

155. *Route Vallon.*
Oil.
Lent by Emile Druet.
Price listed: $324.

156. *Baigneuses.*
Chicago, 131. *Bathers.*
Now called *Landscape with Figures.*
Oil, 1909.
Lent by Emile Druet.
Price listed: $1,620.
Present collection: The Museum of
Modern Art, New York; Gift of
Saidie A. May.

157. *Coimbra.*
Chicago, 132.
Oil.
Lent by Emile Druet.
Price listed: $459.

158. *Vegetation exotique.*
Chicago, 133. *Exotic Vegetation.*

267

Oil.
Lent by Emile Druet.
Price listed: $405.

FRY, Sherry Edmunson
(1879–n.d.)

717. *Bust.*
Bronze.
Catalogued but not received.

FUHR, Ernest (1874–1933)

62. *Etaples.*
Oil.
Lent by the artist.
No price listed.
Present collection: Herbert H.
Brodkin, New York.

63. *Fishing Boat, Etaples.*
Chicago, 134.
Oil.
Lent by the artist.
No price listed.

GAUGUIN, Paul (1848–1903)

173. *Faa iheihe.*
Chicago, 136. Boston, 53.
Oil, dated on entry blank 1898.
Lent by Ambroise Vollard.
Price listed: $8,100.
Present collection: The Tate
Gallery, London.

*** 174.** *Sous les palmiers.*
Chicago, 137. Boston, 54. *Under
Palms.*
Now called *Under the Palm Trees.*
Oil, dated on entry blank 1891.
Lent by Ambroise Vollard.
Price listed: $4,050.
Former collection: Ralph M. Coe
Collection, Cleveland.

175. *L'Esprit du mal.*
Chicago, 138. Boston, 55. *The Spirit
of Evil.*
Now called *Words of the Devil.*
Oil, dated on entry blank 1892.
Lent by Ambroise Vollard.
Price listed: $4,050.
Present collection: National Gallery

of Art, Washington, D.C.; Gift of
Averell Harriman Foundation in
memory of Marie N. Harriman.

176. *Fleurs sur un fond jaune.*
Chicago, 139. Boston, 56. *Flowers.*
Now called *Still Life with Head-
Shaped Vase and Japanese Woodcut.*
Oil, dated on entry blank 1889.
Lent by Ambroise Vollard.
Price listed: $40,500; 150,000F in
record book; $4,050 on entry blank.
Present collection: Museum of
Modern Art, Teheran.

177. *Tête d'homme.*
Chicago, 140. Boston, 57. *Head of
a Man.*
Now called *Head of a Tahitian Man.*
Drawing, black and red crayon,
1891–93.
Lent by Mrs. Chadbourne.
Not for sale.
Present collection: The Art
Institute of Chicago; Gift of Mrs.
Emily Crane Chadbourne.

178. *Femme accroupie.*
Chicago, 141. Boston, 58. *Woman
Stooping.*
Watercolor.
Lent by Mrs. Chadbourne.
Not for sale.

179. *Femme et enfant.*
Chicago, 142. Boston, 59. *Woman
and Child.*
Watercolor.
Lent by Mrs. Chadbourne.
Not for sale.

180. *A la source.*
Chicago, 143. Boston, 60. *At the
Spring.*
Watercolor, 1891–93.
Lent by Mrs. Chadbourne.
Not for sale.
Present collection: The Art
Institute of Chicago; Gift of Mrs.
Emily Crane Chadbourne.

181. *Nature morte.*
Chicago, 144. Boston, 61. *Still Life.*
Oil, dated on entry blank 1888.

Lent by Emile Druet.
Price listed: $5,400.

182. *Atelier.*
Chicago, 145. Boston, 62. *The Studio.*
Now called *The Schuffenecker Family.*
Oil, dated on entry blank 1889.
Lent by Emile Druet.
Price listed: $9,450.
Present collection: Musée d'Orsay, Paris.

581. *Tahitian Scene.*
Chicago, 147. Boston, 64.
Elsewhere called *Promenade au bord de la mer.*
Oil.
Lent by John Quinn.
Not for sale.

615. *Bois sculpté.*
Chicago, 135. Boston, 52. *Wood Sculpture.*
Wood, dated on entry blank 1892.
Lent by Emile Druet.
Price listed: $945.

1066. *Landscape, Tahiti.*
Chicago, 146. Boston, 63.
Oil.
Lent by Mrs. Alexander Tison.
No price listed.

Note: Tahitian Child and *Two Tahitian Women in Landscape*—both now in the Art Institute of Chicago; Gift of Mrs. Emily Crane Chadbourne, and both identifiable in the Chicago Armory Show photographs—may be, respectively, *Femme accroupie* (no. 178) and *Femme et enfant* (no. 179).

Lithographs.
Not listed in New York catalogue, but displayed for sale and order.
Chicago, 148. Boston, 65.
From the evidence available it is impossible to determine which lithographs were exhibited. The sales records indicate the sale of two sets and eleven separate prints. Of these, the identified examples are all from a series of eleven lithographs on zinc executed by Gauguin in 1889 and printed by Ancourt. The plates were sold by Schuffenecker to Vollard, who printed an edition on "Japan" paper. The separate sets seem, because of price, to have no connection with the single prints, nor is the number of prints in a set known.
Lent by Ambroise Vollard.
Price listed: $27 set, $6 single. Two sets sold for $54 to John Quinn, March 10 and June 3, 1913. Single lithographs: Two sold for $12 to Lillie P. Bliss, March 4, 1913: *Pastorales Martiniques* and *Les Cigales et les fourmis* (Present collection: The Museum of Modern Art, New York; Lillie P. Bliss Collection). One sold for $6 to Arthur B. Davies, March 4, 1913. One sold for $6 to Mrs. Charles C. Rumsey, March 6, 1913. One sold for $6 to Allen Tucker, March 7, 1913. One sold for $6 to John Quinn, March 9, 1913. One sold for $6 to Arthur B. Spingarn, March 9, 1913. *Joies de Bretagne* sold for $6 to Katherine S. Dreier, March 13, 1913 (Present collection: Yale University Art Gallery, New Haven, Connecticut; Collection Société Anonyme). *Pastorales Martiniques* sold for $6 to Walter Pach, March 24, 1913, Chicago (Present collection [1963]: Mrs. Walter Pach, New York). *Les Cigales et les fourmis* sold for $6 to John Quinn for Miss Coates, March 25, 1913, Chicago. *Projet d'assiette* sold to Walter C. Arensberg, May 19, 1913, Boston.

GAYLOR, Samuel Wood
(1883–n.d.)

827. *House Boat.* †
Oil.
Lent by the artist.

Price listed: $100.
Present collection (1963): Mrs.
Adelaide L. Gaylor, Glenwood
Landing, New York.

828. *Landscape.* †
Oil.
Lent by the artist.
Price listed: $100.
Present collection (1963): Mrs.
Adelaide L. Gaylor, Glenwood
Landing, New York.

GIBB, Phelan (n.d.)

184. *Three Figures.*
Oil, dated on entry blank 1911.
Lent by the artist.
Price listed: $337.50.

185. *Landscape.*
Oil, dated on entry blank 1911.
Lent by the artist.
Price listed: $675.

186. *Drawings, Nos. 1–12.*
Oil.
Lent by the artist.
No price listed.

GIMMI, Wilhelm (1886–n.d.)

192. *Musikanten.*
Oil.
Lent by Hans Goltz.
Price listed: $136.50.

GIRIEUD, Pierre (1875–1940)

201. *Fleurs.*
Oil.
Lent by Emile Druet.
Price listed: $162.

202. *Vitraux.*
Chicago, 149. Boston, 66. *Stained Glass.*
Oil.
Lent by Emile Druet.
Price listed: $81. Sold for $81 to
John Quinn, March 15, 1913.

203. *Hommage à Gauguin.*
Chicago, 150. Boston, 67. *Homage to Gauguin.*

Gouache, 1906.
Lent by Emile Druet.
Price listed: $189. Sold for $189 to
John Quinn, February 26, 1913.
Present collection: Mr. and Mrs.
Arthur Altschul, New York.

GLACKENS, William J.
(1870–1938)

*****853.** *Family Group.*
Oil, 1910–11.
Lent by the artist.
Not for sale.
Present collection: National Gallery
of Art, Washington, D.C.; Gift of
Mr. and Mrs. Ira Glackens.

854. *The Bathing Hour.*
Chicago, 157.
Oil.
Lent by the artist.
Price listed: $700.

855. *Sailboats and Sunlight.*
Oil.
Lent by the artist.
Price listed: $700.
Present collection (1963):
Kraushaar Galleries, New York.

GLEIZES, Albert (1881–1953)

195. *La Femme aux phlox.*
Chicago, 152. Boston, 68. *Woman and Phlox.*
Oil, dated on entry blank 1910.
Lent by the artist.
Price listed: $189.
Present collection: The Museum of
Fine Arts, Houston; Gift of the
Esther Florence Whinery Goodrich
Foundation.

196. *L'Homme au balcon.*
Chicago, 153. *Man on the Balcony.*
Now called *Man on Balcony.*
Oil, dated on entry blank 1912.
Lent by the artist.
Price listed: $540. Sold for $540 to
Arthur J. Eddy, March 2, 1913.
Present collection: Philadelphia

Museum of Art; Louise and Walter
Arensberg Collection.

GLINTENKAMP, Henry I.
(1887–1946)

84. *The Village Cemetery.* †
Oil.
Lent by the artist.
Price listed: $800.

VAN GOGH, Vincent
(1853–1890)

The number in parenthesis
following each title refers to J. B. de
la Faille, *L'Oeuvre de Vincent van
Gogh: Catalogue Raisonné*, Paris and
Brussels, 1928, 4 vols.

424. *Collines à Arles.* (F. 622)
Chicago, 408. Boston, 213. *Hills at
Arles.*
Now called *Mountains at Saint-
Rémy.*
Oil, 1889.
Lent by Emile Druet.
Price listed: $15,025; $16,200 on
entry blank.
Present collection: Solomon R.
Guggenheim Museum, New York;
The Justin K. Thannhauser
Collection.

*425. *Bal à Arles.* (F. 547)
Chicago, 409. Boston, 214. *Ball at
Arles.*
Elsewhere called *Dance Hall at
Arles.*
Oil, 1888.
Lent by Emile Druet.
Price listed: $8,830; $9,450 on
entry blank.
Present collection: Musée d'Orsay,
Paris.

426. *Le Zouave.* (F. 1482)
Chicago, 410. Boston, 215. *The
Zouave.*
Drawing. (All the evidence,
photographic as well as
documentary, indicates that it was
not an oil as listed.)

Lent by Emile Druet.
Price listed: $1,750; $1,890 on
entry blank.

427. *Montmartre.*
Chicago, 411. Boston, 216.
Oil, dated on entry blank 1888.
Lent by Artz & de Bois.
Price listed: $26,000.

428. *L'Olivier.* (F. 818)
Chicago, 412. Boston, 217. *The
Olive Tree.*
Now called *Landscape with Figures.*
Oil, dated on entry blank 1889.
Lent by Artz & de Bois.
Price listed: $6,500.
Present collection: The Baltimore
Museum of Art; The Cone
Collection.

429. *Dans les bois.* (F. 773)
Chicago, 413. Boston, 218. *In the
Woods.*
Now called *Undergrowth with Two
Figures.*
Oil, dated on entry blank 1889.
Lent by Artz & de Bois.
Price listed: $10,400.
Present collection: Cincinnati Art
Museum; Bequest of Mary E.
Johnston.

430. *Le Grand Olivier.* (F. 711)
Chicago, 414. Boston, 219. *The Big
Olive Tree.*
Now called *The Olive Plantation.*
Oil, dated on entry blank 1889.
Lent by Artz & de Bois.
Price listed: $5,200.
Present collection: Private
collection, Switzerland.

431. *Nature morte. Souliers de bois.*
(F. 607)
Chicago, 415. Boston, 220. *Wooden
Shoes.*
Oil, dated on entry blank c. 1887.
Lent by Artz & de Bois.
Price listed: $2,600.
Present collection: Rijksmuseum
Vincent van Gogh, Amsterdam.

432. *Nature morte. Ecrevisses.*

(F. 256)
Chicago, 416. Boston, 221.
Shrimps.
Oil, dated on entry blank 1887.
Lent by Artz & de Bois.
Price listed: $2,600.
Present collection: Rijksmuseum
Vincent van Gogh, Amsterdam.

433. *Moulin de Montmartre.*
(F. 271)
Chicago, 417. Boston, 222. *Mill,
Montmartre.*
Oil, dated on entry blank 1886.
Lent by Artz & de Bois.
Price listed: $2,600. Reduced to
$1,600, March 25, 1913.
Destroyed by fire, 1967.

434. *Paysage d'Arles.* (F. 708)
Chicago, 418. Boston, 223.
Landscape, Arles.
Now called *Olive Trees: Pale Blue Sky.*
Oil, dated on entry blank 1889.
Lent by Artz & de Bois.
Price listed: $5,200.
Present collection (1970): Mr. and
Mrs. Walter Annenberg.

435. *Des Pommes.*
Chicago, 419. Boston, 224. *Apples.*
Oil, dated on entry blank c. 1884.
Lent by Artz & de Bois.
Price listed: $2,600.

436. *Cruches en étain.*
Chicago, 420. Boston, 225. *Pewter
Pots.*
Oil, dated on entry blank 1882.
Lent by Artz & de Bois.
Price listed: $2,600.

582. *Self-Portrait.* (F. 268)
Chicago, 422. Boston, 227.
Oil, 1886.
Lent by John Quinn.
Not for sale.
Present collection: Wadsworth
Atheneum, Hartford, Connecticut.

1047. *Head and Shoulders of Young
Woman.* (F. 786)
Chicago, 423. Boston, 228.
Now called *Mlle. Ravoux.*

Oil, 1890.
Lent by Katherine S. Dreier.
No price listed.
Present collection: Cleveland
Museum of Art; Leonard C. Hanna,
Jr., Collection.

1048. *Woman Reading.*
Chicago, 421. Boston, 226.
Oil.
Lent by Stephan Bourgeois.
No price listed.

1049. *Red Flowers.* (F. 279)
Chicago, 424. Boston, 229.
Oil.
Lent by Stephan Bourgeois.
No price listed.

1050. *Lillies.*
Chicago, 425. Boston, 230.
Oil.
Lent by Stephan Bourgeois.
No price listed.

GOLDTHWAITE, Anne
(1875–1944)

829. *The Church on the Hill.* †
Now called *The House on the Hill.*
Oil, c. 1911.
Lent by the artist.
No price listed.
Present collection (1963): Miss
Lucy Goldthwaite, New York.

830. *Prince's Feathers.* †
Chicago, 154.
Oil.
Lent by the artist.
No price listed.

GOYA, Francisco (1746–1828)

588. *A Monk and Witch.*
Miniature on ivory.
Lent by John Quinn.
Not for sale.
Present collection: The Art
Museum, Princeton University,
Princeton, New Jersey.

GUERIN, Charles (1875–1939)

211. *Viole d'amour.*
Oil.
Lent by Emile Druet.
Price listed: $1,340; $1,350 on
entry blank.

212. *Dame à la rose.*
Oil.
Lent by Emile Druet.
Price listed: $3,240.

GUSSOW, Bernard (1881–1957)

40. *Movement.*
Oil.
Lent by the artist.
Price listed: $800.

41. *Figures.*
Chicago, 155.
Oil.
Lent by the artist.
Price listed: $300.

GUTMAN

957. Catalogued but not received.

GUTMANN, Bernhard
(1869–1936)

825. *In the Garden.* †
Oil, 1912.
Lent by the artist.
Price listed: $600.
Present collection (1963): Mrs.
Dorothea G. Mollenhauer, New
York.

HALE, Philip L. (1865–1931)

940. *Art Students.*
Oil.
Lent by the artist.
No price listed.
Present collection (1963): Ralph
McLellan, Lakeville, Connecticut.

941. *Studio.*
Oil.
Lent by the artist.
No price listed.
Present collection (1963): Mrs.

Philip L. Hale, Gloucester,
Massachusetts.

HALPERT, Samuel (1884–1930)

23. *Still Life.*
Substituted for *Portrait of a Lady.*
Oil.
Lent by the artist.
Price listed: $300 in Kuhn
catalogue; $400 in MacRae
catalogue.

24. *View of New York.*
Oil.
Lent by the artist.
Price listed: $400.

HARLEY, Charles R. (1864–n.d.)

764. *Freda.* †
Drawing.
Lent by the artist.
Price listed: $25.

HARTLEY, Marsden (1877–1943)

221. *Still Life, No. 1.*
Oil, 1912.
Lent by the artist.
Price listed: $720.
Present collection: Columbus
Museum of Art, Columbus, Ohio;
Gift of Ferdinand Howald.

222. *Still Life, No. 2.*
Oil.
Lent by the artist.
Price listed: $300.

223. *Drawings, No. 1.*
Lent by the artist.
Price listed: $48.

224. *Drawings, No. 2.*
Lent by the artist.
Price listed: $48.

225. *Drawings, No. 3.*
Lent by the artist.
Price listed: $48.

226. *Drawings, No. 4.*
Lent by the artist.
Price listed: $48.

227. *Drawings, No. 5.*
Lent by the artist.
Price listed: $48.

228. *Drawings, No. 6.*
Lent by the artist.
Price listed: $48.

HASSAM, Childe (1859–1935)

71. *Nude Woman with Mirror.*
Oil.
Lent by the artist.
Price listed: $6,000.

72. *The Spanish Stairs.*
Oil, 1897.
Lent by the artist.
Price listed: $6,000.
Present collection: Los Angeles
County Museum of Art; William
Randolph Hearst Collection.

73. *Naples.*
Chicago, 156.
Oil.
Lent by the artist.
Price listed: $4,500.
Present collection: John R. Lehman,
New York.

* **74.** *Vesuvius.*
Oil, 1897.
Lent by the artist.
Price listed: $4,000.
Present collection: Hirshhorn
Museum and Sculpture Garden,
Smithsonian Institution,
Washington, D.C.; Gift of Joseph
H. Hirshhorn.

75. *Posilippo.*
Now called *Bridge at Posilippo,
Naples.*
Oil.
Lent by the artist.
Price listed: $3,000.
Former collection: Ira Spanierman
Inc., New York.
In sale at Christie's, New York,
December 4, 1987.

76. *Cos Cob.*
Oil.

Lent by the artist.
Price listed: $3,000.

96. *Cos Cob, Old House.*
Pastel.
Lent by the artist.
Price listed: $850.

97. *Cos Cob, Old House.*
Pastel.
Lent by the artist.
Price listed: $850.

98. *Cos Cob, Old House.*
Pastel.
Lent by the artist.
Price listed: $650.

99. *Sylph Rock, Appledore.*
Pastel.
Lent by the artist.
Price listed: $650.

100. *The Rain, Connecticut Hills.*
Pastel.
Lent by the artist.
Price listed: $650.

101. *Drawing for Moonrise at Sunset.*
Lent by the artist.
Not for sale.

HAWORTH, Edith (n.d.)

806. *The Birthday Party.* †
Oil.
Lent by the artist.
Price listed: $75.

807. *The Village Band.* †
Oil.
Lent by the artist.
Price listed: $200.

HELBIG, Walter (1878–n.d.)

484. *Liegendes Mädchen.*
Oil.
Lent by Hans Goltz.
Price listed: $260.

HENRI, Robert (1865–1929)

835. *Figure in Motion.*
Chicago, 157.
Oil, 1912.

Lent by the artist.
Price listed: $2,000.
Present collection: Terra Museum
of American Art, Chicago; Daniel J.
Terra Collection.

836. *The Gipsy.*
Now called *The Spanish Gypsy.*
Oil.
Lent by the artist.
Price listed: $1,800.
Present collection: The
Metropolitan Museum of Art,
New York.

*837. *The Red Top.*
Oil.
Lent by the artist.
Price listed: $900. Sold for $900 to
Amos R. E. Pinchot, February 24,
1913.
Present collection (1963): Mrs.
Amos Pinchot, New York.

838. *Drawing.*
Lent by the artist.
Price listed: $25. Sold for $25 to
Mary L. Willard, March 15, 1913.

839. *Drawing.*
Lent by the artist.
Price listed: $25.

HESS, Julius (1878–c. 1935)

243. *Dame mit grünem Schirm.*
Oil, dated on entry blank 1912.
Lent by Heinrich Thannhauser,
#2897.
Price listed: $292.50.

HIGGINS, Eugene (1874–1958)

15. *Hunger under a Bridge.*
Chicago, 158.
Tempera.
Lent by the artist.
Price listed: $250.

16. *Convicts and Guard.*
Drawing.
Lent by the artist.
Price listed: $150.

17. *Weary.*

Oil.
Lent by the artist.
Price listed: $250. Sold for $200 to
George W. Curtis, March 1, 1913.

HOARD, Margaret (1879–1944)

714. *Study of an Old Lady.*
Sculpture.
Lent by the artist.
Price listed: $50 (plaster); $110
(bronze).

HODLER, Ferdinand (1853–1918)

258. *Der Niessen.*
Chicago, 159. Boston, 69. *The
Niessen Mountain.*
Oil, dated on entry blank 1910.
Lent by Heinrich Thannhauser,
#1776.
Price listed: $812.50.

*259. *Die heilige Stunde* (*Fragment*).
Oil, dated on entry blank 1910.
Lent by Heinrich Thannhauser,
#2251.
Price listed: $4,875.

HONE, Nathaniel (1831–1917)

585. *Lough Swilly.*
Oil, 1895.
Lent by John Quinn.
Not for sale.

586. *Hastings.*
Chicago, 160. Boston, 70.
Oil, 1890.
Lent by John Quinn.
Not for sale.

HOPKINSON, Charles
(1869–1962)

69. *Group of Children.*
Now called *Three Girls.*
Oil, 1911.
Lent by the artist.
Price listed: $1,000.
Present collection (1963): Mrs.
Harriot Hopkinson Rive, Dublin.

275

70. *Yachting.*
Oil.
Lent by the artist.
Price listed: $500.

94. *Marine.*
Catalogued but not received.

95. *Landscape.*
Catalogued but not received.

HOPPER, Edward (1882–1967)

751. *Sailing.*
Oil, 1912–13.
Lent by the artist.
Price listed: $300. Sold for $250 to
Thomas F. Vietor, March 14, 1913.
Present collection: The Carnegie
Museum of Art, Pittsburgh; Gift of
Mr. and Mrs. James H. Beal in
honor of the Sarah M. Scaife
Gallery.

HOWARD, Cecil DeB.
(1888–1956)

614. *Woman.*
Chicago, 160½.
Plaster, dated on entry blank 1912.
Lent by the artist.
Price listed: $1,020 (bronze); not for
sale (plaster).

HUMPHREYS, Albert
(n.d.–1925)

723. *Orpheus Charming Animals.*
Sculpture.
Lent by the artist.
No price listed.

724. *Bear Upright.*
Sculpture.
Lent by the artist.
Price listed: $160.

938. *Nocturne, Cape Cod.*
Chicago, 161.
Oil.
Lent by the artist.
Price listed: $500.

939. *Landscape.*
Oil.

Lent by the artist.
Price listed: $500.

1103. *Six Drawings.*
Chicago, 162. Drawings.
Lent by the artist.
Price listed: $25 each; 9 for $200.
One may assume from this that
there were more than six drawings.

HUNT, Mrs. Thomas (n.d.)

752. *The Fishers.* †
Oil.
Lent by the artist.
Price listed: $200.

**HUNTINGTON, Margaret
Wendell** (n.d.)

824. *Cliffs Newquay.* †
Oil.
Lent by the artist.
Price listed: $200.

**INGRES, Jean-Auguste-
Dominique** (1780–1867)

688. *Drawing.*
Chicago, 163. Boston, 71.
Lent by Egisto Fabbri.
Not for sale.

689. *Drawing.*
Chicago, 164. Boston, 72.
Lent by Egisto Fabbri.
Not for sale.

INNES, James Dickson
(1887–1914)

546. *Evening near Arenig, North
Wales.*
Chicago, 165. Boston, 73.
Oil, 1911.
Lent by John Quinn.
Not for sale.

547. *The Rambler's Rest, North
Wales.*
Oil, 1912.
Lent by John Quinn.
Not for sale.

548. *The Cactus.*

Chicago, 166. Boston, 74.
Oil, 1912.
Lent by John Quinn.
Not for sale.
Present collection (1963): Private
collection.

549. *Palm Trees at Collioure.*
Chicago, 167. Boston, 75.
Oil, 1912.
Lent by John Quinn.
Not for sale.

550. *Coast of Cerberre.*
Watercolor, 1911.
Lent by John Quinn.
Not for sale.

551. *Arenig-Fawr.*
Watercolor, 1911.
Lent by John Quinn.
Not for sale.

552. *The Mountain.*
Watercolor, 1911.
Lent by John Quinn.
Not for sale.

JANSEN, F. M. (1885–n.d.)

318. *Vor der Stadt.*
Oil, dated on entry blank 1912.
Lent by the artist.
Price listed: $195.

319. *Ragusa.*
Pastel, dated on entry blank 1911.
Lent by the artist.
Price listed: $19.50. Sold for $19.50
to Mrs. Reginald Fincke, March 11,
1913.

320. *Garda See Riva.*
Etching, dated on entry blank 1912.
Lent by the artist.
Price listed: $19.50. Sold for $19.50
to William P. Chapman, Jr.,
February 22, 1913.

321. *Fiume.*
Colored drawing, dated on entry
blank 1911.
Lent by the artist.
Price listed: $19.50.

322. *Vor der Stadt.*
Watercolor, dated on entry blank
1912.
Lent by the artist.
Price listed: $19.50.

323. *Die Ernte.*
Etching, dated on entry blank 1912.
Lent by the artist.
Price listed: $19.50.

324. *Garda See.*
Etching, dated on entry blank 1912.
Lent by the artist.
Price listed: $19.50. Sold for $19.50
to William P. Chapman, Jr.,
February 22, 1913.

325. *Ein Park.*
Drawing, dated on entry blank
1910.
Lent by the artist.
Price listed: $19.50.

326. *Cypressen.*
Etching, dated on entry blank 1912.
Lent by the artist.
Price listed: $19.50.

327. *Triest.*
Colored drawing, dated on entry
blank 1911.
Lent by the artist.
Price listed: $19.50.

328. *Das Dorf.*
Etching, dated on entry blank 1912.
Lent by the artist.
Price listed: $19.50. Sold for $19.50
to William P. Chapman, Jr.,
February 22, 1913.

329. *Trient.*
Etching, dated on entry blank 1912.
Lent by the artist.
Price listed: $19.50.

330. *Sarajewo.*
Colored drawing, dated on entry
blank 1911.
Lent by the artist.
Price listed: $19.50.

JOHN, Augustus E. (1878–1961)

509. *A Girl's Head.*

277

Chicago, 177 or 178. Boston, 85 or 86.
Drawing, 1911.
Lent by John Quinn.
Not for sale.

510. *Portrait of a Man.*
Drawing, 1911.
Lent by John Quinn.
Not for sale.

511. *A Girl's Head.*
Chicago, 177 or 178. Boston, 85 or 86.
Drawing, 1911.
Lent by John Quinn.
Not for sale.

512. *A Girl's Head.*
Chicago, 177 or 178. Boston, 85 or 86.
Drawing, 1911.
Lent by John Quinn.
Not for sale.

513. *A Draped Figure.*
Drawing, black chalk, 1911.
Lent by John Quinn.
Not for sale.
Present collection: The Metropolitan Museum of Art, New York; Bequest of Stephen C. Clark.

514. *A Stooping Figure, Raising Dress.*
Drawing, 1912.
Lent by John Quinn.
Not for sale.

515. *Studies of a Boy.*
Pencil drawing, 1912.
Lent by John Quinn.
Not for sale.
Present collection: Albright-Knox Art Gallery, Buffalo, New York; Gift of A. Conger Goodyear.

516. *Nude Woman Reclining.*
Chicago, 179. Boston, 87.
Drawing, 1912.
Lent by John Quinn.
Not for sale.

517. *Nude Girl Seated, Side View.*
Chicago, 180. Boston, 88.

Drawing, 1912.
Lent by John Quinn.
Not for sale.

518. *Two Girls and a Boy.*
Chicago, 181. Boston, 89.
Drawing, 1912.
Lent by John Quinn.
Not for sale.

519. *Woman's Head and Shoulders.*
Chicago, 182. Boston, 90.
Drawing, 1912.
Lent by John Quinn.
Not for sale.

520. *Woman Gathering Sticks.*
Drawing, charcoal and gray watercolor, 1912.
Lent by John Quinn.
Not for sale.
Present collection: Albright-Knox Art Gallery, Buffalo, New York; Gift of A. Conger Goodyear.

521. *Design for a Painting.*
Ink drawing, 1912.
Lent by John Quinn.
Not for sale.

522. *A Girl with Cap.*
Charcoal drawing, 1909.
Lent by John Quinn.
Not for sale.

523. *Loving Companions.*
Chicago, 169. Boston, 77.
Tempera, 1912.
Lent by John Quinn.
Not for sale.

524. *Strange Company.*
Chicago, 170. Boston, 78.
Tempera, 1912.
Lent by John Quinn.
Not for sale.

525. *Gitana and Child.*
Chicago, 171. Boston, 79. *Gipsy and Child.*
Tempera, 1912.
Lent by John Quinn.
Not for sale.

** **526.** *The Way Down to the Sea.*

Oil, 1909–11.
Lent by John Quinn.
Not for sale.
Former collection: Lamont Art
Gallery, Phillips Exeter Academy,
Exeter, New Hampshire.

527. *The Olives, Provençal Study.*
Oil, 1910.
Lent by John Quinn.
Not for sale.

528. *The Old Chapel, Provençal
Study.*
Oil, 1910.
Lent by John Quinn.
Not for sale.

529. *Two Boys Bathing, Provençal
Study.*
Oil, 1910.
Lent by John Quinn.
Not for sale.

530. *La Mede, Provençal Study.*
Oil, 1910.
Lent by John Quinn.
Not for sale.

531. *Near Pont du Bonc, Provençal
Study.*
Oil, 1910.
Lent by John Quinn.
Not for sale.

532. *Woman Standing against the
Sky, Provençal Study.*
Chicago, 172. Boston, 80.
Oil, 1910.
Lent by John Quinn.
Not for sale.

533. *Woman Seated in a Garden,
Provençal Study.*
Chicago, 173. Boston, 81. *Woman
in a Garden.*
Oil, 1910.
Lent by John Quinn.
Not for sale.

534. *The Olives by the Pond,
Provençal Study.*
Oil, 1910.
Lent by John Quinn.
Not for sale.

535. *Boy Standing on Cliff,
Provençal Study.*
Oil, 1910.
Lent by John Quinn.
Not for sale.

536. *Boy on Cliff Leaning on a Stick,
Provençal Study.*
Oil, 1910.
Lent by John Quinn.
Not for sale.

537. *Martigues, Provençal Study.*
Oil, 1910.
Lent by John Quinn.
Not for sale.

538. *Woman and Children, Evening,
Provençal Study.*
Oil, 1910.
Lent by John Quinn.
Not for sale.

539. *Girl with Three Children,
Standing, Provençal Study.*
Oil, 1910.
Lent by John Quinn.
Not for sale.

540. *Woman Reading, Provençal
Study.*
Chicago, 168. Boston, 76.
Oil, 1910.
Lent by John Quinn.
Not for sale.

541. *Edyth and Caspar, Dorset
Study.*
Oil, 1911.
Lent by John Quinn.
Not for sale.

542. *Three Little Boys, Dorset Study.*
Chicago, 174. Boston, 82.
Oil, 1911.
Lent by John Quinn.
Not for sale.

543. *Caspar and Pyramus, Dorset
Study.*
Chicago, 175. Boston, 83.
Oil, 1911.
Lent by John Quinn.
Not for sale.

279

544. *Welsh Study: "Rhyd-y-fin."*
Chicago, 176. Boston, 84.
Oil, 1910.
Lent by John Quinn.
Not for sale.
Present collection (1963): Reine
Pitman, London.

545. *Group of Boys Paddling,*
Provençal Study.
Oil, 1910.
Lent by John Quinn.
Not for sale.

1019. *Persian Garden.*
Oil.
Lent by Alexander Morten.
Not for sale.

Boston, 90a. *The Desert.*
Oil.
Lent by the artist.
Price listed: $260.

Boston, 90b. *Pines.*
Oil.
Lent by the artist.
Price listed: $260.

Boston, 90c. *The Orange Frock.*
Oil.
Lent by the artist.
Price listed: $650.

Boston, 90d. *The Coast of Clare.*
Oil.
Lent by the artist.
Price listed: $585.

Boston, 90e. *The Yellow Dress.*
Oil.
Lent by the artist.
Price listed: $780.

Boston, 90f. *The Red Shawl.*
Oil.
Lent by the artist.
Price listed: $650.

JOHN, Gwen (1876–1939)

578. *Girl Reading at the Window.*
Chicago, 183. Boston, 91.
Oil, 1911.
Lent by John Quinn.
Not for sale.

Present collection: The Museum of
Modern Art, New York; Mary
Anderson Conroy Bequest in
memory of her mother, Julia Quinn
Anderson.

579. *A Woman in a Red Shawl.*
Oil, 1912.
Lent by John Quinn.
Not for sale.
Catalogued but not received.

JOHNSON, Grace Mott
(1882–n.d.)

648. *Chimpanzees.*
Chicago, 184.
Bronze.
Lent by the artist.
Price listed: $250.

649. *Chimpanzees.*
Chicago, 184.
Bronze.
Lent by the artist.
Price listed: $200.

650. *Greyhound Pup, No. 2.*
Bronze.
Lent by the artist.
Price listed: $200.

651. *Relief.*
Plaster.
Lent by the artist.
Price listed: $150.

JUNGHANNS, Julius Paul
(1876–1953)

341. *Vieh mit Hirten unter Baumen.*
Oil, dated on entry blank 1911.
Lent by the artist.
Price listed: $260.

KANDINSKY, Wassily
(1866–1944)

*213. *Improvisation.*
Now called *Garden of Love*
(*Improvisation #27*).
Chicago, 185. Boston, 92.
Oil, 1912.
Lent by Hans Goltz.
Price listed: $731.25. Sold for $500

to Alfred Stieglitz, March 8, 1913.
Present collection: The
Metropolitan Museum of Art, New
York; The Alfred Stieglitz
Collection.

KARFIOL, Bernard (1886–1952)

102. *Six Drawings.*
Lent by the artist.
Price listed: $20 each.

786. *Men at Rest.* †
Oil.
Lent by the artist.
Price listed: $50 in Kuhn catalogue;
$100 in MacRae catalogue.

787. *George.* †
Oil, 1909.
Lent by the artist.
Price listed: $100.
Present collection (1963): Mrs.
Bernard Karfiol, Irvington-on-
Hudson, New York.

KELLER, Henry G. (1870–1949)

25. *Wisdom and Destiny.*
Chicago, 186.
Oil.
Lent by the artist.
Price listed: $2,500.
Present collection: Cleveland
Museum of Art.

26. *The Valley.*
Chicago, 187.
Oil.
Lent by the artist.
Price listed: $300.

KING, Edith L. (n.d.)

943. *Statue at Ravello.*
Watercolor.
Lent by the artist.
Price listed: $50.

944. *Bathing Hours, Capri.*
Chicago, 188.
Watercolor.
Lent by the artist.
Price listed: $50.

945. *The Bathers, Capri.*
Watercolor.
Lent by the artist.
Price listed: $50.

946. *The Piccola Marina, Capri.*
Watercolor.
Lent by the artist.
Price listed: $50.

947. *The Marina Grande.*
Chicago, 189.
Watercolor.
Lent by the artist.
Price listed: $50.

KIRCHNER, Ernst Ludwig
(1880–1938)

208. *Wirtsgarten.*
Chicago, 190. Boston, 93. *The Inn
Garden.*
Oil.
Lent by Hans Goltz.
Price listed: $162.50.

KIRSTEIN, Alfred (1863–1922)

357. *Paysage.*
Chicago, 191. Boston, 94.
Landscape.
Watercolor, dated on entry blank
1912.
Lent by the artist.
Price listed: $81.

358. *Paysage.*
Chicago, 192. Boston, 95.
Landscape.
Watercolor, dated on entry blank
1912.
Lent by the artist.
Price listed: $81.

359. *Paysage.*
Chicago, 193. Boston, 96.
Landscape.
Watercolor, dated on entry blank
1912.
Lent by the artist.
Price listed: $81.

KLEIMINGER, Adolph
(1865–n.d.)

281

1. *Farm Yard.*
Oil.
Lent by the artist.
Price listed: $400.

2. *Morning.*
Chicago, 194.
Oil.
Lent by the artist.
Price listed: $400.

KLEINERT, Hermine E.
(1880–1943)

773. *Portrait Study.* †
Oil.
Lent by the artist.
Price listed: $100.

KRAMER, Edward Adam
(1866–1941)

** **881.** *Dawnlit.*
Oil.
Lent by the artist.
Price listed: $700. Sold for $700 to
Charles F. Williams, February 24,
1913.
Present collection: Munson-
Williams-Proctor Institute, Utica,
New York; Gift of Nathan Dolinsky.

882. *Trees of Echo Park.*
Oil.
Lent by the artist.
Price listed: $700.

883. *Meditation.*
Oil.
Lent by the artist.
Price listed: $500. Sold, with no.
884, for $625 to David H. Morris,
March 15, 1913.

884. *Rock Encompassed.*
Chicago, 197.
Oil.
Lent by the artist.
Price listed: $500. Sold, with no.
883, for $625 to David H. Morris,
March 15, 1913.

885. *Hues of Morning.*
Chicago, 198.

Pastel.
Lent by the artist.
Price listed: $150.

886. *Drowsy Afternoon.*
Chicago, 199.
Pastel.
Lent by the artist.
Price listed: $150. Noted as sold in
Kuhn catalogue.

887. *The Evangelist.*
Pastel.
Lent by the artist.
Price listed: $150. Sold for $100 to
Mrs. Samuel Untermeyer, March
11, 1913.

888. *Going to Sleep.*
Drawing.
Lent by the artist.
Price listed: $75.

889. *Quiet and Unseen.*
Drawing.
Lent by the artist.
Price listed: $75.

1107. *Bronx Park.*
Oil.
Lent by the artist.
No price listed.

1108. *The Swing.*
Oil.
Lent by the artist.
No price listed.

1109. *A Tangled Wood.*
Oil.
Lent by the artist.
No price listed.

1110. *Crotona Park.*
Oil.
Lent by the artist.
No price listed.

1111. *The Wood Deep and Quiet.*
Oil.
Lent by the artist.
No price listed.

April(?).
Pastel.
Lent by the artist.

Sold for $100 to Mrs. James E. Watson, February 26, 1913. This picture was called a painting in one letter and a pastel in a later letter by Mrs. James E. Watson, in which it was referred to as *April ?*, hanging near no. 887 and not included in the catalogue. The ledger entry on this sale is in error, listing it as no. 887, which was sold to Mrs. Untermeyer; see above.

Chicago, 195. *In Autumn Vesture.* *
Oil.
Lent by the artist.
No price listed.

Chicago, 196. *Young Woods.* *
Oil.
Lent by the artist.
No price listed.

*Kramer had a penchant for changing the titles of his works, and these paintings may have been in the New York show under other titles.

KROLL, Leon (1884–1974)

85. *Terminal Yards.*
Chicago, 200.
Oil.
Lent by the artist.
Price listed: $600 in Kuhn catalogue; $300 in MacRae catalogue. Sold for $300. According to the artist, the painting was purchased by Arthur J. Eddy; this is supported by a note in the Pach list of sales. However, the records in the MacRae Papers, including statements of purchases by Eddy in his own handwriting, do not list it. The purchase actually was not made through regular channels. The artist in a letter of March 3, 1913, enclosed a check for $30 covering the commission, which was entered in several places in the ledger as from H. Kroll. It may be that the artist sold the painting personally to Eddy and that the signature on the commission check was misread.

Present collection: Flint Institute of Arts, Flint, Michigan; Gift of Mrs. Arthur Jerome Eddy.

KUHN, Walt (1880–1949)

* **862.** *Morning.*
Chicago, 201.
Oil, 1912.
Lent by the artist.
Price listed: $600. Sold for $600 to John Quinn, February 26, 1913.
Present collection: Norton Gallery and School of Art, West Palm Beach, Florida.

863. *Girl with Red Cap.*
Oil.
Lent by the artist.
Price listed: $350. Sold for $350 to John Quinn, February 26, 1913.

864. *Colored Drawing.*
Lent by the artist.
Price listed: $50. Sold for $50 to Mrs. William J. Glackens, March 16, 1913.

865. *Drawing.*
Chicago, 203.
Lent by the artist.
Not for sale.

958. *Nude.*
Chicago, 203.
Pastel.
Lent by Frederick J. Gregg.
Not for sale.

LACHAISE, Gaston (1882–1935)

671. *Statuette.*
Plaster, 1912.
Lent by the artist.
Price listed: $1,000 (original); $500 (reproduction).
Present collection (1963): Landau Gallery, Los Angeles.

LA FRESNAYE, Roger de (1885–1925)

391. *Portrait.*
Chicago, 126. Boston, 48.

283

Oil, dated on entry blank 1911.
Lent by Mme. Duverdier.
Not for sale.

392. *Two Drawings.*
Chicago, 127. *Drawings.*
Lent by the artist.
Price listed: $27 each.

393. *Paysage, No. 2.*
Chicago, 128(?). Boston, 49(?).
Landscape.
Oil.
Lent by the artist.
Price listed: $162.
Present collection (1963): Herbert
and Nannette Rothschild, New
York.

394. *Paysage, No. 1.*
Chicago, 128(?). Boston, 49(?).
Landscape.
Oil.
Lent by the artist.
Price listed: $162.
Present collection: Philadelphia
Museum of Art; Louise and Walter
Arensberg Collection.

LAPRADE, Pierre (1875–1931)

372. *Venise.*
Oil.
Lent by Emile Druet.
Price listed: $1,080.

373. *Roses oranges.*
Chicago, 204. *Orange Roses.*
Oil.
Lent by Emile Druet.
Price listed: $675.

374. *San Giovanni.*
Watercolor.
Lent by Emile Druet.
Price listed: $202.50.

375. *Le Triton.*
Watercolor.
Lent by Emile Druet.
Price listed: $189.

376. *Rome.*
Watercolor.
Lent by Emile Druet.

Price listed: $216.

377. *Villa Borghese.*
Watercolor.
Lent by Emile Druet.
Price listed: $189.

LAURENCIN, Marie
(1885–1956)

383. *Portrait.*
Chicago, 205. Boston, 97.
Watercolor.
Lent by the artist.
Price listed: $81.

384. *Desdemona.*
Chicago, 206. Boston, 98.
Watercolor.
Lent by the artist.
Price listed: $81.

385. *Jeune Fille avec éventail.*
Chicago, 207. Boston, 99. *Girl with Fan.*
Drawing.
Lent by the artist.
Price listed: $81.

386. *Jeune Fille.*
Chicago, 211. Boston, 103. *Young Girl.*
Drawing.
Lent by the artist.
Price listed: $81.

387. *La Toilette des jeunes filles.*
Chicago, 209. Boston, 101. *The Toilet of the Young Girls.*
Oil.
Lent by the artist.
Price listed: $540.

388. *La Poetesse.*
Chicago, 210. Boston, 102. *Poetess.*
Oil.
Lent by the artist.
Price listed: $216.

389. *Nature morte.*
Chicago, 208. Boston, 100. *Still Life.*
Oil.
Lent by the artist.
Price listed: $108.

LAWSON, Ernest (1873–1939)

904. *Cloud Shadows.*
Oil.
Lent by the artist.
Price listed: $800 in Kuhn
catalogue; $1,200 in MacRae
catalogue.

905. *Weeds and Willow Trees.*
Chicago, 212. *Weeds and Willow
Tree.*
Oil.
Lent by the artist.
Price listed: $800 in Kuhn
catalogue; $1,200 in MacRae
catalogue.

1095. *Upper Manhattan.*
Now called *Harlem Winter.*
Oil, 1910.
Lent by the artist.
Price listed: $800 in Kuhn
catalogue; $1,200 in MacRae
catalogue. Sold for $660 to Charles
M. Lincoln, February 26, 1913.
Present collection: Chrysler
Museum, Norfolk, Virginia; Gift of
Walter P. Chrysler, Jr.

LEE, Arthur (1881–1961)

149. *Frame of Drawings.*
Chicago, 213. *Drawings.*
Lent by the artist.
Price listed: $100.

150. *Frame of Drawings.*
Chicago, 213. *Drawings.*
Lent by the artist.
Price listed: $100.

151. *Frame of Drawings.*
Chicago, 213. *Drawings.*
Lent by the artist.
Price listed: $100.

152. *Frame of Drawings.*
Chicago, 213. *Drawings.*
Lent by the artist.
Price listed: $100.

643. *Heracles.*
Bronze.
Lent by the artist.

Price listed: $750 crossed out and
changed to $1,000 in Kuhn
catalogue; $750 in MacRae
catalogue.

644. *Ethiopian.*
Bronze, 1912.
Lent by the artist.
Price listed: $500.
Present collection (1963): Mr. and
Mrs. Knute D. Lee, Brookhaven,
New York.

645. *Virgin.*
Plaster.
Lent by the artist.
Price listed: $750.

646. *Aphrodite.*
Bronze.
Lent by the artist.
Price listed: $500. Sold for $500 to
Tilda Colsman, February 27, 1913.
Present collection (1963): Adalbert
Colsman, Langenberg, Germany.

LEES, Derwent (1885–1931)

553. *Lowering Clouds.*
Chicago, 214. Boston, 104.
Oil, 1912.
Lent by John Quinn.
Not for sale.

554. *Evening.*
Chicago, 215. Boston, 105.
Oil, 1911.
Lent by John Quinn.
Not for sale.

555. *A Sullen Day.*
Oil, 1911.
Lent by John Quinn.
Not for sale.

LEGER, Fernand (1881–1955)

361. *Etude, No. 2.*
Chicago, 216. Boston, 104. *Study.*
Oil.
Lent by the artist.
Price listed: $216.

362. *Etude, No. 1.*
Chicago, 217. Boston, 107. *Study.*

285

Oil.
Lent by the artist.
Price listed: $216.

According to Katharine Kuh (*Léger*, Urbana, Ill.: University of Illinois Press, 1953), *Study for Three Portraits*, 1910–11, now in the Milwaukee Art Museum, was also in the Armory Show.

LEHMBRUCK, Wilhelm (1881–1919)

398. *Drawings, Nos. 1–6.*
Probably etchings; listed as such on entry blank and shipping invoice.
Dated on entry blank 1912.
Lent by the artist.
Price listed: $27 each; $81 set. Sold for $81 to Mrs. Clara S. Davidge, March 6, 1913.

599. *Jeune Femme.*
Now called *Standing Woman*.
Plaster, 1910. Dated on entry blank 1912.
Lent by the artist.
Price listed: $1,620. Sold for $1,620 to Stephen C. Clark, March 1, 1913.
Present collection: The bronze cast in the Museum of Modern Art, New York, was made from the Armory Show plaster in 1916–17, and the latter was then destroyed.

* **600.** *Femme à genoux.*
Chicago, 218. Boston, 108. *Woman Kneeling*.
Plaster, dated on entry blank 1911.
Lent by the artist.
Price listed: $2,160.

LEVY, Rudolph (1875–1943)

260. *Paysage.*
Oil, dated on entry blank 1912.
Lent by Alfred Flechtheim.
Price listed: $325.

LIE, Jonas (1880–1940)

875. *The Black Teapot.*

Oil, 1911.
Lent by the artist.
Price listed: $800.
Present collection: Everson Museum of Art, Syracuse, New York.

876. *At the Aquarium.*
Oil.
Lent by the artist.
Price listed: $1,200.

877. *A Hill Top.*
Oil.
Lent by the artist.
Price listed: $1,200. Sold for $800 to James T. Gwathmey, February 22, 1913.

1078. *The Quarry.*
Chicago, 219.
Oil.
Lent by the artist.
Price listed: $800.

Street.
Not listed, but added in MacRae catalogue, and as *Street Scene* in Kuhn catalogue.
Oil.
Lent by the artist.
Price listed: $500.

LONDONER, Amy (1878–1953)

110. *The Beach Crowd.*
Pastel.
Lent by the artist.
Price listed: $50.

111. *Playing Ball on the Beach.*
Pastel.
Lent by the artist.
Price listed: $50.

112. *The Beach Umbrellas.*
Pastel.
Lent by the artist.
Price listed: $50.

113. *The Life Guards.*
Pastel.
Lent by the artist.
Price listed: $50.

286

LUKS, George B. (1867–1933)

913. *Four O'Clock.*
Oil.
Lent by the artist.
Price listed: $2,500.

*914. *A Philosopher.*
Chicago, 220.
Oil.
Lent by the artist.
Price listed: $750.

915. *A Pennsylvania Dutchwoman.*
Oil.
Lent by the artist.
Price listed: $950.

916. *Studies.*
Drawing(?).
Lent by the artist.
Not for sale.

917. *Ten Studies in the Bronx Zoo.*
Crayon drawings, 1904.
Lent by Edward W. Root.
Not for sale.
Present collection: Addison Gallery
of American Art, Phillips Academy,
Andover, Massachusetts; Gift of
Mrs. Edward W. Root.

918. *Anticipatory Portrait of James
Hunecker.*
Chicago, 221.
Drawing(?).
Lent by Frederick J. Gregg.
Not for sale.

LUNDBERG, A. F. (n.d.)

950. *Lawn Party.*
Oil.
Lent by the artist.
Price listed: $500.
Present collection (1963): Hirschl
& Adler Galleries, New York.

MacKNIGHT, Dodge
(1860–1950)

934. *The Caller.*
Catalogued but not received.

935. *The Hillside.*
Watercolor.
Lent by Desmond Fitz-Gerald.
No price listed.

936. *Coast of Newfoundland.*
Watercolor.
Lent by Desmond Fitz-Gerald.
Not for sale.

937. *Coast of Newfoundland.*
Watercolor.
Lent by Desmond Fitz-Gerald.
No price listed.

MacRAE, Elmer Livingston
(1875–1955)

866. *New York Yacht Club at
Newport.*
Oil.
Lent by the artist.
Price listed: $800. Sold for $800 to
Annie B. Jennings, March 13,
1913.

*867. *Battle Ships.*
Chicago, 222. *Battleships.*
Now called *Battleships at Newport.*
Oil, 1912.
Lent by the artist.
Price listed: $800.
Former collection: The Historical
Society of the Town of Greenwich,
Connecticut.

868. *Fairy Stories.*
Oil.
Lent by the artist.
Price listed: $700.
Present collection: The Parrish Art
Museum, Southampton, New York.

869. *Drawing.*
Crossed out in MacRae catalogue.
Chicago, 223(?). *Drawings.*
Pastel.
Lent by the artist.
Price listed: $200 in Kuhn
catalogue.

870. *Drawing.*
Chicago, 223(?). *Drawings.*
Pastel.

Lent by the artist.
Price listed: $50.
Present collection: Shaw Mudge,
Greenwich, Connecticut.

871. *Drawing.*
Chicago, 223(?). *Drawings.*
Pastel.
Lent by the artist.
Price listed: $50 in Kuhn catalogue;
$200 in MacRae catalogue.
Present collection: Mr. and Mrs.
Howard Kepet.

872. *Drawing.*
Chicago, 223(?). *Drawings.*
Pastel.
Lent by the artist.
Price listed: $50.
Present collection: Shaw Mudge,
Greenwich, Connecticut.

873. *Drawing.*
Crossed out in Kuhn catalogue.
Chicago, 223(?). *Drawings.*
Pastel.
Lent by the artist.
Price listed: $75.
Present collection: Mrs. Walter
Fillin, Rockville Center, New York.

874. *Drawing.*
Crossed out in MacRae and Kuhn
catalogues.
Chicago, 223(?).
Pastel.
Lent by the artist.
No price listed.
Present collection: Shaw Mudge,
Greenwich, Connecticut.

Feeding the Ducks.
Not listed, but added in MacRae
and Kuhn catalogues.
Oil, 1912.
Lent by the artist.
Price listed: $550.
Former collection: The Historical
Society of the Town of Greenwich,
Connecticut.

Chicago, 223. *Drawings* (*Pastel*).
It is not known which or how many

of the drawings from the New York
show went to Chicago.

Note: According to The Fiftieth
Anniversary of the Armory Show
catalogue, nos. 867–74 and *Feeding
the Ducks* were found, after MacRae's
death, in the barn of his home, the
Bush-Holley House, Cos Cob,
Connecticut.

MAGER, Gus (1878–1956)

7. *Tulips and Blue-Flags.*
Chicago, 224.
Oil, c. 1910–12.
Lent by the artist.
Price listed: $300.
Present collection (1963):
Robert A. Mager, Murrysville,
Pennsylvania.

8. *Flowers.*
Oil, c. 1910–12.
Lent by the artist.
Price listed: $300.
Present collection (1963):
Robert A. Mager, Murrysville,
Pennsylvania.

MAILLOL, Aristide (1861–1944)

335. *Dessin, No. 3200.*
Chicago, 227. Boston, 111.
Drawings.
Lent by Emile Druet.
Price listed: $55. Sold for $55 to
Robert Hartshorn, March 2, 1913.

336. *Dessin, No. 1769.*
Chicago, 227. Boston, 111.
Drawings.
Lent by Emile Druet.
Price listed: $50.

337. *Dessin, No. 4114.*
Chicago, 227. Boston, 111.
Drawings.
Lent by Emile Druet.
Price listed: $165.

338. *Dessin, No. 4117.*
Chicago, 227. Boston, 111.

Drawings.
Lent by Emile Druet.
Price listed: $65.

339. *Dessin, No. 4120.*
Chicago, 227. Boston, 111.
Drawings.
Lent by Emile Druet.
Price listed: $38.

340. *Dessin, No. 4118.*
Chicago, 227. Boston, 111.
Drawings.
Lent by Emile Druet.
Price listed: $165.

Note: It is not known which of
these drawings (nos. 335–40) from
the New York show were sent to
Chicago and Boston.

631. *Femme debout.*
Chicago, 225. Boston, 109.
Woman Standing.
Terracotta.
Lent by Emile Druet.
Price listed: $2,160.

632. *Bas-relief.*
Chicago, 226. Boston, 110.
Terracotta.
Lent by Emile Druet.
Price listed: $2,700.

MANET, Edouard (1832–1883)

953. *Portrait.*
Oil.
Lent by Mrs. B. S. Guinness.
No price listed.

1052. *The Bull-Fight.*
Oil, 1866.
Lent by Martin A. Ryerson.
No price listed.
Present collection: The Art
Institute of Chicago; Mr. and Mrs.
Martin A. Ryerson Collection.

1053. *Portrait of Miss Mary Laurent.*
Oil.
Lent by Stephan Bourgeois.
No price listed.

1054. *Still Life.*
Oil.
Lent by Frank Jewett Mather, Jr.
No price listed.
Present collection (1963): Mrs.
Frank Jewett Mather, Jr., Princeton,
New Jersey.
The attribution was later questioned
by Professor Mather.

MANGUIN, Henri (1874–1949)

441. *Le Rocher.*
Chicago, 228. Boston, 112.
The Rock.
Oil.
Lent by Emile Druet.
Price listed: $864.

442. *Baigneuse.*
Chicago, 229. *Bather.*
Oil.
Lent by Emile Druet.
Price listed: $702.

443. *La Toilette.*
Chicago, 236. *The Toilet.*
Oil.
Lent by Emile Druet.
Price listed: $378.

MANIGAULT, Edward Middleton
(1889–1922)

47. *The Clown.*
Chicago, 231.
Oil.
Lent by the artist.
Price listed: $600. Sold for $300 to
Arthur J. Eddy, March 4, 1913.

48. *Adagio.*
Chicago, 232.
Lent by the artist.
Price listed: $750.
Present collection (1963): Mrs.
Edith Kinsley, Sherrill, New York.

**MANOLO (Manuel Martínez
Hugué)** (1872–1945)

621. *Femme nue accroupie.*
Chicago, 232½. Boston, 113.

289

Woman Kneeling.
Bronze.
Lent by Henry Kahnweiler.
Price listed: $202.50. Sold for
$202.50 to John Quinn, February
26, 1913.
Present collection: Mr. and Mrs.
David A. Thompson.

622. *Femme nue debout.*
Bronze, 1912.
Lent by Henry Kahnweiler.
Price listed: $67.50. Sold for
$67.50 to Arthur B. Davies,
March 7, 1913.

623. *Chula.*
Bronze, 1910.
Lent by Henry Kahnweiler.
Price listed: $67.50. Sold for
$67.50 to Alfred Stieglitz,
February 20, 1913.
Present collection: Carl van
Vechten Gallery of Fine Arts, Fisk
University, Nashville; Alfred
Stieglitz Collection.

*****624.** *Buste du peintre Sunyer.*
Bronze, 1912.
Lent by Henry Kahnweiler.
Price listed: $108.

625. *Statuette.*
Bronze.
Lent by Paul Haviland.
Not for sale.

626. *Statuette.*
Bronze.
Lent by Paul Haviland.
Not for sale.

627. *Statuette.*
Bronze.
Lent by Paul Haviland.
Not for sale.

MARIN, John (1870–1953)

139. *Woolworth Building, No. 28.*
Watercolor, 1912–13.
Lent by the artist.
Not for sale.
Present collection: National Gallery
of Art, Washington, D.C.; Gift of
Eugene and Agnes E. Meyer.

140. *Woolworth Building, No. 29*
Watercolor, 1912–13.
Lent by the artist.
Not for sale.
Present collection: National Gallery
of Art, Washington, D.C.; Gift of
Eugene and Agnes E. Meyer.

141. *Woolworth Building, No. 31.*
Watercolor, 1912–13.
Lent by the artist.
Not for sale.
Present collection: National Gallery
of Art, Washington, D.C.; Gift of
Eugene and Agnes E. Meyer.

142. *Woolworth Building, No. 32.*
Watercolor, 1912–13.
Lent by the artist.
Not for sale.
Present collection: National Gallery
of Art, Washington, D.C.; Gift of
Eugene and Agnes E. Meyer.

143. *Broadway, Singer Building.*
Watercolor, 1912.
Lent by the artist.
Not for sale.
Present collection: National Gallery
of Art, Washington, D.C.; Gift of
Eugene and Agnes E. Meyer.

144. *Broadway, St. Paul's Church.*
Now called *St. Paul's, Lower
Manhattan.*
Watercolor, 1912.
Lent by the artist.
Not for sale.
Present collection: Delaware Art
Museum, Wilmington.

145. *Mountain, the Tyrol.*
Watercolor.
Lent by the artist.
Price listed: $300.
Present collection: Mr. and Mrs.
John Marin, Jr.

146. *In the Tyrol.*
Watercolor.
Lent by the artist.

Price listed: $300.

147. *Lake and Mountain, Tyrol.*
Watercolor.
Lent by the artist.
Price listed: $250.

148. *In the Adirondacks.*
Watercolor, 1912.
Lent by the artist.
Not for sale.
Present collection (1963): Weyhe
Collection, New York.

MARIS, Matthew (1835–1917)

590. *Lady of Shalott.*
Oil, 1880–85.
Lent by James G. Shepherd.
Not for sale.

591. *Bride.*
Oil, 1888.
Lent by James G. Shepherd.
Not for sale.

592. *Baby.*
Oil, 1873.
Lent by James G. Shepherd.
Not for sale.

593. *Childhood.*
Oil, 1891.
Lent by James G. Shepherd.
Not for sale.

MARQUET, Albert (1875–1947)

487. *Hambourg.*
Chicago, 234(?). Boston, 115(?).
Hamburg.
Oil.
Lent by Emile Druet.
Price listed: $1,620.

488. *Ste. Adresse.*
Oil.
Lent by Emile Druet.
Price listed: $1,215.

489. *Inondation.*
Chicago, 233. Boston, 114.
Inundation.
Oil.
Lent by Emile Druet.

Price listed: $2,700.

490. *Hambourg.*
Chicago, 234(?). Boston, 115(?).
Hamburg.
Oil.
Lent by Emile Druet.
Price listed: $2,160.

491/492. *Drawings.*
Chicago, 235. Boston, 116.
Drawings.
Lent by Emile Druet.
Price listed:
Druet #4165-7: $21.60.
Druet #5983-34: $27. Sold
for $27 to Stephen C. Clark,
March 1, 1913.
Druet #5983-29: $16.
Druet #4165-10: $32.50.
Druet #5414-16: $54.
Druet #6511-11: $54.
Druet #5414-3: $54.
Druet #5414-2: $54.
Druet #5414-19: $54.
Druet #5414-18: $41.
Druet #5983-21: $41.
Druet #6345-7: $41.

Note: It is not known which or how
many of the Marquet drawings were
included in the Chicago and Boston
exhibitions.

MARVAL, Jacqueline
(1866–1932)

* **204.** *Odalisques au miroir.*
Oil.
Lent by Emile Druet.
Price listed: $675.

MASE, Carolyn C. (n.d.–1948)

781. *September Haze.* †
Pastel.
Lent by the artist.
Price listed: $100.

MATISSE, Henri (1869–1954)

401. *Le Madras rouge.*
Chicago, 237. Boston, 118.

291

Red Madras.
Now called *Red Madras Headdress.*
Elsewhere called *Mme. Matisse:
Madras Rouge.*
Oil, c. 1907–8.
Lent by Michael Stein.
Not for sale.
Present collection: Barnes
Foundation, Merion, Pennsylvania.

402. *Joaquina.*
Chicago, 238. Boston, 119.
Oil.
Lent by Bernheim-Jeune & Cie.
Price listed: $810.

403. *La Coiffeuse.*
Chicago, 239. Boston, 120.
The Hairdresser.
Oil, 1907.
Lent by Michael Stein.
Not for sale.

*****404.** *Les Poissons.*
Chicago, 240. Boston, 121.
Goldfish.
Now called *Goldfish and Sculpture.*
Elsewhere called *Les Poissons
Rouges.*
Oil, 1911.
Lent by the artist.
Not for sale.
Present collection: The Museum of
Modern Art, New York; Gift of Mr.
and Mrs. John Hay Whitney.

405. *Jeune Marin.*
Chicago, 241. Boston, 122.
Young Sailor.
Now called *The Young Sailor, II.*
Oil, 1906.
Lent by the artist.
Price listed: $1,350.
Present collection: Jacques Gelman,
Mexico City.

406. *Panneau rouge.*
Chicago, 242. Boston, 123.
Red Panel.
Now called *Red Studio.*
Elsewhere called *L'Atelier rouge.*
Oil, 1911.
Lent by the artist.

Price listed: $4,050.
Present collection: The Museum of
Modern Art, New York; Mrs.
Simon Guggenheim Fund.

*****407.** *Le Luxe* [II].
Chicago, 244. Boston, 125. *Luxury.*
Casein, c. 1907–8.
Lent by the artist.
Price listed: $1,350.
Present collection: The Royal
Museum of Fine Arts, Copenhagen;
J. Rump Collection.

408. *Portrait de Marguerite.*
Chicago, 245. Boston, 126.
Portrait of Marguerite.
Now called *Girl with a Black Cat.*
Elsewhere called *Marguerite Matisse;
Jeune Fille au chat.*
Oil, 1910.
Lent by the artist.
Not for sale.
Present collection: Private
collection.

409. *Les Capucines.*
Chicago, 246. Boston, 127.
Nasturtiums.
Now called *Nasturtiums and the
Dance, II.*
Oil, 1912.
Lent by the artist.
Price listed: $1,080.
Present collection: The
Metropolitan Museum of Art;
Bequest of Scofield Thayer.

410. *Nature morte.*
Chicago, 247. Boston, 128.
Still Life.
Elsewhere called *Still Life with Greek
Torso.*
Oil, 1908.
Lent by the artist.
Not for sale.

411. *La Femme bleue.*
Chicago, 248. Boston, 129.
The Blue Woman.
Now called *The Blue Nude (Souvenir
de Biskra).*
Oil, 1907.

292

Lent by Leo Stein.
Not for sale.
Present collection: The Baltimore
Museum of Art; The Cone
Collection.

412. *Drawing, No. 839.*
Chicago, 236. Boston, 117.
Drawings.
Lent by Emile Druet, #5839.
Price listed: $67.50.

413. *Drawing, No. 840.*
Chicago, 236. Boston, 117.
Drawings.
Now called *Four Studies of Nude
Woman.*
Lent by Emile Druet, #5840.
Price listed: $67.50. Sold for $67.50
to Mrs. Eliza G. Radeke, March 2,
1913.
Present collection: Museum of Art,
Rhode Island School of Design,
Providence; Gift of Mrs. Gustav
Radeke.

414. *Drawing.*
Stieglitz lent six Matisse drawings to
the Armory Show. Either only one
was hung or the listing should read
"drawings."
Lent by Alfred Stieglitz.
Not for sale.
Present collection: One of the six is
now in The Metropolitan Museum
of Art, New York; The Alfred
Stieglitz Collection; two are in The
Chicago Art Institute; Stieglitz
Collection.

635. *Le Dos.*
Chicago, 243. Boston, 124. *A Back.*
Now called *The Back, I.* Elsewhere
called *Nu de dos, 1ᵉʳ état.*
Plaster, 1910–12.
Lent by the artist.
Price listed: "Not yet known" in
Kuhn catalogue.

1064. *Flowers.*
Chicago, 249. Boston, 130.
Oil.
Lent by Mrs. Howard Gans.

No price listed.

1065. *Study.*
Chicago, 250. Boston, 131.
Now called *Nude in a Wood.*
Elsewhere called *Nu dans les bois.*
Oil, 1905(?).
Lent by George F. Of.
No price listed.
Present collection: The Brooklyn
Museum, New York; Gift of George
F. Of.

MAURER, Alfred (1868–1932)

53. *Landscape.*
Chicago, 251.
Oil.
Lent by the artist.
No price listed.

54. *Old Faïence.*
Oil.
Lent by the artist.
No price listed.

55. *Autumn.*
Oil, c. 1911.
Lent by the artist.
No price listed.
Present collection: Mr. and Mrs. Ira
Glackens, Washington, D.C.

1085. *Still Life.*
Oil.
Lent by the artist.
No price listed.

MAYRSHOFER, Max
(1875–1950)

456. *Wintersport.*
Chicago, 252(?). Boston, 132(?).
Drawings.
Drawing, dated on entry blank
1911.
Lent by Heinrich Thannhauser,
#5249.
Price listed: $25.

457. *Badende Frauen.*
Chicago, 252(?). Boston, 132(?).
Drawings.

293

Drawing, dated on entry blank
1910.
Lent by Heinrich Thannhauser,
#1326.
Price listed: $22.75. Sold for $22.75
to Francis L. Pruyn, February 27,
1913.

458. *Landschaft.*
Chicago, 252(?). Boston, 132(?).
Drawings.
Drawing, dated on entry blank
1912.
Lent by Heinrich Thannhauser,
#1579.
Price listed: $22.75.

459. *Landschaft.*
Chicago, 252(?). Boston, 132(?).
Drawings.
Drawing, dated on entry blank
1911.
Lent by Heinrich Thannhauser,
#1609.
Price listed: $26.

460. *Volksmenge.*
Chicago, 252(?). Boston, 132(?).
Drawings.
Drawing, dated on entry blank
1912.
Lent by Heinrich Thannhauser.
Price listed: $22.75.

461. *Rennreiter.*
Chicago, 252(?). Boston, 132(?).
Drawings.
Drawing, dated on entry blank
1912.
Lent by Heinrich Thannhauser,
#2616.
Price listed: $26.

Chicago, 252. Boston, 132.
Drawings.
Lent by Heinrich Thannhauser.

Note: It is not known how many or
which of the Mayrshofer drawings
were exhibited in Chicago and
Boston. One was sold for $25 to
Mrs. A. L. Farwell, April 11, 1913,
in Chicago, and another for $25 to

Thomas W. Bowers, May 20, 1913,
in Boston.

McCOMAS, Francis (1874–1938)
959. *Monterey, Evening.*
Oil.
Lent by the artist.
Price listed: $200 in Kuhn
catalogue; $150 in MacRae
catalogue.

960. *Landscape, California.*
Oil.
Lent by the artist.
Price listed: "Not for sale" in Kuhn
catalogue; $200 in MacRae
catalogue. Sold for $200 to Mrs.
Eugene Meyer, March 15, 1913.

961. *Arizona Desert.*
Oil.
Lent by the artist.
Not for sale.

McENERY, Kathleen (n.d.)

3. *Going to the Bath.*
Oil, 1912.
Lent by the artist.
Price listed: $600.
Present collection (1963): The
artist.

4. *Dream.*
Chicago, 253.
Oil, 1912.
Lent by the artist.
Price listed: $400.
Present collection (1963): The
artist.

McLANE, Howard (n.d.)

86. *Mott St., Festa.*
Oil.
Lent by the artist.
No price listed.

McLEAN, Hower (n.d.)

739. *Mott Street Fiesta.*
Oil.

Lent by the artist.
Price listed: $800.

Note: Howard McLane and Hower McLean may be the same artist, as the titles of the paintings listed suggest. A search has identified neither.

MELTZER, Charlotte (n.d.)

766. *Hunters.* †
Oil.
Lent by the artist.
Price listed: $200.

767. *Loverene.* †
Chicago, 254.
Oil.
Lent by the artist.
Price listed: $250; crossed out and raised to $500 in Kuhn catalogue; $250 in MacRae catalogue.

MIESTCHANINOFF, Oscar (1884–1956)

633. *Tête de jeune fille.*
Plaster, 1912.
Lent by the artist.
Price listed: $540 (marble); $270 (bronze).
Present collection (1963): The original marble from which the plaster was made belongs to Mrs. Oscar Miestchaninoff, New York.

MILLER, Kenneth Hayes (1876–1952)

49. *The Waste.*
Oil, 1913.
Lent by the artist.
Price listed: $600.
Present collection (1963): Mrs. Louise Miller Smith, Port Washington, New York.

50. *Woman and Children.*
Chicago, 255.
Oil.
Lent by the artist.
Price listed: $750.

51. *Recumbent Figure.*
Oil, 1910–11.
Lent by the artist.
Price listed: $400.
Present collection: Columbus Museum of Art, Columbus, Ohio; Ferdinand Howald Collection.

52. *Primitive Group.*
Oil.
Lent by the artist.
Price listed: $400.

MILNE, David B. (1882–1953)

794. *Little Figures.* †
Chicago, 256.
Watercolor.
Lent by the artist.
Price listed: $70.

795. *Distorted Tree.* †
Oil.
Lent by the artist.
Price listed: $200.

796. *Columbus Circle.* †
Oil.
Lent by the artist.
Price listed: $200.

797. *The Garden.* †
Watercolor.
Lent by the artist.
Price listed: $150.

798. *Reclining Figure.* †
Watercolor.
Lent by the artist.
Price listed: $60.

MONET, Claude (1840–1926)

494. *La Falaise d'Etretat.*
Oil, 1885.
Lent by Durand-Ruel & Sons.
Price listed: $8,200.

495. *Effet de neige, Giverny.*
Oil, 1879.
Lent by Durand-Ruel & Sons.
Price listed: $11,000.

496. *La Promenade à Trouville.*

295

Now called *The Beach at Trouville.*
Oil, c. 1870. Dated 1872 on entry
blank.
Lent by Durand-Ruel & Sons.
Not for sale.
Present collection (1963): Mr. and
Mrs. William Goetz, Los Angeles.

497. *Automne à Jeufosse.*
Now called *Autumn at Jeufosse.*
Oil, 1884.
Lent by Durand-Ruel & Sons.
Price listed: $8,800.
Present collection: Museum of Fine
Arts, Boston.

1073. *Le Bassin aux nymphéas.*
Oil.
Lent by Durand-Ruel & Sons.
Price listed: $7,700.
Present collection (1963): Henry T.
Mudd, Los Angeles.

MONTICELLI, Adolphe
(1824–1886)

1055. *Flowers.*
Now called *Flowers in a Vase.*
Elsewhere called *Field and Garden
Flowers.*
Oil, 1867–77.
Lent by Stephan Bourgeois.
No price listed.
Present collection: Mrs. Virginia L.
Kahn, Cambridge, Massachusetts.

MOWBRAY-CLARKE, John
(1869–1953)

696. *Parasites.*
Bronze.
Lent by the artist.
Price listed: $2,500.

697. *Seared.*
Bronze.
Lent by the artist.
Price listed: $250.

698. *Antiquities.*
Bronze.
Lent by the artist.
Price listed: $350.

* **699.** *The Tree.*
Chicago, 257.
Elsewhere called *The Group.*
Plaster.
Lent by the artist.
Price listed: $400 (bronze).

700. *Aphrodite.*
Bronze.
Lent by the artist.
Price listed: $75.

701. *Happiness.*
Plaster.
Lent by the artist.
Not for sale.

702. *Christ.*
Bronze.
Lent by the artist.
Price listed: $400.

703. *Spring.*
Bronze.
Lent by the artist.
Price listed: $100.

704. *Whither.*
Plaster.
Lent by the artist.
Price listed: $50 (plaster); $250
(bronze).

705. *Portrait, Medal.*
Chicago, 258. *Portrait, Arthur B.
Davies (Medal).*
Bronze.
Lent by the artist.
Price listed: $50.
Present collection (1963): Estate of
Mrs. Mary Mowbray-Clarke, New
City, New York.

706. *Bloomers.*
Plaster.
Lent by the artist.
Price listed: $100. Sold for $200 to
Thomas F. Vietor, March 13, 1913.

MUHRMANN, Henry
(1854–1916)

470. *Boats at Kew.*
Chicago, 259.
Oil.

Lent by the artist.
Price listed: $300.

MUNCH, Edvard (1863–1944)

244. *Woodcuts, Nos. 1–4.*
Chicago, 260. *Lithographs.* Boston,
133. *Lithographs and Woodcuts.*
Lent by the artist.
Price listed: $200 each.
Vampire, lithograph, 4 colors,
1895–1902.
Moonlight, woodcut, 4 colors,
1896–1901.
The Kiss, woodcut, 2 colors,
1897–1902.
Two Beings (The Lonely Ones),
woodcut, 3 colors, 1899–1917.

245. *Lithographs, Nos. 1–4.*
Chicago, 260. *Lithographs.* Boston,
133. *Lithographs and Woodcuts.*
Lent by the artist.
Price listed: $200 each.
Madonna, lithograph, 4 colors,
1895–1902.
Nude with Red Hair, lithograph, 3
colors, 1901.
Jealousy, lithograph, 1896.
Portrait of Leistikow and Wife,
lithograph, 1902.

Note: The Munch prints exhibited
in Chicago as *Lithographs* and in
Boston as *Lithographs and Woodcuts*
were probably identical with those
exhibited at the New York show
under nos. 244 and 245.

MURPHY, Herman Dudley
(1867–1945)

77. *Morro Castle, San Juan.*
Oil.
Lent by the artist.
Price listed: $500.
Present collection: Mr. and Mrs.
Charles Gellman, Valley Stream,
New York.

MYERS, Ethel (1881–1960)

662. *The Matron.*

Elsewhere called *The Fat Woman.*
Plaster, 1912.
Lent by the artist.
Price listed: $85.

663. *Fifth Avenue Gossips.*
Plaster.
Lent by the artist.
Price listed: $160.

664. *Fifth Avenue Girl.*
Sculpture, 1912.
Lent by Mrs. Albert Lewisohn.
Not for sale.

665. *Girl from Madison Avenue.*
Plaster, 1912.
Price listed: $60.

666. *Portrait Impression of
Mrs. D. M.*
Bronze.
Lent by Mrs. Daniel Morgan.
Not for sale.
Present collection: Mrs. Walter
Fillin, Rockville Center, New York.

667. *The Widow.*
Plaster.
Lent by the artist.
Price listed: $70.

668. *The Gambler.*
Plaster, 1912.
Lent by the artist.
Price listed: $60.

669. *Upper Corridor.*
Plaster.
Lent by the artist.
Price listed: $60.

670. *The Duchess.*
Plaster.
Lent by the artist.
Price listed: $60.

MYERS, Jerome (1867–1940)

*__847.__ *Their Life.*
Chicago, 261.
Now called *End of the Walk.*
Oil.
Lent by the artist.
Price listed: $1,000 in Kuhn

297

catalogue; $100 in MacRae catalogue (probably an error). Present collection: Greenville County Museum of Art, Greenville, South Carolina.

848. *The Glow.*
Chicago, 262.
Oil.
Lent by the artist.
Price listed: $600.

849. *15 Drawings.*
Chicago, 263.
Lent by the artist.
Price listed: Heads $150 each in Kuhn catalogue; $75 each in MacRae catalogue.

NADELMAN, Elie (1882–1946)

380. *Drawings, Nos. 1–12.*
Lent by the artist.
Price listed: $40.75 each.

634. *Tête d'homme.*
Plaster.
Lent by the artist.
Price listed: $135.

1099. *Nude.*
Elsewhere called *Femme nue.*
Plaster.
Lent by the artist.
Price listed: $135.
Destroyed.

NANKIVELL, Frank A. (1869–1959)

856. *Apple Picking.*
Oil.
Lent by the artist.
Price listed: $1,500.

857. *Edith.*
Oil.
Lent by the artist.
Price listed: $1,000.

*__**858.** *Pink and Green.*
Chicago, 264.
Oil.
Lent by the artist.
Price listed: $1,000.

859. *Fowls.*
Chicago, 266. *Fowls (Color Print).*
Watercolor from wood blocks.
Lent by the artist.
Price listed: $30.

860. *Football Player.*
Chicago, 267. *Football Player (Color Print).*
Watercolor from wood blocks.
Lent by the artist.
Price listed: $25.

861. *New York in the Making.*
Etching, c. 1912.
Lent by the artist.
Price listed: $50.

1097. *Landscape.*
Oil.
Lent by the artist.
Price listed: $400.

1098. *Laughing Boy.*
Oil.
Lent by the artist.
Price listed: $150.

Harbor after Regatta.
Not listed but added in MacRae catalogue.
Chicago, 265. *After the Regatta.*
In the Chicago shipping list it is crossed out and *Blackstone Library at Branford* is substituted.

NILES, Helen J. (n.d.)

956. *Phyllis.* †
Oil.
Lent by the artist.
Price listed: $600.

OPPENHEIMER, Olga (n.d.)

453. *Woodcuts, Nos. 1–6.*
Illustrations for "Van Zanten's Glückliche Zeit" by Laurids Bruun.
Chicago, 268. Boston, 134.
Dated on entry blank 1911.
Lent by the artist.
Price listed: $16.25 each.

ORGAN, Marjorie (1886–1931)

107. *Drawings, Nos. 1–6.*
Chicago, 269.
Lent by the artist.
Price listed: $50 each.

PACH, Walter (1883–1958)

263. *Flowers.*
Oil.
Lent by the artist.
Price listed: $87.50. Sold for $87.50
to Henry C. Frick, March 4, 1913.

264. *Portrait.*
Now called *Portrait of Gigi Cavigli.*
Oil, 1912.
Lent by the artist.
Price listed: $350.
Present collection (1963): Mrs.
Nikifora L. Pach, New York.

265. *Girls Bathing.*
Oil.
Lent by the artist.
Price listed: $195.

266. *Casentino Mountains.*
Chicago, 270.
Oil.
Lent by the artist.
Price listed: $180.

267. *The Wall of the City.*
Chicago, 271.
Oil.
Lent by the artist.
Price listed: $195.

268[a]. *Mary.*
Chicago, 273½.
Etching.
Lent by the artist.
Price listed: $10.

268[b]. *Renoir's "Liseuse."*
Etching.
Lent by the artist.
Price listed: $10. Sold for $10 to
Mrs. Richard Sheldrick, March 13,
1913.

269[a]. *Gothic Virgin.*
Chicago, 272.

Etching, 1912.
Lent by the artist.
Price listed: $10.

269[b]. *St. Germain-des-Près—
Night.*
Chicago, 273.
Etching.
Lent by the artist.
Price listed: $10.

270. *St. Germain-des-Près—Day.*
Chicago, 273.
Etching.
Lent by the artist.
Price listed: $10.
The original catalogue listing under
268, 269, and 270 is confusing,
probably garbled in typesetting.

PADDOCK, Josephine
(1885–1964)

808. *Swan on the Grass.* †
Watercolor, 1910.
Lent by the artist.
Price listed: $50.
Former collection: The artist,
New York.

809. *Swan Study—Peace.* †
Watercolor, 1910.
Lent by the artist.
Price listed: $50.
Former collection: The artist,
New York.

810. *Swan Study—Aspiration.* †
Watercolor, 1910.
Lent by the artist.
Price listed: $50.
Former collection: The artist,
New York.

PASCIN, Jules (1885–1930)

472. *Expectancy.*
Engraving.
Lent by the artist.
Price listed: $65. Sold for $65 to
John Quinn, March 1, 1913.

473. *Watercolor.*
Lent by the artist.

299

Price listed: $65. Sold for $65 to
John Quinn, March 1, 1913.

474. *A Visit.*
Now called *The Visit.*
Chicago, 276. Boston, 137.
Drawing, pen and pencil.
Lent by the artist.
Price listed: $65. Sold for $65 to
John Quinn, March 1, 1913.
Present collection: The Museum of
Modern Art, New York; Gift of
A. Conger Goodyear.

475. *No. 9. At the Antiquarians.*
Chicago, 277. Boston, 138.
Drawing.
Lent by the artist.
Price listed: $65.

476. *No. 8. In the Salon.*
Drawing.
Lent by the artist.
Price listed: $65. Listed as sold in
the Kuhn catalogue.

477. *No. 7. The Music Lesson.*
Chicago, 278. Boston, 139.
Drawing.
Lent by the artist.
Price listed: $65.

478. *No. 6. Interior.*
Chicago, 279. Boston, 140.
Drawing, pen and watercolor.
Lent by the artist.
Price listed: $50. Sold for $50 to
John Quinn, March 1, 1913.

479. *No. 5. Beggars.*
Drawing, dated on entry blank
1912.
Lent by the artist.
Price listed: $65.

480. *No. 4. Siesta.*
Drawing, pen and pencil, dated on
entry blank 1912.
Lent by the artist.
Price listed: $32.50. Sold for $32.50
to John Quinn, March 1, 1913.

481. *No. 3. In the Park.*
Watercolor, dated on entry blank
1912.

Lent by the artist.
Price listed: $81.50. Sold for $81.50
to John Quinn, March 1, 1913.

482. *Three Girls.*
Chicago, 275. Boston, 136.
Drawing, dated on entry blank
1912.
Lent by the artist.
Price listed: $65.

485. *No. 1. Venus.*
Chicago, 274. Boston, 135.
Engraving, dated on entry blank
1912.
Lent by the artist.
Price listed: $48.75.

PELTON, Agnes (1881–1961)

11. *Vine Wood.*
Oil, c. 1910.
Lent by the artist.
Price listed: $100.
Present collection (1963): Agnes
Pelton Estate, Cathedral City,
California.

12. *Stone Age.*
Chicago, 280.
Oil.
Lent by the artist.
Price listed: $100.

PEPPER, Charles H. (1864–1950)

42. *Irene.*
Oil.
Lent by the artist.
Price listed: $1,000.

43. *In the Woods.*
Oil.
Lent by the artist.
Price listed: $1,000.

986. *Sunny Window.*
Chicago, 281.
Watercolor.
Lent by the artist.
Price listed: $100.

987. *The Caller.*
Watercolor.
Lent by the artist.

300

Price listed: $100.

988. *The Hillside.*
Watercolor.
Lent by the artist.
Price listed: $250.

PERRINE, Van Dearing
(1869–1955)

*105. *When the Wind Blows.*
Oil.
Lent by the artist.
Price listed: $750. Sold for $650 to
Mrs. N. M. Pond, March 7, 1913.

106. *The Ice Floes.*
Oil.
Lent by the artist.
Price listed: $2,000.
Present collection: Whitney
Museum of American Art,
New York.

PHILLIPS, Harriet Sophia
(1849–1928)

774. *Head.* †
Chicago, 282.
Oil.
Lent by the artist.
Price listed: $75.

PICABIA, Francis (1878–1953)

*415. *La Danse à la source.*
Chicago, 283. *The Dance at the
Spring.*
Now called *Dances at the Spring.*
Oil, 1912.
Lent by the artist.
Price listed: $675. Sold for $400 to
Arthur J. Eddy, March 2, 1913.
Present collection: Philadelphia
Museum of Art; Louise and Walter
Arensberg Collection.

416. *La Procession, Seville.*
Chicago, 288. Boston, 141.
The Procession, Seville.
Oil, 1912.
Lent by the artist.
Price listed: $1,080.

Present collection: Private
collection.

417. *Paris.*
Chicago, 285. Boston, 142.
Oil.
Lent by the artist.
Price listed: $486.
Present collection: Private
collection.

418. *Souvenir de Grimaldi, Italie.*
Chicago, 286. Boston, 143.
Souvenir of Grimaldi, Italy.
Oil.
Lent by the artist.
Price listed: $405.

PICASSO, Pablo [listed in
catalogue as Paul] (1881–1973)

345. *Nature morte No. 1.*
Chicago, 288. Boston, 145.
Still Life.
Oil.
Lent by Leo Stein.
Not for sale.

346. *Nature morte No. 2.*
Chicago, 289. Boston, 146.
Still Life.
Oil.
Lent by Leo Stein.
Not for sale.

347. *Les Arbres.*
Chicago, 290. Boston, 147. *Trees.*
Now called *Landscape.*
Gouache, dated on entry blank
1907.
Lent by Henry Kahnweiler.
Price listed: $243. Sold for $243 to
Arthur B. Davies, March 7, 1913.
Present collection: Philadelphia
Museum of Art; Louise and Walter
Arensberg Collection.

348. *Mme. Soler.*
Chicago, 291. Boston, 148.
Oil, dated on entry blank 1903.
Lent by Henry Kahnweiler.
Price listed: $1,350.
Present collection: Staatsgalerie
Moderner Kunst, Munich.

349. *Tête d'homme.*
Chicago, 292. Boston, 149.
Head of a Man.
Oil, dated on entry blank 1912.
Lent by Henry Kahnweiler.
Price listed: $486.

* 350. *La Femme au pot de moutarde.*
Chicago, 293. Boston, 150.
The Woman and the Pot of Mustard.
Now called *Woman with Mustard Pot.*
Oil, 1910.
Lent by Henry Kahnweiler.
Price listed: $675.
Present collection: Haags
Gemeentemuseum, The Hague.

351. *Drawing.*
Chicago, 287. Boston, 144.
Now called *Female Nude.*
Charcoal, 1910.
Lent by Alfred Stieglitz.
Not for sale.
Present collection: The
Metropolitan Museum of Art, New
York; The Alfred Stieglitz
Collection.

598. *Bust.*
Now called *Head of a Woman.*
Bronze, 1909.
Lent by Alfred Stieglitz.
Not for sale.
Present collection: The Art
Institute of Chicago; Alfred Stieglitz
Collection.

PIETRO (n.d.)

726. *The Proletariat.*
Oil.
Lent by the artist.
No price listed.

PISSARRO, Camille (1830–1903)

498. *Neige, soleil couchant.*
Oil, 1894.
Lent by Durand-Ruel & Sons.
Price listed: $4,400.
Present collection: Mrs.
Frederick M. Stafford, New York.

499. *Pontoise.*

Oil, dated on entry blank 1872.
Lent by Durand-Ruel & Sons.
Price listed: $3,850.

500. *La Bêcheuse.*
Oil, 1882.
Lent by Durand-Ruel & Sons.
Price listed: $5,500.
Present collection: Caroline
Godfroy, Paris.

501. *Paysannes ramassant des herbes.*
Oil.
Lent by Durand-Ruel & Sons.
Price listed: $1,650.

1056. *Woman at Mirror.*
Oil.
Lent anonymously.
No price listed.
Present collection: Private
collection, New York.

PLEUTHNER, Walter K.
(1885–n.d.)

740. *Winter.* †
Oil.
Lent by the artist.
Price listed: $200.

POPE, Louise (n.d.)

735. *Portrait of Mrs. P.* †
Chicago, 294.
Oil.
Lent by the artist.
Not for sale.

POTTER, Louis (1873–1912)

695. *Spirit of the Winds.*
Bronze.
Catalogued but not received.

POWERS, T. E. (n.d.–1939)

968. *Landscape.*
Catalogued but not received.

969. *Landscape.*
Catalogued but not received.

PRENDERGAST, Maurice Brazil
(1858–1924)

893. *Crépuscule.*
Chicago, 295.
Oil, c. 1912.
Lent by the artist.
Price listed: $500.
Present collection: Miss Antoinette
Kraushaar, New York.

* **894.** *Sea Shore.*
Chicago, 296.
Oil.
Lent by the artist.
Price listed: $650 in Kuhn catalogue;
$625 in MacRae catalogue.

895. *Landscape with Figures.*
Oil, 1912.
Lent by the artist.
Price listed: $800. Sold for $800 to
Edward W. Root, March 15, 1913.
Present collection: Munson-
Williams-Proctor Institute, Utica,
New York; Edward W. Root
Bequest.

896. *Under the Trees.*
Watercolor.
Lent by the artist.
Price listed: $200.

897. *The Red Rock.*
Watercolor.
Lent by the artist.
Price listed: $200.

898. *Marblehead Rocks.*
Chicago, 297.
Watercolor.
Lent by the artist.
Price listed: $150.
Present collection (1963): George
May, Kingston, Pennsylvania.

899. *Study.*
Watercolor.
Lent by Mrs. William J. Glackens.
Not for sale.
Present collection: Mr. and Mrs. Ira
Glackens, Washington, D.C.

PRESTON, James (1873–1962)

64. *Landscape.*
Oil.

Lent by the artist.
Price listed: $250.

65. *Landscape.*
Oil.
Lent by the artist.
Price listed: $300.

PRESTON, May Wilson
(1873–1949)

68. *Girl with Print.*
Chicago, 298.
Oil.
Lent by the artist.
Price listed: $1,000.
Present collection (1963): Heirs of
James Preston.

PRYDE, James (1866–1941)

399. *The Little Tower.*
Chicago, 299.
Now called *A Small Tower*
(*Moonlight*).
Oil.
Lent by the artist.
Price listed: $390. Sold for $390 to
George F. Porter, March 7, 1913.
Present collection: The Art
Institute of Chicago; George F.
Porter Collection.

PUTNAM, Arthur (1873–1930)

628. *Bacchus.*
Sculpture.
Lent by William Macbeth.
No price listed.

629. *Deer and Puma.*
Sculpture.
Lent by William Macbeth.
No price listed.

630. *Puma Resting.*
Sculpture.
Lent by William Macbeth.
No price listed.

1040. *Lions.*
Sculpture.
Lent by Mrs. F. S. McGrath.
No price listed.

303

PUVIS DE CHAVANNES, Pierre Cécile (1824–1898)

483. *Pastel.*
Lent by Walter L. Taylor.
No price listed.

556. *La Décollation de St. Jean Baptiste.*
Oil, 1869.
Lent by John Quinn.
Not for sale.
Present collection: The Barber Institute of Fine Arts, The University of Birmingham, Birmingham, England.

557. *Femme nue.*
Oil.
Lent by John Quinn.
Not for sale.

588. *Etude pour le Grand Amphithéâtre de la Sorbonne.*
Crayon drawing, 1888.
Lent by John Quinn.
Not for sale.

559. *Etude pour "Ludus Pro Patria."*
Crayon drawing, 1882.
Lent by John Quinn.
Not for sale.

560. *Etude pour "Ave Picardia Nutrix."*
Crayon drawing, 1865.
Lent by John Quinn.
Not for sale.

561. *Etude pour le plafond de l'Hôtel de Ville de Paris, Victor Hugo.*
Crayon drawing, 1889.
Lent by John Quinn.
Not for sale.

562. *Etude de mains décoration de l'Hôtel de Ville de Poitiers.*
Sanguine drawing, 1875.
Lent by John Quinn.
Not for sale.

563. *Etude pour la décoration de l'Hôtel de Ville de Paris.*
Pastel, 1891.
Lent by John Quinn.
Not for sale.

564. *Le Pêcheur.*
Sanguine drawing, 1878.
Lent by John Quinn.
Not for sale.

565. *Dessin pour "Victor Hugo offrant la lyre à la Ville de Paris."*
Drawing, 1889.
Lent by John Quinn.
Not for sale.

566. *Etude de femme pour "La famille du pêcheur."*
Pencil drawing, 1875.
Lent by John Quinn.
Not for sale.

567. *L'Homme, assis.*
Pencil drawing.
Lent by John Quinn.
Not for sale.

568. *Torse de femme.*
Crayon drawing.
Lent by John Quinn.
Not for sale.
Present collection (1963): Mlle. Marguerite Mespoulet, Paris.

1057. *Decorative Panel.*
Now called *The Fisherman's Family.*
Oil.
Lent by Martin A. Ryerson.
No price listed.
Present collection: The Art Institute of Chicago; Mr. and Mrs. Martin A. Ryerson Collection(?).

Note: This is the only work by Puvis given to the Art Institute of Chicago by Mr. Ryerson; it may be the *Decorative Panel* he lent to the Armory Show.

RASMUSSEN, Bertrand (1890–n.d.)

785. *The Tree of Knowledge.* †
Oil.
Lent by the artist.
Price listed: $200.

REDON, Odilon (1840–1916)

271. *Geranium.*
Chicago, 300. Boston, 151.
Oil.
Lent by Marcel Kapferer.
Price listed: $1,080.

272. *Le Bouquet aux feuilles rouges.*
Chicago, 301. *The Bunch of Red Leaves.* Boston, 152. *The Bouquet with Red Leaves.*
Oil.
Lent by Marcel Kapferer.
Price listed: $1,620.

273. *Fleurs (fond rouge).*
Chicago, 302. Boston, 153. *Flowers (Red Background).*
Oil, c. 1905.
Lent by Marcel Kapferer.
Price listed: $1,350. Sold for $1,350 to Mrs. Wendell T. Bush, March 14, 1913.
Present collection (1963): Private collection, Venezuela.

274. *Pégase sur un roc.*
Chicago, 303. Boston, 154.
Pegasus on a Rock.
Oil.
Lent by Marcel Kapferer.
Price listed: $2,700.

275. *Fécondité (étude).*
Chicago, 304. *Study.* Boston, 155. *Fecundity (Study).*
Oil.
Lent by Marcel Kapferer.
Price listed: $2,700.

276. *Vase de fleurs avec geranium, No. 115.*
Chicago, 305. *Vase of Geraniums.* Boston, 156. *Vase of Flowers with Geranium.*
Oil, dated on entry blank 1912.
Lent by Joseph Hessel.
Price listed: $1,620.

277. *Papillons, No. 121.*
Chicago, 306. Boston, 157.
Butterflies.
Oil, dated on entry blank 1908.

Lent by Joseph Hessel.
Price listed: $405. Sold for $405 to Miss E. McKinney, March 15, 1913.
Present collection (1963): Miss Sally Connor, New York.

278. *Roses sur fond vert, No. 116.*
Chicago, 307. Boston, 158. *Roses.*
Oil, dated on entry blank 1912.
Lent by Joseph Hessel.
Price listed: $810.

279. *Papillon, No. 38.*
Chicago, 308. Boston, 159.
Butterflies.
Oil.
Lent by Joseph Hessel.
Price listed: $1,350.

280. *Profil noir sur fond or, No. 111.*
Chicago, 309. Boston, 160.
Profile against Gold Background.
Now called *Imaginary Portrait of Paul Gauguin.*
Oil, dated on entry blank 1912.
Lent by Joseph Hessel.
Price listed: $1,350.

281. *Fleurs, No. 75.*
Chicago, 310. Boston, 161.
Flowers.
Oil, dated on entry blank 1911.
Lent by Joseph Hessel.
Price listed: $2,700.

282. *Phaeton, No. 114.*
Chicago, 311. Boston, 162.
Now called *The Fall of Phaeton.*
Oil, dated on entry blank 1912.
Lent by Joseph Hessel.
Price listed: $2,160.
Present collection (1963): Mr. and Mrs. Werner E. Josten, New York.

283. *Deux Têtes dans les fleurs.*
Chicago, 312. Boston, 163.
Two Heads among Flowers.
Oil, c. 1905.
Lent by Marcel Kapferer.
Price listed: $2,160 in Kuhn catalogue; no price listed in MacRae catalogue.

305

Present collection (1963): Private collection, Cambridge, Massachusetts.

284. *Vieillard.*
Chicago, 313. Boston, 164.
Old Man.
Oil, dated on entry blank 1912.
Lent by Joseph Hessel, #117.
Price listed: $1,350.

285. *Muse sur Pégase, No. 110.*
Chicago, 314. Boston, 165.
Muse on Pegasus.
Oil, dated on entry blank 1912.
Lent by Joseph Hessel.
Price listed: $2,160.

286. *Barque.*
Chicago, 316. Boston, 167. *Boat.*
Oil.
Lent by Joseph Hessel, #1073.
Price listed: $2,700.

287. *Le Char d'Apollon.*
Chicago, 317. Boston, 168.
The Chariot of Apollo.
Oil.
Lent by Joseph Hessel, #161.
Price listed: $4,050.

288. *Fleurs dans un pot de grès.*
Chicago, 318. *Flowers in Vase.*
Boston, 169. *Flowers in Porcelain Vase.*
Oil.
Lent by Joseph Hessel, #77.
Price listed: $2,160.

289. *Initiation à l'étude.*
Chicago, 319. Boston, 170.
Initiation to Study.
Oil.
Lent by Wilhelm Uhde.
Price listed: $675. Sold for $675 to John Quinn, February 22, 1913.
Present collection: Dallas Museum of Art.

290. *Fleurs.*
Chicago, 320. Boston, 171. *Flowers.*
Pastel.
Lent by Wilhelm Uhde.
Price listed: $205. Sold for $205 to Mrs. Henry W. Hardon, March 6, 1913.

291. *Profil mystique.*
Chicago, 321. Boston, 172.
Mystic Profile.
Black chalk, dated on entry blank 1885.
Lent by Artz & de Bois.
Price listed: $780.

292. *Songe d'Orient.*
Chicago, 322. Boston, 173.
Dream of the Orient.
Pastel, dated on entry blank 1885.
Lent by Artz & de Bois.
Price listed: $650.

293. *Corbeille de fleurs.*
Chicago, 323. Boston, 174.
Basket of Flowers.
Oil, dated on entry blank 1910.
Lent by Artz & de Bois.
Price listed: $195. Sold for $195 to Mrs. Porter Norton, March 7, 1913.

294. *Coquelicots.*
Chicago, 324. Boston, 175. *Poppies.*
Oil, dated on entry blank 1909.
Lent by Artz & de Bois.
Price listed: $520. Sold for $520 to Daniel H. Morgan, February 19, 1913.

295. *Barque.*
Chicago, 325. Boston, 176. *Ships.*
Oil, dated on entry blank 1900.
Lent by Artz & de Bois.
Price listed: $390. Sold for $390 to Ira N. Morris, March 17, 1913.

296. *Vase de fleurs, bleu.*
Oil, dated on entry blank 1912.
Lent by Artz & de Bois.
Price listed: $520. Sold for $520 to Daniel H. Morgan, February 19, 1913.

297. *Vase de fleurs, gris.*
Oil, dated on entry blank 1912.
Lent by Artz & de Bois.
Price listed: $520. Sold for $520 to Daniel H. Morgan, February 19, 1913.

298. *Prometheus.*
Chicago, 327. Boston, 178.
Oil, dated on entry blank 1900.
Lent by Artz & de Bois.
Price listed: $390.

299. *Tête en fleurs.*
Chicago, 328. Boston, 179.
Head among Flowers.
Oil, dated on entry blank 1900.
Lent by Artz & de Bois.
Price listed: $300. Sold for $300 to
Gertrude Watson, March 3, 1913.

300. *Le Silence.*
Chicago, 329. Boston, 180. *Silence.*
Oil, c. 1911.
Lent by the artist.
Price listed: $540. Sold for $540 to
Lillie P. Bliss, February 26, 1913.
Present collection: The Museum of
Modern Art, New York; Lillie P.
Bliss Collection.

301. *Monstre et Angélique.*
Oil, dated on entry blank 1906.
Lent by Artz & de Bois.
Price listed: $455.

302. *Deux Etres sublunaires ailes
dans l'espace.*
Chicago, 326. Boston, 177.
*Two Sublunary Beings Winging
through Space.*
Oil, dated on entry blank 1909.
Lent by Artz & de Bois.
Price listed: $585.

303. *Ohannès.*
Chicago, 330. Boston, 181.
Oannès.
Oil, dated on entry blank 1900.
Lent by Artz & de Bois.
Price listed: $520.
Present collection: Haags
Gemeentemuseum, The Hague.

304. *Tête de femme.*
Chicago, 333. Boston, 184.
Woman's Head.
Pastel.
Lent by Mrs. Chadbourne.
Not for sale.

305. *Fleurs des champ dans un vase.*
Chicago, 334. Boston, 185.
Wild Flowers in a Vase.
Now called *Lilas, geranium,
capucines et folles avoines dans un
pot noir.*
Pastel.
Lent by Marcel Kapferer.
Price listed: $1,080.
Present collection (1963): Marcel
Kapferer, Paris.

306. *Roger and Angelica.*
Pastel, c. 1910. Dated on entry
blank 1912.
Lent by the artist.
Price listed: $810. Sold for $810 to
Lillie P. Bliss, February 26, 1913.
Present collection: The Museum of
Modern Art, New York; Lillie P.
Bliss Collection.

307. *Tête d'Orphée.*
Chicago, 336. Boston, 186.
Head of Orpheus.
Now called *Orpheus.*
Pastel.
Lent by the artist.
Price listed: $405.
Present collection: Cleveland
Museum of Art; Gift of J. H. Wade.

308. *Lithographies, Nos. 1–29.*
Chicago, 315. *Lithographs.*
Lent by the artist, except for a set,
containing an unknown number,
that was lent by Ambroise Vollard.
Prices listed: $12.50, $15, $20, $25.
The titles of these lithographs are
not listed. However, the sales and
other records note titles that may be
at least tentatively identified. The
number in parenthesis following
each title refers to André Mellerio,
*L'Oeuvre graphique complet d'Odilon
Redon*, Paris, 1913.

*Le Souffle qui conduit les êtres est aussi
dans les sphères.* 1882. Plate V of the
portfolio "A Edgar Poe." (M. 42)

Unidentified lithograph from "Les
Origines," 1883.

Les Prêtresses furent en attente. 1886.
Plate V of the portfolio "La Nuit."
(M. 66)

L'Idole. 1888. Frontispiece of "Les
Soirs." (M. 74)

Les Débâcles. 1889. Frontispiece of
"Les Débâcles" by Emile Verhaeren.
(M. 101)
Sold for $12.50 to Arthur B.
Spingarn, March 9, 1913.

Pégase captif. 1889. (M. 102)
Sold for $25 to Lillie P. Bliss,
February 26, 1913.
Present collection: The Museum of
Modern Art, New York; Lillie P.
Bliss Collection.

Serpent auréole. 1890. (M. 108)

Six plates from "Songes," 1891.
I. C'était un voile, une empriente.
(M. 110)
II. Et là-bas l'idole astral, l'apothéose.
(M. 111)
Sold for $25 to Katherine S. Dreier,
March 13, 1913.
Present collection: Yale University
Art Gallery, New Haven,
Connecticut; Collection Société
Anonyme.
III. Lueur précaire, une tête à l'infini
suspendue. (M. 112)
Sold for $25 to Lydia S. Hays,
March 15, 1913.
IV. Sous l'aile d'ombre, l'être noir
appliquait une active morsure.
(M. 113)
V. Pèlerin du monde sublunaire.
(M. 114)
VI. Le Jour. (M. 115)
Sold for $12.50 to Lillie P. Bliss,
February 26, 1913.
Present collection: The Museum of
Modern Art, New York; Lillie P.
Bliss Collection.

Druidesse. 1892. (M. 117)
Sold for $15 to Lillie P. Bliss,
February 26, 1913.
Present collection: The Museum of
Modern Art, New York; Lillie P.

Bliss Collection.

Initiation à l'étude; Entretien mystique.
1892. (M. 118)
Sold for $12.50 to John Quinn,
March 11, 1913.

L'Arbre. 1892. (M. 120)

L'Aile. 1893. (M. 122)
Sold for $25 to Lillie P. Bliss,
February 22, 1913.
Present collection: The Museum of
Modern Art, New York; Lillie P.
Bliss Collection.

Lumière. 1893. (M. 123)
Sold for $25 to Mrs. Arthur T.
Aldis, March 1, 1913.

Brünnehilde (Crépuscule des dieux).
1894. (M. 130)
Sold for $25 to Harriet Monroe,
April 16, 1913, Chicago.

L'Art céleste. 1894. (M. 131)
Sold for $25 to Mrs. Arthur T.
Aldis, March 1, 1913.

Centaure visant les nues. 1895.
(M. 133)
Sold for $20 to Lillie P. Bliss,
March 14, 1913.
Present collection: The Museum of
Modern Art, New York; Lillie P.
Bliss Collection.

Oannès: Moi, la première conscience
de chaos . . . 1896. Plate 14 from
the "Tentation de Saint-Antoine"
by Gustave Flaubert. (M. 147)

Tête d'enfant avec fleurs. 1897.
(M. 169)

Puis l'ange prit l'encensoir. 1899.
Plate IV from the "Apocalypse de
Saint-Jean," one of the Vollard set.
(M. 177)
Sold for $25 to Lillie P. Bliss,
February 22, 1913.

. . . Une Femme revêtue du soleil.
1899. Plate 6 from the "Apocalypse
of Saint-Jean." (M. 179)
Sold for $25 to Mrs. Arthur T.
Aldis, March 1, 1913.

308

Edouard Vuillard. 1900. (M. 190)

Pierre Bonnard. 1902. (M. 191)

Maurice Denis. 1903. (M. 193)
Sold for $20 to John Quinn,
February 26, 1913.

Mlle. Juliette Dodu. 1904. (M. 195)

309. *Eaux fortes, Nos. 1–7.*
Lent by the artist.
Prices listed: $12.50, $15, $20, $25.
The titles of these etchings are not
listed. However, the sales and other
records note titles that may be at
least tentatively identified. The
number in parenthesis following
each title refers to André Mellerio,
*L'Oeuvre graphique complet d'Odilon
Redon,* Paris, 1913.

Lutte de Cavaliers. 1865. (M. 4)
Sold for $12.50 to Arthur B. Davies,
February 21, 1913.

Bataille. 1865. (M. 5)
Sold for $13.50 to Robert W.
Chanler, February 26, 1913.

La Peur. 1865. (M. 6)
Sold for $12.50 to Robert W.
Chanler, February 26, 1913.

Mauvaise Gloire. 1886. (M. 17)

Petit Prélat. Drypoint, 1888. (M. 19)
Sold for $12.50 to Lillie P. Bliss,
February 26, 1913.
Present collection: The Museum of
Modern Art, New York; Lillie P.
Bliss Collection.

Perversité. 1891. (M. 20)

Sainte Thérèse. Drypoint, 1892.
(M. 24)
Also called *Le Livre.*
Sold for $12.50 to Pauline Stein,
March 4, 1913.

310. *Le Bateau rouge.*
Chicago, 332. Boston, 183.
The Red Boat.
Oil.
Lent by Wilhelm Uhde.
Price listed: $270. Sold for $270 to

Mary L. Willard, March 15, 1913.

1059. *Le Christ.*
Chicago, 335. *Christ.*
Oil.
Lent by F. R. Lillie.
No price listed.

Chicago, 331. Boston, 182.
Ophelia.
Oil.
Listed in the Boston catalogue as
lent by Wilhelm Uhde, but records
show no such loan.
Price listed: $1,200.

RENOIR, Pierre-Auguste
(1841–1919)

502. *L'Ombrelle.*
Oil, 1878.
Lent by Durand-Ruel & Sons.
Price listed: $13,200.
Present collection (1963): Mme.
Edouard Jonas, Paris.

503. *Algérienne assise.*
Now called *Algerian Girl.*
Oil, 1881.
Lent by Durand-Ruel & Sons.
Not for sale.
Present collection: Museum of Fine
Arts, Boston.

504. *Pivoines.*
Oil, 1882.
Lent by Durand-Ruel & Sons.
Not for sale.

505. *Dans le jardin.*
Oil, 1884.
Lent by Durand-Ruel & Sons.
Price listed: $16,500.
Present collection (1963): John L.
Booth, Grosse Pointe, Michigan.

1051. *Elise.*
Oil.
Lent by Stephan Bourgeois.
No price listed.

Lithographs.
Not listed in the New York
catalogue but displayed for sale
and order.

Chicago, 337–47. Boston, 187.
From available evidence it is
impossible to determine which or
how many lithographs there were
and how they were priced. The
Vollard loan is listed as including
sets of three at 300 francs, but the
Chicago catalogue lists eleven.
Lent by Ambroise Vollard.
Three sold for $81 to Lillie P. Bliss,
February 22, 1913.
Six sold for $162 to John Quinn,
March 10, 1913.
One sold for $40 to Mrs. Richard
Sheldrick, March 13, 1913.
One sold for $20 to Elmer L.
MacRae, May 10, 1913.

REUTERDAHL, Henry
(1871–1925)

952. *Blast Furnaces.* †
Oil, 1912.
Lent by the artist.
Price listed: $250.
Present collection: The Toledo
Museum of Art, Toledo, Ohio.

RHOADES, Catherine N.
(1895–c. 1938)

736. *Talloires.* †
Chicago, 348.
Oil.
Lent by the artist.
Price listed: $400.

RIMMER, Dr. William
(1816–1879)

1102. *4 Drawings.*
Chicago, 349. *Drawings.*
Lent by Miss Rimmer.
No price listed.

ROBINSON, Boardman
(1876–1952)

1002. *3 Drawings.*
Chicago, 350. *Nude.*
This was probably one of the three
drawings in the New York show.
Lent by the artist.

Prices listed: $25 for two small
drawings, $50 for one large in Kuhn
catalogue; $25 each in MacRae
catalogue. Red chalk drawing sold
for $25 to A. E. Gallatin, March 11,
1913.

1003. *2 Cartoons.*
Chicago, 351.
Lent by the artist.
Price listed: $30 each.

ROBINSON, Theodore
(1852–1896)

729. *Debacle.*
Now called *La Débâcle.*
Oil, 1892.
Lent by John Gellatly.
Not for sale.
Present collection: Scripps College,
Claremont, California; Gift of
General and Mrs. Edward Clinton
Young.

730. *In the Orchard.*
Oil.
Lent by William Macbeth.
Price listed: $500.
Present collection: The Art
Museum, Princeton University,
Princeton, New Jersey.

731. *Two in a Boat.*
Oil, 1891.
Lent by William Macbeth.
Price listed: $500. Sold for $350 to
George D. Pratt, February 26, 1913.
Present collection: The Phillips
Collection, Washington, D.C.

732. *Hillside, Summer.*
Catalogued but not received.
Oil.
Lent by William Macbeth.
Price listed: $500.

1077. *Bay Shore.*
Oil.
Lent by Alexander Morten.
No price listed.

RODIN, Auguste (1840–1917)

1015. *Figure of Man.*

310

Bronze.
Lent by Mrs. Gertrude Kasebier.
Not for sale.
A letter in the Kuhn papers from
the assistant secretary of the AAPS
states that there was no Rodin
sculpture in the exhibition.

1016. *Seven Drawings.*
Chicago, 352.
Pencil and watercolor.
Lent by Mrs. Gertrude Kasebier.
Although a letter in the Kuhn
papers states that they were not for
sale, there is a note in the Kuhn
catalogue, "Two in Redon room
$250 each." One of these, the
"green one," was sold for $250 to
Miss Lydia S. Hays, March 15,
1913; the other, "The muse and the
poet," was sold for $250 to W. R.
Valentiner, March 11, 1913.
Present collection (1963): Four of
these drawings are in the collection
of Miss Minna Turner, New York.

ROGERS, Mary C. (1881–1920)

791. *Portrait.* †
Chicago, 353.
Oil, 1911.
Lent by the artist.
Price listed: $150.
Present collection (1963): Miss
Catherine L. Rogers, Clearwater,
Florida.

ROHLAND, Paul (1884–c. 1950)

744. *Still Life.* †
Chicago, 354.
Oil.
Price listed: $175. Sold for $175 to
Mrs. V. P. Snyder, March 7, 1913.

745. *Waterfalls.* †
Oil.
Lent by the artist.
Price listed: $200.

746. *Still Life.* †
Oil.
Lent by the artist.

Price listed: $200. Noted as sold
in the Kuhn catalogue, but it is
no. 744 that is listed as sold in the
financial ledgers.

ROINE, Jules Edouard
(1857–1916)

637. *Medals.*
Lent by the artist.
No price listed.

638. *Medals.*
Lent by the artist.
No price listed.

639. *Medals.*
Lent by the artist.
No price listed.

ROOK, Edward F. (1870–1960)

58. *Grey Sea. Monhegan.*
Called *Snow, Ice and Foam* in Kuhn
catalogue.
Oil.
Lent by the artist.
Price listed: $1,500.

59. *White-faced Chasm.*
Oil.
Lent by the artist.
Price listed: $800.

ROUAULT, Georges (1871–1958)

437. *Compositions, Nos. 3109–
3118.*
Chicago, 356. Boston, 189.
Drawings.
Lent by Emile Druet.
Price listed: $810—frame.

438. *La Parade.*
Chicago, 355. Boston, 188.
The Parade.
Gouache and pastel, 1907.
Lent by Emile Druet.
Price listed: $540.

439. *Compositions, Nos. 3100–
3108.*
Chicago, 356. Boston, 189.
Drawings.
Lent by Emile Druet.

311

Price listed: $810—frame.

440. *Nu.*
Chicago, 357. Boston, 190. *Nude.*
Gouache, 1907.
Lent by Emile Druet.
Price listed: $540.

ROUSSEAU, Henri-Julian
(1844–1910)

381. *Le Centennaire [de la
Revolution].*
Chicago, 358. Boston, 191.
The Centennial of the Revolution.
Oil, 1892.
Lent by Alfred Flechtheim.
Price listed: $6,750.

382. *Cheval attaqué par un jaguar.*
Chicago, 382. Boston, 192.
Horse Attacked by a Jaguar.
Oil, 1910.
Lent by Ambroise Vollard.
Price listed: $1,350.
Present collection: Pushkin Museum,
Moscow, U.S.S.R.

978. *Jardin de Luxembourg.*
Oil.
Lent by Max Weber.
No price listed.

979. *Vue de Malakoff.*
Now called *Street Scene* (*Sketch for
View of Malakoff*).
Oil, 1898.
Lent by Max Weber.
No price listed.
Former collection: Mrs. Max
Weber; now deceased.

980. *Nature morte [avec cerises].*
Now called *Still Life.*
Elsewhere called *La Bougie rose.*
Oil, 1900–8.
Lent by Max Weber.
No price listed.
Former collection: Mrs. Max
Weber; now deceased.

981. *La Famille.*
Oil.
Lent by Max Weber.

No price listed.

982. *La Maison, environs de Paris.*
Now called *House, Outskirts of Paris.*
Elsewhere called *Maison de campagne
à St.-Cloud.*
Oil, 1905–7.
Lent by Max Weber.
No price listed.
Former collection: Mrs. Max
Weber; now deceased.

983. *Paysage avec un taureau.*
Oil.
Lent by Robert J. Coady.
No price listed.

984. *Patâche d'aval quai.*
Now called *River Scene, Quai
d'Auteuil.*
Ink drawing, 1885.
Lent by Max Weber.
No price listed.
Former collection: Mrs. Max
Weber; now deceased.

985. *Quai d'Auteuil.*
Ink drawing, 1885.
Lent by Max Weber.
No price listed.
Former collection: Mrs. Max
Weber; now deceased.

ROUSSEL, K[er]-X[avier]
(1867–1944)

1063. *Maenads with Head of
Orpheus.*
Chicago, 359½. Boston, 193.
Oil.
Lent by Bernheim-Jeune & Cie.
No price listed.

RUMSEY, Charles C.
(1879–1922)

692. *A Fountain.*
Sculpture.
Lent by the artist.
No price listed.

693. *Bayard Boyesen.*
Sculpture.
Lent by the artist.

No price listed.
This was listed in the catalogue as *Beyond Boyesen*, probably a misspelling of "Bayard." Bayard Boyesen was an American poet of Norwegian descent.

694. *Indians and Buffaloes.*
Chicago, 360.
Sculpture.
Lent by the artist.
No price listed.

RUSSELL, George W. (AE)
(1867–1935)

574. *The Waders.*
Oil, 1907.
Lent by John Quinn.
Not for sale.

575. *The Bather.*
Chicago, 361. Boston, 194.
Oil, 1906.
Lent by John Quinn.
Not for sale.

576. *The Waders.*
Chicago, 362. Boston, 195.
Oil.
Lent by Frederick J. Gregg.
Not for sale.

577. *The Lake.*
Oil.
Lent by Frederick J. Gregg.
Not for sale.

RUSSELL, Morgan (1886–1953)

253. *Portrait.*
Oil.
Lent by the artist.
Price listed: $120.

254. *Capucines.*
Oil, dated on entry blank 1912.
Lent by the artist.
Price listed: $60. Sold for $60 to Mary L. Willard, March 15, 1913.

RYDER, Albert Pinkham
(1847–1917)

962. *A Pastoral Study.*

Oil.
Lent by John Gellatly.
Not for sale.
Present collection: National Museum of American Art, Smithsonian Institution, Washington, D.C.; Gift of John Gellatly.

963. *Moonlight Marine.*
Oil.
Lent by N. E. Montross.
No price listed.
Present collection: The Metropolitan Museum of Art, New York; Samuel D. Lee Fund.

964. *Moonlight on Beach.*
Now called *Moonlit Cove.*
Oil, 1880–90.
Lent by Alexander Morten.
Not for sale.
Present collection: The Phillips Collection, Washington, D.C.

965. *Diana.*
Chicago, 364.
Oil, c. 1900.
Lent by Alexander Morten.
Not for sale.
Present collection: The Chrysler Museum, Norfolk, Virginia; Gift of Walter Chrysler, Jr.

966. *Hunter and Dog.*
Chicago, 365.
Now called *Hunter's Rest.*
Oil.
Lent by Alexander Morten.
Not for sale.
Present collection: The Nebraska Art Association; Thomas C. Woods Memorial Collection; Sheldon Memorial Art Gallery, University of Nebraska, Lincoln.

967. *Interior of Stable.*
Chicago, 366.
Now called *In the Stable.*
Oil.
Lent by Mrs. Lloyd Williams.
No price listed.
Present collection: National Museum of American Art, Smithsonian

313

Institution, Washington, D.C.; Gift of John Gellatly.

1079. *St. Agnes Eve.*
Now called *The Lovers.*
Oil.
Lent by Mrs. Lloyd Williams.
No price listed.
Present collection: Vassar College Art Gallery, Poughkeepsie, New York; Gift of Mrs. Lloyd Williams.

1080. *Pegasus.*
Chicago, 363.
Oil, 1887.
Lent by J. R. Andrews.
No price listed.
Present collection: Worcester Art Museum, Worcester, Massachusetts.

1081. *Resurrection.*
Oil, 1885.
Lent by N. E. Montross.
Not for sale.
Present collection: The Phillips Collection, Washington, D.C.

1082. *At the Ford.*
Oil.
Lent by N. E. Montross.
No price listed.
Present collection (1963): David B. Findlay Art Galleries, New York.

SALVATORE, Victor D.
(1884–1965)

727. *Harriman Baby.*
Marble bust.
Lent by the artist.
Not for sale.

728. *Richardson.*
Now called *Bust of a Child.*
Marble.
Lent by the artist.
Not for sale.
Present collection: The Brooklyn Museum, New York.

SCHAMBERG, Morton L.
(1881–1918)

18. *Study of a Girl.*

Chicago, 367(?).
Oil, c. 1909.
Lent by the artist.
Price listed: $100.
Present collection: Williams College Museum of Art, Williamstown, Massachusetts; Bequest of Lawrence H. Bloedel.

19. *Study of a Girl.*
Chicago, 367(?).
Oil.
Lent by the artist.
Price listed: $100.

20. *N.E.A.*
Oil.
Lent by the artist.
Price listed: $100.

21. *Figure.*
Oil.
Lent by the artist.
Price listed: $100.

22. *Landscape.*
Oil.
Lent by the artist.
Price listed: $100. Sold for $100 to Mrs. H. Orme Wilson, February 28, 1913.

SCHUMACHER, William E.
(1870–1931)

737. *Her Blue Skirt.* †
Oil.
Lent by the artist.
Price listed: $400.

738. *The Lady, Maid and Child.* †
Chicago, 368.
Oil.
Lent by the artist.
Price listed: $400.

SEGONZAC, André Dunoyer de
(1884–1974)

246. *Paysage No. I.*
Chicago, 115. *Landscape.*
Oil, dated on entry blank 1912.
Lent by the artist.

314

Price listed: $216. Sold for $216 to Arthur J. Eddy, March 1, 1913.

247. *Scène de pâturage.*
Chicago, 116. *Pasturage.*
Now called *Pasture.*
Oil, dated on entry blank 1912.
Lent by the artist.
Price listed: $216. Sold for $216 to Arthur J. Eddy, March 1, 1913.
Present collection: The Art Institute of Chicago; Arthur Jerome Eddy Memorial Collection.

248. *Paysage No. III.*
Chicago, 117. *Landscape.*
Oil, dated on entry blank 1912.
Lent by the artist.
Price listed: $216.

249. *Paysage.*
Drawing, dated on entry blank 1912.
Lent by the artist.
Price listed: $54.

250. *Drawings, Nos. 1 to 5.*
Chicago, 119.
Elsewhere called *Nudes.*
Dated on entry blank 1912.
Lent by the artist.
Price listed: $54 each. Three sold for $162 to John Quinn, March 11, 1913.

251. *Paysage No. II.*
Oil, dated on entry blank 1912.
Lent by the artist.
Price listed: $216.

252. *Une Bucolique.*
Chicago, 118. Boston, 47.
A Pastoral.
Oil, dated on entry blank 1912.
Lent by the artist.
Price listed: $405.

SERRET, Charles (1824–1900)

1090. *Three Drawings.*
Chicago, 369. Boston, 196.
Lent by Arthur B. Davies.
No price listed.

SEURAT, Georges (1859–1891)

454. *Honfleur.*
Chicago, 370. Boston, 197.
Oil.
Lent by Emile Druet.
Price listed: $2,020.

455. *Les Poseuses.*
Chicago, 371. Boston, 198. *Models.*
Oil, 1888.
Lent by Alphonse Kann.
Not for sale.
Present collection: Private collection.

SEYLER, Julius (1873–1949)

194. *Nordischer Fischerhafen.*
Oil, dated on entry blank 1911.
Lent by Heinrich Thannhauser, #2825.
Price listed: $325.

SHANNON, Charles H. (1865–1937)

1083. *Toilet of Venus.*
Chicago, 372. Boston, 199.
Oil.
Lent by William Macbeth.
Price listed: $3,500.

SHAW, Sidney Dale (1879–1946)

29. *California.*
Oil.
Lent by the artist.
Price listed: $500.

30. *Southwestern Country.*
Chicago, 373.
Oil.
Lent by the artist.
Price listed: $350.

31. *Topanza.*
Oil.
Lent by the artist.
Price listed: $350.

315

SHEELER, Charles R.
(1883–1965)

972. *Red Tulips.*
Oil, 1912.
Lent by the artist.
Price listed: $150.
Present collection: The Regis
Collection, Minneapolis.

973. *Landscape.*
Oil, 1913.
Lent by the artist.
Price listed: $150.
Present collection: Private
collection, Boston.

974. *The Waterfall.*
Chicago, 374.
Oil.
Lent by the artist.
Price listed: $150.
Present collection: Raymond
Balasny, New York.

975. *The Mandarin.*
Oil, 1912.
Lent by the artist.
Price listed: $200.
Present collection: Munson-
Williams-Proctor Institute, Utica,
New York.

976. *Dahlias and Asters.*
Oil, 1912.
Lent by the artist.
Price listed: $200.
Present collection: Corcoran
Gallery of Art, Washington, D.C.;
Gift of Mrs. F. H. Detweiler.

977. *Chrysanthemums.*
Chicago, 375.
Oil, 1912.
Lent by the artist.
Price listed: $250.
Present collection: Whitney Museum
of American Art, New York; Gift of
the artist.

Note: Sheeler sent his works to the
Domestic Committee although he
had apparently been invited. His
entries are listed in the notebook
but were not judged.

SICKERT, Walter (1860–1942)

378. *Noctes Ambrosianae.*
Oil, dated on entry blank 1906.
Lent by Walter L. Taylor.
Not for sale.
Present collection: Castle Museum,
Nottingham, England.

379. *S. Rémy, Dieppe.*
Chicago, 376. Boston, 200.
Now called *Church in Dieppe.*
Oil, dated on entry blank 1912.
Lent by the artist.
Price listed: $1,675.
Present collection: Queensland Art
Gallery, Brisbane, Australia.

SIGNAC, Paul (1863–1935)

395. *Marseilles, Calm Sea.*
Now called *Port of Marseilles.*
Chicago, 377. Boston, 201.
Oil, 1901.
Lent by Bernheim-Jeune & Cie.
Price listed: $945.
Present collection: Mr. and Mrs.
William Mazer, New York.

396. *La Bonne Mère.*
Catalogued but not received.
A variety of evidence indicates that
this was an alternative title for
no. 395.

397. *15 Aquarelles.*
Chicago, 378. Boston, 202.
Watercolors.
Lent by Emile Druet.
Price listed: $135 each. Druet
#2771 sold for $135 to John Quinn,
March 1, 1913. Druet #6727 sold
for $135 to John Quinn, March 1,
1913.
Price listed: $90 each. Druet #2491.
Druet #2492. Druet #2498–99
(framed). Druet #2764. Druet
#2773. Druet #2774. Druet #2775.
Druet #6915. Two sold for $180 to
Robert Hartshorn, March 2, 1913.
One sold for $90 to John Quinn for
Miss Coates, March 15, 1913.
Price listed: $65. Druet #2508–9
(framed), sold for $65 to Gertrude

Watson, March 4, 1913. Druet #2510–11 (framed), sold for $65 to Mrs. Eliza G. Radeke, March 2, 1913. Now framed separately and called *Seascapes* (Present collection: Museum of Art, Rhode Island School of Design, Providence; Gift of Mrs. Gustav Radeke).
Another of these watercolors, called *The River,* is now in the Norton Gallery and School of Art, West Palm Beach, Florida.

SISLEY, Alfred (1839–1899)

506. *Vieilles Chaumières à Veneux.*
Oil, 1881.
Lent by Durand-Ruel & Sons.
Price listed: $3,750.

507. *Chemin du vieux, Bac-a-By.*
Oil, 1880.
Lent by Durand-Ruel & Sons.
Price listed: $3,300.
Present collection: The Tate Gallery, London.

508. *Prairie inondée.*
Oil, 1878.
Lent by Durand-Ruel & Sons.
Price listed: $4,400.
Present collection (1963): Mr. and Mrs. Nathan L. Halpern, New York.

SLEVOGT, Max (1868–1932)

400. *Weinberg-Arbeiter.*
Chicago, 379. Boston, 203.
The Worker in the Vineyard.
Oil, dated on entry blank 1909.
Lent by Heinrich Thannhauser, #2838.
Price listed: $1,950.

SLOAN, John (1871–1951)

906. *Sunday, Girls Drying Their Hair.*
Now called *Sunday, Women Drying Their Hair.*
Chicago, 380.
Oil, 1912.
Lent by the artist.
Price listed: $650.

Present collection: Addison Gallery of American Art, Phillips Academy, Andover, Massachusetts.

907. *McSorley's Ale House.*
Elsewhere called *McSorley's Bar.*
Oil, 1912.
Lent by the artist.
Price listed: $500.
Present collection: The Detroit Institute of Arts; Gift of the Founders' Society.

908. *Girl and Beggar.*
Etching, 1910.
Lent by the artist.
Price listed: $10.

909. *Portrait of Mother.*
Etching, 1906.
Lent by the artist.
Price listed: $15.

910. *Night Windows.*
Etching, 1910.
Lent by the artist.
Price listed: $10.

911. *Anchutz's Talk on Anatomy.*
Etching, 1912.
Lent by the artist.
Price listed: $15.

912. *The Picture Buyer.*
Etching, 1911.
Lent by the artist.
Price listed: $10. Sold for $10 to William Macbeth, March 14, 1913.

SOUSA-CARDOZO, Amadéo de (1887–1918)

462. *Marine.*
Chicago, 381. Boston, 204.
Watercolor, dated on entry blank 1912.
Lent by the artist.
Price listed: $13.50. Sold for $13.50 to Robert W. Chanler, February 26, 1913.

463. *Château fort.*
Chicago, 382. *The Stronghold.*
Oil, dated on entry blank 1912.
Lent by the artist.

317

Price listed: $81. Sold for $81 to
Arthur J. Eddy, April 10, 1913,
Chicago.
Present collection: The Art
Institute of Chicago; Arthur Jerome
Eddy Memorial Collection.

464. *Le Prince et la meute.*
Chicago, 383. Boston, 205.
The Prince and the Pack.
Oil, dated on entry blank 1912.
Lent by the artist.
Price listed: $324.

*465. *Avant la corrida.*
Chicago, 384. Boston, 206.
Before the Bullfight.
Oil, dated on entry blank 1912.
Lent by the artist.
Price listed: $216. Sold for $216 to
Robert W. Chanler, February 26,
1913.

466. *Return from the Chase.*
Chicago, 385.
Oil, dated on entry blank 1912.
Lent by the artist.
Price listed: $54. Sold for $54 to
Manierre Dawson, April 10, 1913,
Chicago.
Former collection: Manierre Dawson,
Ludington, Michigan; now deceased.

467. *Saut du lapin.*
Chicago, 386. *Rabbit Jump.*
Now called *The Leap of the Rabbit.*
Oil, dated on entry blank 1912.
Lent by the artist.
Price listed: $67.50. Sold for $67.50
to Arthur J. Eddy, April 10, 1913,
Chicago.
Present collection: The Art
Institute of Chicago; Arthur Jerome
Eddy Memorial Collection.

468. *Paysage.*
Chicago, 387. *Landscape.*
Oil, dated on entry blank 1912.
Lent by the artist.
Price listed: $81. Sold for $81 to
Arthur J. Eddy, April 10, 1913,
Chicago.

467. *Pêcheur.*

Chicago, 388. Boston, 207.
Fisherman.
Oil, dated on entry blank 1912.
Lent by the artist.
Price listed: $135. Sold for $135
to Mrs. Elizabeth S. Cheever,
March 14, 1913.

SPRINCHORN, Carl
(1887–1971)

753. *Distant Rain.* †
Chicago, 389.
Oil, 1911.
Lent by the artist.
Price listed: $250.
Former collection: The artist,
Selkirk, New York.

754. *Stockholm.*
Chicago, 390.
Pastel, 1910.
Lent by the artist.
Price listed: $50.
Former collection: The artist,
Selkirk, New York.

755. *The Balcony.*
Watercolor, 1910.
Lent by the artist.
Price listed: $50.
Former collection: The artist,
Selkirk, New York.

756. *Mordkin and Pavlova.*
Chicago, 391.
Watercolor.
Lent by the artist.
Price listed: $50.

STEER, Philip Wilson (1860–
1942)

87. *Landscape.*
Chicago, 392. Boston, 208.
Oil.
Lent by Mrs. B. S. Guinness.
No price listed.

STELLA, Joseph (1880–1946)

818. *Nature morte.* †
Catalogued but not received.
Oil.

Lent by the artist.
Price listed: $600.

819. *Still Life.*
Oil.
Lent by the artist.
Price listed: $500 in Kuhn
catalogue; $600 or $200 in MacRae
catalogue.

Chicago, 393. *Landscape.*
Oil.
Lent by the artist.
No price listed.

Note: Stella submitted to the
Domestic Committee five works,
one of which was accepted. No. 819
and Chicago no. 393 must have
been invited later.

STEVENS, Frances Simpson
(n.d.)

779. *Roof Tops of Madrid.* †
Oil.
Lent by the artist.
Price listed: $200.

STINEMETZ, Morgan (n.d.)

747. *Landscape.* †
Oil.
Lent by the artist.
Price listed: $100.

748. *Sailboat.* †
Oil.
Lent by the artist.
Price listed: $100.

TARKHOFF, Nicolas (Nicolai A. Tarchov) (1871–n.d.)

360. *Sous la lampe.*
Chicago, 394. *Lamplight.*
Elsewhere called *Mother and
Children.*
Oil.
Lent by Emile Druet.
Price listed: $540.

TAYLOR, Henry Fitch
(1853–1925)

878. *Omen.*
Oil.
Lent by the artist.
Price listed: $2,500.

879. *Prostitution.*
Chicago, 395.
Oil.
Lent by the artist.
Price listed: $800.

*** 880.** *Dusk of Morning.*
Oil.
Lent by the artist.
Price listed: $800.

TAYLOR, William L. (1854–1926)

83. *Decorative Panel, Spring* (two
panels).
Chicago, 396.
Oil.
Lent by the artist.
Price listed: $750. Both panels sold
for $600 to Arthur J. Eddy, March 4,
1913.

Chicago, 398. *Drawings.*
Lent by the artist.
No price listed.

TOBEEN, Felix E. (1880–n.d.)

421. *Ciboure.*
Chicago, 400½. Boston, 211.
Oil.
Lent by the artist.
Price listed: $270.

422. *L'Ecuyère.*
Chicago, 399. Boston, 209.
The Circus Rider.
Oil.
Lent by the artist.
Price listed: $270.

423. *Les Pelotaris.*
Chicago, 400. Boston, 210.
The Pelota Players.
Sketch.
Lent by the artist.
Price listed: $135.

319

TOULOUSE-LAUTREC, Henri de (1864–1901)

333. *Affiche "Le Divan Japonais."*
Chicago, 401. *Poster, the Japanese Divan.*
Color lithograph, 1892.
Lent by Emile Druet.
Price listed: $675.

334. *La Tresse.*
Chicago, 402. Boston, 212.
The Tress of Hair.
Oil, 1891.
Lent by Bernheim-Jeune & Cie.
Price listed: $3,240.

1060. *Woman in Garden.*
Oil.
Lent by Stephan Bourgeois.
Price listed: $6,600.

1061. *Woman Sitting at Table.*
Now called *La Buveuse.*
Oil, 1889.
Lent by Stephan Bourgeois.
No price listed.
Present collection: Fogg Art Museum, Harvard University, Cambridge, Massachusetts; Maurice Wertheim Collection.

1062. *Red-Haired Woman Sitting in Conservatory.*
Oil, 1889.
Lent by Sir William Van Horne.
No price listed.
Present collection: Private collection, U.S.A.

TOUSSAINT, Gaston (1872–1946)

636. *Faunesse.*
Bronze.
Lent by the artist.
Price listed: $405.

TUCKER, Allen (1866–1939)

* **900.** *Mount Aberdeen.*
Chicago, 404.
Elsewhere called *Mount Aberdeen, Sunny Afternoon.*
Oil, 1912.
Lent by the artist.
Price listed: $400.
Present collection (1963): Allen Tucker Memorial Collection, New York.

901. *Study in Rose and Black.*
Oil, 1912.
Lent by the artist.
Price listed: $900.
Present collection: Staten Island Institute of Arts and Sciences, New York; Gift of the Allen Tucker Memorial.

902. *Rain on Victoria.*
Oil.
Lent by the artist.
Price listed: $400.
Present collection (1963): Allen Tucker Memorial Collection.

903. *Storm in the Rockies.*
Oil, 1912.
Lent by the artist.
Price listed: $400.
Present collection (1963): Allen Tucker Memorial Collection.

1091. *Portrait.*
Chicago, 403.
Elsewhere called *Blue and Gold.*
Probably identical with *Blue and Gold* added in pencil to the catalogue listing by both MacRae and Kuhn.
Oil.
Lent by the artist.
Price listed: $350.

TWACHTMAN, Alden (1882–n.d.)

777. *El Punta Delacantara.* †
Oil.
Lent by the artist.
Price listed: $150.

778. *Coronation Week—Madrid.* †
Chicago, 405.
Oil.
Lent by the artist.

320

Price listed: $100. Sold for $100 to Mary L. Willard, March 15, 1913.

TWACHTMAN, John H.
(1853–1902)

733. *Hemlock Pool.*
Oil, 1902.
Lent by John Gellatly.
Not for sale.
Present collection: Addison Gallery of American Art, Phillips Academy, Andover, Massachusetts.

734. *The Sea.*
Oil.
Lent by William Macbeth.
Price listed: $6,000.

VALLOTTON, Félix-Edouard
(1865–1925)

369. *La Route.*
Oil.
Lent by Emile Druet.
Price listed: $594.

370. *La Coiffure.*
Chicago, 406. *Woman Dressing Her Hair.*
Oil.
Lent by Emile Druet.
Price listed: $1,620.

371. *La Lecture.*
Chicago, 407. *Woman Reading.*
Oil.
Lent by Emile Druet.
Price listed: $1,620.

VILLON, Jacques (1875–1963)

444. *Arbres en fleurs.*
Chicago, 426. Boston, 231.
Flowering Trees, Puteaux.
Listed on entry blank as *Les Fumées et les arbres en fleur.* Now called *Puteaux: Les Fumées et les arbres en fleur.*
Oil, dated on entry blank 1912.
Lent by the artist.
Price listed: $270. Sold for $270 to Arthur B. Davies, March 7, 1913.

Present collection (1963): Mr. and Mrs. Dan R. Johnson.

445. *Fillette au piano.*
Chicago, 427. Boston, 232.
Girl at the Piano.
Oil, dated on entry blank 1912.
Lent by the artist.
Price listed: $270. Sold for $270 to John Quinn, February 20, 1913.
Present collection (1963): Mrs. George Acheson, New York.

446. *Etude pour jeune femme.*
Chicago, 428. *Study of a Young Woman.*
Now called *Study for Young Woman.*
Oil, dated on entry blank 1912.
Lent by the artist.
Price listed: $135. Sold for $135 to John Quinn, February 20, 1913.
Present collection (1963): Mr. and Mrs. Alister Cameron.

447. *Etude pour Puteaux, No. 1.*
Subtitled on entry blank *Les Fumées et les arbres en fleur.* Now called *Smoke and Trees in Bloom, No. 2.*
Chicago, 429. Boston, 235.
Puteaux, Study.
Oil, dated on entry blank 1912.
Lent by the artist.
Price listed: $81. Sold for $81 to Walter C. Arensberg, May 19, 1913, Boston.
Present collection: Philadelphia Museum of Art; Louise and Walter Arensberg Collection.

448. *Etude pour Puteaux, No. 2.*
Subtitled on entry blank *Les Fumées et les arbres en fleur.*
Chicago, 430. Boston, 233 or 234.
Puteaux, Study.
Oil, dated on entry blank 1912.
Lent by the artist.
Price listed: $108. Sold for $108 to Miss L. Parsons, March 16, 1913.

449. *Etude pour Puteaux, No. 3.*
Subtitled on entry blank *Les Fumées et les arbres en fleur.* Elsewhere called *Etude pour les arbres en fleur.* Now

321

called *Study for Puteaux, No. 3.*
Chicago, 431. Boston, 233 or 234.
Puteaux, Study.
Oil, dated on entry blank 1912.
Lent by the artist.
Price listed: $108. Sold for $108 to
Hamilton E. Field, March 7, 1913.
Former collection: Robert Laurent,
Bloomington, Indiana; now
deceased.

450. *Etude pour Puteaux, No. 4.*
Subtitled on entry blank *Les Fumées
et les arbres en fleur.*
Chicago, 432. Boston, 233 or 234.
Puteaux, Study.
Oil, dated on entry blank 1912.
Lent by the artist.
Price listed: $108. Sold for $108 to
Dr. Helen C. Loewenstein, March 9,
1913.

Notes to Puteaux Studies, nos.
447–50:
The Chicago catalogue numbers
given here are based on the
assumption that the Studies were
numbered in sequence, as they were
in New York. The same is true of
the Boston catalogue except that
only three of the paintings were
shown. The original catalogue
listing, "Lent by M. Lemaitre," is
incorrect. On the entry blank, the
address "7 Rue Lemaitre à Puteaux,"
had been written on the line
reserved for the lender and, since
the script was not clear, it was read
as "M. Lemaitre à Puteaux."
The sales records for the four
Puteaux studies are not entirely
consistent; the buyer cited is the
most likely in view of all the
evidence.

451. *Etude pour fillette au piano.*
Chicago, 433. Boston, 236.
Study for Girl at the Piano.
Oil, dated on entry blank 1912.
Lent by the artist.
Price listed: $135. Sold for $135 to
John Quinn, February 22, 1913.

452. *Jeune Femme.*
Chicago, 434. *Young Woman.*
Now called *Young Girl.*
Oil, dated on entry blank 1912.
Lent by the artist.
Price listed: $270. Sold for $270 to
Arthur J. Eddy, March 1, 1913.
Present collection: Philadelphia
Museum of Art; Louise and Walter
Arensberg Collection.

VLAMINCK, Maurice de
(1876–1958)

189. *Tower Bridge.*
Oil, dated on entry blank c. 1910.
Lent by Heinrich Thannhauser,
#2447.
Price listed: $162.50.

190. *L'Estuaire de la Seine.*
Chicago, 436. Boston, 237.
Branch of the Seine.
Oil.
Lent by Henry Kahnweiler.
Price listed: $202.50.

191. *Les Figues.*
Chicago, 437. Boston, 238. *Figs.*
Oil.
Lent by Henry Kahnweiler.
Price listed: $162. Sold for $162 to
Dr. Albert C. Barnes, March 6,
1913.
Present collection: Barnes
Foundation, Merion, Pennsylvania.

1067. *Rueil.*
Chicago, 435.
Now called *Village (Rueil).*
Oil, dated on entry blank 1912.
Lent by Henry Kahnweiler.
Price listed: $224. Sold for $224 to
Arthur J. Eddy, March 2, 1913.
Present collection: The Art
Institute of Chicago; Arthur Jerome
Eddy Memorial Collection.

VONNOH, Bessie Potter
(1872–1955)

719. *Dancing Figure.*
Bronze.

322

Lent by the artist.
No price listed.

720. *Nude.*
Terracotta.
Catalogued but not received.

721. *Study.*
Terracotta.
Catalogued but not received.

VUILLARD, Edouard
(1868–1940)

471. *Les Journaux.*
Chicago, 438. Boston, 239.
The Newspapers.
Oil.
Lent by Bernheim-Jeune & Cie.
Price listed: $405 in Kuhn catalogue
(probably correct); $504 in MacRae
catalogue.

Lithographs.
Not listed in the New York
catalogue but displayed for sale
and order.
Chicago, 439. Boston, 240.
From the evidence available it is
impossible to determine which and
how many were exhibited.
Lent by Ambroise Vollard.
Price listed: $12 each. One sold for
$12 to Lillie P. Bliss, March 6,
1913. One sold for $12 to Mrs.
Clara S. Davidge, March 6, 1913.
Thirteen sold for $112 to E. Horter,
March 9, 1913. One sold for $12 to
Walter C. Arensberg, March 11,
1913; returned May 19, 1913,
Boston. Four sold for $48 to Arthur
J. Eddy, April 10, 1913, Chicago.
One sold for $12 to Thomas W.
Bowers, May 20, 1913, Boston.

WAGNER, Fred (1864–1940)

66. Catalogued but not received.

67. Catalogued but not received.

WALKOWITZ, Abraham
(1880–1965)

127. *In the Opera.*

Now called *At the Opera.*
Oil, 1908.
Lent by the artist.
Price listed: $500.
Present collection (1963): Dr. and
Mrs. George Piner, Brookline,
Massachusetts.

128. *Anticoli Corrado.*
Oil, 1907.
Lent by the artist.
Price listed: $500.
Present collection (1963): Dr. and
Mrs. George Piner, Brookline,
Massachusetts.

129. *On the Avenue.*
Oil, 1905.
Lent by the artist.
Price listed: $250.
Present collection: Mr. and Mrs.
Nathan Weisman, New York.

130. *Man—Woman.*
Oil.
Lent by the artist.
Price listed: $200.

131. *A Bit of Venice.*
Oil.
Lent by the artist.
Price listed: $500.
Present collection: University
Gallery, University of Minnesota,
Minneapolis; Collection of Ione and
Hudson Walker.

132. *Drawing.*
Lent by the artist.
Price listed: $100.

133. *Drawing.*
Lent by the artist.
Price listed: $100.

134. *Drawing.*
Lent by the artist.
Price listed: $100.

135. *Drawing.*
Lent by the artist.
Price listed: $100.

136. *Drawing.*
Lent by the artist.

323

Price listed: $100.

137. *Monotype* (*color*).
Lent by the artist.
Price listed: $100.

138. *Watercolor.*
Lent by the artist.
Price listed: $100.

WALTS, F. M. (n.d.)

951. *Four Frames of Drawings.*
Chicago, 440.
Lent by the artist.
Price listed: $125 each.

WARD, Hilda (1878–1950)

108. *The Hound.*
Pastel, 1910.
Lent by the artist.
Not for sale.

109. *The Kennels.*
Drawing, 1910.
Lent by the artist.
Not for sale.

WARSHAWSKY, Alexander L.
(1887–n.d.)

771. *Madame F.* †
Oil.
Lent by the artist.
Price listed: $500.

772. *Nature morte.* †
Oil.
Lent by the artist.
Price listed: $250.

WEBER, F. William (n.d.)

5. *Winter.*
Oil.
Lent by the artist.
Price listed: $300.

6. *French Village.*
Oil.
Lent by the artist.
Price listed: $350.

WEBSTER, E. Ambrose
(1869–1935)

1032. *Sunlight, Jamaica.*
Chicago, 441.
Oil.
Lent by the artist.
No price listed.
Former collection: Karl F. Rodgers,
Provincetown, Massachusetts; now
deceased.

1033. *Old Hut, Jamaica.*
Oil.
Lent by the artist.
No price listed.
Present collection: Private
collection.

WEINZHEIMER, F. A.
(1882–n.d.)

419. *Inferno.*
Chicago, 443. Boston, 241.
Drawing.
Lent by the artist.
Price listed: $130.

420. *Badende Frauen.*
Chicago, 444. Boston, 242.
Women Bathing.
Drawing.
Lent by the artist.
Price listed: $97.50.

WEIR, J. Alden (1852–1919)

78. *Factory Village.*
Also known as *A New England
Village* and *Willimantic.*
Oil, 1899(?).
Lent by the artist.
Price listed: $5,000.
Present collection: The Metropolitan
Museum of Art, New York; Gift of
Mrs. Charles Burlingham.

79. *Flowers.*
Oil.
Lent by the artist.
Not for sale.

80. *Head Profile.*
Oil.

324

Lent by the artist.
Price listed: $3,500.

81. *Portrait.*
Oil.
Lent by the artist.
Not for sale.

82. *The Orchid.*
Oil.
Lent by the artist.
Price listed: $2,500.
Present collection: Huntington
Library and Art Gallery, San Marino,
California; Virginia Scott Steele
Collection.

991. *Landscape and Figure.*
Etching.
Lent by the artist.
No price listed.

992. *Watercolor.*
Chicago, 442(?). *Watercolors.*
Lent by the artist.
No price listed.

993. *Watercolor.*
Chicago, 442(?). *Watercolors.*
Lent by the artist.
No price listed.

994. *Watercolor.*
Chicago, 442(?). *Watercolors.*
Lent by the artist.
No price listed.

995. *Watercolor.*
Chicago, 442(?). *Watercolors.*
Lent by the artist.
No price listed.

996. *Watercolor.*
Chicago, 442(?). *Watercolors.*
Lent by the artist.
No price listed.

1041. *The Pond.*
Oil.
Lent by the artist.
No price listed.

1042. *The Orchard.*
Oil.
Lent by the artist.
Price listed: $2,500.

12 Etchings.
Not listed, but added in Kuhn
catalogue.
Lent by the artist.
Price listed: $500 for lot.

WEISGERBER, Albert
(1878–1915)

486. A painting promised by
Heinrich Thannhauser was not
received.

WENTSCHER, Julius, d.j.
(1881–n.d.)

390. *Warriors Fighting.*
Tempera.
Lent by the artist.
Price listed: $270.

WHISTLER, James A. McNeill
(1834–1903)

657. *Andromeda* (copy after
Ingres).
Oil, 1857.
Lent by William Macbeth.
Price listed: "Open to offer."

658. *Portrait.*
Oil.
Lent by William Macbeth.
Price listed: $8,500.

1058. *Study in Rose and Brown.*
Oil.
Lent by William Macbeth.
Price listed: $8,500.
Present collection: Muskegon
Museum of Art, Muskegon,
Michigan.

1086. *The Little Blue Bonnet.*
Oil.
Lent by Mrs. Herbert Pratt.
No price listed.

WHITE, Charles Henry
(1878–1969)

761. *The Valley of Unrest.* †
Etching.

325

Lent by the artist.
Price listed: $25.

762. *Fulton Market.* †
Etching, 1905.
Lent by the artist.
Price listed: $25.

763. *The Condemned Tenement.* †
Etching, 1906.
Lent by the artist.
Price listed: $25.

WILSON, Claggett (1887–1952)

780. *Moorish Girl.* †
Oil.
Lent by the artist.
Price listed: $100.

WOLF, Leon (n.d.)

742. *Trees.* †
Oil.
Lent by the artist.
Price listed: $150.

WORTMAN, Denys, Jr.
(1887–1958)

760. *Waterfront, Bermuda.* †
Oil.
Lent by the artist.
Price listed: $200.

YANDELL, Enid (1870–1934)

690. *The Five Senses.*
Bronze.
Lent by the artist.
Price listed: $75.

691. *Indian and Fisher.*
Lent by the artist.
Price listed: $15(?).

YEATS, Jack B. (1871–1957)

352. *A Stevedore.*
Oil.
Lent by the artist.
Price listed: $118.

353. *The Barrel Man.*
Oil.

Lent by the artist.
Price listed: $118.

354. *Strand Races.*
Oil.
Lent by the artist.
Price listed: $118. Sold for $118 to
George F. Porter, March 13, 1913.
Ex-collection: The Art Institute
of Chicago; George F. Porter
Collection. Sold: Parke-Bernet,
March 2, 1944, no. 2.

355. *The Last Corinthian.*
Oil.
Lent by the artist.
Price listed: $118.

356. *The Circus Dwarf.*
Oil, 1912.
Lent by the artist.
Price listed: $590.
Present collection: Private
collection, Montreal.

587. *The Political Meeting.*
Chicago, 447. Boston, 243.
Watercolor, 1909.
Lent by John Quinn.
Not for sale.

YOUNG, Arthur (Art)
(1866–1943)

933. *Drawings* [6].
Chicago, 448.
Lent by the artist.
Not for sale. Kuhn catalogue lists
Nice Young Man, $75, and *Peace of
a Summer Evening*, $100.

Chicago, 449. *This World of Creepers.*
Drawing.
Lent by the artist.
Not for sale.

YOUNG, Mahonri (1877–1957)

929(A). *Founding the
Commonwealth*, Relief for the
Sea Gull Monument, Salt Lake
City, Utah.
Sculpture.
Lent by the artist.

No price listed.

930(B). *The Arrival of the Sea Gulls,* Relief for the Sea Gull Monument, Salt Lake City, Utah.
Sculpture.
Lent by the artist.
No price listed.

931. *Mother and Son.*
Bronze.
Lent by the artist.
Price listed: $150.

932. *Rembrandt, Old.*
Plaster.
Lent by the artist.
Price listed: $200.

1093. *Man with Boys on Shoulder.*
Sculpture.
Lent by the artist.
No price listed.

1094. *Man Shoeing a Horse.*
Sculpture.
Lent by the artist.
No price listed.

Coal Carrier.
Not listed, but added in Kuhn catalogue as *Carrying Coal.*
Chicago, 450.
Sculpture.
Lent by the artist.
Price listed: $150.

Chicago, 451. *Drawings.*
Lent by the artist.
No price listed.

ZAK, Eugene (1884–1926)

233. *Le Berger.*
Chicago, 452. *The Shepherd.*
Oil.
Lent by the artist.

Price listed: $540. Sold for $540 to Arthur J. Eddy, February 27, 1913.
Present collection: The Art Institute of Chicago; Arthur Jerome Eddy Memorial Collection.

234. *En Eté.*
Chicago, 453. Boston, 244.
In Summer.
Oil.
Lent by the artist.
Price listed: $340. Sold for $340 to John Quinn, February 22, 1913.

ZORACH, Marguerite
(1888–1968)

782. *Study.* †
Oil.
Lent by the artist.
Price listed: $600.

ZORACH, William (1887–1966)

783. *Portrait.* †
Oil.
Lent by the artist.
Price listed: $800.

784. *An Arrangement.* †
Oil.
Lent by the artist.
Price listed: $500.

1089. *Early Cubist Study.*
This was probably by Luca Cambiaso.
See Theodore Earl Butler, no. 1089.

1112. "The plan for the interior of the mansion (Façade architectural) [see Raymond Duchamp-Villon, no. 609] by M. Raymond Duchamp-Villon is by M. André Mare. The design for the garden is the work of M. G. Ribemont-Desseignes."

327

A selection of art books
lent by Ambroise Vollard and Artz & de Bois
was displayed for sale at the Armory Show.

Gaspard de la nuit by Louis Bertrand, illustrated with 213 wood engravings by Armand Seguin, published by Ambroise Vollard, Paris, 1904.
Lent by Ambroise Vollard.
Price listed: $40.50.

A Van Gogh portfolio of 9 collotype reproductions of his paintings, published by Artz & de Bois.
Lent by Artz & de Bois.
Price listed: $76.

L'Imitation de Jesus-Christ, anonymous translation of the 17th century, illustrated with 216 wood engravings by Maurice Denis, published by Ambroise Vollard, Paris, 1903.
Lent by Ambroise Vollard.
Price listed: $67.50. Sold for $50 to Arthur B. Davies, May 1, 1913.

Le Jardin des supplices by Octave Mirbeau, illustrated with 20 lithographs by Auguste Rodin, published by Ambroise Vollard, Paris, 1902.
Lent by Ambroise Vollard.
Price listed: $54.

Odilon Redon—Oeuvre graphique com- plet, published by Artz & de Bois, The Hague, 1913, 2 vols.
Lent by Artz & de Bois.
Price listed: $35. Sold for $35 to George F. Of, February 27, 1913. Listed as "portfolios."

Parallelment by Paul Verlaine, illustrated with 109 lithographs and 9 wood engravings by Pierre Bonnard, published by Ambroise Vollard, Paris, 1900.
Lent by Ambroise Vollard.
Price listed: $54.

Les Pastorales de Longus, ou Daphnis et Chloë, translated by J. Amyot, illustrated with 151 lithographs by Pierre Bonnard, published by Ambroise Vollard, Paris, 1902.
Lent by Ambroise Vollard.
Price listed: $60.75.

Sagesse by Paul Verlaine, illustrated with 72 wood engravings by Maurice Denis, published by Ambroise Vollard, Paris, 1911.
Lent by Ambroise Vollard.
Price listed: $59.40.

328

APPENDIX 1
CONSTITUTION OF THE AMERICAN
PAINTERS AND SCULPTORS

ARTICLE I:—NAME

The name of this Association shall be the AMERICAN PAINTERS AND SCULPTORS.

ARTICLE II:—OBJECT

The object of this Association is to provide adequate place for, and to hold periodically, national and international exhibitions of the best examples procurable of contemporary art in New York or wherever else the Association may hereafter designate.

ARTICLE III:—MEMBERSHIP

Section 1.
The membership is unlimited and shall be of two degrees: Active Members and Honorary Members.

Active Members shall consist of such members as are present at the adoption of this Constitution and are accepted as charter members of the Association; of such non-resident or foreign painters and sculptors as have been duly invited by unanimous ballot at the meeting of the incorporators; and such as may hereafter be elected to become Active Members in the manner hereinafter provided. The management of the affairs of the Association shall be confined to the Active Members.

Honorary Members are men of distinction in the fine arts, whom the Association wishes to honor, and are elected by a three-fourths majority at an Annual Meeting of Active Members.

Section 2:—Qualifications for Active Membership
Distinguished ability in one of the fine arts.

Any person over the age of twenty-five, after having been duly represented at three of the Association's exhibitions—which means the public exhibition of his or her work—becomes without further presentation or voucher eligible for active membership.

Such an artist upon being duly proposed and seconded shall have his name balloted upon for membership in the Association at the Annual Meeting.

A four-fifths majority of those present balloting in favor shall be necessary to elect him or her an Active Member.

Section 3:—Expulsion
Any member may be expelled for cause.

Any breach of conduct agreed upon by three Active Members to be to the dishonor of the Association, may upon written and duly signed and sealed complaint to the President compel trial by the Active Members. A true copy of such complaint shall be forwarded to the defendant. A three-fourths vote shall be necessary to expel or degrade any member.

329

Section 4:—Resignation

Resignation of membership shall be made in writing to the Secretary.

No resignation shall be accepted unless all indebtedness to the Association of the member resigning shall have been paid.

Section 5:—Dues

The annual dues of Active Members are $20.00.

In addition the Active Members shall be assessed $25.00 each year when an Annual Exhibition is held.

All dues must be paid in advance. Exhibition assessments must be paid fourteen days before the Exhibition opens.

Active Members whose dues are unpaid after nine months shall forfeit the right of voice at the Association's meetings; and should the dues continue unpaid at the Annual Meeting following they shall lose their right to vote; should dues and other charges remain unpaid for two years the delinquent members shall be placed on the retired list.

ARTICLE IV:—GOVERNMENT

Section 1:—Board of Trustees

The Association shall be governed by a Board of Trustees, which shall consist of twelve Active Members, six of whom shall be painters and six of whom shall be sculptors. They shall be elected in classes of four each—two painters and two sculptors—at the Annual Meeting, each class to serve three years, except those elected at the first meeting of the Association in 1912. Of these the term of the first four—known as the first class—expires the second Tuesday in 1915; the term of the second class of four expires the second Tuesday in 1914; that of the third class of four expires the second Tuesday in 1913. All Trustees elected after 1912 shall hold office for three years or until their successors are elected.

A majority of the ballots cast is necessary for the election of a Trustee.

Should a vacancy occur or should any member be absent or unable to attend to his duties as Trustee for two months, the Board shall appoint a substitute who shall hold office in the interim or until the next Annual Meeting.

The Board of Trustees shall direct the affairs of the Association in harmony with the policy of the Association.

Any of its regular or special meetings may be open to Active Members upon written request of three of the Active Members.

A majority of the Board shall constitute a quorum.

The Board shall create the necessary standing and special committees; both painters and sculptors being represented on all such committees.

Section 2:—Executive Officers

The Executive Officers shall be:

President
Vice-President
Treasurer
Secretary

who shall be elected annually from the Board of Trustees.

The President or Vice-President shall not hold the same office for more than two successive years; and after their retirement an interval of two years must elapse before they can hold again the same office. These offices shall be held alternately by a painter and a sculptor: i.e., if the President be a painter the

Vice-President shall be a sculptor and vice versa. And a painter may not succeed a painter nor a sculptor a sculptor in office unless it be to fill an unexpired term of office, when a painter or a sculptor shall succeed to the unfulfilled term of painter or sculptor.

Section 3:—Duties of Officers

(a) The President shall preside at all meetings of the Association and the Board of Trustees. He shall with the Secretary execute all agreements on behalf of the Association. He is ex-officio member of all committees and shall perform such other duties as the Board of Trustees shall assign to him.

(b) The Vice-President shall perform all the duties of the President in case of his absence or disability.

(c) The Treasurer shall receive all moneys and valuables that become the property of the Association, and enter upon the books of the Association full account of the same. He shall act as official custodian of all effects of the Association and shall keep and hold for the Trustees and the Association all such properties, and surrender none whatsoever without an order from the Board or a committee of the Board designated by the chairman or President.

The Board may at its discretion demand a bond from the Treasurer.

The funds of the Association shall be deposited in some bank approved by the Trustees and may not be withdrawn except upon written order, under authority as above described.

(d) The Secretary shall give notice of all meetings of the Association, keep a record of the minutes of the Annual Meetings and with the President sign all agreements on behalf of the Association and Board of Trustees. He shall keep the minutes of all the meetings of the Board of Trustees and notify the members of their appointment upon committees.

ARTICLE V:—MEETINGS

Section 1:

The Annual Meeting for the Election of officers, receiving reports of officers, Board of Trustees and Standing Committees shall be held on the evening of the second Tuesday of every year, at eight o'clock. A printed notice of the Annual Meeting shall be mailed to each Active Member ten days prior to such meeting.

Section 2:—Quorum

Two-thirds of the resident Active Members in the Metropolitan District shall constitute a quorum at an annual or special meeting of the Association.

ARTICLE VI:—EXHIBITIONS

Section 1:—Character

It is the purpose of the Association to hold annually in New York at least one comprehensive exhibition of the best examples procurable of contemporary art. The character, as to medium, shape or nature of work is not here designated. This Association, organized for the advancement of the fine arts, does not attempt to suggest the medium by which an artist shall express himself, recognizing the master artist to be one through whom nature speaks in varying technical terms according to his individuality.

331

Section 2:—Member's Work

Each Active Member shall exhibit by right of his position in the Association. The space his work may occupy in the exhibition shall be determined by an exhibition committee, which shall allot the exhibition area available to each member, reserving a due proportion for invited work. No work not invited will be exhibited.

APPENDIX 2
FINANCIAL CONTRIBUTORS
TO THE ARMORY SHOW

This list is based on one contained in the MacRae Papers, Ledger 3, page 1, with additional information derived from the cash entries in Ledger 1 (cashbook), also in the MacRae Papers, and from various correspondence.

The name in parenthesis is that of the person to whom the donation was given.

Mrs. George Blumenthal (*Mrs. C. S. Davidge*), March 1, 1913 ..	$100.00
Mrs. John Jay Chapman (*Mrs. C. S. Davidge*), January 11, 1913 .	100.00
(*Mrs. E. S. Dodge*), January 21, 1913	500.00
Mr. Edward S. Clark (*Mrs. C. S. Davidge*), March 1, 1913	200.00
Mr. Stephen C. Clark (*Mrs. C. S. Davidge*), January 10, 1913 ...	200.00
Mrs. Seymour Cromwell (*Mrs. C. S. Davidge*), March 1, 1913 ...	25.00
Mrs. Clara Sydney Davidge, March 1, 1913	5.00
Mr. Arthur B. Davies, September 10, 1912	150.00
September 12, 1912	2,500.00
February 7, 1913	800.00
February 15, 1913	600.00
Mrs. Edwin Shurrill Dodge (*Mrs. C. S. Davidge*), March 1, 1913 .	200.00
Elizabeth Sage Goodwin (*Arthur B. Davies*), March 3, 1913	500.00
Miss Marian Hague (*Mrs. C. S. Davidge*)	10.00
Mrs. Edward Henry Harriman, March 1, 1913	600.00
(*Mrs. C. S. Davidge*), March 1, 1913	400.00
Miss Lydia S. Hays (*John Mowbray-Clarke*), February 11, 1913 ...	100.00
Miss Husted (*Mrs. C. S. Davidge*), March 1, 1913	25.00
Miss Alice Lewisohn (*J. Mowbray-Clarke*), September 20, 1912 ..	100.00
Miss Luquer (*Mrs. C. S. Davidge*), March 1, 1913	10.00
Mrs. Howard Mansfield (*Mrs. C. S. Davidge*), March 1, 1913	25.00
Mrs. John J. Milburn (*Mrs. C. S. Davidge*), March 1, 1913	25.00
Mrs. Victor Morowitz (*Mrs. C. S. Davidge*), March 1, 1913	25.00
Mr. John Mowbray-Clarke, February 7, 1913	700.00
Mrs. David Rumsey (*Mrs. C. S. Davidge*), March 1, 1913	25.00
Mr. William Salomon (*Mrs. C. S. Davidge*), January 10, 1913 ...	100.00
Mrs. Dorothy Whitney Straight (*Mrs. C. S. Davidge*), January 31, 1913	1,000.00
Miss Ruth Twombly (*Mrs. C. S. Davidge*), March 1, 1913	25.00
Mrs. Harry Payne Whitney (*Mrs. C. S. Davidge*), January 24, 1913	1,000.00

333

APPENDIX 3
INDEXES OF LENDERS AND BUYERS

LENDERS

BUYERS

336

Duchamp, 241.

Tucker, Allen: Gauguin, lithograph.

Untermeyer, Mrs. Samuel: Kramer, 887.

Valentiner, W. R.: Rodin, 1016.

Vandergrift, Dr. D. D.: Beach, 655.

Van Gerbig, Mrs. Barend: Freund, 820.

Van Horne, Sir William: Bourdelle, 605.

Vietor, Thomas F.: Hopper, 751;

Mowbray-Clarke, 706.

Watson, Gertrude: Denis, 2 lithographs; Redon, 299; Signac, 397.

Watson, Mrs. James E.: Kramer.

Willard, Mary: Henri, 838; Redon, 310; Russell, M., 254; Twachtman, A., 778.

Williams, Charles F.: Kramer, 881.

Wilson, Mrs. H. Orme: Schamberg, 22.

337

BIBLIOGRAPHY

Since the Armory Show is discussed in every book that addresses 20th-century American art, only works that deal with the Armory Show specifically or at some length are included here. (For a more comprehensive bibliography of the period and the effects of the Armory Show, consult Milton W. Brown, *American Painting from the Armory Show to the Depression*.) Entries are in alphabetical order, with the exception of catalogues, which are in chronological order. Newspapers have not been cited because that material is so extensive and so scattered. However, much of the newspaper material is available in the large collection of clippings in the Press Scrapbooks of the Kuhn Papers; smaller collections can be found in the MacRae Papers and the Museum of Modern Art Library.

UNPUBLISHED SOURCE MATERIAL

Armory Show Material. Museum of Modern Art Library, New York.
The Kuhn Papers, The Myers Papers (microfilm only). Archives of American Art, Smithsonian Institution, Washington, D.C.
The MacRae Papers. Hirshhorn Museum and Sculpture Garden, Smithsonian Institution, Washington, D.C.
The Pach Papers.
The Quinn Papers. New York Public Library, Manuscript Division, New York.

CATALOGUES

Sonderbundes Westdeutscher Kunstfreunde und Kunstler. *Internationale Kunstausstellung*. May 25–September 30. Cologne, 1912.

Grafton Galleries. *Second Post-Impressionist Exhibition*. October 5–December 31, 1912. London, 1912.

Association of American Painters and Sculptors. *Catalogue of International Exhibition of Modern Art, at the Armory of the Sixty-Ninth Infantry*. February 15–March 15, 1913. New York, 1913.

Supplement of Catalogue Containing Additions, Errata and Exhibits Catalogued But Not Received. New York, 1913.

The Art Institute of Chicago. *International Exhibition of Modern Art, Association of American Painters and Sculptors, Inc.* March 24–April 16, 1913. Chicago, 1913.

Copley Society of Boston. *International Exhibition of Modern Art, Under the Auspices of Association of American Painters and Sculptors, Incorporated, Copley Hall*. April 28–May 19, 1913. Boston, 1913.

PAMPHLETS

Association of American Painters and Sculptors. *For and Against: Views on the International Exhibition Held in New York and Chicago*. Edited by Frederick J. Gregg. New York, 1913.

Faure, Elie. *Cézanne.* Translated by Walter Pach. New York, 1913.

Gauguin, Paul. *Extracts from "Noa-Noa."* Translated by Walt Kuhn. New York, 1913.

Pach, Walter. *Odilon Redon.* New York, 1913.

———. *A Sculptor's Architecture.* New York, 1913.

MEMOIRS

Du Bois, Guy Pène. *Artists Say the Silliest Things.* New York, 1940, pp. 165–75.

Kuhn, Walt. *The Story of the Armory Show.* New York, 1938.

Myers, Jerome. *Artist in Manhattan.* New York, 1930, pp. 32–39.

Pach, Walter. *Queer Thing, Painting; Forty Years in the World of Art.* New York, London, 1938, pp. 192–203.

CONTEMPORARY COMMENT

Adams, Adeline. "The Secret of Life." *Art and Progress* 4 (April 1913): 925–32.

"An Art Awakening." *American Art News* 11 (March 15, 1913): 4.

"An Opportunity to Study New Art Tendencies." *Outlook* 103 (March 1, 1913): 466–67.

"Art Revolutionists on Exhibition in America." *American Review of Reviews* 47 (April 1913): 441–48.

"Bedlam in Art." *Current Opinion* 54 (April 1913): 316–17.

Brinton, Christian. "Evolution Not Revolution in Art." *International Studio* 49 (April 1913): 27–35.

———. "Fashions in Art—Modern Art." *International Studio* 49 (March 1913): 9–10.

Cortissoz, Royal. "The Post-Impressionist Illusion." *Century* 85 (April 1913): 805–15.

Cox, Kenyon. "The Modern Spirit in Art." *Harper's Weekly* 57 (March 15, 1913): 10.

Davies, Arthur B. "Chronological Chart Made by Arthur B. Davies Showing the Growth of Modern Art." *Arts and Decoration* 3 (March 1913): 150.

———. "Explanatory Statement: The Aim of the A.A.P.S." *Arts and Decoration* 3 (March 1913): 149.

Dodge, Mabel. "Speculations, or Post-Impressionism in Prose." *Arts and Decoration* 3 (March 1913): 172, 174.

Du Bois, Guy Pène. "The Spirit and the Chronology of the Modern Movement." *Arts and Decoration* 3 (March 1913): 151–54, 178.

Fisher, William M. "Sculpture at the Exhibition." *Arts and Decoration* 3 (March 1913): 168–69.

Glackens, William J. "The American Section: The National Art." *Arts and Decoration* 3 (March 1913): 159–64.

"The Greatest Exhibition of Insurgent Art Ever Held." *Current Opinion* 54 (March 1913): 230–32.

Gregg, Frederick J. "The Attitude of the Americans." *Arts and Decoration* 3 (March 1913): 165–67.

————. "The Extremists: An Interview with Jo Davidson." *Arts and Decoration* 3 (March 1913): 170–71, 180.

Laurvik, J. Nilson. *Is It Art? Post-Impressionism, Futurism, Cubism.* New York, 1913.

"Lawlessness in Art." *Century* 86 (May 1913): 150.

Mather, Frank J., Jr. "Art Old and New." *Nation* 96 (March 6, 1913): 240–43.

————. "Newest Tendencies in Art." *Independent* 74 (March 6, 1913): 504–12.

Meltzer, Charles H. "New York Sees Things." *Hearst's Magazine* 23 (April 1913): 635–36.

Mechlin, Leila. "Lawless Art." *Art and Progress* 4 (April 1913): 840–41.

"Mob as Art Critic." *Literary Digest* 46 (March 29, 1913): 708–9.

"New Tendencies in Art." *American Review of Reviews* 48 (August 1913): 245.

Pattison, James W. "Art in an Unknown Tongue." *Fine Arts Journal* 27–29 (May 1913): 293–307.

Phillips, Duncan. "Revolutions and Reactions in Painting." *International Studio* 51 (December 1913): sup. 123–29.

Quinn, John. "Modern Art from the Layman's Point of View." *Arts and Decoration* 3 (March 1913): 155–58, 176.

Roberts, Mary F. "Science in Art, as Shown in the International Exhibition of Painting and Sculpture." *Craftsman* 24 (May 1913): 216–18.

Roosevelt, Theodore. "A Layman's View of an Art Exhibition." *Outlook* 103 (March 29, 1913): 718–20.

Simons, Theodore LeF. "The New Movement in Art; From a Philosophic Standpoint." *Arts and Decoration* 3 (April 1913): 214.

SUBSEQUENT ACCOUNTS

Albright Art Gallery. *50th Annual Exhibition: 50 Paintings, 1905–1913.* May 14–June 12, 1955. Introduction by Robert J. Goldwater. Buffalo, N.Y., 1955.

Amherst College. *The 1913 Armory Show in Retrospect.* February 17–March 17, 1958. Introduction by Frank A. Trapp. Amherst, Mass., 1958.

"The Armory Show 1913–1963: Fiftieth Anniversary." *Art in America* 51 (February 1963): 29–63. Various authors.

Blesh, Rudi. *Modern Art U.S.A.: Men, Rebellion, Conquest, 1900–1956.* New York, 1956, pp. 41–67.

Breuning, Margaret. "Critic's Notebook: Reflections on the Armory Show." *Arts Digest* 29 (April 1, 1955): 4, 32.

Brooks, Van Wyck. "John Sloan and the Armory Show." *Arts Digest* 29 (February 1, 1955): 6–8, 35.

Brown, Milton W. *American Painting from the Armory Show to the Depression.* Princeton, N.J., 1955.

Buffet-Picabia, Gabrielle. "Introduction à l'art moderne aux Etats-Unis." XXᵉ *Siècle*, n.s. 40 (June 1973): 63–68.

Cincinnati Art Museum. *Pictures for Peace: A Retrospective Exhibition Organized from the Armory Show of 1913.* March 18–April 16, 1944. Introduction by Walter H. Siple. Cincinnati, 1944.

Dwight, Edward H. "The Armory Show—New York 1913." *Canadian Art* 20 (March–April 1963): 118–19.

Genauer, Emily. "Can You Predict What a Painting Will Be Worth?" *Today's Living*, March 22, 1959, pp. 12–15.

Glackens, Ira. *William Glackens and the Ashcan Group: The Emergence of Realism in American Art.* New York, 1957, pp. 180–84.

Hunter, Sam. *Modern American Painting and Sculpture.* New York, 1959, pp. 62–79.

Kruty, Paul. "Arthur Jerome Eddy and His Collection: Prelude and Postscript to the Armory Show." *Arts Magazine* 61 (February 1987): 40–47.

Kuhn, Walt. "The Story of the Armory Show." *Artnews Annual* 37 (1939): 63–64, 168–74.

Lynes, Russell. *The Tastemakers.* New York, 1954, pp. 196–222.

Masheck, Joseph. "Teddy's Taste: Theodore Roosevelt and the Armory Show." *Artforum* 9 (November 1970): 70–73.

McCoy, Garnett. "The Post-Impressionist Bomb." *Archives of American Art Journal* 20 (Winter 1980): 12–17.

Mellquist, Jerome. "Armory Show 30 Years Later." *Magazine of Art* 36 (December 1943): 298–301.

———. *The Emergence of an American Art.* New York, 1942, pp. 213–39.

Munson-Williams-Proctor Institute and the Henry Street Settlement. *The Armory Show, 50th Anniversary Exhibition.* February 17–March 31, 1963. New York, 1963.

Nassau County Museum of Fine Art. *The Shock of Modernism in America.* April 29–July 29, 1984. Text by Constance H. Schwartz. Roslyn, New York, 1984.

Perlman, Bennard B. "The Story behind a Great Art Event." *American Artist* 27 (February 1963): 26–29+.

Phillips, Sandra S. "The Art Criticism of Walter Pach." *Art Bulletin* 65 (March 1983): 106–21.

341

Saarinen, Aline B. *The Proud Possessors*. New York, 1958, pp. 206–49.

Sachs, Samuel, II. "Reconstructing the 'Whirlwind of 26th Street.'" *Artnews* 61 (February 1963): 26–29+.

Schapiro, Meyer. "Rebellion in Art." In *America in Crisis*. Edited by Daniel Aaron. New York, 1952, pp. 203–42.

Tillim, Sidney. "Dissent on the Armory Show." *Arts Magazine* 37 (May–June 1963): 96–101.

Trapp, Frank A. "Armory Show Revived by Amherst." *Art in America* 46 (Spring 1958): 63–66.

———. "The Armory Show: A Review." *Art Journal* 23 (Fall 1963): 2–9.

Whitney Museum of American Art. *Pioneers of Modern Art in America*. April 9– May 19, 1946. Introduction by Lloyd Goodrich. New York, 1946, pp. 11–16.

Zilczer, Judith K. "The Armory Show and the American Avant-garde: A Re-evaluation." *Arts Magazine* 53 (September 1978): 126–30.

Index

Abbot, Holker, 216

Adams, Adeline, 170–71

Ahern, Maurice L., 138

Aldis, Arthur T., 72, 189, 190, 191, 194, 208, 213

Alexander, John White, 142, 171

American Art News, 106, 124, 126, 136, 150, 156, 166, 231, 238

Anciens de l'Académie Julian, 141

Anderson, Karl, 49, 83, 228

Andrews, J. R., 98

Archipenko, Alexander, 67, 70, 75, 129, 197; *Le Repos*, 206

Architectural League, 140

Arensberg, Louise, 128

Arensberg, Walter, 127–29, 131, 218, 239; Arensberg Collection, 128–29, 239

Armory Show: American artists in, 84–90, 98, 116, 135–36, 225–26; artists, effect on, 234–38; art market, effect on, 238–39; attendance, 109, 110, 118, 187–88, 213, 214, 217–18; Boston Exhibition, 215–19; catalogs, 92, 205, 221; Chicago Exhibition, 189–214; collecting works for, 67–76; collectors, impact on, 239; conception and model for, 64–67; critical evaluations of, 153–86; defenders of modern art, 178–86; Delaunay conflict, 147–49; documents of, 15–23; educating American taste, 112–17; end of show, 219–22; financial outcome of, 117–18, 230, 231, 233; floor plan, *115*; fundraising for, 94–95; hanging of, 107–8, 114–17; historical importance of, 234–40; "immorality" of modern art, 163–66; invitations to exhibit in, 63–64; last day of, 187–89; layout of, 93–94, 98, 108, 114–17; loan form, American, 90; loans of art, 96–98; number of works in, 110–11; office, 80; opening of, 41–45; photographs of, 43, *114*, *197–202*; "political threat" of modern art, 166–68; poster for, 91; press reactions to, 45, 84, 108–9, 110, 136–40, 141, 142, 149–52, 153–86, 206, 210–13; publications accompanying, 92–93, 205, 221; publicity for, 78, 91–92, 106, 118, 146–52; public reactions to, 45, 133–42, 143–46, 205–10, 240; sale of artworks, 119–32, 134–36, 213, 218, 221–22; space chosen and rented, 61–62; spoofs, hoaxes, and jokes, 136–42, 146, 149, 152, 209–10; taste of public, impact on, 240

Art and Progress, 167, 170

Art Institute of Chicago, 18, 22, 23, 72, 80, 96, 239; show in Chicago, 189–214

Art Nouveau, 236

Arts and Decoration, 83, 112–14, 150, 156

Art Students League, Chicago, 210

Arts Students League, New York, 106, 142

Artz & de Bois, 67, 221

Ash Can School, 51, 52, 55–56, 83, 129, 131, 155, 224, 225. *See also* The Eight; Realists (New York)

Ashwell, Thomas E., 150

Association of American Painters and Sculptors (AAPS), 15, 16, 17, 18, 20, 41, 42, 43, 44, 45, 64, 68, 72, 212, 213, 214; Borglum crisis, 99–106; Chicago Exhibition, control of, 189–96; closing the show, 219–22; Davies, Arthur, as president, 82–85, 223–33; discord and end of, 224–33; formation of, 48–62; Healy's Restaurant party, 149–52; Manhattan Hotel, final meeting at, 228–30; party for "friends and enemies," 149–52; praises for, 109; preparations for show, 79–98; resignations, final, 228–33

Astor, Mrs., 143

Ayer, Margaret Hubbard, 165

Barnard, George Grey, 52, 108; *The Prodigal Son and His Father*, 101, 116

Barnes, Dr. Albert C., 127

Barr, Alfred H., Jr., 97

Bartlett, Paul, 52

Beach, Chester: *The Big Wave*, 213

Becker, Maurice, 90

Bellows, George, 51, 52, 83, 104, 142, 224, 226, 229, 230, 235, 236; *Circus*, 37

Bergson, Henri, 181

Berliner Neue Sezession, 185

Bernard, Joseph, 196

Bernheim-Jeune & Cie., 71

Blanchet, Alexandre, 122

Blashfield, Edwin H., 140, 142

Blaue Reiter group, 185

Bliss, Lillie P., 70, 120, 121, 239

Bluemner, Oscar, 90, 237

Boldini, Giovanni, 169

Bonnard, Pierre, 71, 72

Borglum, Gutzon, 49, 50, 51, 52, 53, 55, 60, 62, 83, 85, 94, 137, 147, 163; resignation from AAPS, 99–106

Borglum, Solon, 146–47

Boston Exhibition, 215–19

Boston *Transcript*, 157, 162–63, 164, 171, 174

Bourdelle, Emile A., 70, 196

Bourgeois, Stephan, 97, 221–22; Bourgeois Gallery, 238

Bowers, Thomas W., 218

Brancusi, Constantin, 68, 70, 133–34, 181,

343

Dawson, Manierre, 213, 232
de Chirico, Giorgio, 68
Degas, Edgar, 85, 96, 113, 117
Delacroix, Eugène, 44, 96, 112, 113, 116
de La Fresnaye, Roger, 67, 70, 79
Delaunay, Robert, 67, 70, 79; conflict with 147–49; *Ville de Paris*, 147–49, 219
Denis, Maurice, 71, 72, 159, 197, 213
Derain, André, 67, 72, 75, 122, 148; *La Forêt à Martigues*, 124; *Window at Vers*, 220
de Zayas, Marius, 239
Diaghileff ballet, 67
Dimock, Edith, 122, 130
Dirks, Rudolph, 110
documents of show, 15–23; buyers ledger, page of, 19; catalog, 14; invitation, 18; poster, 25; priced catalog, 21
Dodge, Mabel, 94, 95, 113
Dorr, Charles Henry, 155, 156
Dove, Arthur, 237, 238
Downes, William H., 157, 164, 171, 174
Drake, Alexander W., 96
Dreier, Katherine S., 97, 129, 239
Dresdener Brücke, 184
Druet, Emile, 71, 72, 221
du Bois, Guy Pène, 15, 52, 58, 78, 83, 113, 150, 156, 229, 230, 231, 232
Duchamp, Marcel, 67, 70, 128, 129, 135, 213; *Le Roi et la reine entourés des nus vites*, 124; *Nude Descending a Staircase No. 2 (Nu descendant un escalier)*, 32, 128, 131, 136–37, 139, 142, 146, 172, 174, 188, 205, 207; *Portrait de joueurs d'échecs*, 124
Duchamp-Villon, Raymond, 67, 93, 122, 135; *Danseurs*, 120, 129; *Torso of a Young Man*, 102
Duchamp-Villon family, 70
Dufrenoy, Georges Leon, 70
Dufy, Raoul, 70
Durand-Ruel & Sons, 72, 96

Eakins, Thomas, 98
Eddy, Arthur J., 122, 123–24, 136, 183, 194, 195, 205, 208, 213, 239
The Eight, 48, 51, 88, 225, 235, 238. See also Ash Can School; Realists (New York)
Eilshemius, Louis, 90
Epstein, Jacob, 79
Everybody's, 137
Expressionists, 114, 116

Farwell, Arthur Burrage, 206
Farwell, Mrs. A. L., 213
Faure, Elie, 93
Fauves, 66, 67, 70, 72, 135, 154, 162, 168, 181, 183, 235, 236
Field, Hamilton Easter, 127, 129
Fisher, William M., 113
Fitzgerald, Charles, 149, 155
Flechtheim, Alfred, 75
Folsom Gallery, 238
Francke, Benjamin A., 141
Fraser, James E., 49, 50, 52, 53
Freisz, Othon, 70
French, Daniel Chester, 100
French, William M. R., 189, 190, 191, 192, 196
Freud, Sigmund, 181
Frick, Henry C., 126–27; Frick Collection, 127
Fry, Roger, 72–73, 83, 152
Fry, Sherry, 53, 230, 231
Futurism, 67, 79, 113, 114, 138, 140, 141, 142, 147, 162, 172, 177, 183, 185, 205

Gallatin, Albert E., 127, 129; Gallatin Collection (Gallery of Living Art), 239
Gamut Club, 239
Gans, Mrs. Howard, 97
Gauguin, Paul, 66, 71, 72, 76, 79, 85, 96, 97, 113, 117, 121, 129, 130, 132, 154, 157, 159, 161, 162, 173, 186, 197, 199, 213; *Faa Iheihe*, 160–61; *Fleurs sur un fond jaune*, 132; *Noa-Noa*, 18, 76, 93, 207; *Words of the Devil*, 26, 206, 207
Gaynor, William J., 152
Gellatly, John, 98
German Expressionists, 66
Gewey, Edward, 91
Girieud, Pierre, 75, 122
Glackens, William, 49, 51, 59, 83, 104, 113, 122, 127, 228, 232, 235, 236; *Family Group*, 36
Gleizes, Albert, 67, 70; *L'Homme au balcon*, 124
Goltz, Hans, 67, 221
Goya, Francisco, 44, 112, 116
Grafton shows, 72–73, 75, 76, 152, 185
Greeley-Smith, Nixola, 163
Greenwich Historical Society, 17
Gregg, Frederick J., 81, 82, 83, 85, 95, 111, 113, 145, 150, 155, 178, 192, 193, 195–96, 203, 207, 208, 209, 214, 217, 218
Gris, Juan, 67
Griswold, J. F., 136
Guinness, Mrs. B. S., 96

Haelstrom, Jens, 207
Hagelstein Brothers, 192
Halpert, Samuel, 89, 147, 148, 237
Hapgood, Hutchins, 179
Harper's Weekly, 159, 209

345

Photography Credits

The photographers and the sources of photographic material other than those indicated in the captions are as follows: David Heald: page 27; Hirshhorn Museum and Sculpture Garden, Smithsonian Institution, Washington, D.C.: pages 14, 19, 21, 25 (photograph by Lee Stalsworth), 46, 56, 65, 69, 122, 150, 151, 197–202; Alex Jamison, Washington, D.C.: page 40, top; Metropolitan Museum of Art, New York: page 28, bottom; Museum of Fine Arts, Boston: page 39, top.